THE EXPERIMENTAL IMAGINATION

THE EXPERIMENTAL IMAGINATION

Literary Knowledge and Science in the British Enlightenment

TITA CHICO

Stanford University Press • Stanford, California

Stanford University Press
Stanford, California

© 2018 by the Board of Trustees of the Leland Stanford Junior University. All rights reserved.

No part of this book may be reproduced or transmitted in any form or by any means, electronic or mechanical, including photocopying and recording, or in any information storage or retrieval system without the prior written permission of Stanford University Press.

Printed in the United States of America on acid-free, archival-quality paper

Library of Congress Cataloging-in-Publication Data

Names: Chico, Tita, 1970– author.
Title: The experimental imagination : literary knowledge and science in the British Enlightenment / Tita Chico.
Description: Stanford, California : Stanford University Press, 2018. | Includes bibliographical references and index.
Identifiers: LCCN 2017050808 (print) | LCCN 2018002879 (ebook) | ISBN 9781503606456 (ebook) | ISBN 9781503605442 (cloth) | ISBN 9781503613591 (paper)
Subjects: LCSH: Literature and science—Great Britain—History—18th century. | Knowledge, Theory of—Great Britain—History—18th century. | English literature—18th century—History and criticism. | Enlightenment—Great Britain. | Imagination.
Classification: LCC PR448.S32 (ebook) | LCC PR448.S32 C55 2018 (print) | DDC 820.9/36—dc23
LC record available at https://lccn.loc.gov/2017050808

Cover design: John Barnett, 4 Eyes Design

To Dr. Beverly Berghaus Chico,
my mother

CONTENTS

	Acknowledgments	ix
	Introduction	1
1	Literary Knowledge	17
2	Immodest Witnesses	44
3	Scientific Seduction	76
4	Political Science	104
5	When Science Becomes Literature	134
	Notes	169
	Bibliography	209
	Index	233

ACKNOWLEDGMENTS

A book such as this depends on research libraries and the resources to access them. I have been very lucky on both counts. I wish to thank the librarians at the British Library, the Bodleian Library, the Wellcome Library, the Folger Shakespeare Library, the Library of Congress, the New York Public Library, the Huntington Library, and the Newberry Library. Pat Herron of the University of Maryland Library deserves special appreciation.

My scholarship has been supported by a range of fellowships that have given me valuable time away from teaching, including the Visiting Fellowship at Chawton House Library and Research Centre; the Visiting Research Fellowship in the Institute of English Studies at the School for Advanced Study, University of London; the Research and Scholarship Semester Award from the University of Maryland; the ASECS/Andrew W. Mellon Foundation Research Fellowship at the Harry Ransom Center; the University of Maryland General Research Board Semester Award; and a Grant-in-Aid from the Folger Institute. The University of Maryland's College of Arts and Humanities ADVANCING Scholarship Initiative, along with the Department of English, provided funding for my manuscript workshop, which was invaluable.

I have had the great fortune to share my work with colleagues in the United States and Britain at numerous conferences, including the American Society for Eighteenth-Century Studies, the British Society for Eighteenth-Century Studies, the Society for Literature, Science, and the Arts, and the Modern Language Association. I am grateful to audience members at various institutions for considering my work with such care and consideration, including the University of York Centre for Eighteenth-Century Studies, Georgetown University, Chawton House Library and Research Centre, Birkbeck College/University of London, the University of Illinois, Queen Mary University of London, the Foundling Museum, the University of Warwick, Columbia University, Southern Methodist University, the Folger Institute, the CUNY Graduate Center, the University of Pennsylvania, the University of Colorado-Boulder, Tufts University, the Center for Eighteenth-

Century Studies at Indiana University, and the University of Oklahoma. These conversations made my work sharper and stronger.

Three people read the entire manuscript, one of them twice: Laura Brown (twice!), Bob DeMaria, and Jonathan Kramnick. They saw what my book as a whole could do and helped me figure out how I could do it. I will be forever grateful for their guidance. I am also thankful for the friends who responded to sections of my book: Toni Bowers, Kandice Chuh, Lisa Freeman, Suvir Kaul, Kathy Lubey, Ruth Mack, Bob Markley, Megan Kate Nelson, Nush Powell, Cristobal Silva, Courtney Weiss Smith, Alok Yadev, and Chi-ming Yang.

At the University of Maryland, I have brilliant, insightful colleagues, and I thank several for reading chapters and talking with me extensively over the years: Ralph Bauer, Chuck Caramello, Maud Casey, Bill Cohen, Theresa Coletti, Kim Coles, Jane Donawerth, Oliver Gaycken, Michael Israel, Matt Kirschenbaum, Ted Leinwand, Bob Levine, Zita Nunes, Randy Ontiveros, Jerry Passannante, Carla Peterson, Sangeeta Ray, Kellie Robertson, Laura Rosenthal, Jason Rudy, Mary Helen Washington, Christina Walter, and Orrin Wang. My chairs, Kent Cartwright, Bill, and Amanda Bailey, have been unflagging in their support. Karen Nelson heroically read the final draft, improving it greatly with her keen editorial eye. Jonathan Williams read the proofs with his characteristic care. My graduate and undergraduate students at the University of Maryland enliven me with their intelligence and creativity. I thank them for taking up the difficulties of true thinking.

I also thank the many friends with whom I have conversed about this book, our collective work, and the futures of intellectualism, politics, and the humanities: Dave Alff, Misty Anderson, Jennie Batchelor, Luisa Calè, David Clark, Lucinda Cole, Alison Conway, Helen Deutsch, Carolyn Dever, Tom DiPiero, Gillian Dow, Markman Ellis, Rod Ferguson, Lynn Festa, Dustin Griffin, Anita Guerrini, Donna Heiland, Laura Kang, Joanne Long, Devoney Looser, Tina Lupton, Elaine McGirr, Lisa Moore, Melissa Mowry, Danny O'Quinn, Mary Poovey, Joe Roach, Slaney Chadwick Ross, Sean Silver, Chloe Wigston Smith, Siobhan Somerville, Kristina Straub, Rajani Sudan, David Taylor, Helen Thompson, Cindy Wall, and Gena Zuroski.

Emily-Jane Cohen of Stanford University Press is the editor we all want: rigorous, reasonable, and smart. It has been a pleasure to work with her. Faith Wilson Stein offered me impeccable editorial advice as I prepared the final manuscript. I thank them both deeply. I am also grateful for the assistance from Tim Roberts, Beverly Miller, and Stephanie Adams.

My life was very different when I began this book, but it also remains profoundly the same, a world made up of loving connections. In Alyssa Alston, Isabel Borland, Toni, Bill, Lisa F., Daryle and Steven Fretwilliams, Nicole King, Matt K., Carla, Cristobal, Gita Panjabi Trelease, and Randy Trumbach, I find deep support and care. With Filiz Turhan, Robin Peck, Zita, Kandice, and Megan, I have sister-like friendships. These women have astounding hearts and minds, and they embrace me with happiness and love. Plus, we laugh a lot.

And my family. My father, Raymundo José Lorenzo Chico, has accomplished so much and has taught me about research, commitment, and independence. My brother, Greg Chico, lovingly cares for me as he has my whole life: he reads my work, fixes up my homes, and counsels me on the finer, mundane, and ridiculous things of life. I am also so deeply happy that Adam Martinez, my brother-in-law, is now family. Matt Chico, my brother, and Laura Shipler Chico, my sister-in-law, gave me a soft landing in London while I drafted this book. Their love and compassion, the countless dinners, conversations, and special outings were exactly what I needed and wanted. I have a home in theirs, in all ways. My nephews, Ben and Dylan Chico, bring me joy; I adore being their aunt and cherish seeing everything anew with them. I thank Tomás, Nico, Sebastian, and Florencia Foxley for their affection and the fun we have together. Alex Foxley recognized me the moment we met—it left me breathless then, and still does. I thank him for his love, kindness, and humor.

I dedicate this book to my mother, Dr. Beverly Berghaus Chico, who taught me to be fierce in my curiosity and unrelenting in my dedication. From the time I was a little girl, she showed me the complexity and power of art and the beautiful lessons of history. She also instilled in me a deep commitment to feminism—in theory, history, and practice. My mother sees the world in everything around her and taught me to do the same. With this accomplished, worldly woman as my role model, I grew up expecting that I could do exactly what I wanted. And I am doing just that, with the knowledge that I would not be where I am without her. Mom, I love you and I thank you.

THE EXPERIMENTAL IMAGINATION

INTRODUCTION

The memory, senses, and understanding are, therefore, all of them founded on the imagination, or the vivacity of our ideas.

David Hume, *A Treatise of Human Nature* (1739)

This is a book about the experimental imagination in the British Enlightenment. It tells the story of how literariness came to be distinguished from its epistemological sibling, science, as a source of truth about the natural and social worlds. I begin with the argument that early science formulated itself through literary knowledge. What does this mean? Natural philosophy in the late seventeenth century—the term for *science* at this time—relied on literariness to present experimental findings; the textual representation of such discoveries necessitated an extensive use of figurative language. More radically, I argue, the main technologies that made natural philosophy intellectually possible were so because they could be articulated in literary terms. Early science's observed particular and modest witness together formed the backbone of evidence and authority in this new episteme. They both drew on empirical experience, of course, but weighed much more heavily on the imaginative possibilities afforded by literary knowledge. Early scientists used metaphor to define the phenomenon they studied. They also used metaphor to imagine themselves into their roles as experimentalists.

And yet this is only the beginning of my story. British literature of the long eighteenth century includes countless references to early science, whether as themes, tropes, or characters. Certainly, cultural consumers in London ate up science in an assortment of fora, eager to associate themselves with its fashionability. My book understands these mentions as much more than reflections of a culture's increased fascination and familiarity with natural philosophy. There is such a multiplicity and diversity of allusions to science in the literary archive because numerous writers used the topic to make the case for the epistemological superiority of literary knowledge. Representing natural philosophy occasions a deliberation about its efficacy and shortcomings, particularly in contrast to the insights and truths conveyed by literariness. I use the phrase *the experimental imagination* to capture this simultaneously intellectual and aesthetic process.

Through the experimental imagination, the representation of early science persistently discloses its literary status—not merely in the tropological nature of scientific writing and practice, but also through the metaphorics of science that allow writers to posit alternative models of authority and evidence. The narrative I tell in this book is one of other possibilities, paths imagined as viable, reasonable, and superior to the unreliability and even danger of scientific knowledge and its acquisition.[1] The truths of literary knowledge, I argue, challenge the dominant account we have inherited that identifies the scientific revolution as the sine qua non epistemological innovation of the long eighteenth, an event leading to the modern celebration of and dependence on scientific rationalization. I recover doubts about science's efficacy and beliefs in literature's insights, and adjust our critical lens so we can see clearly the historical moment when what we now think of as literature and science were not settled as distinct epistemologies, but were understood as deeply, if sometimes awkwardly, implicated in one another. The often noisy satiric rancor and just as pervasive quiet concern that natural philosophy generated among an array of writers, including science advocates, dramatists, satirists, essayists, and poets, together reveal a doubled epistemological trajectory: experimental observation uses imaginative speculation, and imaginative fancy enables new forms of understanding. Early scientific practice requires yet often obscures that imaginative impulse; literary knowledge embraces this impulse as a way of understanding the world at large.

The Experimental Imagination argues that the debates, contradictions, and alignments that later shape the disciplinarity associated with, and even attributed to, the British Enlightenment register a profound awareness of the literariness of science and a growing sense of literary knowledge as an independent, viable epistemology. Writers during this period understood the fictionality of objectivity and details, representing science as not only forged but also improved by the literary imagination. Taken together, the texts I examine articulate an emerging category of literary knowledge, which is drawn from literature as well as from literary interpretive methods and protocols, no matter the discipline. Literary knowledge gains value because it relies on the imagination as a source of truth, simultaneously reflecting the limits of experimental philosophy and formulating the lines of difference that eventually define the boundary between the arts and sciences. As a specifically modern form, literary knowledge facilitates a redefinition of authority and evidence. It also reveals the newly modern categories of things and observed particulars to be figurative, as well as the social, financial, and even sexual costs of objectivity.

The *experimental imagination* encapsulates the process and effects of literary knowledge as an epistemology. My use of the term *experiment* draws on its two predominant meanings as connoting experience and as tentative. Samuel Johnson's definition of *experiment* aptly summons the idea of process: as a noun, it is a "trial of anything," and as a verb, it is "to try."[2] As a realm of experience, experiment pertains to scientific process; indeed, experimentation and observation are key forms of knowledge production developed in the period.[3] For Ian Hacking, experimenting is "not stating or reporting but *doing* [emphasis added]."[4] It is an action. Understood as an attempt or a trial or a "doing," something akin to Montaigne's *essai,* experiment is likewise a discursive, rhetorical mode, an act of imaginative work tied to the protocols of genre and, more broadly, a sense of literariness. Experiments make abstractions visible, theories tangible.[5] Robert Mitchell makes the compelling point that *experiment* in the late eighteenth century came to be appropriated from science to literature at a moment when interest in vitalism took hold.[6] But long before then, long before the disciplinarity that needs to exist for such a discursive transfer to occur, reading texts and observing phenomena were understood to be far more similar than different. If, by the late eighteenth century, Coleridge and Wordsworth presented poetry as an entirely self-referential epistemology, then their Restoration and early-eighteenth-century predecessors used the tools of literary representation to find and make truths about the world.[7] Specialized language, a hallmark of disciplinary difference from the late eighteenth century to now, had not yet taken hold. Figurative language, and the imaginings and means of knowing that it facilitated, were deeply imbricated with representation of the natural world, whether through the perspective of a seventeenth-century microscope or an eighteenth-century Georgic poem. Tropes made the world newly visible—and newly imaginable.

KEYWORDS AND INTERVENTIONS: LITERARY KNOWLEDGE, SCIENCE, TROPE, AND GENDER; OR, WHAT IS DISTINCTIVE ABOUT THIS BOOK

The study of literature and science has been greatly enabled by the work of Steven Shapin and Simon Schaffer, historians of science who make literariness central to their reading of late seventeenth-century British experimentalism.[8] Shapin and Schaffer's *Leviathan and the Air-Pump: Hobbes, Boyle, and the Experimental Life* argues that Robert Boyle's and Thomas Hobbes's debates about the experimental method reveal the nascent protocols of facticity and modest witnessing. While Boyle and his acolytes actively defended the plausibility and accuracy of such knowledge, Hobbes insisted that such practices were logically incoherent—particularly the vacuum at the center of Boyle's air pump—and would produce dangerous social upheaval and discord.[9] These arguments also offer an important lesson: problems of knowledge and social order are mutually constitutive.[10] Both Hobbes and Boyle, along with their supporters, were keenly aware of the pressing need to develop a "means of guaranteeing assent" to establish an "indefeasible civil order."[11] In their account, Shapin and Schaffer formulate the concept of "virtual witnessing," that is, a literary technology wherein an experiment would be represented in a text for others to corroborate, as an important mechanism for the legitimization and circulation of scientific knowledge.[12] But "virtual witnessing" and their central conceit of early modern objectivity, the "modest witness," both depend on a literary imagination that is well beyond the scope of Shapin and Schaffer's analysis, as we shall see in Chapter 1.

For many scholars (including several historians of science who gleaned the significance of literary and language studies before literary critics did), the literary strategies of Boyle and his Royal Society followers often aim exclusively for realism, a claim that inheres to an understanding of literary representation more generally as an empirical mode.[13] Subsequently, numerous studies of the relationship between literature and science in the eighteenth century focus on the empiricism of the novel, a characterization posited over fifty years ago by Ian Watt's "rise of the novel" thesis in which seventeenth-century empiricism required the descriptive writing made available through what we now call the novel.[14] A great deal of critical attention has been paid to the novel as a formal expression of natural philosophy's empiricism.[15] As Helen Thompson has recently argued, the empirical-realist assumption at the core of Shapin and Schaffer's account dovetails with the critical trend of reading the eighteenth-century novel as emerging from and indebted to experimental philosophical practices.[16] When Shapin and Schaffer miss the implications of figuration, so too does scholarship that focuses exclusively on narrative as realistic.

Recent scholarship has been more capacious in thinking about literature and science. Rajani Sudan, Lucinda Cole, and Al Coppola provide vibrant cultural studies approaches to scientific discourse.[17] And Jonathan Kramnick, Jayne Elizabeth Lewis, Wolfram Schmidgen, Helen Thomson, and Courtney Weiss Smith focus on novelistic and poetic representations that challenge the science-realism assumption.[18] *The Experimental Imagination* is a book about the unique effects of the literary, and, as a consequence, it sees cultural awareness as an occasion to think through the terms of representation. Drawing on the cultural studies' sense of representation as always socially networked, and combining this with a rigorous attention to literariness, the fundamental premise of *The Experimental Imagination* is that **science** is a literary trope.

My argument demands that we attend to science as a form of figuration, a kind of literary act. I do so throughout this book with keywords: **literary knowledge**, **science**, **trope**, and **gender**. Keywords, as Raymond Williams defines them, "are significant, binding words in certain activities and their interpretation; they are significant, indicative words in certain forms of thought."[19] They simultaneously connote praxis and theory—in Williams's terms, activity and thought. In *The Experimental Imagination*, these keywords index how form and thought combine to shape new ways of understanding.

My choice of the keyword **literary knowledge** (rather than *literature*) points to literariness as a form of epistemology. Of course, the word *literature* in the long eighteenth century was not confined to the modern sense of creative literature, but connoted literacy; in Johnson's *Dictionary*, literature is "Learning; skill in letters." Literary knowledge still includes the representational workhorses of form and content, but it expands our notion to insist on this work as intellectual, not merely creative. Literary knowledge conveys the period's investment in seeing the literary as a way of ascertaining truth about the world. I also view literariness as a form of practice: that is, the literary imagination makes material possible. Literariness is itself a form of making.

By *science*, I mean the sense available in the long eighteenth century, yet now obscure, as the state of knowing; I also draw on the definition science accrued during this same period as signifying a specific branch of study based on observation and experiment.[20] Scientific practices linger in our cultural history as the discipline's major innovation; indeed, the experimental work of natural philosophers transformed how natural phenomena were understood. Natural philosophy's practitioners and supporters found cause to assert and defend an empirical methodology, inherited from a Baconian ideal. This is the narrative we tell ourselves as we navigate our technocratic world: the instrumentalism of scientific practice yields insight, progress, and improvement. There are solutions to problems, cures of ailments, and fixes for social ills. These are the promises of the Enlightenment, a heuristic born out of late eighteenth-century political debates that were later incorporated into the historiography of the period writ large.[21]

But as a heuristic, the Enlightenment embodies a specific perversion: it requires the subordination of its own misgivings.[22] Late seventeenth-century debates between the ancients and the moderns, the *querelle des Anciens et des Modernes*, over which sort of knowledge was superior—traditional or discovered—expose, rather than suppress, such apprehensions and reveal that positive attitudes toward modernity emerged fitfully and unevenly, in no small part because modernity demanded a reconsideration and redefinition of authority and evidence.[23] The late seventeenth century, when these fights unfolded, displays an epistemological uncertainty well in advance of the Enlightenment logic that enabled the sealing off and circumvention of its own subversions.

To recover the tentative, imaginative qualities at the core of natural philosophy, I use science as a relatively loose and commodious category of intellectual, cultural, and aesthetic work. Many scholars have studied particular sciences and their literary iterations.[24] But natural philosophy as I use it in this book may mean experimental or observational science. It could mean mathematics. Or astronomy or microscopy. I narrate the larger difference emerging between natural philosophy and literariness rather than the discipline-specific literary histories or histories of specific sciences or genres or a single connotation embedded in practice. My goal is to suspend that disciplinary division, even as an end point, to develop the language and rubric to apprehend the possibilities that long eighteenth-century writers and thinkers imagined, cherished, and even disregarded. To study this material without understanding our own predilection for their division threatens to obscure the important and interconnected interpretive work that took place among a range of writers, thinkers, and practitioners.

The challenge we face is how to understand the relationship between literature and science. To think about a moment such as the British Enlightenment tempts one to ask what the temporal and causal relation between literature and science might be. Which came first? Does literature influence science? Or does science influence literature? With traditional and new historicisms popular in literary studies, especially eighteenth-century studies, contextual approaches that imagine history as an interpretive key are tempting. Allusive readings of *Gulliver's Travels*, for example, are structurally embedded in how the satire has been published.[25] Editors of *Gulliver's Travels* frequently narrow Swift's satire to specific political allegories: in this mode of interpretation, the political hijinks in Lilliput are satiric versions of English politics. Blefuscu is France. Such historicism can provide insight into the literary text and, indeed, *The Experimental Imagina-*

tion situates self-consciously literary texts in their milieu. But relying solely on science—or anything else, for that matter—as a historical context can too easily presume that the context is well established and stable in its signification and import and that a literary text unproblematically reflects its historical context.

Metaphor accomplishes a conflation by virtue of its transformative effects: a metaphor compares two things, but in the process, it seems to convert the original into its figurative companion. As a result, the logic of metaphoric thinking concludes with a signified that exists beyond the confines of the text itself. To depend uncritically on historical and contextual reading short-circuits the work of critical interpretation, leading to overly simple conclusions that present *Gulliver's Travels* as "about," and only "about," historical events, people, and places. In this model, the good reader will figure out who and what Swift is satirizing. Alexander Pope capitalized on and mocked the allusive reading model when he published *A Key to the Lock; Or, a Treatise Proving, Beyond All Contradiction, the Dangerous Tendency of a Late Poem, entitled* The Rape of the Lock, *to Government and Religion* (1715) a year after his famous mock epic.

The stakes of allusive reading are even higher when considering the relation of science and literature. In the case of *Gulliver's Travels*, allusive reading suggests that Swift appropriates scientific discourse and, in so doing, produces a textual belatedness.[26] The influence argument is unilateral: we move from scientific innovation—or failure—to its literary reflection. Swift makes fun of early scientific practitioners, but puts his money on the losing team: those practitioners go on to win in the course of history. From this point of view, science in *Gulliver's Travels* is not fundamentally flawed as an enterprise, just poorly executed. But this conclusion reads retrospectively, seeing the present in the past, seeing the British Enlightenment's uneven, experimental, and fanciful forays into new forms of knowledge making as successful before they were accepted. Long ago, Hayden White insisted that text and context are both artifacts of their political and ideological moments.[27] The case of satire is especially resonant, for, as Fredric V. Bogel reminds us, "referentiality" and even "factuality are essential conventions, products of certain rhetorical strategies" in satire.[28] In *Designing Women: The Dressing Room in Eighteenth-Century English Literature and Culture*, I took up this methodological question directly, discovering that the dressing room of history was a world away from the dressing room of literature.[29] As a trope, the dressing room accomplished things related to, but fundamentally at odds with, what the dressing room conveyed as a physical space, including how it was experienced. I argued that this divergence discloses the uneasy and laborious formulation of gender difference.

Yet the idea that literature follows the scientific remains a powerful narrative, perhaps because of our collective agreement that science itself is the greatest source of truth and knowledge, that science is, as it were, right. Separating a consideration of literature from that of science, represented by C. P. Snow's "two cultures" of disciplinarity, has the obscuring effect of negating their shared cultural status.[30] "So internalized has the distinction between science and the arts become," writes L. J. Jordanova, "that we greet any sign of a bridge between them with surprise."[31] Even with these correctives, the apparent stability of this disciplinary divide is deeply evident in our own time, where these distinctions not only shape funding and budget decisions in the modern university, but also shape public policy about what sorts of knowledge matter, with STEM (science, technology, engineering, and math) receiving the lion's share of support and praise.[32] Writing with an awareness of this divide-yet-to-come, some literary scholars have conceptualized the seventeenth- and eighteenth-century moment as predisciplinary, a rubric that inevitably leads to the culmination of the familiar disciplinary divide and hierarchy.[33]

The problem is that such approaches presume the predominance of scientific over literary regimes long before the verdict had been issued, a fact we know from the archive of history but that gets obscured in theoretical terms. The challenge for scholars of the British Enlightenment is to acknowledge the peculiarity between then and now, and to hold that peculiarity as simultaneously disorienting and illustrative. How do we get out from the teleology that sees science as a winner of history and literature as its debased sibling, scampering to catch up? What, in other words, comes after belatedness? Or, as Gillian Beer asks, "How to explain the concurrent appearance of similar ideas in science and in literature without inevitably forging causal links?"[34] An invigorating response is Peter Galison's concept of a "trading zone" in which the individuals, resources, and activities necessary to produce modern experiments converge.[35] Visualizing literature and science cohabitating in a conceptual trading zone presents a metaphor to apprehend the similarity of and differences between the protocols and practices of literature and science.[36] However, the trading zone has it limits. As a figure for commerce, the trading zone emphasizes exchange without parsing out what these particular relations might be. It also presumes that the players involved are fully formed as they enter into this marketplace, a presumption anachronistic to the long eighteenth century.

The broader questions we must ask, therefore, are these: What happens when one turns to a context that is in flux and imagined through and apart from the means of its representation? What happens when we step back to ask, "What are these texts reflecting?" The category of reflection as a mode of critical interpretation desperately needs reconsideration because it has the tendency to institute a temporality of cause and effect. The idea of representation as reflection builds in a belatedness that can never be overcome, a belatedness that echoes the binary privileging of speech over writing in Western philosophy Derrida revealed to us many years ago.[37]

To offer a revitalized approach to these questions, I turn to a tract by Robert Boyle, founding member of the Royal Society, powerful advocate for the experimental method, and brilliant chemist. Boyle's *The Excellency of Theology* illuminates the meanings and relationship of literary knowledge and science that animate my thinking in this book. In this treatise, Boyle announces, "The two great Books, of Nature and of Scripture, have the same Author."[38] Boyle's statement can be understood as an expression of physico-theology, a "quest for a single system of representation that articulates its equally strong commitments to experimental philosophy and to theology."[39] When Boyle and his contemporaries link the book of nature and the book of scripture, they are able to imagine a prelapsarian quality to their intellectual project, divorcing experimental knowledge from the vagaries of a degraded, subjective self. As a consequence, the early scientist could be conceptualized as an Adam figure, a subject imagined to redeem the fallen world and to institute a divinely ordained political stability.[40]

However, Boyle's intellectual project veers toward a specific form of literariness. Scripture certainly has its place, but for the purposes of an analogical exegesis of the natural philosophical process of discovery, Boyle earlier in *The Excellency of Theology* likens the book of nature to literature. These two sorts of books, and these two sorts of epistemologies, have a similar effect on the individual. One comparison is to *Aesop's Fables*, another to romances. Boyle writes, "For when you have brought an Experiment to an Issue, though the Event may often prove such as you will be pleas'd with; yet it will seldome prove such as you can acquiesce in. For it fares not with an Inquisitive mind in studying the Book of Nature, as in reading of *Aesop's Fables*, or some other collection of Apologues of differing sorts."[41] Boyle is concerned here with the limits of knowledge, particularly inductive knowledge. The expression of this realm of unknowability relies on an uneasy confluence of the scientific and the literary, a conjunction to which Boyle returns when he writes, "The full discovery of Natures Mysteries, is so unlikely to fall to any mans share in this Life, that the case of the Pursuers of them is at best like theirs, that light upon some excellent Romance, of which they shall never see the latter parts."[42] The process of acquiring knowledge is like reading a book, a romance, that one can never finish. The natural philosopher is like a reader who has access to only the first volume of a multivolume work. The literary here stands for what can never be completed, a characterization in tension with the exigencies of closure associated with plot more generally. Natural philosophy is partial, incomplete, and never ending, and this quality finds expression in Boyle's sense of the literary. Boyle's allusions to *Aesop's Fables* and romances ground his claims for science, but they also provide an instance of a much larger network of associations that are the subject of my study: figurative language and the imaginings it facilitated were deeply enfolded with representing the natural world.

The Experimental Imagination concentrates on possibilities imagined, if not fully developed, when writers contemplate what a natural philosophical approach to the world might be. For many in the long eighteenth century, natural philosophy requires the imaginative impulses available within a literary framework.[43] Natural philosophy is not merely a practice or a form of knowledge: it is a trope.[44] I use **trope** as a keyword because it vividly records the shifting and intricate relationship of early science and literary knowledge. A trope, of course, is a figure of speech; as the *Oxford English Dictionary* explains, a trope "consists in the use of a word or phrase in a sense other than that which is proper to it."[45] Etymologically, *trope* conveys motion; it embodies a turning. Thus understood, a trope exploits the figuration made possible through language, making connections and relations that may or may not be "proper" to the original object. Not far from its rhetorical sibling the metaphor, which draws on the idea of a transfer from one thing to another but is wider in its connotative and dynamic possibilities, the concept of trope provides a lens to view the representational work of early science and literature as itself a mechanism for making meaning.

My use of trope stresses that early science finds its intellectual and conceptual footing in the metaphoric thinking available through literary knowledge and that literary writers in turn wield natural philosophy as a figure for the importance and unique insights of literary knowledge. While early experimental philosophers were often fearful that the imagination would lead to corruption and demean their tenuous claims to objectivity, they were simultaneously aware of its significance to the protocols of observation and the circulation of their methodology. Literary writers more commonly embraced the imaginative potential of such witnessing and the fanciful observed particulars it might produce. The topic of science occasions vibrant considerations of character, plot, and metaphor, enabling writers to use natural philosophy metaphorically to move well beyond its intellectual and ideological limits. The authors we now know as literary emphasized and exploited the imaginative potential that those whom we now call scientists used often with ambivalence. In this book, I tell the story of how the imaginative qualities of literature told the truth.

Science as a literary trope precipitates epistemological and ideological changes that often get worked out as questions of **gender**, my final keyword. Gender can be an identity or a relation. The feminist commitment of this book sees in these texts the architecture of social connections, a playing out of the shifts in evidence and authority that scientific and textual practices could facilitate. With my attention to gender, I am able to identify a wider and more expansive archive central to reading science as a trope. Consider a text that one does not ordinarily encounter in approaches to science and literature, Eliza Haywood's *Eovaai* (1736). Haywood's novel is a political allegory featuring a deposed queen of the same name. Eovaai is trained in Lockean philosophy to rule her country, but she has been seduced by the phantasmagorical Ochihaton, a stand-in for Walpole, whose power derives from a magical wand. In his mystified state, Ochihaton is handsome and charming, luring Eovaai into treacherous amatory and political waters. At the height of this danger, a genie appears to give Eovaai a telescope and urges her to "behold your Lover as he really is: all Delusions of the *Ypres* [the supernatural spirits helping him] vanish before this sacred Telescope, nor can even they themselves, invisible as they are to human Sight, escape detection by the Eye that looks through this."[46] This "sacred Telescope" also has night vision, enabling the viewer to "see all as clearly as at Noon-day."[47]

Eovaai's telescope allows her to see the truth of bodies. However, Eovaai can see "clearly" not only because she is in possession of the magical telescope, but also because she is subjectively situated in a scenario that requires her discovery of this knowledge. She is at a point of sexual peril—a moment of heightened physical vulnerability in which all she is is a body. Eovaai here exists solely as a female body subject to the erotic control and abuse of Ochihaton. As is so familiar in the period, a heroine's vulnerable embodiment becomes, paradoxically, the source of her agency. She is emphatically not the objective scientist, the modest witness: she is instead an immodest witness who derives her wisdom and power from her embodiment and subjectivity. To apprehend her presence and effect is to constitute the archaeology of the modest witness topos, a figure that was and remains as fictional as Jonathan Swift's Laputans in need of their flappers to return themselves to their bodies. The erasure of the female body from the subject position of the natural philosopher is a fundamentally patriarchal move; it depends on a now tired binary of female embodiment and masculine abstraction. To insist on the body, particularly the scientific body, the *legitimate* scientific body, is, in turn, a powerfully feminist rejoinder.[48]

In this book, *gender* as a keyword measures the migratory patterning of scientific subjectivities. By observing gender while simultaneously observing matters of literary knowledge and science, we can glimpse the wider social, ideological, and imaginative structures taking shape and coming to determine what experience, evidence, and authority could be in the British Enlightenment—including for and by whom. I understand some of these possibilities in this book as dramatized in the relations of gender and, in this way, uniquely provide a consistently feminist account of literature and science in the period. Thinking figuratively— thinking through the experimental imagination—offers a potentially liberatory mode of subjectivity. New ways of imagining agency and self-improvement for an expanded population emerged, which included, most dramatically, unmarried women.

BRIEF OVERVIEW OF THE BOOK

I begin the story of *The Experimental Imagination* with literary knowledge, particularly as it is expressed and utilized in natural philosophical texts. Chapters 1 and 2 argue for the literary knowledge available through figuration, with dedicated attention to individuals who imagine themselves to be scientists. In Chapter 1, I study the texts of Samuel Pepys, Robert Boyle, Robert Hooke, Henry Power, Thomas Sprat, Benjamin Martin, and Henry Baker—all enthusiasts of natural philosophy who penned diary entries, experiments, guidebooks, treatises, and instrument guides. I make the case that the writing of natural philosophical experiments depends heavily on the metaphoric possibilities of literary language and that modernity, a concept bound up with experimental philosophy, also relied on figuration. But this is only my first critical intervention. These aspects of description merely hint at the more radical revelation that literariness enables a whole-scale imagining of the proper object of natural philosophical inquiry as well as the subject proper to carry it out. The development of the observed particular (the thing) and the modest witness (the neutral observer) as the key protocols of scientific method might be presented as a priori, but these protocols are crafted through the imaginative logic of literariness.

In Chapter 2, I turn to bad scientists, variously satirized and pilloried in plays and periodicals of the long eighteenth century. I argue that failed scientists and scenes of scientific failure allow playwrights and essayists to scrutinize scientific observational practice. A self-consciously literary framework allows for the exploration of the inherent immodesty of the witness whose interest, rather than disinterest, productively factors into scientific debate, education, and civic society. Immodest witnesses index the self-interest, sexual desire, and circulation of wealth implicitly bound up with the practice of experimental philosophy. The characterization of Gimcracks (a proper noun for foolish scientists) in Thomas Shadwell's *The Virtuoso*, James Miller's *The Humours of Oxford*, and Susannah Centlivre's *The Basset-Table* and coquettes in Joseph Addison and Richard Steele's the *Spectator* and Eliza Haywood's the *Female Spectator* all depend on immodesty, a quality that foregrounds self-interest. As surprising as they may be in a scientific context, these characters lay bare the embodiment inherent in scientific observation. If the ideal natural philosopher (always a male of gentlemanly status) removed himself to achieve objectivity and to speak only for the object under examination, then the Gimcrack and coquette were defined by an inability to overcome prejudice and desires, speaking for himself or herself rather than for the object. For some, this form of bias leads only to self-delusion, eroticism, and social obstruction; for others, it allows a new form of self-directed agency and social, even moral, improvement.

These two opening chapters expound the role that literary knowledge, visible as metaphor, plot, and characterization, plays in the formulation of the intellectual and social effects of the experimental imagination. Following my deliberation on the scientific subjects and subjectivities that literary knowledge exposes, I address how one might enter into this intellectual community. Chapter 3 reads scientific dialogues to understand the process of learning science correctly—how one comes to believe in the discoveries of natural philosophy. I concentrate on two dialogues translated into English, Bernard de Fontenelle's study of Copernican and Cartesian cosmology, *Entretiens sur la pluralité des mondes* (1686), translated by Aphra Behn as *A Discovery of New Worlds*, and Francesco Algarotti's rendering of Newtonian optics, *Il Newtonianismo per le dame, ovvero, dialoghi sopra la luce e i colori* (1737), translated by Elizabeth Carter as *Sir Isaac Newton's Philosophy Explain'd for the Use of the Ladies*. Both dialogues adopt the literary plot of seduction to explain how scientific instruction works. Mathematicians, we learn, are like lovers—persuasive and persistent, ultimately demanding submission. To understand Cartesianism, Copernicanism, or Newtonianism necessitates new ways of thinking that are possible only with one's "fancy." These scientific dialogues reframe erotic relations to promote intellectual and moral self-improvement, qualities posited as uniquely modern and widely available to the texts' readers.

Seduction moves an individual from one set of beliefs to another—from ignorance to enlightenment—and the process of scientific seduction introduces the question of what sort of community is subsequently possible. Chapter 4 answers this query by considering sociopolitical formations available through the practice of natural philosophy. The three prose texts I examine all use the conventions of literary knowledge to express their scientific-political visions: Thomas Sprat's scientific manifesto, *The History of the Royal Society*; Margaret Cavendish's utopic romance, *The Blazing World*; and Jonathan Swift's Menippean satire, *Gulliver's Travels*. The experimental imagination mobilized in these three texts uses literariness—including genre and metaphor—to envisage, in turn, an idealized civil government, an absolutist monarchy, and imperialism.

If the trope of science authorizes writers to imagine new forms of evidence and new forms of observation, as well as new processes of learning and geopolitical formation, then it also provokes numerous poets in the early eighteenth century to turn to a specifically aesthetic register. Aesthetics mediates and, as a consequence, supersedes the promised insights of natural philosophy, as poets consider what can be observed, how it can be represented, and who is equipped and authorized to do both (or even either) of these. With Chapter 5, I conclude *The Experimental Imagination* by studying poems that self-consciously utilize a scientific referent to posit aesthetics as epistemologically superior to natural philosophy. Scientific tropes provide shape to eighteenth-century aesthetics and therefore expose the reciprocity of scientific and literary epistemologies. These poems all fully exploit their allegiance to literary knowledge by aestheticizing science. Alexander Pope's *The Rape of the Lock*, poems inspired by Queen Caroline's homage to British theological and scientific accomplishments in her Richmond

Hermitage, and James Thomson's *The Seasons* emphasize the epistemological limitations of science, build an argument for the superiority of literariness, and reimagine subjectivity.

I have collected an extensive archive in the chapters that follow. It includes experiments published under the auspices of the Royal Society; guidebooks by instrument makers selling to enthusiasts; plays staged in Restoration and early eighteenth-century playhouses; periodicals sold in and circulated among the London coffeehouses; English translations of scientific dialogues that redact Copernicus, Descartes, and Newton; sprawling scientific manifesto, utopic romance, and Menippean satire; and poetry concerned with the London elite, British intellectual worthies, and the Georgic landscape. In all of these texts, scientific themes, characters, objects, and plots play pivotal roles. But beyond their thematic work, these instances imagine past the boundaries natural philosophers impose, whether through technological limitation or in an effort to shore up their credibility, and signal moments of deep literariness as they do so. Let loose, scientific tropes generate profound reconsiderations of what authority might be, who has it, and how it might be transformed. And ultimately, scientific tropes shape the types of stories that we tell about ourselves.

1 LITERARY KNOWLEDGE

How did what came to be known as science differ from earlier intellectual work about the natural world? We can track the change in the shifting connotations of the term *experiment*. Before the seventeenth century, experiment conveyed explanation; facts were commonly known phenomena, generalized and universalized. In experiment's explanatory mode, the particular instance of a phenomenon was irrelevant, if not entirely absent.[1] In the Scholastic tradition, *object* and *objective* "referred to the presentation of an intelligible entity, universal essence, or 'species' to consciousness"; the "objective state of an entity's essence [was] the mental mode in which the essence existed in the knowing mind."[2] Understanding the world was a matter of mental labor.

Historians of science have charted the emergence of early scientific practice from this earlier model of textual exegesis.[3] Beginning in the seventeenth century, *experiment* came to mean discovery. Experiment in the epistemological world of Baconianism signified finding out new things. But this activity of experiment, of discovering, in turn introduced concerns about the authority one might have or not have to make such claims. As a result, modern experiment concomitantly required "means of protecting the discoverers from being disbelieved."[4] The discourse of objectivity began to take shape to provide a buffer of authority for experimentalists, converting the meanings of *object* and *objective*, as well as *subject* and *subjective*, into their modern, more familiar forms. To underscore the transformation: *object* and *objective*, which earlier understood the knowability of things as a feature of the mind, now indicated an independence from that same mind.

My excursus on experiment opens up the central concern of this chapter: the extent to which literariness is at the heart of the observational practices of experimental philosophy. The experimental imagination of this book's title focuses our attention on the literary qualities of experimental philosophy as a mode of knowledge acquisition that redefined the natural world as well as the individual who understood it. Alongside efforts to construct objectivity as separate from the vagaries and influences of the imaginative mind, experimental philosophy also depended in fundamental ways on the possibilities available exclusively through the realm of the imagination. It is not too much of a surprise that natural philosophers in the seventeenth and eighteenth centuries drew on a repository of metaphors to represent their findings. As we shall see, in spite of an overt caution about figurative language, literariness served a vital, definitional function in the textual rendering of early scientific knowledge. Textuality, of course, requires metaphors, but early advocates of natural philosophy variously utilized, acknowledged, and promoted figurative language in a descriptive capacity. They also endorsed figurative language—literariness—as necessary to their conception of science, specifically what it studies and who practices it.

Critical discussions of metaphors in science writing have become increasingly frequent, and their prominence attests to the inevitable interconnections of literariness and science. Historian of science Nancy Lays Stepan, studying the analogy in life sciences between race and gender in the nineteenth century, calls for "a critical theory of scientific metaphor" that reveals metaphors' cultural referents and how metaphors shape scientific thinking.[5] Within the context of late seventeenth-century scientific practice, Stephen Shapin and Simon Schaffer argue that Robert Boyle and his colleagues developed a scientific strategy that adopts "literary technology" in two ways. The first relates to the descriptions natural philosophers produce "to make representations that reliably imitated the act of unmediated seeing."[6] Shapin and Schaffer animate their own critical observations with a tour through Svetlana Alpers's pictorial criticism of Dutch painting, drawing on the notion that descriptive practices in the seventeenth century use a "craft of realist representation" to "reliably imitate the act of unmediated seeing."[7] Pace Alpers, and Shapin and Schaffer's admission that the comparison between these two domains does not always make sense; "realist representation" is left unacknowledged as a literary form, an assumption that unquestioningly replicates its effects.

The idea of "literary technology" for Shapin and Schaffer performs a second explanatory function: the concept of "virtual witnessing" through which experimental knowledge is both authorized and circulated relies on natural philosophers' reading these descriptive accounts and, as a result, becoming convinced by them. Shapin and Schaffer specify that such witnessing occurs not in person, but in the reader's imagination, and their own language is illuminating:

The technology of virtual witnessing involves the production in a *reader's* mind of such an image of an experimental scene as obviates the necessity for either direct witness or replication. Through virtual witnessing the multiplication of witnesses could be, in principle, unlimited. It was therefore the most powerful technology for constituting matters of fact. The validation of experiments, and the crediting of their outcomes as matters of fact, necessarily entailed their realization in the laboratory of the mind and the mind's eye.[8]

The account of how scientific knowledge acquires credibility admits that storytelling makes the difference. To phrase it this way reminds us that virtual witnessing—without which there would be no large-scale epistemological transformation—demands a literary quality that, in its effect, it also seems to deny. The term *laboratory* to describe the reader's "mind and the mind's eye" performs its own figurative transformation. The scene of experimental discovery is not bound by time and space, but is in effect created through the imagination.

To read a description of an experiment and then to *see* it is an act of imagination. Shapin and Schaffer's explication of Boyle's literary technology discloses this only insofar as it goes, which is to say that they stop short of considering figuration. The association of "realist representation" with early scientific writing (and Dutch painting) is suggestive, but presumes a stability and familiarity to what that might mean—not to mention that realism as a literary aesthetic emerges in the nineteenth century, not the seventeenth. The process of virtual witnessing relies on a conception of the imagination that cannot account for the fact that imaginative thinking occurs in the domain of the fictional. The imagination is metaphorical: figurative language is figurative because of its connections between two things that are unrelated but that one can imagine as related. In fact, figurative language requires the individual to forge those connections. Perception, the lifeblood of experimentalism, is short-circuited in the process, even though the imagination may seem to be like perception—which, indeed, is part of its efficacy. The protocols of Boyle and other Royal Society members are, in sum and essence, the work of the experimental imagination. Shapin and Schaffer impart a framework that begins to consider the literariness in experimental knowledge production. Yet it does not adequately account for the workings and possibilities of the figurative language that describes—and also constitutes—experimental knowledge production.

The Royal Society's commitment to literariness shaped its lucrative bookselling business. As a new entity, the Royal Society brought together various scientific groups of the Interregnum, but it was chronically underfunded and needed to be financially self-sufficient.[9] In 1662, a royal charter authorized the Royal Society to publish and sell books as a means of generating revenue, an endeavor that contributed significantly to the society's financial health. The first titles were John Evelyn's *Sylva* and Robert Hooke's richly engraved *Micrographia*. As part of this publishing program, Robert Boyle issued forty-nine works, contributing "more than anyone else to the scientific book trade."[10] The popularity of the Royal Society's *Philosophical Transactions*, first edited in 1665 by the society's secretary, Henry Oldenburg, prompted reissues for an even broader audience, including the three-volume *Miscellenia Curiosa* (1705–1707; revised and corrected edition by William Derham, 1723–1727) and *Memoirs of the Royal Society; Being a New Abridgement of the Philosophical Transactions* (1739).

Within the context of this publishing initiative, the case of Hooke is significant. The title of his seminal *Micrographia: or Some Physiological Descriptions of Minute Bodies Made by Magnifying Glasses* (1665) reflects the centrality of literariness to experimental philosophy. Hooke does not title his volume *microscopy*, but uses the word *micrographia*, with its linkage to the Greek *graphia*, the written word. In a title of an official publication of the Royal Society, a volume designed to draw readers into its intellectual purposes and to generate revenue, the qualities of textuality and writing cannot be separated from the development and legitimization of experimental philosophy.

In this chapter, I argue that natural philosophy in the long eighteenth century connoted a sense of modernity and enlightenment, attributes that bound science to meanings in excess of its practice and consumption, especially for enthusiasts in the London marketplace. The pliancy of science as a trope finds support in Boyle's, Hooke's, and others' reflections on language as a scientific tool. Finding the best figure, the most salient metaphor, to represent one's findings, Boyle contends, is part of the process of disseminating knowledge; at the heart of this principle is a belief in the experimental imagination as a source of intellectual illumination. Readers understand things better if they can visualize those things in familiar terms. This urgency for visualization applies to all experimental knowledge, but takes on greater consequence in Boyle's studies of combustion with the air pump and Hooke's of the *subvisibilia* with the microscope. In these experiments, Boyle and Hooke develop the literary principles that sustain their intellectual work. Natural philosophers may articulate their objects of study and their own subject positions through recourse to the imagination, itself an effect of literariness. Observation is not merely a rhetorical device, "hypotyposis," a detailed rendering, but also a "key learned practice and a fundamental form of knowledge."¹¹ Observation is at once a figure and a scientific technology, and it can be so only through its reliance on imaginative work. As a consequence, I argue, the two dominant technologies of the experimental imagination are the observed particular and the modest witness. Observed particulars of empirical study are those nuggets of data that disclose themselves and, in their revelation, produce knowledge. The modest witness is the individual who is objective by virtue of erasing himself through his privilege. In readings of Boyle, Hooke, and others, I argue that both of these concepts, vital to the successful promotion of experimental knowledge, are possible only through imaginative thinking. At their core, scientific subjects, both the object of study and the individual who studies, require literariness to exist. Tropes are literary tools that not only enable practitioners to describe scientific findings, but also enable an even more fundamental component of experimentalism: literariness makes possible the conceptualization of scientific findings and the individual who produces them.

METAPHORS OF MODERNITY

Aristotle's natural philosophy persisted for nearly two thousand years, reformulated and reimagined, up until Francis Bacon's new work in the early seventeenth century. Where Aristotelian natural philosophy sought out teleological explanations for natural phenomena and promoted textual exegesis as the means to provide them, Baconian natural philosophy aggressively turned to a highly regulated program of experiment to learn about the natural world. The analysis of nature, according to Bacon's plan in *Novum Organon* (1620), was founded on a methodology of observation and experiment, principles embraced and pursued by the founders of the Royal Society.¹²

This is a familiar history.

But what did science *mean* in the long eighteenth century? It could connote variously: insight or blindness; discovery or irrelevance; individual agency or wasteful self-interestedness; legitimacy or illicitness; civil society or social upheaval; modern enlightenment or trivial novelty. It could signal moral self-improvement and disinterestedness, or it could leave practitioners socially outcast and helpless in the marketplace. It could be conservative. It could be subversive.¹³

In his *Diary*, Samuel Pepys privately records a casual meeting in August 1666 on the streets of London that captures the multiplicity of these associations:

Up, and with Reeves walk as far as the Temple, doing some business in my way at my bookseller's and elsewhere, and there parted, and I took coach, having first discoursed with Mr. Hooke a little, whom we met in the streete, about the nature of sounds, and he did make me understand the nature of musicall sounds made by strings, mighty prettily; and told me that having come to a certain number of vibrations proper to make any tone, he is able to tell how many strokes a fly makes with her wings (those flies that hum in their flying) by the note that it answers to in musique during their flying. That, I suppose, is a little too much refined; but his discourse in general of sound was mighty fine.[14]

As is the case throughout the *Diary*, the actors in Pepys's report reflect new, urban practices and pastimes. Richard Reeve was the most prominent London instrument maker in the 1650s and 1660s, offering detailed tutorials for customers in his shop or their homes.[15] Reeve, according to Christopher Wren, "makes the best of any microscopes to be had."[16] Although he came from relatively humble beginnings, Hooke was a brilliant and central figure in the newly established Royal Society, serving in a variety of posts, including curator of experiments (1662), Cutlerian Lector in Mechanics (1664), and Gresham Professor in Geometry (1664). He was also a special advisor to Reeve's shop.[17] Pepys, clerk of the acts to the Navy Board and later member of Parliament, was admitted as a fellow of the society in 1664–1665 and served as its president from 1684 to 1686. He is also famous for his love of wine, women, and the playhouse—this same entry includes details of meeting with one Mrs. Burroughs and "having much pleasure with her."[18]

In August 1664, two years before this chance encounter on the street, Pepys had bought a microscope from Reeve. Its outer tube would have been covered in dyed vellum (or a thicker leather) and adorned with decorative gold tooling, similar to book bindings.[19] On delivery, Reeve gave Pepys a portable camera obscura called a scotoscope. With his typical concern about finances, Pepys marveled at the expense of the instrument. The microscope is "a most curious bauble" and the scotoscope "is of value; and a curious curiosity it is to look at objects in a darke room with."[20] That evening, Pepys consulted Henry Power's *Experimental Philosophy in Three Books* (1664) "to enable me a little how to use and what to expect from my glasse" and then tried it out with his wife, Elizabeth, the following day.[21] The experience of excitement and frustration was typical for a new user. Samuel and Elizabeth embarked "with great pleasure," but it was "with great difficulty before we could come to find the manner of seeing any thing by my microscope."[22] After the new year, Pepys spotted *Micrographia* at his booksellers, "bespoke" it on January 2, and collected it on January 20, at which point he calls Hooke's text "a most excellent piece, and of which I am very proud," and "most ingenious book that ever I read in my life."[23] The next night, Pepys stayed up until two in the morning reading it.

I enumerate these details to characterize what early science meant to a man such as Pepys. His purchase and use of scientific instruments and natural philosophy texts signal membership in an urban circle that mixed at the playhouse, the Royal Exchange, and the Royal Society. Pepys's purchases are in company in the *Diary* with social events, cultural offerings, and commercial exchanges; that is, they are one of many ways that Pepys seeks entertainment and intellectual enlightenment, how he keeps up with the current modes of sociability in London. For Pepys, ownership of these items communicates his fashionability as a Londoner who was just as likely to receive a short lecture in the street from Robert Hooke as he was to patronize the playhouse tiring room and converse with Nell Gwyn. Pepys consumed information about the scientific instrument he bought and fell into the imaginative wonder available because of these new views, even because of the possibility of these new views. He then wrote about the experience, bringing the work of experimental discovery into the textual domain. Practicing experimentalism meant doing experiments and imagining how they might be done and, in the process, reformulating one's sense of self as a specifically modern subject, a discoverer of natural knowledge—or at least a witness to it.[24]

In the example of Pepys, we can see that experimental philosophy connoted a sense of modernity, a new mode appropriate to the current time. Thomas Sprat, who was commissioned to write *The History of the Royal Society* not long after its founding, explains that natural philosophy produces a collective focus on the present rather than the past. Our bodies even confirm this forward-looking sensibility: while we "easily upon occasion turn about to look behind us; yet [nature] has plac'd the *Eyes*, the chief *Instruments* of *Observation*, not in our *Backs* but in our *Foreheads*."[25] Sprat conjoins physical and temporal presence. The body's eyes not only function as veritable instruments for observation, but they also hold a connotative purpose as well. This is looking forward as both a physical, embodied practice and a metaphor. Sprat's image correlates to the wider project of promoting natural philosophy. The experience of conducting or witnessing a scientific experiment produces a specific cognitive effect: the subject attends to the present and, as a result, is aware of being a modern individual, here and now. Experiments are therefore inherently about modernity, and this modernity is specifically English.

The processes of performing experiments and reading about them "give us a perfect Sight of what is before us; they bring us home to our selves; they make us live in *England*, and not in *Athens* or *Sparta*, at this present time, and not three thousand Years ago."[26] James Fortescue, in the following century, lauds the teachings of Bacon, Boyle, and Newton because they "Pierc'd the obscure, and taught us to be men."[27] Experiments produce specific knowledge, but they also perform the figurative work of expressing the practitioner's identity. Experiments "bring us home to ourselves; they make us live in *England.*" They "taught us to be men." The acts of practicing science and writing about science produce modern, enlightened subjects—masculinized and privileged certainly, but modern, enlightened subjects nonetheless. Science in this period "became public, fashionable and a matter of cultural status."[28] It was available through the Royal Society or the marketplace, in coffee houses and shops.[29] (By these means, according to Margaret C. Jacob and Larry Stewart, it was also established as a major force in economic development, a fulfillment of Sprat's earlier vision of improving England's "*Industry*" and the Royal Society functioning as "the general *Bank* and Free-port of the World."[30]) Microscopy and other forms of experimental philosophy became fashionable and, in the process, facilitated the articulation of what it meant to be a modern, enlightened subject. Scientific instruments and instruction gave consumers the promise of transforming themselves into experimental philosophers, delving into the natural and social worlds. Such enthusiasm reflects a vibrant commercial market for scientific instruments.[31] The example of the microscope is illustrative. Small single lenses known as "flea glasses," for instance, were widely available and extremely popular.[32] In his 1691–1692 Cutlerian Lecture to the Royal Society, Hooke lamented that only the Dutch naturalist Antoni van Leeuwenhoek, inducted an "overseas member" of the Royal Society in 1680, still used microscopes for science.[33] For others, it was merely a "Diversion and Pastime."[34] By the mid-eighteenth century, "the Moderateness of the Price" enhanced microscopes' availability and appeal, and they were used in homes and lecture halls.[35]

Collecting scientific instruments became increasingly popular for display, use, and edification.[36] The instrument maker Benjamin Martin gave courses, lectures, and demonstrations in his shop on Fleet Street (Martin's son, J. L. Martin, became his partner in 1780, two years before Benjamin's death). In *Lettres astronmiques* (1771), J. Bernoulli observes, Martin's "shop is one of the best equipped, and his courses are well attended."[37] Martin also published over thirty guides and instruction books, most of which were aimed at converting readers into practitioners.[38] He made science a matter of public and fashionable knowledge, rather than being confined merely to "the country homes of the aristocracy or to those whom the Court chose to patronize."[39] Martin's *The Young Gentleman and Lady's Philosophy* (1759–1763) portrays a conversation between a young woman (Euphrosyne) and her brother (Cleonicus), who has just returned from university. Cleonicus praises his sister's intellectual curiosity in no small part because it is à la mode: "Philosophy is the darling Science of every Man of Sense, and is a peculiar Grace in the Fair Sex; and depend on it, Sister, it is now growing into a Fashion for the Ladies to study Philosophy."[40] Cleonicus—sounding like Martin the instrument maker plying his wares—argues that consumers will want to buy microscopes, for example, because they "are very apt to be affected with Grandeur and Magnificence, in every Shape; and the Microscope, to many People, as much recommends itself by a pompous Appearance, as by its useful Effects."[41] Young women will appreciate that they are "neatly disposed in their Cases, with a Number of little Trinkets about them, all of elegant Workmanship."[42] Arthur Devis's *The John Bacon Family* (1742–1743) features a domestic interior furnished with numerous scientific instruments, including a quadrant, telescope, air pump, a microscope, and two globes (see Figure 1.1). And even Jonathan Swift contemplated buying a microscope for his close friend, Esther Johnson, whom he called Stella.[43]

Experimental philosophy's allure in the cultural marketplace was that it could represent newness and modernity, urbanity and sophistication. Whether as a practice, a theory, or a consumer good, experimental philosophy served as a metaphor through which advocates, enthusiasts, and consumers could imagine themselves and their worlds anew.

LITERARINESS

The commercial association of natural philosophy with metaphors of modernity was possible because of the imaginative connotations built into the practice, description, and aspirations of natural philosophers. Yet from the early days of the Royal Society, such figurative associations were admonished, particularly with regard to reporting scientific discoveries. The 1663 statutes governing its establishment and functioning deliberately outline what an experimental thing might be: "In all Reports of Experiments to be brought into the Society, the matter of fact shall be barely stated, without any prefaces, apologies, or rhetorical flourishes;

FIGURE 1.1. Arthur Devis, *The John Bacon Family* (1742–1743). Paul Mellon Collection at the Yale Center for British Art.

and entered so in the Register-book, by order of the Society."⁴⁴ In other words, it is language that is emphatically not literary. The genre of the report suggests a purely descriptive quality to the writing, which is expected to obscure both its authorship and its existence as a piece of writing. An experimental report submitted to the Royal Society needs to be distinguished from the implied vagaries and indulgences of literariness. The purpose of the dictum is to inoculate experimental discoveries from the charge of incredulity. And the effect of this dictum is to institute an association and opposition—literariness with the imagination in contrast to experimentalism with the empirical.

The shorthand for this difference was *words* and *things*.⁴⁵ Abraham Cowley's encomium to the Royal Society praises Bacon for loosening the grip of "Words, which are but Pictures of the Thought,/(Though we our Thoughts from them perversely drew)," in favor of "Things, the Mind's right Object."⁴⁶ Hooke shuns literariness as inferior to things, the former drawing on the imagination and the latter on observation: "The truth is, the science of nature has been already too long made only a work of the brain and the fancy: It is now high time that it should return to the plainness and soundness of observations on material and obvious things."⁴⁷ With mock humility, he turns away from "the brain and the fancy" as the source of figuration by demurring that "works of wit and imagination are above my weak abilities."⁴⁸ In this same vein, Sprat asserts that things facilitate social harmony, enjoining readers that "the most effectual Remedy to be us'd [against "Animosities"], is, first to assemble about some *calm* and *indifferent* Things, especially *Experiments*. In them there can be no cause of mutual *Exasperations*: In them they may agree, or dissent without Faction or Fierceness."[49]

If the institutional documents of the Royal Society promoted, in Cowley's words, "Things, the Mind's right Object," in Hooke's, "material and obvious things," and in Sprat's, "*calm* and *indifferent* Things," then the society's members meditated on the explanatory role figurative language might serve in the reporting of experimental findings. Jonathan Lamb finds a turn to the imaginative in Locke's empiricism, but the writings of Robert Boyle—chemist, physicist, a member of the "invisible college" of the 1640s, and later a founder of the Royal Society—vividly reflect the uneasy and yet persistent tension, characteristic of seventeenth-century natural philosophical texts, between the need to be spare and the need to draw on the reader's imagination in order to make findings imaginable and thus not incredible but credible.[50] Such pieces of writing, though dedicated to presenting scientific facts as inviolable, were often self-consciously literary, imbued with pleasure and promoting enjoyment.[51]

Boyle is famed for his endorsement of the plain style in writing experimental philosophy, a view that simultaneously maligns what he calls in *A Proemial Essay* (1661) "rhetorical ornaments in setting down an experiment."[52] In the essay, Boyle addresses the representation of experiments, not the experiments themselves. The imperative to persuade an audience outside those available to observe a singular experiment relied on the production of texts, facilitating the virtual witnessing central to the Royal Society's process of authenticating experimental knowledge.[53] Scholars have noted Boyle's reliance on narrative, rather than mere description, as a way of constructing a text's authority.[54] Boyle cautions that these reports have an obligation to "inform readers, not to delight or persuade them."[55] Figuration, that is, the use of literary language, confirms this distinction. He continues, "to affect needless rhetorical ornaments in setting down an experiment, or explicating something abstruse in nature, were little less improper, than it were (for him that designs not to look directly upon the sun itself) to paint the eyeglasses of a telescope, whose clearness is their commendation."[56] The image of a telescope provided fodder for advocates and satirists alike. In *Entretiens sur la pluralité des mondes* (1686), dedicated to explaining Copernican and Cartesian cosmology, Bernard de Fontenelle endorses the use of telescopes, but understands them figuratively as tools for naturalists to imagine traveling to the moon, while the poet Samuel Butler ridicules a natural philosopher who claims to discover an elephant on the moon when in fact a mouse has "mistaken its Way and got into his Telescope."[57] The painted telescope lens is a central conceit of Aphra Behn's *The Emperor of the Moon* (1687), wherein the patriarch-naturalist is duped by such images into believing he sees a royal court on the moon.

Yet Boyle's comparison between "rhetorical ornaments" and adorned lenses accomplishes more than a satiric end. The potential for telescopes to reveal and obscure was always at issue, but the image of a painted telescope lens, as Boyle imagines it, transforms this concern about the reliability of optical perception into a denunciation of figuration—that is, rejecting metaphors as unreliable. "Rhetorical ornaments" and painted lenses convey aesthetic, not empirical, knowledge; in this they are similar. But they are also significantly distinct, as Boyle's own simile confirms. If the painted lens corrupts the transparency—the "clearness"—of the observation possible through a telescope, then the metaphor relies on a firm belief in optical instrumentation as reliable and true, an assumption that was not yet historically settled.[58] But the comparison between an aesthetically modified lens and aesthetically modified language as similarly misleading presumes a stability to figurative language that, we shall see, Boyle's own writing rejects.

The metaphor of clarity to bolster the credibility of experimental writing exfoliates a double bind: scientific writing requires literary knowledge but suppresses it simultaneously. A few years after Boyle's *A Proemial Essay*, Cowley praises Sprat's *History* for the author's "candid Stile [which] like a clean Stream does slide," unmarked by pollution.[59] Here, Cowley uses a simile. Here, too, language is transparent. Ennobling the simile by alluding to an unwavering faith in first causes, Cowley characterizes the currents of the Thames as guided gently by God's "judicious hand."[60] Verbal clarity is not only accurate; it also serves as the vehicle for physico-theology.

In contrast to his statements against literary language in *A Proemial Essay*, Boyle confesses in *The Christian Virtuoso Shewing that by Being Addicted to Experimental Philosophy, a Man is Rather Assisted than Indisposed to be a Good Christian* (1690), "I think myself here obliged to acknowledge, once for all, that I did it [used metaphors] purposely."[61] The justifications are twofold. "Comparisons fitly chosen" help a reader understand science better. They also serve as "a kind of Argument."[62] In the latter case, Boyle offers a theory of language that reverses his earlier position. Metaphors, like microscopes, advance scientific learning: "Proper Comparisons do the Imagination almost as much Service, as Microscopes do the Eye."[63] The optical instrument "gives us a distinct view of divers minute Things, which our naked Eyes cannot well discern."[64] So, too, does the proper metaphor: "a skilfully chosen, and well-applied, Comparison much helps the Imagination, by illustrating Things scarce discernible, so as to represent them by Things much more familiar and easy to be apprehended."[65] Boyle claims that metaphors bring the object into view. Here, literary language operates as a scientific instrument unto itself, one that uncovers, rather than distorts or creates, natural phenomena.

The Christian Virtuoso embraces the potential for literary knowledge to function as an effective translator of scientific knowledge. Boyle's concern with making "a skilfully chosen, and well-applied, Comparison" plays out in an early treatise, *New Experiments Physico-mechanical, Touching the Spring of the Air, and its Effects* (1660), which recounts the results from experiments conducted in Oxford using an air pump designed and constructed by Hooke and Ralph Greatorex. The air pump introduced technology to visualize combustion and respiration, and it enabled the study of "airs," which were ordinarily detected only through their effect on other objects. Boyle faces a rhetorical and intellectual challenge—how to convey his discovery that common air has elasticity. He famously conceptualized this feature as a spring, which, as Jayne Elizabeth Lewis notes, points in two directions, to air's "measurable and defining attribute" and its "difference from the infinite fluency of aether."[66] If air is simultaneously measurable and unmeasurable, then a spring is illustrative for Boyle because it requires a limit: a spring "needs a wall to hit if it is to happen in the first place."[67]

Spring in Boyle's usage is not a verb but a noun.[68] What does air's spring—its elasticity—look like? In answer, Boyle, like many others following him, turns to the logic of similitude by referring to things from everyday life, a move that uses figurative language for two ends. Such metaphors make air visible imaginatively and also underscore its familiarity, even ubiquity. Boyle does not merely slip into metaphor: he actively searches for the right one, skillfully choosing and applying well. First, he selects a sponge, and then suggests that the pressure of air against bodies is akin to the tension one feels in a stretched bow.[69] Yet neither metaphor suits fully. Boyle continues to cast about and finally encourages the reader to picture

the Air near the Earth to be such a heap of little Bodies, lying one upon another, as may be resembled to a Fleece of Wooll. For this (to omit other likenesses betwixt them) consists of many slender and flexible Hairs; each of which, may indeed, like a little Spring, be easily bent or rouled up; but will also, like a Spring, be still endeavouring to stretch it self out again.[70]

The care to eliminate a broad comparison "to omit other likenesses betwixt them" is palpable. The metaphor of wool does not specify whether it is still attached to the sheep's body, whether it continues to grow or is held in organic suspension. The singular likeness on which Boyle grounds the justness of the comparison is the curved buoyancy of air particles. The reader cannot *see* air: it is invisible to the naked eye except as an effect on other objects. Leaves flutter. Feathers lilt. But air remains stubbornly transparent and, by extension, unknowable. Boyle's figuration transforms that transparency into the material form of wool. The exactness of this demarcation requires, not suspends, the experimental imagination.

Yet Boyle's wool metaphor is not merely a visual substitute: the metaphor simultaneously endows air with tactile qualities. Boyle elaborates the somatic effects of air particles in a discussion of "the compactness and pressure of Inferior Air."[71] Wool operates as an effective metaphor because it replicates specific qualities of air. Rather than conjure the experience of wind, Boyle provides a tactile comparison:

when a man squeezes a Fleece of Wool in his hand, he may feel that the Wool incessantly bears against his hand, as that which hinders the hairs it consists of, to recover their former and more natural extent. So each parcel of the Air about the Earth, does constantly endeavour to thrust away all those contiguous Bodies, whether Aerial or more gross, that keep them bent, and hinder the expansion of its parts.[72]

The order of information contributes to Boyle's figuration. We begin with the vehicle—the detailed experience of compressing wool in one's hand and how the substance feels against one's skin. The man's hand forms the boundary against which the wool, structurally designed to expand into springs, presses. As both a visual and somatic metaphor, the tangibility of wool in one's hand illuminates Boyle's arguments about air, but it does so through figuration. Then an adjunctive "So" signals the pivot of the metaphor's meaning making, turning to the particles of air and their relation to earth. In material substance and action, the metaphor registers the experimentalist's need to convert specialized knowledge into common knowledge.[73] The choice of wool is not so casual either: it is a specifically English commodity that Daniel Defoe later argues is the cornerstone of the national and patriotic economy.[74] The metaphor of wool thus encourages readers to think of Boyle's experiments with air as especially English—familiar and necessary. The literariness built into Boyle's accounts of combustion and respiration exposes a sustained use of metaphoric language to describe experiments. The crux for Boyle is selecting the best comparison to convey his findings, in no small part because the process of finding that comparison is equally important. The metaphor's vehicle conveys meanings that enable the naturalist to make his observations comprehensible. It serves as a sort of tutor for the reader, translating science analogically.

A metaphor's effect, however, introduces the potential that figuration may displace the referent altogether. Henry Power's vivid account of a horse fly captures the ever-present possibility that a naturalist's object of study comes to be transformed through its description. Power, a member of the Royal Society who primarily worked independently on his Yorkshire estate (a practice that Sprat endorsed), published *Experimental Philosophy in Three Books* (1664) a year before Hooke's richly engraved *Micrographia*. The section devoted to microscopy faces a challenge similar to Boyle's study of combustion and respiration: How can Power describe something that the human eye cannot perceive? He relies on simile: the horse fly's "eye is an incomparable pleasant spectacle . . . it looks like green silk Irish-stich, drawn upon a black ground, and all latticed or chequered with dimples . . . her body looks like silver in frost-work, only fring'd all over with wise silk."[75] Power's use of one form of visual perception (microscopy) to study another (the eye of an insect) is a self-conscious meditation on the process of experimental observation. If Power assumes a transparency to microscopy as an instrument, then his metaphors present these microscopic findings as aesthetic objects, surprisingly rendering an insect beautiful. Certainly microscopy in particular "had an immediate aesthetic appeal."[76] But this does not capture the literariness of microscopic demonstrations. The fly's eye "looks like" silk, jewelry, brocade, and lace. Power's rhetoric draws not only on similes, but also on the literary trope of ekphrasis, the "verbal representation of visual representation," something that is itself the result of artistic labor.[77] Silk, jewelry, brocade, and lace may be consumer goods, but they are also manufactured aesthetic objects.

Power's "skilfully chosen, and well-applied" similes create the effect of displacing the object under view such that the reader comes to imagine the fly's eye as made up of these jeweled, filigreed, and latticed parts. If the air pump's air figuratively converts into wool, then the microscope's insect transforms into a work of art. Metaphors, whether of wool or jewelry, enable experimental philosophers to describe things, but in so doing, metaphors simultaneously endow these things with a value and meaning that exceeds their original state. Inert bodies become active agents.[78] Through the imaginative power of metaphor, the eye of a horse fly transmutes into a beautiful luxury item. This is the basic lesson a metaphor teaches. Literariness, that "skilfully chosen, and well-applied, Comparison," instructs readers in the work of experimental observation: what you see is visible to you through your own imaginative activity.

OBSERVED PARTICULARS

As we have seen, experimentalists persistently use tropes to make their findings visible, if only in the reader's imagination. Metaphor is necessary because air and insects' eyes share the quality of invisibility. Both the air pump and the microscope facilitate the observation of things that cannot be seen with the naked eye—gases and the *subvisibilia*. Literariness produces visibility, which, within an optical regime, connotes knowability.[79]

Yet the role of literary figuration in early science exceeds a merely descriptive function: textual visibility and thus knowability of natural phenomena require these sustained acts of imagination. Experimentalists study the natural world, and thereby they consistently use literariness not solely to represent, but also to understand and conceptualize the objects under their purview. If Boyle encourages the use of "a skilfully chosen, and well-applied, Comparison" in the writing up of experimental discoveries, then Hooke demonstrates that a similar method of selection and application shapes the process that determines which natural phenomena count as significant—what is an observed particular and what is not. For Hooke, microscopy's observed particulars are "*exceeding small Bodies*, or *exceeding small Pores*, or *exceeding small Motions*," though not just any "exceeding small" thing will do: "there should be a *scrupulous* choice, and a *strict examination*, of the reality, constancy, and certainty of the Particulars that we admit."[80] The range of phenomena is capacious—bodies, pores, and motions—but each is subjected to discrimination that decides its validity, which Hooke measures as "reality, constancy, and certainty." They are chosen and they are examined, and "the most severe, and most impartial diligence, must be imployed."[81] Hooke modifies his nouns with rigorous adjectives: *scrupulous*, *strict*, *severe*, and *impartial*. Mary Poovey explains that Baconian facts "always carried an aura of theory."[82] But for Hooke, exactness is what endows observed particulars with their usefulness; as he explains, "above all, the most *instructive* are to be entertain'd."[83] Experimental philosophy's observed particular needs to meet the criteria of instructiveness.

Selecting a metaphor bears an uncanny resemblance to identifying an observed particular. Both must be well chosen. And by virtue of their analogous requirement for application (in Boyle's words, "well-applied") and "diligence," qualities that characterize a process of construction, metaphors and observed particulars likewise demand a practitioner's skill.

The science of microscopy presents an illustrative case study for the identification and certification of observed particulars in experimental practice more generally. The obstacle the experimentalist faces is determining an observed particular's "true form" or "true appearance," phrases that Hooke utilizes as synonyms for the legitimizing criteria of "reality, constancy, and certainty."[84] The experimentalist arrives at that "true form" or "true appearance" not through a singular observational instance but through a series of lookings. Microscopy requires repeated viewings, under a variety of conditions—in different light and with different lenses. The quest for a "true form" presupposes the stability of an object under view, of course, as well as a certainty that multiple viewings will ultimately unveil it, even though these viewings inevitably produce a synthesis. Hooke explains that "the same Object [may] seem quite differing, in one position to the Light, from what it really is, and may be discover'd in another."[85] Faced with different images under the microscope, images that may or may not resemble each other, Hooke does not enumerate his method apart from an insistence that he performs "many examinations in several lights, and in several positions to those lights."[86] Peering through the microscope repeatedly, Hooke explains, enables the production of experimental knowledge: thus, "I had discover'd the true form."[87] Repetition is methodology. An observed particular is an attempt to render a thing's "true form," an *essai*, and Hooke's clarification here highlights the difference between the observed particular and the thing itself. In "Discourse concerning Telescopes and Microscopes," Hooke nods to the provisional status of observed particulars when he explains that scientific instruments enable the "perfecting and compleating the Knowledge of those Particulars which have been already, in Part, detected."[88] The gerunds are telling. Experimental knowledge and its observed particulars are works in progress.[89] The observed particular is ultimately a process and a compilation, a result of piecing together various images that combine to represent a thing's "true form" and "true appearance." For Hooke in the seventeenth century, the multiply-viewed object as a concept was designed to convey authority and reliability specifically because it avoided the singular, and potentially inaccurate, observation.[90] Yet what the naturalist presents is a singularity, not the imaginative process behind the scientific sense of a singular instance.

The observed particular occupies the same figurative territory as a metaphor. Hooke's observed particular requires the scientist's mind to make connections among various images as a way of determining, and thus producing, the object's "true form"; as such, the observed particular draws on the imagination. Some have characterized Hooke's natural philosopher as "an automaton-scribe," but this reading ignores the role Hooke imagines for the learned mind.[91] As Boyle's writing demonstrates, representing experimental findings relies on the imaginative possibilities inherent to figurative language. The process of demarcating an observed particular—identifying it, justifying it—likewise utilizes the logic of figuration. Microscopy, and any other experimental practice, is not just about looking at things: observed particulars exist because natural philosophers determine that they are worthwhile. Built into this formulation is a claim about essence that operates retrospectively, the minute particular as an ontological effect. A thing's assigned value is presented as its inherent value, a claim that conceals the imaginative discernment at the core of experimental knowledge production.

Hooke strongly endorsed the Royal Society's Baconianism, which he expressed as a resistance to theorizing.[92] Even so, Hooke criticized the accumulation of data merely as data. He explicitly cautions against the temptation to record every phenomenon as if it were an observed particular: "the storing up of all, without any regard to evidence or use, will only tend to darkness and confusion."[93] While tapping his own visual metaphor, Hooke uses the generic term *all* to avoid naming these bits that fail to rise to the level of observed particulars. The production of experimental knowledge is a form of acquisition and, as such, needs to seek things that are valuable: "We must not therefore esteem the riches of our Philosophical treasure by the *number* only, but chiefly by the *weight*."[94]

And yet for all of Hooke's rhetorical and intellectual work to explicate what may count as an observed particular, *Micrographia* implicitly challenges Hooke's own words with its spectacular engravings. Whereas the Dutch natural philosopher Leeuwenhoek was a poor draftsman and needed to be convinced to use an illustrator, Hooke devoted himself to sketching images for the detailed engravings that contributed to his book's immense popularity.[95] Hooke and Christopher Wren synthesized scientific images for artists to reproduce for publication in an aesthetic practice recently described as "wicked intelligence."[96] These images produced an important effect. There was no way to demonstrate his microscopical findings except to individuals, one at a time, so the engravings provided ocular demonstration of what Hooke saw or what the microscope revealed, depending on one's emphasis. This is virtual witnessing, but with images rather than words. Perhaps microscopy in particular requires visual supplementation.[97] But Hooke's reliance on figuration does not halt with the images themselves: these too are for the mind's eye. The images of the *subvisibilia* rely on techniques of engraving that produce an effect of magnification in line with the experience of looking through a microscope: a reader of *Micrographia* must unfold the famous plate of the flea, an act that simulates the wonder one would have felt with the original microscopical view. Hooke produces an aesthetic experience as a way of intimating microscopical scrutiny. The technology of a book comes to represent the instrumentation of a microscope.

MODEST WITNESSES

My discussion of literariness and the observed particular has excavated the far-reaching and productive role of the experimental imagination to the textual representation of scientific knowledge and, even more radically, to the conceptualization of the things that warrant experimental observation, those "things" of natural philosophy. Spiraling outward, my argument turns now to the role of the scientist, that producer of text and discoveries. As we shall see, the subject position that natural philosophers construct for themselves requires yet more imaginative acts. These are the modest witnesses of early modern objectivity, instrumental to the work of experimentalism and yet simultaneously obscured from view.

To articulate the ideal viewer, one must also evoke its opposite. When Boyle explains, in *Considerations Touching the Usefulness of Experimental Natural Philosophy* (1663), "there are many things in Nature, which to a superficial Observer seem to have no relation to one another," he draws a contrast between an untrained and trained viewer.[98] The "superficial Observer" skims over surfaces, glances at things, and misses the fullness of the phenomena that could be, even ought to be, under consideration—anticipating the "regime of the eye" that Peter de Bolla associates with William Hogarth's early eighteenth-century aesthetic theory.[99] The difference between this possibility and its opposite turns on the adjective *superficial*. In the following clause, Boyle's adjective explicitly refers to learning, whether in the form of training, experience, or some other method altogether: "a *knowing* Naturalist . . . is able to discern [nature's] secret Correspondences and Alliances [emphasis added]."[100] Boyle contends that knowledge is waiting to be gathered by those who might pay attention to the "obvious phaenomena of nature": "attention alone might quickly furnish us with one half of the History of Nature," while the other half might be acquired through experiments.[101] Offering his own biography as an example, Boyle recounts that he resisted reading earlier philosophers such as Descartes and Gassendi so that "I might not be prepossess'd with any Theory or Principles"; the absence of traditional learning allows him to be attentive to the natural world.[102] And the cultivation of attentiveness preoccupied naturalists throughout the seventeenth and eighteenth centuries.[103]

To the "superficial Observer," the world looks chaotic; to the "knowing Naturalist," it appears coherent. Experimental philosophy discovers and reports connections that comprise what Henry Power calls the "great Machine of the World."[104] Power uses the metaphor of a clock to convey the specialized skills and knowledge of natural philosophers. Like Boyle, Power uses a contrast, but he differs from Boyle by making it clearer what he rejects, Scholasticism. Power associates inferior observation with the intellectual predecessors of natural philosophers. These were, according to Power, "old Dogmatists and Notional Speculators, [who] onely gaz'd at the visible effects and last Resultances of things."[105] Power charges that they "understood no more of Nature, than a rude Countrey-fellow does of the Internal Fabrick of a Watch, that onely sees the Index and Horary Circle, and perchance hears the Clock and Alarum strike in it."[106] The watch metaphor is telling: a watch measures the passage of time, but it also represents two forms of knowledge. The first type pertains to recognizing the measurability of time. But the second requires an understanding of how the mechanism that is measuring time works. The former is available to any "rude Countrey-fellow." The latter, to the elite, learned, and regulated natural philosophers of the Royal Society. Within the imagistic equivalences of Power's language, "old Dogmatists and Notional Speculators" are similar to, if not now themselves, "rude Countrey-fellow[s]." Power's characterization overlays a generational critique with the hierarchies of rank, status, and urbanity; as we shall see, the latter gesture to rank and status features regularly in advocates' arguments for the legitimacy and superiority of the experimental method.[107]

The acuity, creativity, and attentiveness of the "knowing Naturalist" distinguish him (more on the masculinity of the experimentalist shortly) from an ordinary observer. But who is this experimental philosopher? From its earliest days, a major preoccupation of the Royal Society was training that observer, which Shapin and Schaffer, and later Donna Haraway, have described as the "modest witness" of late seventeenth-century experimental practice.[108] The observer needed to be believed to be reliable.[109] That observer was also not necessarily the experimenter; few members of the Royal Society performed their own experiments, and most relied on men of lower rank. Hooke is the notable exception to this practice. He was a brilliant experimenter and thinker: he was an engineer, surveyor, and architect, and he invented numerous scientific instruments. Hooke lectured on optics, light, color, heat, meteorology, astronomy, gravity, combustion, and comets. And he was also overworked.[110] But he was not a gentleman. In later years, the president and luminary, Isaac Newton, who came to loathe Hooke, at one point removed Hooke's name from the Royal Society records and destroyed his portrait.[111] Science was not the domain of professionals as we would now understand it but rather was attached (for Hooke, especially) to the social exclusivity of rank.[112]

Just as with the concept of the observed particular, the notion of the modest witness relies on figuration that exposes its literariness. The "knowing Naturalist," the modest witness is a masculine figure of authority, gentility, and privilege, admired for his morality and knowledgeability and, just as notable, distinguished from women and laboring men.[113] He embodies, paradoxically, a privileged absence, a model of spectatorship that conveys authority through its claim to be free from the limitations of self-interest. As Shapin and Schaffer explain, "The literary display of a certain sort of morality was a technique in the making of matters of fact. A man whose narrative could be credited as mirrors of reality was a *modest* man; his reports ought to make that modesty visible."[114] Through a "parajuridical metaphor," Boyle creates a source of authority founded on the consensus of a collection of modest witnesses who together confirm the existence of a fact but steer clear of speculating about its cause.[115]

Modesty here expressly safeguards—and, in so doing, it articulates—the subject who understands himself as impervious to individualistic opinion and as persuaded only by collectively agreed-on facticity. In Hooke's words, the natural philosopher only "record[s] the things themselves as they appear."[116] Haraway points out that such modesty, emblematized by a "witness whose accounts mirror reality," "must be invisible, that is, an inhabitant of the potent 'unmarked category,' which is constructed by the extraordinary conventions of self-invisibility."¹¹⁷ Male modesty referred to the mind; female modesty referred to the body.¹¹⁸ Male modesty is the modesty of objectivity and takes for granted an invisibility that settles into a trope of universalized transparency. Thus, the mirror metaphor recurs as scholars describe the rhetoric of a male modest witness's findings. In contrast, female modesty is subjectivity, which—as I discuss in Chapter 2—connotes experiential authority that is individualized, particularized, and biased.

The mirror as a metaphor for mimesis is just one form of figuration that conveys modesty. Another is the human body: the modest witness could be imagined as a tool because of the centrality of scientific instrumentation as a technology and a metaphor of early experimental practice. The air pump and the microscope, in particular, were showpieces of the Royal Society, associated with Boyle and Hooke, respectively, and brought out for demonstrations when visitors arrived.¹¹⁹ Conceptually, scientific instruments serve two purposes. They provide a mechanism for the modest witness to erase himself from the processes of observation and experiment. They also produce the observed particulars that stand as the currency of experimental practice. Descriptions of instrumental experiments presume and present observed particulars as stable, discoverable facts, not the works in progress that we saw earlier.¹²⁰

In *Micrographia*, Hooke uses the metaphor of optical instruments to imagine the scientist. Hooke's defense of sense perception is at the heart of his understanding of scientific instrumentalization: "because [we previously] rely'd upon the strength of humane Reason alone, [we] have begun anew to correct all *Hypotheses* by sense."¹²¹ Sensory perception is amplified, not distorted, by scientific instruments. "Artificial Instruments," he explains, provide "a reparation made for the mischiefs, and imperfection, mankind has drawn upon it self."¹²² John Locke vehemently disagrees with Hooke's optimism; the potential for sensory perception, according to Locke, is located within the human body only. Hooke's "Artificial Instruments" will only lead to faulty perceptions. Locke's refutation of scientific instrumentation, in turn, views the human body as an instrument in its own right, one that ought not be subject to adaptation or modification. He explains that "our Senses, Faculties, and Organs" are already "fitted" "to the conveniences of Life, and the Business we have to do here."¹²³ Although Locke presents the human body instrumentally, he disagrees with Hooke's endorsement of prosthetics. Locke is especially skeptical of microscopy, contending that it produces blindness rather than insight. Locke imagines that human eyes are replaced by the lenses of a microscope: "if by the help of such Microscopical Eyes (if I may so call them,) a Man could penetrate farther than ordinary into the secret Composition, and radical Texture of bodies, he would not make any great advantage by the change, if such an acute Sight would not serve to conduct him to the Market and Exchange."[124] Locke's imagery is vivid. Microscopic perception may help discover minute qualities, but an individual with these optical skills will falter in the main corridors of life. We are left with the picture of a man whose eyes have been replaced by microscopes, groping as he futilely attempts to navigate the commercial and social world.

Locke's skepticism finds its opposite in Hooke's enthusiasm: endorsing instrumentation enables Hooke to imagine the modest witness metonymically. Within an instrumental framework, Hooke figures the modest witness as "a sincere Hand and a faithful Eye," a metaphor that converts the human body into a scientific instrument.[125] Hooke even represents himself as an instrument for others to use. Hooke refers to his work with a simile to instrument makers: "all my ambition is, that I may serve to the great Philosophers of this Age, as the makers of my Glasses did to me."[126] Hooke's modest witness and Hooke himself are instruments that facilitate the production of experimental knowledge. Not only is the individual modest witness metonymically reduced, but so, too, is the corporate body of the Royal Society, according to Sprat, into a "*Union* of *Eyes, and Hands.*"[127] Sprat's version denudes the instrumentalized body of any subjective qualities and, through the plural, imagines a community through metonymy. But the body of the modest witness in *Micrographia* is reduced to metonymies, the hand for representation (writing) and the eye for observation (seeing). Even instrumentalized body parts, separated from the body as a whole, still require adjectival modification with their adjunctive *sincere* and *faithful*. These qualities shore up the metaphor of a human body as a reliable instrument and also evoke the subjective human peering through the microscope's lens and writing about these sights.

Within his own experimental accounts, Boyle takes Hooke's figuration a step further by removing the human body altogether, leaving no trace of it even adjectivally. In *New Experiments Physico-Mechanicall, Touching the Spring of the Air, and its Effects* (1660), Boyle explains that, thanks to the air pump, combustion and respiration "constantly and regularly offer it self [themselves] to our observation, as depending upon the Fabrick of the Engine [the air pump] it self, and not upon the nature of this or that particular Experiment which 'tis employed to try."[128] Boyle's verbal construction, "offer it self to our observation," conceives the phenomenon under observation making itself available to the air pump; this is a machine that interacts with the natural world, apparently without human intervention, receiving its data unadulterated. Boyle sidesteps the unanswered question of an instrument's mediation. He also employs a rhetorical sleight of hand to ensure the self-effacement that defines the modest witness. All we perceive is the generalized "our" of "our observation."

These figurations of the modest witness limit the presence of the human body and dramatize the sort of invisible subject required to produce experimental knowledge. Yet the modest witness cannot erase the subjectivity of the experimenter completely, for these accounts serve a double duty: they not only must convey the protocols that legitimize experimental findings, but they must also transmit enthusiasm for the project altogether. Advocates meet a subject's modesty with the imaginative quality of wonder in equal measure. If the modest witness requires imaginative figuration, then the process of engaging in experimentalism is linked to the affective responses of wonder and delight.[129] The pared down quality of the modest witness seems to be at odds with the lure of the imagination, yet these figurations are part of the same project. This doubleness is embodied in Hooke himself, who, as Michael Hunter argues, was "a 'scientist' in a full, modern sense, yet this was not exclusive of his being something of a 'wonder-monger,'" selling his findings rhetorically wrapped in the cloak of amazement.[130]

In *The Microscope Made Easy* (1742), Henry Baker is keen to convey how the imagination will be stimulated by experimental practice.[131] Baker was a fellow of the Royal Society, member of the Society of Antiquaries, author of poems on natural philosophy, Daniel Defoe's son-in-law, and memorialized in the 1798 edition of *Biographia Britannica* as "an ingenious and diligent Naturalist," as well as an "active and zealous instrument in carrying on [the Royal Society's] laudable purposes."[132] In a section of *The Microscope Made Easy* devoted to the examination of blood under a microscope, Baker proclaims, "No Words can describe the wonderful Scene [of circulation] that was presented before our Eyes!"[133] "No words can describe," so the reader's imagination will have to take over—a common trope. Baker's promise is specific: take up a microscope to encounter an extra-linguistic experience of wonder and amazement. Then you will "pass those leisure Hours agreeably and usefully in contemplating the wonders of the Creation, which otherwise would be spent in tiresome Idleness, or perhaps, some fashionable and expensive Vice."[134] The fashionability of experimental knowledge is implied through its contrast to idleness and vices, but this is only part of its appeal. Experimental philosophy draws people because of its expansive imaginative possibilities.

As powerful as the lure of the imagination could and needed to be, however, it required moderation and policing. The conceptualization of the modest witness pivots between celebrating and eschewing the imagination. If promoters such as Baker celebrate the imagination in an experimental context, then they synchronously share a cautious skepticism about its efficacy and potential to derail true and reliable experimental practice. The concern was to prove that experimental accounts in no way embellished the details—that is, natural philosophers had to assure readers that accounts did not draw on the imagination in any overt or identifiable way.[135] Sprat's *History* pursues the problem of weighing both a favorable and a skeptical view of the role of the imagination in the production of experimental knowledge. Sprat evokes the critics of the Royal Society who contend that experimentalists are subject to their imaginative whims. To naysayers, experimental philosophy "makes [fellows] *Romantic*, and subject to frame more perfect Images of Things, than the Things themselves will bear."[136] Sprat's treatment of this possibility illuminates the intellectual balancing act of justifying and controlling their recourse to the powers of the imagination. Sprat explains that because the wonder epitomized by enthusiastic advocates could easily be interpreted as an uncritical and delusional response, the idea of the imagination serving a purpose in natural philosophy always needs to be folded back into the larger project of experimentalism. Sprat's text models this recuperation in its argument that natural philosophy produces the opposite, sober response to a "Romantic" one: the practitioner of natural philosophy "endeavours rather to know, than to admire."[137] Intellectual mastery is captured by the term *know* and contrasted with the "Romantic" quality of admiration. The former comes across as means to establish distance and difference between the observer and the observed. The latter conveys identification and a loss of self. Sprat's natural philosopher aims "to enlarge, and amend his *Knowledge* . . . [and is] modest in his *Judgment*."[138]

Modesty here is an externalization of one's morals and wisdom. Sprat's scientist has modest judgment that emerges from a rigorous interplay of the figurative and the empirical. Modesty does not merely render the body metonymic or invisible, as in Hooke's and Boyle's metaphors. It also mobilizes the imagination and simultaneously contains it. In a later elaboration of the modest judgment Sprat hails, Baker contends that modesty and candor are the most vital attributes for any individual desiring to produce or to contribute to experimental knowledge. In a letter addressed to the president of the Royal Society, Martin Folkes, Baker explains that "knowledgeable people are modest and that ignorant people are arrogant: therefore consider Things with Modesty and Candour."[139] Baker initially posits knowledgeability as the attribute that produces modesty and ignorance as that which produces its opposite, arrogance. But he quickly and subtly reverses his stance. Expressed in the logical turn of a single word, *therefore*, Baker subsequently cautions experimentalists that they need to be modest, even though he has just claimed that "knowledgeable people"—presumably those reading these texts and practicing natural philosophy—already are. Baker's syntax carries the burden of turning a claim about knowledgeable people more generally into an imperative for experimentalists. The implicit command is that if experimentalists are modest, then they will be knowledgeable: "A truly wise Man is so fully sensible how little he knows, and what Things he once was ignorant of, which he is now acquainted with, that he is far enough from supposing his own Judgment a Standard of the Reality of Things."[140] For Baker, the human mind is inclined to careful examination because of its native propensity to satisfy curiosity and seek novelty, inclinations that may lead to intellectual growth, moral self-improvement, and pleasure. Curiosity has been recuperated from its deep associations with original sin.[141] Modesty curtails the curious mind, serving as a vital corrective to the lures of "Prejudice and Obstinacy," the "Delusions of Imagination," and the ensnaring limitations of "Opinion."[142] All of these are potentially pernicious, Baker contends, because they lead the observer to maintain "the Belief that we know Things sufficiently already."[143] Curiosity is the engine for discovery, modesty for knowledge.

The cultivation of modernity in the British Enlightenment found active practitioners in natural philosophers. For science to be understandable and to be associated with the contemporary moment, experimentalists relied on figuration, rendering the work of natural philosophy visible through the logic of comparison inherent to metaphor. Yet as we have seen in this chapter, science was not merely represented through metaphor. Science was enabled by metaphor: natural philosophers were able to articulate their objects of study and their own observational stances because of the figuration that literariness made available. The observed particular and the modest witness are forged as scientific technologies through this process of figuration. It is no wonder, then, that others took up the mantle of figuration to imagine these same objects and subjects, but through the interconnected lenses of satire and critique.

From these modest witnesses, therefore, we now turn to their antithesis: immodest witnesses.

2 IMMODEST WITNESSES

Natural philosophers in the seventeenth and eighteenth centuries were devoted to creating and safeguarding the objectivity of the modest witness and his scientific findings, particularly with recourse to the imaginative possibilities available through literary knowledge. These representations were designed to portray good, successful naturalists—they were modest in their judgment and in their bodies, instrumentally divorcing themselves from anything that might suggest bias.

But if there are good scientists, there are also bad scientists. The long eighteenth-century literary archive provides seemingly innumerable examples, often in the form of satires: Samuel Butler's natural philosopher mistakes a mouse in his telescope for an elephant on the moon; Margaret Cavendish pillories the bear-men in *The Blazing World* for their narrow and speculative views; Aphra Behn dupes and ultimately reprimands Ballarido, with his twenty-foot-long telescope in *The Emperor of the Moon*; Swift satirizes the projectors in the Academy of Lagado; and Ned Ward's *The London Spy* and William King's *Dialogues of the Dead* ridicule virtuosi as impractical and myopic. Beyond satirizing science as self-interested folly, what do these characterizations accomplish?

The character of the immodest witness equips writers to explore both the limits and potential of scientific observational practice. In this chapter, I focus on two literary characters that embody the possibilities of an immodest witness, the Gimcrack (a proper noun for foolish scientists) and the coquette. They are not only ubiquitous in the Enlightenment archive; they also demonstrate the imaginative work possible through literariness. The Gimcrack and the coquette are often viewed as performers and dissemblers, devoted to advancing their own social standing and self-interest. They are deeply social characters, portrayed within a web of relations—affective, sexual, financial, and intellectual—although they often obstruct the normal functioning of those connections. Gimcracks ignore society and social demands in favor of studying insects. And coquettes refuse to cede their moment of agency on the marriage market by endlessly deferring the choice of a husband. Through their interactions with others, these characters reveal the social embeddedness of scientific practice, both its costs and benefits.

The Gimcracks and coquettes in this chapter appear in dramas and periodicals, respectively, a fact that provides an occasion to consider the genres' affinities. Of course, drama and periodicals have distinct conventions and expectations, evident in drama's links to playhouse culture and the periodical's proliferation through print media. However, I focus on their common investment in performance as a literary device.[1] The literary characterization of Gimcracks and coquettes relies on performance to explain their coherence, motivation, and expression; they are individuals performing roles to advance their self-interest. Plays and periodicals share features that instructively relate to the practice of natural philosophy: these genres implicitly imagine sociability, whether in the form of audience members or readers, and they enact vivid examples of affective relations. Drama allows the opportunity to witness a character in a social context, interacting with others and maneuvering according to the dictates of the author's plot. Plays provide a special view of the experimental philosopher in company and in relation to his or her other social roles. While theatricality in natural philosophy credentials practitioners and advocates, theatricality in plays with Gimcracks locates the operation of science in a larger social network.[2] In the production of scientific knowledge, performance acts as the means of acquiring consensus and credibility; on the playhouse stage, performance functions as a mechanism that reveals and determines social relations. Performance in the genre of the periodical, in which the coquette frequently appears, is a mode of observational behavior. Eidolons import theatricality into print, as they draw on the rhetoric of display and disclosure to convey meaning. The tension between experimental philosophy and the periodical brings to light competing modes of ocularity and a metacritical discourse on observation and authority.

I begin this chapter by discussing the quality of immodesty in the literary archive of the long eighteenth century, demonstrating that it is a photographic negative of the idealized modest witness that practitioners of experimental philosophy imagine. Scientific instrumentation and observation always run the risk of deviating into the terrain of the immodest, whether as a vehicle solely for self-aggrandizement or through the eroticization of the body. I then turn to the theatrical Gimcrack, a character first imagined by Thomas Shadwell in *The Virtuoso* and who has a long afterlife in plays, poems, and periodicals. The Gimcracks I consider—Shadwell's Sir Nicholas Gimcrack, James Miller's Lady

Science, and Susannah Centlivre's Valeria—are all self-interested observers intent on blocking systems of sociability. Gender here plays an important, revelatory role: Gimcracks are ordinarily men, but female Gimcracks uncover the plasticity of the characterization and the social relations that natural philosophy puts at stake. I conclude with a discussion of the periodical's coquette, who might seem to be an unlikely player in the discourses of natural philosophy. The coquette in the *Spectator* and the *Female Spectator* serves both as an example of the shared trivialness and self-delusion of the beau monde and the experimental project, and as a paragon for the necessity of this self-interested viewpoint to observe and appreciate the natural and social worlds. The coquette can be an object of futile scientific scrutiny, or she can express and even acquire the moral quality of good taste by devoting herself to natural philosophy. Taken together, these immodest witnesses bear out the logic of self-interest undergirding claims to objectivity, revealing its limitations and contradictions, as well as the literariness of their characterizations that in some instances promise superior insight.

IMMODESTY

The modest witness of natural philosophy is attentive and self-effacing, devoted to producing credible information about natural phenomena. The concept of the modest witness draws on metaphoric language and thinking to make this subject position possible. And the modest witness ends up being a winner of history—it is the source of modern scientific objectivity. However, the alternative discourse of the virtuoso as an immodest witness emerged alongside the modest witness and came to function as its cultural and ideological antithesis.[3] Some seventeenth-century skeptics even suspected that the modest witness might actually devolve into a virtuoso.

The term *virtuoso* was first recorded in English in 1598 and was not closely allied with natural philosophy until the 1640s; by the 1660s, it connoted an exclusively scientific interest.[4] Robert Boyle uses the term in *New Experiments Physico-Mechanical: Touching the Spring of the Air and their Effects* (1661) when recounting a German experiment, a citational practice that demonstrates the cosmopolitanism of experimental philosophy, the networks of authority on which it relies, and the significance of virtual witnessing. The German practitioner is a "great Virtuoso": "And a Learned Man a while since inform'd me, That a great *Virtuoso*, friend to us both, has, with not unlike success, tryed the same Experiment in the lower and upper parts of a Mountain in the West of *England*."[5] The ranks of "a Learned Man" and "a great Virtuoso" are explicit signals that Boyle's claims are built on already-established privileges and authority. To be a virtuoso, one needed wealth and leisure; "he is a gentleman."[6]

As evident in Boyle's account, *virtuoso* originally had positive associations, referring to a man of learning. However, once the Royal Society acquired its first charter in 1662, the meaning of the term quickly transformed into a person engaged in "futile and indiscriminate study."[7] In this later sense, the virtuoso was understood to be motivated by a desire for reputation and social standing, even "snob-appeal."[8] Mary Astell, when discussing the "Character of a Virtuoso," asks, "What Knowledge is it? What Discoveries do we owe to their Labours? It is only the Discovery of some few unheeded Varieties of Plants, Shells, or Insects, unheeded only because useless."[9] When John Dryden's character Sir Martin Marr-All, in the play of the same name, pretentiously announces that he is known as a virtuoso, his companion comedically asks, "Is not *Vertue* enough, without O so?"[10] The connotation persisted well into the eighteenth century: Samuel Johnson's *The Idler* parodies the attempts of one "Tim. Ranger" to fashion himself into a "*fine Gentleman*" by becoming a virtuoso.[11]

Two poems published within a year of each other exemplify the potential blurring of the modest witness and the immodest one, between the virtuoso who is admired and one who is maligned. Both titled "The Microscope," these poems imagine microscopic views for markedly different ends. Tipping Silvester's 1733 poem celebrates polite science. Silvester's "The Microscope" figuratively represents the experience of examining natural phenomena under the microscope, including a bee, a spider, a fly, a silkworm, and various liquids. Silvester contrasts the sights under a microscope to the limited vision of artists, concluding that art without the microscope produces "pleasing Error" and, with it, "gross Defects."[12] Under the microscope, engravings of grape vines on a silver cup are roughly and coarsely hewn, grotesque even. Artists are the tricksters of early modern image making, and Silvester turns to reprimand women as exemplars of such dissembling. In the mode that Swift made famous in "The Lady's Dressing Room" (1732), Silvester turns the microscope on women's clothes, hair, fingernails, and hands, imagining women enraged by the microscopic revelation that female beauty is superficial and cannot sustain further inspection: "if by chance their dirty Nails they spy,/Their scaly Hands, and brisly Hairs; O fie!"[13] The labor and magic of the toilet vanish in the magnified view.

The previous year, another poem of the same name was published in *Female*

Inconstancy Display'd (1732). The anonymous "The Microscope" tells the story of an absent-minded father, a natural philosopher who has succumbed to the allure of the microscope to examine "Flies and Maggots by the Hour."[14] The microscope is an appropriate prosthetic for a man who cannot see beyond his own nose. The character of the distracted, self-involved scientist was often portrayed as declining the normal obligations of polite society, selfishly abdicating convention, and squandering the privileges and fortunes of a gentleman.[15] The father's fascination with the natural world in "The Microscope" unveils his obliviousness to the social world. But if the father is blind, the poem is not. Elaborating what the father cannot see, "The Microscope" pictures "Which way his Daughters were inclin'd."[16] Sally and Jenny's inclination is explicitly erotic: they experiment "For Lechery and Learning sake," turning the microscope to measure their sleeping brother's penis and then using it to view one of their own vaginas.[17]

The contrast between these two poems demonstrates that scientific instrumentation could be imagined as modest and immodest. Even with Silvester's Swiftian interlude to scrutinize female beauty, his microscope remains a stable, reliable tool for knowledge production, promoting optical scrutiny and the aesthetics of the natural world. In the other "The Microscope," Sally and Jenny reduce the optical instrument to an erotic plaything. The explicit sexualization of "The Microscope" might seem surprising, but it is analogous to Gulliver's bawdy experiences in Voyage II of *Gulliver's Travels*, wherein he synecdochally becomes a microscope examining naked ladies-in-waiting.[18]

My juxtaposition of the two microscope poems also intends to underscore that eroticism, particularly masturbatory eroticism, was written into microscopy from its early usage. Antoni van Leeuwenhoek's specimens included human semen, the microscopic examination of which yielded the discovery of human spermatozoa in 1677, findings he published in *Philosophical Transactions* the following year.[19] In 1718, Alexander Pope met a Mr. Hatton, a clockmaker "who is like wise curious in microscopes and [who] showed my mother some of the *semen masculinum*, with animascula in it."[20] And Henry Baker includes a chapter on the "Animalcules in Semine Masculino," with engravings of seven samples, in *The Microscope Made Easy* (1742); it draws heavily on Leeuwenhoek's work.[21] Even within the practice of a credentialed and influential modest witness, immodesty—in this case, the sexualized body, regardless of gender—is always possible.

Gimcracks and coquettes are defined by an inability to overcome prejudice and desires, speaking for himself or herself rather than for the object. Rather than conclude that immodest witnesses are merely failures, merely bad scientists, I analyze them for the observational practices they imply. Drawing on techniques of literary convention including characterization, plot, and the imagination, numerous writers of the long eighteenth century embrace, rather than deny, the witness's inherent immodesty.

GIMCRACKS

The proper noun *Gimcrack* was widely associated with buffoonish virtuosi throughout the seventeenth and eighteenth centuries: it was a synonym for a bad scientist. Sir Nicholas Gimcrack is the lead character in Thomas Shadwell's 1676 play, *The Virtuoso*. After Hooke attended a performance of the play on June 12, 1676, at Dorset Garden, he complained in his diary that the audience knew the characterization of "Sir Nicholas Gimcrack, F. R. S." satirized him: "Damned dogs. *Vindica me Deux*. People almost pointed."[22] His peers and acquaintances peppered him with questions about the play, drawing out the allusion. Hooke was an astute choice for Shadwell's satire. Many of the Royal Society's weekly meetings, especially during its first two decades, involved staging experiments and reading about others, work that heavily depended on Hooke's labor and expertise.[23] Due to his publications and roles within the organization, Hooke was the public face of experimentalism. But Hooke's status was precarious. He was vulnerable to being viewed as a professional mechanic rather than a gentlemanly natural philosopher. And he "lost" the seventeenth-century public relations battle for scientific innovation to Isaac Newton.[24]

Shadwell's characterization was prescient, for the character Gimcrack lingered in the long eighteenth-century literary archive.[25] As we shall see, the "afterlife," or "imaginative expansion," of Gimcrack is rich and varied, pointing to this literary character's timeliness, resilience, and pliability.[26] In *Reflections upon Ancient and Modern Learning*, William Wotton refers to Gimcrack as an embarrassment, complaining of "the sly Insinuations of the Men of Wit, That no great Things have ever, or are ever likely to be perform'd by the *Men of Gresham*, and, That every Man whom they call a *Virtuoso*, must needs be a *Sir Nicolas Gimcrack*."[27] In their satires, William Congreve, Joseph Addison, and John Hildrop caricature Gimcrack.[28] Gimcrack captures a variety of imaginative possibilities, from his first appearance on stage—as an occasion for Hooke's humiliation in the theater—to texts serious and satiric, pedantic and playful. What is it about the original Sir Nicholas Gimcrack in Shadwell's *The Virtuoso* that generates such a literary heritage?

The answer resides in Shadwell's literary strategy: Gimcrack's characterization. This is an independent yet deluded gentleman who fritters away his time and wealth on nonsensical experiments. His ultimate failing is not that he is obsessed with experimental philosophy, but that he is obsessed with experimental philosophy at the expense of his other duties and responsibilities as a wealthy gentleman and guardian. Through a vast number of examples, humorous in their extravagance, the play ensures that Gimcrack's expenditures of financial and social capital are seen as ludicrous, even worthy of censure. Gimcrack exhausts a substantial portion of his income on expensive specimens and instruments, including, his nieces complain, £2,000 on "microscopes, telescopes, thermometers, barometers, pneumatic engines, strentrophonical tubes, and the like."[29] On a smaller financial scale, Gimcrack spends 10 shillings each on eggs, hoodwinked into believing they have hair on them. Other curiosities include a spider that he claims to have tamed and to have taught that it was named "Nick" (after him); a vault stocked with bottles of air from around England, air that he boasts is of various weights; and rotten wood and putrid flesh that he vows produce light enough for reading. We first meet him in his study learning to swim. The location is not unexpected, for the home was the primary site of experimental philosophy in the seventeenth century.[30] Yet the sight of Gimcrack lying prone on his library desk, imitating the movements of a frog in a bowl of water next to him, is comedic and satiric. He scoffs at the idea of practicing in a pool: "I content myself with the speculative part of swimming; I care not for the practic. I seldom bring any thing to use, 'tis not my way. Knowledge is my ultimate end" (II.ii.84–86). Sir Formal Trifle, an adoring orator, quickly adds, "To study for use is base and mercenary" (II.ii.89). The obviously erroneous quality of Gimcrack's observations provides a hearty rejoinder to his statement that "Knowledge is my ultimate end." The character Gimcrack is defined by his desire for any kind of purportedly experimental knowledge that in turn blinds him to actual observable phenomena.

If Gimcrack is focused on what he thinks he sees, then the play is designed to show us what he refuses to notice. Gimcrack announces, "'Tis below a virtuoso to trouble himself with men and manners. I study insects" (III.iii.86–89), but "men and manners"—that is, matters of one's socially experienced life, including affective and sexual relations—plague him. *The Virtuoso*, like so many of Shadwell's other plays, imagines uncontrolled female sexuality and desire.[31] Gimcrack's own marriage binds him to a wife (his second) known for her sexual promiscuity.

His nieces mock Lady Gimcrack for her sexual experience and pretensions, and Lady Gimcrack later has quick liaisons with their beaus.

Most of the transactions between the play's characters are determined by their desire for sex, and Shadwell engineers the plots so that most are ridiculed or pilloried. The marriages of the nieces are socially legitimate forms of sexual desire, but these are comparatively minor events in the play, haphazardly arranged. Even these are subject to the imperatives of performance: because Gimcrack refuses to allow any sort of marriage plot for his nieces, Clarinda and Miranda, their suitors, Bruce and Longville, pretend to be virtuosos to visit the Gimcrack household. The young men take up the traditional roles of the clever and resourceful beaux, determined to find a way around an obstinate guardian. Their full-bodied parody of natural philosophy matches Gimcrack's earnest, if self-interested, performance in tone and effect. From the guardian's blinded, self-interested point of view, these men are perfect acolytes.

With all of this plotting and counter plotting, *The Virtuoso* stages sexual farce. But the play also imagines the origin of Gimcrack's obtuseness: his passion for natural philosophy, as superficial and misguided as it is, is the primary cause of his demise. Gimcrack's experimentalism is a vehicle for his self-aggrandizement. Craving more fawning and praise from Bruce and Longville, Gimcrack begins to make far-fetched claims about the effects of various inventions. For example, a "speaking trumpet" or a "stentrophonical tube" (V.ii.43, 44) will replace clergy, allowing one parson to preach to the entire country and the monarchy to seize church lands. This same invention could eliminate the need for ambassadors and their expense to the state. Gimcrack's bragging about technology replacing people begins to circulate beyond his domestic orbit and elicits a particularly dangerous response from the laboring classes: a mob of ribbon weavers protests that Gimcrack's proposed mechanical loom will leave them without work. In hasty and frightened response to the threats of the crowd, Gimcrack renounces the utility of experimental philosophy altogether: "Hear me, Gentlemen, I never invented an engine in my life. As Gad shall sa' me you do me wrong. I never invented so much as an engine to pare cream cheese with. We virtuosos never find out any thing of use, 'tis not our way" (V.iii.76–79). Shadwell may have been alluding to a 1675 uprising of silk weavers who were protesting the invention of an automatic loom, a historic example of labor unrest and social upheaval in the face of scientific advancement.[32]

Whether the threat of protest is too potent or too irrelevant for the play to contemplate, the threat of a mob attack serves another purpose, for it precipitates the dramatization of the sexual and domestic costs of experimental philosophy. The undoing of Sir Nicholas hinges on his embrace of science. He has been too preoccupied with experiments and with talking about them to notice that his wife is as unfaithful to their marriage as he is. The couple find themselves in a scene of mutual discovery and they reach a stalemate of accusation, each spouse pretending to be injured by the other's sexual infidelity. Even these conjugal betrayals do not tell the whole story: through asides, the audience learns that the spouses' lovers, Flirt and Hazard, have been having their own affair. Once the nieces are paired off with their suitors, the play stages a final showdown between Sir Nicholas and Lady Gimcrack. The virtuoso swears to his wife that he'll be "reveng'd on all your lewdness" and Lady Gimcrack promises the same (V.vi.1). Gimcrack attempts to throw his wife out of the house and replace her with Flirt, but his outburst has no effect: Lady Gimcrack announces that she is financially independent with "a settlement for separate maintenance" and that she has proof of his criminal conversation (V.vi.11). Sir Nicholas, with little bargaining power of his own, both offers and asks for forgiveness: without missing a beat, he preposterously offers a truce at the moment he is outwitted.

Abject as he is, the play swiftly compounds Gimcrack's sexual humiliation in financial terms. The Steward announces, "Several engineers, glassmakers, and other people you have dealt with for experiments" have seized "all your estate in the country" (V.vi.27–29). Grasping for something to save him, Gimcrack turns again to Lady Gimcrack, now looking at her as a source of income, and repeats his promise to forgive her. Lady Gimcrack's rejection of his now wholly worthless offer is complete: "No, Sir, I thank you; my settlement is without incumbrance" (V.vi.36). And Snarl—Gimcrack's uncle—turns out to have just married his own mistress, Figgup, thus ensuring that Gimcrack will not inherit Snarl's estate. Gimcrack's final economic alternative resides in his nieces, and so he proposes that they lend him money. Clearly having already sensed a bad money manager in their uncle (among his other flaws), Miranda and Clarinda defer to their new financial guardians, their husbands. With his monetary future doomed, Sir Nicholas tries to comfort himself by reflecting that he still has Flirt. But Flirt has no interest in an impoverished lover. "Deserted by all," Gimcrack is left with only his experimental philosophy to comfort him (V.vi.130). Humbled, Sir Nicholas promises to reform, vowing to devote himself to practical study. The play concludes with Gimcrack claiming that experimental philosophy must be for utility rather than merely for speculation and its associated pleasures: "Well, now 'tis time to study for use: I will presently find out the philosopher's stone; I had like to have gotten it last year, but that I wanted May-dew, being a dry season" (V.vi.130–32).

The objects of the play's critique are various. In terms of experimental philosophy, Gimcrack's enthusiasm for fancy and speculation are absurd in the face of common sense. While experiments to him are always grounded in the material world and are not, in essence, instances of magical thinking, divine intervention, or astounding miracles, they are presented to the audience and to the majority of the characters in the play as outlandish and fundamentally unbelievable. They seem to be imaginable, following the encouragement of natural philosophical advocates, but they are *too* imaginative to be real. Missing from Gimcrack's practice is the authenticating process practiced by the modest witness, in which experiments were considered a performance subject to collective adjudication. In the world of *The Virtuoso*, everyone performs to advance his or her own self-interest. The authorizing structure built into the production of natural philosophical knowledge is reduced to a parodic performance in the scenes where Bruce and Longville pretend to agree with Gimcrack only so they may be close to Clarinda and Miranda.

Is the play's point that Gimcrack is a fool or that experimental philosophy is foolish? One could argue that the play imagines experimental philosophy could be enacted legitimately, in which case the problem here is merely Sir Nicholas's selfishness and shortsightedness.[33] His vanity all too easily allows him to replace a collective of like-minded experimentalists with the flattering tones of Sir Formal, Bruce, and Longville. But *The Virtuoso* also implies that the practice of experimental philosophy encourages and even requires such buffoonish and self-interested behavior. *The Virtuoso* does not merely make Gimcrack a blinded fool who could, but does not, practice science well: the sexual plotting of Shadwell's play suggests that experimental philosophy is yet another form of self-interested folly. The play wraps up with Gimcrack financially depleted and sexually abandoned. He seems to learn a little bit by the end, but this is a limited and parodic reformation. The lesson Gimcrack takes away from his humiliations is that he needs experimental philosophy to produce for him, to effect tangible results. The possibility of Gimcrack being productive, however, is unlikely. The cumulative effect of these disgraces is that natural philosophy is a nongenerative activity. Within a play dramatizing so many forms of sexual plotting, Shadwell's message is clear: experimental philosophy is epistemologically dubious and socially destructive, for it simultaneously impedes the circulation of wealth and the reproduction of the family.

Shadwell's literary descendent, James Miller, transforms the character of Sir Nicholas Gimcrack into a woman, Lady Science, in order to insist on natural philosophy's intellectual and social legitimacy. Miller's play, *The Humours of Oxford* (1730), bears out the fruitlessness, inappropriateness, and inaccuracies of experimental practice when taken up by a woman. The change of Gimcrack's gender enables a plot that polices scientific women as interlopers and emphasizes the social relations that such female characters threaten, in effect signaling a danger well beyond the ignominy that Sir Nicholas suffers.

Miller's Lady Science is a wealthy widow with a marriageable daughter; her niece makes the connection to Shadwell's original by mocking her aunt as "Lady Gimcrack."[34] For Lady Science, science is a metaphor, always conveying figurative connotations. In this, Lady Science performs the literariness embedded in natural philosophy as a theory and practice. But her success as a natural philosopher ends here. We meet Lady Science mid-lament: "I profess it grieves me to the very Center of my Heart, to think that I have any Mode of Relation to such an empty *Cilinder*, such an *exhausted Receiver*—Surely, we need no longer doubt the Existence of a *Vacuum*; for the Skulls of the young Girls and Fops of this Age, are Demonstrations sufficient of it" (12–13). Lady Science's characterization of fashionable society through metaphors of instrumentation conflates the now-familiar air pump experiments with a dramatic stock-in-trade, a stalwart of the older generation lamenting the manners and attitudes of the current age. From the guardian's point of view, the next generation is as weightless as a vacuum, a metaphor that evokes a concept from experimental philosophy to make social commentary.

Lady Science's conclusions about the beau monde may well be apt, but she is characterized as a fool, a scientific Mrs. Malaprop. If experimental philosophy represents a mode of knowing and understanding the natural world, then the joke *The Humours of Oxford* develops is that Lady Science's words consistently, and comically, reveal precious little knowing and even less understanding. Lady Science utters scientific words without recognizing their meanings, bending natural philosophical language to her own self-interested and self-deluded ends. When she meets a potential suitor for her daughter, who pretends he is a fellow naturalist to gain her approval, Lady Science queries, "Which *Hypothesis are you of*—the *Ptolemaick,* or *Copernican*?" and "Have you any Skill in *Judicial Astrology*—I think it absolutely necessary, for one who has a Family, to be a considerable Proficient in that useful Science" (57, 58). The point of Lady Science's characterization is that she has been caught up in science merely as a novelty. Clarinda, her niece, lampoons Lady Science's devotion to natural philosophy as substituting one form of frivolous fashion and novelty for another. It is as if "a Beau [were] encompass'd with Telescopes and Globes, instead of Looking-Glasses, and Peruke-Blocks; and a Coquette with *Euclid* and *Newton* on her Toilet, instead of *Waller* and *Congreve*; and stript of all her Patches, to mark the Planets in the Solar System, ha, ha!" (13). If beaux and coquettes were to take up experimental philosophy and to trade their looking glasses and peruke blocks for telescopes and globes, it would only be in an attempt to out-fashion each other once again. In Miller's universe, this competition would evacuate natural philosophy of intellectual significance, even though science's fashionability was one of its powerful and alluring connotations. Clarinda's witty description insinuates that the social context of the beau monde forestalls a genuine engagement with substantive intellectual work and practice. The implication is that Lady Science could just as easily have become ensnared in cards, liquor, sex, or any other form of urban dissipation. As we saw in Chapter 1, the naturalist Henry Baker made a similar point in his advocacy of scientific practice, but he did so to insist on its superiority. For Miller, Lady Science's devotion to natural philosophy embodies self-pleasure, self-indulgence, and self-delusion.

The Humours of Oxford links its satiric characterization of Lady Science as a fool to a deep discomfort with her power and independence as a widow. Her self-aggrandizement leads her to believe she is a natural philosopher; her wealth provides the resources to pursue this fiction, enabling her, for example, to take up residence in Oxford "that she might be within the Pales of *Parnassus,* and at the Fountain-head of Erudition" (3). As a mother and a widow, Lady Science has the legal, social, and ethical right to determine her daughter's future. Yet she is an intransigent and silly guardian who, in the logic of the play's plot, must be tricked. She refuses to inform Victoria of a £10,000 inheritance from Victoria's grandmother and takes an unyieldingly patriarchal approach to her daughter's amatory prospects: "Pray, Mistress, who taught you to have any Inclinations but what I think proper?" (46). Victoria must obey all her mother's whims or risk being cut off, which Lady Science does anyway in Act V.

Following the model of Shadwell's Bruce and Longville, who purport to be virtuosos to gain the favor of an inflexible guardian, Victoria's suitor pretends to be "Mr. Mudbrains," a "Fellow of Brazen-Nose-College" (46). In their interview, Lady Science's misunderstandings of scientific ideas and discoveries are flagrant, even though she self-consciously justifies her queries with the claim that "in the Disposal of my Daughter I am principally concern'd for the Improvement of her Intellectual Faculties" (57). Lady Science explains her hope that Victoria will be altered into a version of herself, urging "Mr. Mudbrains" to "use your utmost Endeavours to make her more like her Mother" (59). From Lady Science's point of view, such a transformation would ensure Victoria's position; from everyone else's, of course, it would render her a fool. If Lady Science's hopes for Victoria are self-interested, then so too is her perception of Gainwell-as-Mr.-Mudbrains. She sees herself in him: "I perceive this is a Man of very great Learning (for he thinks and saith just as I do)" (58). Lady Science is so blinded by her self-image that she cannot see the facts in front of her, not even that Gainwell is wearing a pillow under his coat and telling her only what she wants to hear. She finds Mr. Mudbrains appropriate because he mimics what she believes about the world and, more important, about herself. Enhancing the comedy and satire, when she questions the young suitor, he only occasionally affirms "absolutely" or mumbles a list of similar nouns; more frequently, she answers for him. If one considers the interview an opportunity for Lady Science to evaluate this young man—to conduct, as it were, an experiment to determine Gainwell's suitability as a match for her daughter—then it of course fails miserably. Lady Science's assessment of Gainwell merely confirms her opinions, biases, and image. The play heightens its ridicule of Lady Science by having Gainwell's ruse discovered by an idiot, one Ape-all, "an Oxford Scholar, a trifling ridiculous Fop, affecting Dress and Lewdness, and a Contemner of Learning" (x). Lady Science may be perfectly convinced by Gainwell's garbled and sycophantic responses, but even a bona-fide fool can figure out the truth.

Lady Science's flaw is not merely that she is a vain, selfish, and deluded guardian. It is also that she is a woman. The play's censure and reformation of Lady Science concentrate on her gender, punishing her with amatory humiliation. Haughty, a college fellow, pretends to admire Lady Science but only for her £50,000, and she, in turn, warmly welcomes his attention. She is seduced by his seemingly learned company, which in fact replicates the dynamic of rhetorical assent played out in her interview with Gainwell. Haughty vehemently takes her side in the debate with Clarinda (and, to a lesser extent, Victoria) about the worth of natural philosophy (21–23). Drawn to Haughty's image of her, Lady Science agrees to what turns out to be a sham marriage, the truth of which is disclosed by the appearance of Haughty's wife shortly thereafter. Humiliated, Lady Science faints. When she recovers, she swiftly reprimands herself: "I am justly made a Fool of" (79). Her remorse does not focus merely on having been tricked by her misguided desire for Haughty, but also on her ill-formed aspiration, as a woman, to "be a Philosopher" (79). The problem that Lady Science represents is scientific thinking in the wrong hands: Lady Science fails to understand it properly and also uses this ill-learned habit merely to promote herself as fashionable. Intellectually and socially, she fails. She has a dull mind and is fooled easily by the machinations of others.

Lady Science's womanhood opens her to an even sharper punishment within the logic of Miller's play. She is not merely humiliated by her fake marriage to Haughty. She is also subject to a searing rebuke from the normative Gainwell, who announces that "The Dressing-Room, not the Study, is the Lady's Province—and a Woman makes as ridiculous a Figure poring over Globes, or thro' a Telescope, as a Man would with a Pair of *Preservers* mending Lace" (79). Gainwell's spatialization of gender difference utilizes a conservative eighteenth-century ideology that associates beautification with women and intellectual production with men, a figuration challenged by the complexity of the dressing room trope.[35]

The marriage plot of *The Humours of Oxford* depends on Lady Science's shaming and reformation, for only then might she be powerless to impede Victoria's match with Gainwell. She shares humiliation with her literary predecessor, Sir Nicholas Gimcrack, but she deviates from his path when she rejects natural philosophy altogether. Sir Nicholas promises to become a good scientist, as unlikely as this may be; Lady Science vows to abandon it altogether. While the action of the play moves quickly at this point, taking only a few minutes longer to conclude, Lady Science's pledge to give up natural philosophy is markedly belabored and takes up a sizeable amount of time on stage:

I will destroy all my *Globes, Quadrants, Spheres, Prisms, Microscopes,* and *Magick-Lanthorns*—I'll throw out all my Lumber of *Load-stones, Peble,* and *Petrified Shells,* to pave my Door—I'll convert my *Air-Pump* into a *Water-Pump,* send all my *Serpent's Teeth, Mummy's-Bones,* and *monstrous Births,* to the *Oxford Museum;* for the Entertainment of other as ridiculous Fools as my self; and then I will immediately fly from this abominable Place. (79)

When Lady Science promises to speak no longer of natural philosophy, she does so with an inventory of how she will extract it from her life—destroying, repurposing, or disposing of her instruments and specimens. The almost excessive detail of her concluding speech seems to connote a thorough refashioning of Lady Science before she will "fly," but suggests an uneasy, even anxious desire on the part of the playwright to eradicate the material objects that have represented the widow's self-interest—along with all evidence that she was able to act on this self-interest. The peculiar thoroughness of the play's repudiation of Lady Science in these concluding lines suggests that the capacity of a widow to assert her self-interest through the languages of science, though not successful in this instance, retains a particularly unsettling potential.

Sir Nicholas Gimcrack and Lady Science hold the power of wealth and guardianship in their respective plays, and the dramas use natural philosophy in obviously ridiculous ways to undo that knot of self-interested and self-perpetuating authority. In the examples of Sir Nicholas Gimcrack and Lady Science, Shadwell and Miller repudiate experimental philosophy as selfish and nongenerative. Both characters are domineering, self-interested fools who bend their social worlds to their delusions. Nevertheless, their failures differ. Lady Science exposes herself as a bad scientist, and Sir Nicholas subject to the bad influence of science. The dramatic unfolding of these breakdowns offers the audience an opportunity to witness situations that by necessity require remedying. Shadwell's and Miller's plays cannot end without such renunciations: natural philosophy introduces problems that the plotting—of the dramatist and of other characters—must solve.

In *The Virtuoso* and *The Humours of Oxford,* the Gimcrack character has financial and legal independence, conditions that ease a lifestyle devoted to experimental philosophy. Centlivre's *The Basset-Table* (1705) alternatively turns to an individual without guaranteed social power, but for whom the practice of science has the potential to facilitate a self-determination that might otherwise be impossible legally, financially, or morally. The character Valeria does not have an independent fortune nor does she maintain legal independence. She is the unmarried daughter of a boorish and old-fashioned squire, Sir Richard. Early in the play, a potential suitor calls her a "Philosophical Gimcrack."[36] Valeria lives as Lady Science recommends in *The Humours of Oxford*: she inhabits the beau monde as a devotee of natural philosophy. But Centlivre's Gimcrack is earnest, not frivolous, and serious, rather than misguided.

For Centlivre, the practice of experimental philosophy is an opportunity to redefine what a fashionable young woman's life might be. Valeria transforms her dressing room into a domestic laboratory where she uses her prized microscope to perform experiments on various specimens, including a "huge Flesh Fly" (a present from her beau, Mr. Lovely) and a fish that she begins to dissect under the microscope (217, 227). To acquire suitable specimens, Valeria sends her servants out for vermin and turns normally fashionable accoutrements into gross bodily matter. She reports with pride that she has "dissected [her] Dove" and tries to trade a piece of jewelry for her cousin's "*Italian* Greyhound" (218). Valeria consistently transforms materials of female fashionability and sophistication into objects for scientific scrutiny. While Lady Science is told to leave the gentleman's study and stay in her dressing room, ironically, the unmarried and dependent Valeria has the freedom to define her dressing room as a laboratory. Her dressing room is not a site of theatricality, artifice, or illicit sexuality, but rather evokes the space's figurative and historic associations with women's education, autonomy, and possible independence.[37]

Valeria's dedication to natural philosophy is not merely an isolated or idiosyncratic characterization, for it occurs within the larger social possibilities envisaged in *The Basset-Table*. Valeria's story is a subplot in a play devoted to representing women's inclinations. The main action concerns Lady Reveller's basset table, a place where fortunes and reputations are raised and dashed with a turn of the cards. Gambling was tied to aristocratic self-display and to the possibility that gamblers were merely performing that identity. A vehicle for the unpredictable transfer of wealth, the gaming table threatened to undo traditional social hierarchies because participants, such as the underclass or women, could acquire power through this newfound, if "irrationally" acquired, wealth.[38] In *The Basset-Table*, Centlivre knots gambling to female agency. Lady Reveller rebuffs her uncle's censure by insisting on her autonomy: "Lookye, Uncle, do what you can, I'm resolv'd to follow my own Inclinations" (206).

Read in relation to the play's main gambling plot with its performative display of rank and power, irrational circulation of wealth, and potential to upend social hierarchies, Valeria's experimental philosophy should also be considered a performance. It is a form of play and self-fashioning, a means for a young woman to articulate and manage her self-interest and value. Valeria's experiments also function figuratively: her practice of science enables her to imagine her own self-determination. When enacted by an authority figure such as Sir Nicholas Gimcrack or Lady Science, the effects are obstructionist. When performed by one who does not have the assurance of authority, wealth, or privilege, the results make possible a self-interest that these structures and institutions by definition deny. Valeria refuses her lover's proposal that they elope and explains that her angry father will destroy her laboratory: "What," she asks, "and leave my Microscope, and all my Things, for my Father to break in Pieces?" (228). Her refusal is to the point. Centlivre not only displaces paternalistic fury from the daughter's body onto her belongings and presents the specter of the patriarch's tyrannical authority (only to undermine it later, when her father is bamboozled to accept Lovely), but also gives Valeria the language to insist on her worth apart from the marriage market. By transforming her dressing room into a laboratory and her luxury goods into specimens and by valuing her "Microscope, and all [her] Things" more than an elopement with Mr. Lovely, Valeria momentarily at least holds on to her self-fashioning as a virtuosa devoted to—and safeguarded by—her own theater of experimental philosophy. In many ways, Valeria can be viewed as proto-feminist.[39]

Valeria may be determined to follow her inclinations in her dressing room/laboratory, but Centlivre's endorsement of the virtuosa in *The Basset-Table* is uneven, seemingly tolerant but not unequivocal. While Valeria is not humiliated or exposed as Gimcrack and Lady Science are by the end of *The Virtuoso* and *The Humours of Oxford*, she is not fully successful within the play. This young Gimcrack epitomizes Centlivre's "feminist individualism," which introduces the possibility of female agency only to explore its contradictions.[40] Valeria's characterization leaves her susceptible to her lover and vulnerable to her father. For all that she practices scrutiny of the natural world, Valeria cannot see Lovely's motives. She believes he shares her enthusiasm for natural philosophy, but his lack of interest is evident to the play's audience when she invites him to peer into her microscope: "O Mr. *Lovely*! come, come here, look through this Glass, and see how the Blood circulates in the Tale of this Fish" (227). His response calls attention to the erotic, rather than philosophical, nature of his attentions: "Wonderful! but it Circulates prettier in this fair Neck" (227). Valeria's dressing room to Lovely is a place for sexual play and indulgence, a figure for female sexuality. Lovely is not only uninterested but also only indulging Valeria's fancy for experimentalism until he can secure her acceptance. After Valeria announces that she has discovered a tapeworm in a dog's cadaver, he mutters, "I wish they be not got into thy Brain," and then quickly recovers himself to flatter her, "Oh you charm me with these Discoveries" (227). One need only recall Mr.

Lovely's opening conversation with his friends, in which he brags that he makes fun of her experiments behind her back. A cad at heart, Lovely believes that he "deserve[s] her by mere dint of Patience" (210). The motivation for Lovely's attention? Wealth. Valeria is worth £20,000 to her future husband, and Lovely, a soldier, needs to raise his own fortune.

A second way that Centlivre diminishes Valeria's agency is in relation to her father: her attempts at self-determination are sharply curtailed by Sir Richard, who dreams of English colonial expansion and values his daughter exclusively in those terms. To him, she is merely a reproductive machine for the first empire. *The Basset-Table* attaches a desire for empire to the domestic concern of a daughter's marriage, forging a relationship between colonial and national concerns that shapes many plays of the period.[41] When approached by the fictitious "Captain Match" (Valeria's beloved, Mr. Lovely, in disguise), Sir Richard delights in the idea that his daughter will marry a sailor bound to travel and who, like himself, hates the French. The prospect of an alliance between Valeria and "Captain Match" warms Sir Richard's jingoistic, patriarchal heart. To him, Valeria is a vehicle for her father's descendants who will help to found a global Britannia; he muses that his grandsons (and they will be grandsons) will be "Heroes of my Nation.—Boys, all Boys,—and all Soldiers./ *They shall the Pride of France pull down, / And add their Indies to our English Crown*" (241). Sir Richard's inclination is to produce a militaristic legacy to enlarge the dominion of the nascent British Empire, with little care for his future son-in-law's fortune, much less his daughter's thoughts; for him, the goal is to recuperate the patriarchal loss that a daughter institutes in the newly capitalistic economy of the eighteenth century.[42] He views that compensation in imperialistic terms.

If we read *The Basset-Table* solely through characterization, Valeria's experimental philosophy offers only a temporary and ultimately unsuccessful means through which she pursues her amatory and intellectual inclinations. Indeed, Sir Richard increases the pressure on Valeria to the point of forcing her into marriage, although she does not know that Captain Match is actually her beloved Lovely. But the question of Centlivre's view of Valeria's experimental philosophy is not exclusively evident in the heiress's characterization and requires that we turn to the narrative of the play's plot. Centlivre's plots won praise from her contemporary critics, most notably Richard Steele in the *Tatler*, who admires their "Subtilty of Spirit."[43] Centlivre's plots reflect her views of society and function as a means to improve social relations.[44] Plot in Centlivre's plays is a site of ideological critique and reformulation, "imagining how the bold strokes of theatrical action might render the plots of patriarchy obsolete."[45] Plot, moreover, is a form of literary knowledge: it produces story.

In *The Basset-Table*, Centlivre's plotting ensures that Valeria may maintain her two inclinations—experimental philosophy and Lovely. Centlivre's plotting also stymies Sir Richard's attempts to throw his fortune and his daughter's future into the service of the fledgling empire. In the face of these plots, *The Basset-Table* locates Valeria's sense of independence in experimental philosophy: it allows Valeria to thwart the conventions of female sociability and fashion, and also gives her the intellectual means of valuing herself outside the marriage market. With Lovely's ruse to trick Sir Richard almost complete, and of which Valeria remains unaware, she continues to refuse her assent. Sir Richard scoffs at his daughter in revealing terms: "Ay, you and your Will may philosophize as long as you please,—Mistress,—but your Body shall be taught another Doctrine,—it shall so,—Your Mind,—and your Soul quotha! . . . 'Tis the Flesh Housewife, that must raise Heirs" (240–241). In this response, the playwright gives full voice to the father's blustery and ultimately unsuccessful attempt to define Valeria solely as "the Flesh Housewife." However, at the moment that he insists his daughter's value is only to extend the patriarchal line, Sir Richard is being tricked into condoning the spouse of her choice, a simultaneity that indicates the sharpness of Centlivre's critique. The plot of *The Basset-Table* punishes the jingoistic, patriarchal father for reducing his daughter to a sexual commodity. Therefore, the final circumvention of Sir Richard confirms the efficacy, as tenuous as it may be, of experimental philosophy to redefine what it means to be a young woman in London. Centlivre recuperates the virtuosa from satire and celebrates her agency and intellectual independence, even if those qualities are not fully imagined or possible.

Read together, the significance of *The Virtuoso*, *The Humours of Oxford*, and *The Basset-Table* resides in their presentation of experimental philosophy within the context of domestic and affective relations. The playwrights' thematic treatment of science correlates to acts that either enhance or diminish one's status and hopes for success, as well as those of one's family. And yet the plays' characterizations of Gimcracks and their uses of performance and plotting point to the literariness of these explorations. These plays insist on a persistent association among the practice of experimental philosophy, sexual regimes, and the circulation of wealth. Shadwell's prescient drama, *The Virtuoso*, renders those associations embarrassingly visible, while envisaging the potential for wholescale loss endemic to hopes for technological advancement. The original Sir Nicholas Gimcrack is humiliated not by the ridiculousness of his experiments, but by a series of sexual and financial losses that are, by implication, endemic to the natural philosophical project. Miller's *The Humours of Oxford* unremittingly characterizes the wealthy widow Lady Science as a fool guided only by self-interest and desire. Its conservatism impugns Lady Science for imagining that she can participate in the project of experimentalism, rendering her engagement superficial and self-aggrandizing; despite its punitive conclusion, the play's plot displays such a woman's agency as socially disruptive and dangerous. *The Basset-Table* converts Gimcrack from a wealthy gentleman or a wealthy widow into a dependent heiress, in the process exposing the institutional privileges of natural philosophy and reconfiguring them in the service of feminine, possibly feminist, self-determination. Centlivre posits, even if ambivalently, a model of agency available through the practice of experimental philosophy, in which a virtuosa does not embody the privileged and self-effacing objectivity of the modest witness or an obstructionist self-indulgence of the typical Gimcrack. She instead has the opportunity, albeit limited, to speak for herself.

COQUETTES

In my discussion of Gimcracks, I have focused on three characters: a gentleman, a widow, and an heiress—a man and two women, the latter of whom are in vastly different social positions from each other. In so doing, I develop an archaeology of a subjectivity associated with the practice of science, a character type known to embrace experimentalism in the service of self-advancement. Gimcracks are always social beings, under pressure to perform a particular role within a community where everyone seems to be dissembling.

My second literary character, the coquette, may not seem to have as strong of an association with natural philosophy as the Gimcrack, yet the connection recurs in the eighteenth-century literary archive. Why? Coquettes are problems. They are social problems because they refuse to capitulate to the demands of the marriage market, rejecting the imperative that they choose a single suitor. Committed to life á la mode, the coquette appears to her critics to be an excessive consumer of male attention: rather than committing to one admirer, she collects many. She also seems to be an excessive consumer of the vast array of luxury goods newly available in the London marketplace. According to Eliza Haywood's narrator in *The History of Miss Betsy Thoughtless*, coquettes value themselves "on the number and quality of their lovers, as they do upon the number and richness of their clothes."[46] The coquette Betsy Thoughtless is known for her vanity, love of flattery, and the "little Lightness of her Mind."[47] Her lifestyle implies that a coquette exists only to attract the admiration of men and the envy of women, playing with "courtship rituals without following through on their promise—consummation within marriage."[48] Because the coquette by definition delays and defers marriage, she is, in fact, "in open rebellion against the standard rules of courtship."[49] But because she dresses beautifully and fashionably, she is likewise a key and desired actor in dramas about affective relations. Coquettes present an ideological crisis because they expose the vulnerability of a patriarchal system that requires their acquiescence. They are immovable. They refuse the trajectory of the marriage plot and insist on perpetually living in the moment of a woman's greatest power—courtship.[50]

Coquettes are social problems, but they are also epistemological problems: they invite attention yet thwart inspection. One cannot tell whom a coquette truly favors; this is what makes her frustrating to male admirers. She hides her specific intentions and desires beneath a beautiful and alluring surface. One cannot know what a coquette genuinely thinks, much less what she truly is. For critics, there is also the distinct possibility that a coquette has no inside to hide and that she is simply a mirage of brilliant surfaces—a social creation with no knowable or discoverable interiority.

The coquette appears as a character to generate desire and discouragement, an occasion for scrutiny and condemnation and a symbol of rebellious excess. In what follows, I argue that as a character to be observed, she elicits an exploration of the limits of experimental knowledge acquisition. As a character to be imitated, she introduces the possibility of enlightened subjectivity.

The character of the coquette recurs in Addison and Steele's the *Spectator*. Her primary effect within the periodical is frustration. Men, women, and Mr. Spectator find the coquette's willfulness and refusal to play by the rules alluring, annoying, and even dangerous. And the *Spectator*'s coquette exists within a periodical actively devoted to crafting its own model of observational wisdom and authority. The paper's eidolon, Mr. Spectator, is present but not seen, and he writes under the cover of anonymity.[51] Alongside its configuration of spectatorship, the periodical expresses deep skepticism about experimental observation. In a discussion of his paper's popularity, Mr. Spectator ironically praises the Royal Society: "The Air-Pump, the Barometer, the Quadrant, and the like Inventions were thrown out to those busie Spirits, as Tubs and Barrels are to a Whale, that he may let the Ship sail without Disturbance, while he diverts himself with those innocent Amusements."[52] From Mr. Spectator's viewpoint, experimental philosophy does not have any intrinsic value; its import dwells in its tactical function, which safeguards the body politic.

In two issues published a week apart (nos. 275 and 281), the *Spectator* intensifies its derision by conjoining satire of natural philosophy and satire of the beau monde. The periodical's fiction is this: after meeting with a group of experimental philosophers to discuss a human dissection and microscopic examination, Mr. Spectator's imagination is fired so vividly that these new scientific ideas, "mixing with those which were already there, . . . employed my Fancy all the last Night, and composed a very wild Extravagant Dream" (2:594). The result is a "Visionary Dissection" of a beau's brain and of a coquette's heart (2:594). In the *Spectator*, dreams provide access to certain types of knowledge, particularly social, cultural, and political positions that the periodical wishes to promulgate. The dream about Lady Credit is an especially famous example. The dream is an instrument of observation, grounded in imaginative insight. It is, most important, a literary device.

The plot is this. An anatomist cuts open a body and observes its parts under a microscope. Within the fiction of the dream, the microscopic examination of the beau's brain confirms that it is "only something like" a real brain (2:571). Magnification reveals things "imperceptible to the naked eye," namely cavities, ducts, and bladders filled with all manner of "Trumpery": "Ribbons, lace and Embroidery," "Billet-doux, Love-Letters, pricked Dances," "Fictions, Flatteries, and Falshoods," "Vows, Promises, and Protestations," "Oaths and Imprecations," and "Sonnets and little musical Instruments" (2:571). The dissection of the coquette's heart unveils a similar literalization. The anatomist proclaims her heart the most difficult he has tried to dissect because of its "many Labyrinths and Recesses" where she hides her true intentions and desires (2:594). Twisted like a Gordian knot, her heart has no anatomical connection to her tongue and is "stuffed with innumerable sorts of Trifles" (2:594). Its surface bears millions of scars from lovers' "innumerable Darts and Arrows," none of which seem to have broken through the surface, that is, until they discover in its inner cavity a "little Figure, which, upon applying our Glasses to it, appeared dressed in a very fantastic manner" (2:595–596). The beau resides deep within the recesses of the coquette's heart, visible only with the tools of experimental philosophy. This ocular demonstration ultimately confirms Mr. Spectator's assessment of the coquette more generally. She who is obsessed with being fashionable and commanding male attention has a heart stuffed full of fashionable accoutrement and a miniature of her cherished, fickle beau. The discovery of the beau in the coquette's heart suggests that her rebellion against the rules of courtship fails. She might refuse to choose a lover openly, but the "Visionary dissection" confirms that she nonetheless loves the beau.

The results of the dissections are what an eighteenth-century reader of Addison and Steele's periodical might expect. Scientific observation in both cases exposes literalization. The beau and coquette, preoccupied by the whims of social climbing and erotic pleasures, turn out to be made of them, a metonymic rendering that Alexander Pope exploits in *The Rape of the Lock*. The beau and the coquette embody the objectification and commodification that their behavior perpetuates. Yet Mr. Spectator's "Visionary Dissection[s]" do not solely indict the superficial values of the beau monde. His dreams simultaneously implicate experimental philosophy in ridicule and critique, a provocation the paper elaborates by questioning the validity of knowledge gained from sensory perception, the hallmark of experimental knowledge production.

The *Spectator*'s dream transforms the beau's brain and the coquette's heart into instruments. As evident in Hooke's *Micrographia*, the conversion of body parts into scientific instruments supports the erasure of a practitioner's bias. But according to Addison, instrumentalization of the body only exacerbates prejudice and error. The beau's ear contains a canal filled with "Wind or Froth" that leads directly to a cavity linked to the beau's tongue filled with a "Spongy Substance, which the *French* Anatomists call *Galimatias*, and the *English*, Nonsense" (2:571). The anatomical structure Mr. Spectator details literalizes a process wherein the beau hears cant and repeats it. As an instrument for sensory perception, the beau's ear bypasses any filter of judgment or reasoning, transforming that perception into its own organic substance, nonsense. The beau's vision is equally inadequate: while his "Ogling Muscles, were very much worn and decayed with use," his "Elevator" muscle—looking upward to heaven—is undeveloped and unused (2:571). Even a feature of the brain that is not related to the senses per se indicates the mechanistic self-justification of the beau's brain and, by implication, of such ocular practices. When Mr. Spectator takes the microscope to the beau's "pineal gland," arguably the "Seat of the Soul," he sees "a thousand little Faces or

Mirrours, which were imperceptible to the naked Eye, insomuch that the Soul, if there had been any here, must have been always taken up in contemplating her own Beauties" (2:571). What should be the physical manifestation of the beau's soul, in other words, is a machine for self-observation and self-love—that is, narcissism. The imaginative dissection of the beau's body exposes instruments of sensory perception that result in nonsense, ogling, and self-admiration.

The imaginative dissection of the coquette's heart heightens this skepticism because of her gender. The beau may be selfish and foolish, but the coquette threatens the economy of sexual relations and patriarchal authority by refusing to subject herself to its rules. As a consequence, her characterization in Mr. Spectator's "Visionary Dissection" is even sharper. The coquette's heart, scarred and hiding her true feelings, is encased in a "thin reddish Liquor," which it turns out has "all the Qualities of that Spirit which is made use of in the Thermometer, to see the Change of Weather" (2:596). In a lengthy description, Mr. Spectator recounts an experiment conducted on the same liquid from another dissection of a coquette's heart. The movement of this fluid "shewed him the Qualities of those Persons who entered the Room where it stood" (2:596). The coquette's "Liquor" responds with animation to "the Approach of a Plume of Feathers, an embroidered Coat, or a Pain of fringed Gloves; and that it fell as soon as an ill-shaped Perriwig, a clumsy Pair of Shoes, or an unfashionable Coat came into his House" (2:596). The liquid remains of the coquette's heart react quickly and passionately, rising and falling based on the proximity of pleasurable and valued fashions.

Hearts, of course, are not organs of sensory perception. Nevertheless, this instrumentalization of the coquette's body, achieved through the abstraction of organic liquid from the body itself, impugns the valuation of sensory perception at the core of experimental knowledge: sensory perception is inherently biased and flawed, even in its instrumental manifestations.

Tackling the dominant experimental sense, Mr. Spectator's instrumentalization of the coquette's dissected body widens to her eyesight: "We could not but take Notice likewise, that several of those little Nerves in the Heart which are affected by the Sentiments of Love, Hatred, and other Passions, did not descend to this before us from the Brain, but from the Muscles which lie about the Eye" (2:596). Microscopic examination in this instance reveals the mechanics of pure sensory perception. The coquette's visual perception bypasses her mind and directly fuels her sentiments, without the benefits of intellectual reflection and moderation. The coquette's vision embodies the myopia of "the uncritical and coquettish eye [that] was easily duped by petty illusion and maggoty marvels."[53] Mr. Spectator's characterization of the coquette's ocular apprehension assails her sensory perception and sensory perception more generally as a way to obtain knowledge. When the body reacts—when only the senses shape human behavior—the results are impetuous, even irrational.

In the *Spectator*'s "Visionary Dissection," both the beau and the coquette come under the periodical's judgmental purview. But the beau is not as much of a problem in the plot of social relations; he is not unknowable, merely frivolous. For Mr. Spectator, the coquette is both a specimen and observer, failing in both roles to produce meaningful, valuable knowledge. The dissection of the coquette's heart lays bare heartlessness, a quality that comes as no surprise to Mr. Spectator and his agreeable readers. But it also discloses the dangers of sensory perception. As an instrument, the coquette's heart displays how sensory perception works, the transformative process by which external stimuli are rendered into observations. In Mr. Spectator's dream, her perceptions merely accord with the frivolous value system of the beau monde and with her insistence on her importance, both of which challenge the paternalistic, commercial world Addison and Steele envisage throughout the periodical. A coquette's eyes and optical instruments inappropriately and similarly value small, trivial, and ultimately superficial things. For Mr. Spectator, coquettes and experimental philosophy not only share but also deepen these flaws, a stance in accord with the larger project of the *Spectator*'s promotion of an urban, masculine sociability and standard of taste.[54]

As in the case of Shadwell's Gimcrack, Addison's coquette finds an important afterlife. In the hands of Eliza Haywood, the midcentury periodical the *Female Spectator* reconfigures Mr. Spectator's evocation of coquettes: not only is the Spectator reborn as the Female Spectator, but the Female Spectator is a reformed coquette herself. The Female Spectator is a version of Haywood's heroine Betsy Thoughtless at the end of the novel by the same name: still conversant in the urbanized world, fashions, and desires of eighteenth-century London, though reformed into good judgment, discrimination, and gentility.[55]

The *Female Spectator* self-consciously draws on the *Spectator* as its model and target.[56] The eidolon's status as a reformed coquette is only part of Haywood's rejoinder: in a pair of related issues, Haywood recuperates the coquette through her practice of experimental philosophy. She is not the object of inspection or subject to the mediation of Mr. Spectator's dreaming technology. The *Female Spectator* reimagines the coquette as an avid and productive practitioner of scientific scrutiny. Haywood narrates an excursion to the country in which the Female Spectator and her club are inculcated into the pleasures and curiosities of natural philosophy. The club includes the unmarried Euphrosine, the married Mira, and a widow, together representing the social roles available to a woman over her lifetime. When the sun begins to shine at Mira's country estate, the women sally "forth with our Microscopes" to examine the natural wonders in the garden.[57] They observe numerous caterpillars, noting their coloration, and collect hillocks into pots, examining them daily to see what changes they can detect (17:296). To the naked eye, the hillocks have a coarse and ugly covering, "like the Bristles of a Boar," but under the microscope, their "Skin [is] perfectly enameled with Gold and Purpose" (17:293). "When you come to examine them," the Female Spectator writes, "you will find Beauties you little expected"; they are admirable, "graceful and majestic," well designed, and medicinally useful (17:293, 299). The women's scientific curiosity is also piqued by the prospect of using a neighbor's thirty-six-foot telescope, which is housed in a specially designed turret. Furnished with a pair of globes, a writing table, a bookcase, and a dozen chairs, the turret connotes privilege, intimate society, and knowledge production.[58] The Female Spectator looks through the telescope and observes that peculiar dark spots and shadows on the moon counter its brightness, phenomena that the group interprets as evidence of the plurality of worlds.

Haywood honors fashionable London women who practice experimental philosophy together. Within the pages of the *Female Spectator,* the experience of natural philosophy produces sustained, careful observation of nature and new topics of conversation. The Female Spectator summarizes her intention: "All that was aimed at . . . was to shew the Female Subscribers and Encouragers of this Undertaking, how much Pleasure, as well as Improvement, would accrue to them by giving some few hours, out of the many which they have to spare, to the Study of Natural Philosophy" (17.318). With an apology for any inadvertent errors, she hopes that women will imitate her example. Haywood's story and encouragement that women pursue scientific inquiry can be read as one of many ways the periodical offers sensible and appealing instruction for readers. The few pages devoted to "Recreations" in Richard Steele's *The Ladies Library,* for instance, address only the things women ought not do.[59] Haywood provides positive models: such diversions will safeguard her audience from the allure of other dangerous urban pleasures; they also introduce the possibility of intellectual and social equality with men.[60] Hers is the sophisticated and intelligent version of Lady Science's enthusiasm. Haywood also echoes Celia Fiennes's claim that London's fashionable would improve greatly were they "curious to inform themselves and make observations of the pleasant prospects, good buildings, different producers and manufacturers of each place, with the variety of sports and recreations they are adapt to."[61] Haywood goes so far as to suggest all women and all men of leisure ought to practice experimental philosophy.

But filling women's leisure time is not Haywood's primary goal: the practice of natural philosophy sets up the means for a powerful conversion narrative that undergirds the periodical. By applying themselves to the study of natural philosophy, coquettes have the potential to reform themselves and become versions of the Female Spectator herself. A correspondent "Philo-Naturae" clarifies that coquettes are the intended audience. It is not merely "the Ladies," but more specifically "the Enliveners of Society" who must be taught the advantages of natural philosophy (15:144)—coquettes. Experimental philosophy enhances the social world of the coquette, providing innumerable topics for discussion: "here they never can want Matter:—new Subjects of Astonishment will every Day, every Hour start up before them, and those of the greatest Volubility will much sooner want Words than Occasions to make Use of them" (15:153–154). Philo-Naturae's case for natural philosophy implicitly relies on an association with being á la mode without indicting the value of novelty, as Mr. Spectator does.

The suitability of the coquette to natural philosophy goes beyond replacing one topic of conversation for another. The coquette as a character has observational training that prepares her well to engage in scientific observation. If one is instructed in the logic of the fashions and diversions associated with the dressing room, then one has the skills appropriate to the practice of experimental philosophy:

If we become early Connoisseurs in the Mode, can make smart Remarks on the Dress of every one we see at the Ball, the court, the Opera, or any other public Place, take so much Delight in hearing and reporting every little Accident that happens in Families we are acquainted with,—how much more Pleasure should we find in examining the various and beautiful Habits with which Natures cloathes those Plants and Flowers which adorn our Gardens. (15:139)

The Female Spectator's journey to the country with her club produces such observations, illuminating that the discriminating eye of a fashionable woman is an excellent observational instrument:

There are *Microscopes* which will shew us such magnificent Apparel, and such delicate Trimming about the smallest Insects, as would disgrace the Splendor of a Birth-day:— Several of them are adorned with Crowns upon their Heads, have their Wings fringed with Colours of the most lively Dye, and their Coats embroidered with Purple and with Gold. (15:147)

Haywood overtly frames the Female Spectator's microscopical observation in language from the contemporary world of sartorial fashion. Words such as *apparel* and *trimming* and the allusion to ornate clothing one would wear for the king's birthday overlay the observations of these insects such that the language of fashion shares and even brings forth the aesthetic values of experimental philosophy. The Female Spectator's description evokes the literariness of Robert Boyle's "skilfully chosen, and well-applied, Comparison" and Henry Power's aesthetic rendering of a horse fly's eye. Written into this account is a privileging of the coquette's view—she, among observers, can identify and assess such things as trimming, crowns, dye, and embroidery. The coquette's schooling in fashionable London life prepares her for astute observations of the natural world. She also has the possibility of contributing to the nationalist project of the Royal Society (see 15:151, 153–154).

Even for the author of *Betsy Thoughtless,* whose coquettish heroine reforms, the transformation of a coquette into a natural philosopher is radical. The *Female Spectator*'s investment in science for women comes from a conviction that it allows for the expression—and even the acquisition—of good taste. Haywood introduces the topic of natural philosophy in the *Female Spectator* through a discussion of reason, curiosity, and intellectual beautification. She builds the case that making one's mind beautiful is no different from doing the same with one's body, conjoining the connotations of the dressing room as a space for cosmetic adornment and intellectual improvement: women "can find means to purify their Complexions, to take out Pimples, Freckles, and Morphew from the Skin . . . will not Reason and Reflection enable us to erase whatever is a Blemish in the Mind?" (15:131–132). Reason and reflection are the tools of intellectual self-improvement and available through three "Amusements, Diversions, and Employments": studying history, reading travel narratives, and practicing natural philosophy (15:132). These are forms of intellectual work that provide the commensurate benefit of "more solid Reflections," "enlarging the Ideas, informing the Understanding, and above all, of inspiring in us a Love and Reverence for the great Author, Director, and sole Disposer of every thing in Nature" (15:139–140). At the core of this pedagogy, the Female Spectator imagines inculcating a model of the self in which "We shall be enabled to prize every thing according to its real Value, and be entirely free from all Prejudice and partial Attachments" (15:140).

The Female Spectator envisages the reformed coquette as a subject position to which her readers may aspire. Haywood's model of observation embodied by the reformed coquette does not deny the experiential but depends on it. The "Amusements, Diversions, and Employments" that the Female Specatator endorses are valuable because they serve as barometers of an individual's powers of discrimination, skills that are available because of that individual's engagement with, not detachment from, the world.

The coquette's transformation embodies the larger pedagogical goal of the periodical—the reformation and education of its readers—and is possible through, and confirmed by, the acquisition of good taste. The "Amusements, Diversions, and Employments" of history, travel narratives, and natural philosophy allow for the measurement of one's taste, for in them, "our good or bad Taste are chiefly discoverable" (15:132). As appropriate observers, Haywood explains, "We shall be possessed of all those useful and agreeable Talents, which in their Assemblage compose of what may justly be called the *true fine Taste*" (15:140). Taste is an eighteenth-century aesthetic category inextricable from a sense of fashionability, moral quality, rank, and social status. To be in possession of good taste in the eighteenth century connoted modesty, restraint, practicality, and decorum in distinction to bad (aristocratic) taste corrupted by ideologically retrogressive qualities of personal ostentation, irrational excess, arbitrary election, and libertine abandon.[62] Good taste is both a personal and a social quality and, as such, can serve as a mechanism to inculcate female restraint and (in its absence) as a measure of female license.[63] To have good taste was to be seen as a discerning, refined individual. To have good taste was to be seen as a moral individual. At the same time, the culture of taste embodied "repressive tendencies" that labored to obscure its structural relation, for example, to the institution of slavery.[64]

The *Female Spectator*'s conjunction of taste and natural philosophy is hardly accidental. As in the case of eighteenth-century aesthetic theory more generally, which I discuss at length in Chapter 5, the quality of taste could be linked to refined sensory perception. David Hume makes this connection in a discussion of perception; with heightened perception comes heightened sensibility. Taste and sentiment are inseparable.[65] Hume argues that "the perfection of the man, and the perfection of the sense or feeling, are found to be united."⁶⁶ To have "delicacy of taste," the pinnacle of accomplishment, "enlarges the spheres both of our happiness and misery, and makes us sensible to pains as well as pleasures, which escape the rest of mankind."⁶⁷ Pain and pleasure are, in turn, "a way of knowing."⁶⁸ For Hume, this experience of pleasure is specifically designed for judgment. The skill of discernment may be achieved if one practices appropriately: "But allow him to acquire experience in those objects, his feeling becomes more exact and nice."⁶⁹ It takes doing. With practice, "the organ acquires greater perfection in its operations; and can pronounce, without danger of mistake, concerning the merits of every performance."⁷⁰ Hume's evocation of experimental philosophy is clear: the most refined "organ" of sensory perception will produce, in the end, "the perfection of man."⁷¹ This turn to natural philosophy depends on an analogy between mental and physical taste, what the mind and body process.⁷² Perceiving well, for Hume, is inextricably linked to one's archive of knowledge and one's embodiment.

Along with Hume, Haywood imagines good taste as something that may be acquired through practice because good taste is not "morally impossible for any one to be possessed of" (15:137). Readers of the periodical may convert their bad taste into good through the right exercise. With proper instruction and training, a person can join the morally and socially superior individuals in possession of good taste: "But they who can once resolve to employ themselves in such a manner as becomes a Person of *fine Taste*, however repugnant they may be at first, will, by Degrees, be brought insensibly to have it in reality" (15:138). By imagining that an individual may receive an education in good taste, the Female Spectator envisages and promotes techniques of self-improvement and self-transformation. From the periodical's opening pages, the Female Spectator focuses on good taste, enjoining her readers to practice it: "It is very much by the choice we make of subjects for our entertainment, that the refined taste distinguishes itself from the vulgar and more gross" (1:1). Good taste is revealed by our choices. But Haywood suggests that this may be obtained: if you perform good taste, eventually you will have it.

The periodical's message for its female readers is unequivocal: transform yourself from a vain and trivial coquette into a serious and morally judicious lady, and you will simultaneously convert yourself from a woman of bad taste to good. Coquettes, after all, are singled out by Mr. Spectator as those who cannot hope to have any of these qualities and who have no potential for improvement. The Female Spectator argues the opposite. The possibility of a coquette's reformation, rather than her imagined death and dissection, does not negate her earlier activities and amusements but readjusts her focus and the ends. Through this conversion narrative, the Female Spectator repudiates a competitive social network in which coquettes battle for admirers and attention, and instead promotes an intellectual and social community where women learn from each other as a means of developing and promoting good taste. The conversion narrative's availability to coquettes ultimately is the import of the embedded story of the journey to Mira's country estate. The account of their country excursion shows good taste in action, thereby promoting a new mode of female society populated by modern, self-improving, and discerning individuals. A coquette's experience in the fashionable world and her acquisition of good taste through the practice of natural philosophy suggest a specific model for British modernity: the coquette may be an unlikely and unexpected exemplar, but she is emphatically imagined as at once enlightened and á la mode.

Immodest witnesses, so often maligned as bad scientists with poor judgment and blinded by self-importance, disclose the structural, cultural, and ideological qualities bound up with the scientific project more generally. One may dismiss the Gimcracks and coquettes of the world as, at best, comic buffoons and, at worst, obstructionist retrogrades. These bad scientists, however, expose a more nuanced account of the natural philosophical project. They embody the inescapability of immodesty: the self-interest of knowledge production, which in turn provides material for critique and endorsement. The scientific project runs the risk of being only a mechanism, variously, for self-interest, sexual pleasure, and the accumulation of wealth. The lesson that the immodest witness teaches is that this proclivity for self-interest is written into the characterization of the modest witness. Yet this predisposition has the perhaps unexpected effect of ennobling subjects ordinarily marginalized by traditional social structures. For this reason, Centlivre and Haywood see an opening. Natural philosophy offers a means to translate the inherent subjectivity of scientific observation into an unlikely model for female agency. Centlivre portrays the potential for a dependent heiress to be independent through the intellectual work of experimental philosophy, and Haywood imagines the reformation of a coquette accomplished through the same method, adding to it the promise of acquiring that sparkling aesthetic and moral quality of having good taste in the process. The Gimcrack and the coquette thus transform into avatars of modern enlightenment.

What emerges next, and the subject to which we turn in the following chapter, is the narrative structure that produces scientific believers: the seduction plot.

3 SCIENTIFIC SEDUCTION

The previous two chapters have concentrated on the centrality of literary knowledge to the representation of natural philosophy and to natural philosophers' own ways of thinking about themselves and the natural world. Metaphor provides experimental philosophers an instrument to imagine two things: the phenomena they study as observed particulars worthy of attention and themselves into their roles as modest witnesses who objectively scrutinize the world. Satiric parodies of the modest witness uncover an ever-present potential for self-interest, self-aggrandizement, and eroticism lurking in the experimental project. Literary characters that embody these forms of immodesty, Gimcracks and coquettes, thwart the normative functioning of social relations. This is the story of how literary knowledge—in the form of metaphor, plot, and characterization—constructs and yet also flays the principle of objectivity as an epistemology and subject position. These scenes of science bring about ruminations on the intellectual and social effects of the experimental imagination.

Whether advocates, practitioners, or literary characters, the individuals we have encountered for the most part already believe experimental philosophy, legitimately or not. The genre of scientific dialogues displays the education that occurs before these other texts begin. To become adherents of natural philosophy, characters in scientific dialogues undergo a process of seduction. Scientific education is viable and codified through the specific literary convention of the seduction plot.

To begin with the obvious question: What do science and seduction have to do with each other? Eliza Haywood's 1719 seduction novel, *Love in Excess*, provides an answer. The "matchless Melliora" mingles grief for her father's death with sexual desire for her guardian (who is married) and, thanks to her self-awareness, she concludes that Count D'Elmont is "not an object to be safely gazed at."[1] Following a bitter fight with his wife, D'Elmont encounters Melliora reading. He finds her beautiful and alluring, "lying on a green bank, in a melancholy but a charming posture," so completely engrossed in reading that "she saw not the Count 'till he was close enough to her to discern what was the subject of her entertainment."² D'Elmont seizes Melliora's reading as an occasion for flattery, insisting that if the author had "ever seen Melliora ... he would have been able to write of nothing else but love and her," to which Melliora demurs that what she cherishes is the "improvement ... this book has given me."³ "Thank heaven then madam," D'Elmont responds, "that you were born in an age successive to that which has produced so many fine treatises of this kind for your entertainment."⁴ Such compliments resolve into their first sexual encounter, the inaugural moment in the novel when they act on their mutual desire.⁵

What is Melliora reading with such focus and commitment? A volume of "Phylosophy" by "Monsieur L'fontenelle."⁶ The work for which Fontenelle was most famous was a volume explicating Copernican and Cartesian cosmology, *Entretiens sur la pluralité des mondes*.⁷ With Fontenelle in her lap, D'Elmont sees love in Melliora's eyes. In terms of Haywood's narrative action, Melliora's reading Fontenelle hastens the love affair: Haywood alludes to Fontenelle in a novel of seduction at the moment of seduction. And the characterization of Melliora as a reader of Fontenelle operates on two fronts. It revises the traditionally "ruined" female in a seduction narrative, making Melliora at once virtuous and sexually desiring.⁸ Her characterization also redefines the seduction plot of *Love in Excess* as one that is simultaneously affective and intellectual.

Haywood's reference to Fontenelle transpires within an established tradition of figurative associations that couple sexual seduction and scientific knowledge. Natural philosophy texts, beginning with Francis Bacon, frequently present scientific practice as heteronormative, erotic quests. Bacon's metaphors expressly identify the early scientist as a masculine seducer: the naturalist, according to Bacon, wants to "penetrate into the inner and further recesses of nature" and to "find a way at length into her inner chambers."⁹ If the natural philosopher seduces, then nature submits: "it is no wonder if nature will not give herself into their hands."¹⁰ When Bacon's writings represent nature as female, they imagine that scientific scrutiny is both a form of sexual analysis and an occasion for "conquest and containment" by the masculinized naturalist.¹¹ Within the rationale of Baconianism, sexual, affective relations permit the practice of science and the production of scientific knowledge. The correspondence between sexual seduction and natural philosophical inquiry was not confined to Bacon. Others regularly represented scientific practice as an erotic, seductive plot involving a masculinized experimentalist aspiring to dominate a feminized nature. Male natural history collectors articulated their intellectual desire through allusions to Ovid's *Metamorphoses*.[12] Abraham Cowley's "Ode. Upon Dr. Harvey" (1657), in its descriptions of Harvey's discoveries about the circulation of the blood, presents nature as a "Coy virgin," who "When Harveys violent passion she did see,/Began to tremble, and to flee," while he "pursues" her.[13] And even Hooke's *Micrographia* draws on the "eroticization of sight" in its story of magnification and discovery.[14] (In a provocative reversal of the association between eroticism and science, the dialogue *The Whores Rhetorick* [1686] features the bawd Mrs. Creswell teaching carnal knowledge with allusions to the Royal Society.[15])

Although the conceptualization of natural philosophy is embedded in Haywood's seduction plot, experimentalists differ from Melliora, for they imagine generating scientific knowledge. Haywood's heroine does not create knowledge but devotes herself to understanding natural philosophy and, in so doing, believing it. Among its myriad connotations, Melliora's reading Fontenelle is a form of scientific education.

A few words about seduction. Seduction plots as literary devices explore who has legitimate authority by imagining social relations as determined by power and feeling. The problem that seduction plots confront is the possibilities, or impossibilities, available to an individual with less power. For every Melliora, there are countless heroines exploited, humiliated, and wronged. These power relations often unmask an epistemological quandary—a desire for sex displaced by or imagined as a desire to know something.[16] Seduction stories disclose the precarious, unstable division in the period between the notion of consent associated with seduction and the refusal assumed to be inherent to rape.[17] Indeed, the differences among rape, seduction, and courtship demand that a heroine in a seduction story can distinguish between men's violence, coercion, and courtship, even if the men's behavior in all three cases seems all too similar.[18] The "specter of rape" conveys with seduction scenes, and it becomes difficult to apprehend the putative difference between consent and refusal since rape, seduction, and courtship share fundamental assumptions about power and desire between men and women.[19] Seduction stories roll out a sleight-of-hand to imagine that such divisions are possible. This may be rape, this may be seduction, this may be courtship, but the difference among the three in the long eighteenth century was fraught, if not indistinguishable.

Thus understood, seduction stories accomplish several things simultaneously. They stage power relations among unequal participants, conjoin sexual desire with a desire for knowledge, narrate a character's changing state and status, and imagine affect as an epistemology.

This chapter analyzes seduction plots in texts devoted to teaching scientific ideas. These narratives picture their characters undergoing an intellectual conversion. I focus on two dialogues translated into English from French and Italian: Bernard de Fontenelle's study of Copernican and Cartesian cosmology, *Entretiens sur la pluralité des mondes* (1686), and Francesco Algarotti's rendering of Newtonian optics, *Il Newtonianismo per le dame, ovvero, dialoghi sopra la luce e i colori* (1737). In a book about the British Enlightenment, a chapter on a French and Italian might seem anomalous, yet both Fontenelle's and Algarotti's works were immensely popular with the English reading public as translations, a genre with its own particular conventions and possibilities.

I begin by discussing translations of Fontenelle and Algarotti by two eminent female writers of the British long eighteenth century, Aphra Behn and Elizabeth Carter. The best-known female translator of the time, Behn prefaces her translation of Fontenelle with a treatise that sharply critiques his science and style. Carter translated Epictetus with great critical and financial success, contributed vitally to the Blue Stockings Society (which promoted women's education), and was renowned for impeccable classical and scientific learning; she leaves her intellectual mark in editorial corrections of Algarotti. Both translations embrace the suitability of natural philosophical education for women.

Following these arguments in support of women's scientific instruction, I then turn to Fontenelle and Algarotti directly. For both, learning about science mandates undergoing a process of seduction. Philosophical, intellectual seduction uproots sexual, bodily seduction, though the connotations of the latter persist: Fontenelle and Algarotti portray the acquisition of natural philosophical knowledge as acquiescence to the seductive power of one's educator. Yet while the ideas of Copernicus, Descartes, and Newton seduce, they accomplish transformation through a redactor. The "philosopher" character in each dialogue positions himself as seduced by scientific ideas and by his female interlocutor, but he also presents himself as a seducer of his female interlocutor. The innovation and allure of Copernican, Cartesian, and Newtonian ideas prove compelling, convincing the philosopher, the lady, and presumably the readers to assent. While imagining a traditional gendering of seduction wherein a male teacher seduces a female pupil, this form of scientific education also opens up space for men to be seduced and for women to be seducers.[20]

TRANSLATING SCIENCE: BEHN AND CARTER

In the British context, the market for translations, particularly those in the vernacular, was growing during this period.[21] Translators worked for sundry levels of compensation and had varying degrees of proficiency.[22] Conceptually, the work of translation in the long eighteenth century evoked the premodern notion of transmission of power and learning while also merging with the newly modern sense of translation "as a national-cultural project."[23] Behn and Carter both produced translations that signaled their own intellectual authority, delivering science education to a British reading public eager for it.

To begin with Fontenelle in Britain. Within two years of the Paris publication, Sir W. D. Knight (Dublin, 1687), John Glanvill, a fellow of the Royal Society (London, 1688), and Aphra Behn (London, 1688) all produced translations, and three additional translations appeared in the eighteenth century.[24] Knight's and Glanvill's volumes address Fontenelle's female readership and promote British nationalism. Knight evokes Anglo-Franco rivalry, suggesting "we have hitherto outdone the French by the Progress of our Arms in *this World*, why should we fall short of them in our Discovery of *others*."[25] His stated accomplishment is to have "rectify'd [Fontenelle's] French Telescope the best I could for the use of an English Eye."[26] Knight takes a conservative view of the text's imagined audience, contending that women are merely ornamental and do not have the intellects to understand science: it is "a Work more proper for Men."[27] For Glanvill, the act of translation is also an action of nationalism. His *Conversations with a Lady, on the Plurality of Worlds* replaces French references with English ones, many of which specifically allude to the Royal Society. Glanvill's modifications resonate with the popularizing impulse of the Royal Society's publication program.[28]

Behn's *A Discovery of New Worlds* is significant in both literary and intellectual terms. It opens with "An Essay on Translated Prose," an extended discussion of her translation theory and estimation of Fontenelle's intellectual contributions.[29] Published months before Glanvill's translation, Behn's volume went through four editions by 1737.[30] Behn's translation, she explains, is faithful to Fontenelle: it delivers "*the* French *Book into* English"; to do otherwise would be "*to give you the subject quite changed and made my own*."[31] As a result, the setting is Paris, as in Fontenelle's original, not England, as in Glanvill's (86).

Behn explains that she was attracted to *A Discovery of New Worlds* for three reasons: Fontenelle's reputation, the "novelty" of cosmology written in English, and the female participant, that is, "*the Authors introducing a Woman as one of the speakers in these five Discourses*" (73). The final reason elicits an elaboration. Behn connects the idea of a female interlocutor to her own status as a woman writer: "*I thought an* English *Woman might adventure to translate any thing, a* French *Woman may be supposed to have spoken*" (73). The phrasing is notable: her language accommodates the fictionality of Fontenelle's dialogue with the phrase "may be supposed to have spoken." The marchioness is a literary character and Behn expresses a commitment to ventriloquize her. Unacknowledged by Behn, though obviously the case and equally significant, is the fact that she as a translator also gives voice to Fontenelle's male philosopher. If Behn's stated sympathy is with the marchioness, the result is that she, as a translator, acquires full control over representing the teaching and learning of natural philosophy.

Although Behn's primary role is as a translator, she also insists on her own authorship. The scientific dialogue teaching about the cosmos, in this English translation, is associated with Behn's authorship, not Fontenelle's. Behn's name features prominently on the title page, while Fontenelle's is dropped. Within "An Essay," Behn expands her role as translator and author to include that of literary critic when she chastises Fontenelle for his characterization of the French woman. Fontenelle strains credulity by featuring a "*Woman of Quality . . . whom he feigns never to have heard of any such thing as Philosophy before*" (77). From Behn's point of view, the marchioness is, at turns, too naive and too sophisticated to be believable. Behn complains that Fontenelle "*makes* [the marchioness] *say a great many very silly things, tho' sometimes she makes Observations so learned, that the greatest Philosophers in* Europe *could make no better*" (77). There is a subtle yet defining difference that Behn's sentence registers. Fontenelle is a sort of puppeteer who "makes her say" things, while the lady is presented as an autonomous being who "makes Observations." Why does this difference matter? With a turn of phrase, Behn places any blame for the literary characterization of this woman at Fontenelle's feet and any praise for her intellectual insights, which rival the best philosopher's, as a credit to the fictional woman's character. By switching subjects within a single sentence, moving from author to character, Behn fabricates a literary character into a fully and admirably intellectual female mind.

Behn's skepticism about Fontenelle's characterizations establishes her credentials as a literary critic, but she again claims another role for herself when she corrects the science in Fontenelle's dialogue. In one instance, she fixes a matter of fact concerning "*the heighth of our Air of Sphere of Activity of the Earth*" (86). She attributes the original confusion to a printer's error. The effect is to bind her work as translator and critic to her intellectual acumen as a learned natural philosopher. In addition to such granular revisions, Behn challenges Fontenelle's primary scientific claim that there are other worlds beyond our own. Fontenelle "*gives a magnificent* Idea *of the vastness of the Universe, and of the almighty and infinite Power of the Creator,*" which can be "*comprehended by the meanest Capacity*" and which "*he proves judiciously*" (77). However—and this is the crucial point—Fontenelle "*hath urged this Fancy too far*" (77). Behn cautions that Fontenelle will confuse readers with "*trifling and airy*" ideas about other worlds rather than "*what is truly solid (or at least, probable)*" (77). In Behn's criticism of Fontenelle, she discloses an understanding of the universe as vast yet fundamentally incomprehensible; it can be intuited, not understood.[32] Fontenelle's interpretations of Descartes, in particular, are excessive. In Behn's language, they are "wild": a "*wild* Notion *of the* Plurality of Worlds" spawned by Fontenelle's "*wild Fancy*" (77). Behn alters Fontenelle's Cartesianism to reflect the contemporary scientific preference for Newtonian voluntarism.[33] Her translation, as a consequence, confirms a sophisticated understanding of contemporary scientific debate.[34]

Forty-one years after Behn rendered Fontenelle, Carter translated Algarotti. She was twenty-two years old. Even by this young age, Carter was already a regular contributor to the *Gentleman's Magazine*, spending time with the publisher Edward Cave and his family when she was in London.[35] In 1738, the *Gentleman's Magazine*, which had published her first poem four years earlier, featured her verse, "While clear the Night, and ev'ry Thought serene." The poem showcased a sophisticated astronomical knowledge. It also paid tribute to Newton's protégé, John Theophilus Desaguliers (1683–1744), and to the astronomer and mathematician, Thomas Wright of Durham (1711–1786). In the same year as the Algarotti volume (1739), she translated *An Examination of Mr Pope's Essay on Man, From the French of M. Crousaz*. Both texts required that she have substantial knowledge and mastery of Newtonian theories.

Carter's intelligence and learning were stunning, her erudition rivaling that of any man in the academic establishment.[36] She learned Greek, Latin, Hebrew, and French in the company of her brothers; she taught herself Italian, Spanish, German, and some Portuguese and Arabic.[37] In the 1730s, she exerted a formidable influence on Samuel Johnson, who, Carter would remember, "had said, speaking of some celebrated scholar, that he understood Greek better than any one whom he had ever known, except Elizabeth Carter."[38] Her friend Thomas Birch praised Carter publicly in *History of the Works of the Learned*—at the same time revealing her authorship of the Algarotti translation—as an "extraordinary Phaenomenon in the Republick of Letters."[39] Later in life, contemporaries described Carter as a college don or a "university of ladies."[40]

Carter chose to translate Algarotti's Newton over Boethius, likely motivated by her long-term interest in mathematics and astronomy.[41] Her decision to publish Algarotti's Newton and Crousaz's Pope reflects Carter's ambitions as a professional writer (even though she ended up returning home to Deal, Kent, shortly thereafter and living in the country for the next twenty years).[42] Later, her translation of the works of the stoic philosopher Epictetus was the first complete English version and earned Carter critical renown. It also paid her the princely sum of £1,000 (an amount at the very upper end of the pay scale for translations), which ensured her financial security.[43]

Algarotti's text presented Carter a unique opportunity. Translating the Italian redactor enabled Carter to bring Newton home to a British reading public. With this translation, Carter participated in a larger cultural production of Newtonianism that resulted in myriad texts, lectures, and demonstrations in early eighteenth-century London. Newtonian science held a "public status" that ultimately permeated British economics, politics, and society. This influence was accomplished not through Newton's direct engagement, but instead through "the practitioners, the audience, the new public, the buyers and consumers" of early science.[44] Even fashionable women were expected to acquire familiarity with Newtonian science through such interlocutors.[45] John Harris's *Astronomical Dialogues Between a Gentleman and a Lady* (London, 1719), for example, is devoted to educating women in Newtonian cosmology.

The historical record does not include any direct statements from Carter articulating her intentions. We can only speculate that Carter may have been drawn to Algarotti's original for reasons similar to Behn's interest in Fontenelle. Perhaps part of the dialogue's appeal to her as a translator, writer, and thinker was its association with the Italian salon, with its roles available to women.[46] Both Naples and Milan in the eighteenth century supported a vibrant salon culture, much as one would find in Paris, with learned women playing prominent roles.[47] Lady Mary Wortley Montagu observed in 1753, "the character of a learned woman is far from being ridiculous in [Italy]," "the greatest Familys being proud of having produce'd female Writers"; she goes on to describe with great enthusiasm the public prominence of Laura Bassi, one of the first women to earn a doctorate and the first to hold a university professorship (at the University of

Bologna).[48] Wortley Montagu could well have been referring to her own experience in England. The rest of the letter amplifies the differences between the two nations, arguing (as she does elsewhere) that English society degrades women by not allowing them to be educated properly. "I think it the highest Injustice," she laments, "to be debarr'd the Entertainment of my Closet, and that the same Studies which raise the character of a Man should hurt that of a Woman."[49] Just like Behn before her, Carter chooses a scientific text that narrates and, by extension, advocates for the intellectual education of women—in Wortley Montagu's words, those "same Studies."

Though overt statements are not available, there is evidence that Carter translated Algarotti rigorously and thoroughly. Her translation bears evidence of her own intellectual critique. In the footnotes, she draws extensively from Pierre Bayle's *General Dictionary*, which Birch was translating and adapting. She also criticizes Algarotti's generalizations on philosophy and his inclusion of unattributed poetry.[50] The effect of these editorial reservations is to signal the translator's learning and wisdom, qualities that bear out the appropriateness of natural philosophical study for women.

Translation for Behn and Carter constituted political acts, a form of sexual politics even.[51] Behn brought Copernicus and Descartes to England; Carter delivered Newton back to England. In both instances, the translator leaps over the redactor to assert (overtly for Behn, implicitly for Carter) a direct engagement with and mastery of Copernicus, Descartes, or Newton. These translations, through their editorial apparatuses, commingle the translators' reputations and claims for intellectual authority with those of their originals. Translating Fontenelle and Algarotti enabled Behn and Carter to demonstrate the suitability of science for women.

COPERNICAN AND CARTESIAN SEDUCTION: FONTENELLE

Bernard de Fontenelle was a major figure of the French Enlightenment for the duration of his long—nearly one hundred years—life.[52] In 1686, he published his most famous work, *Entretiens sur la pluralité des mondes*, an explication of Copernican and Cartesian cosmology.[53] In France, it was "an instant best-seller," resulting in four editions in three years and thirty-three more editions up to the author's death in 1757.[54] In a sign of its influence and radicalism, *Discovery* was placed on the Papal Index in 1687.[55] Fontenelle's scientific reputation was forged on the basis of *Discovery*.⁵⁶ Following its publication, he was elected to the Académie Française and the Académie des Inscriptions, and in 1697, he began his appointment as perpetual secretary of the Académie des Sciences, which he held until 1740. In this position, Fontenelle served as a gatekeeper of French science studies as author of *Histoire du renouvellement de l'Académie des Sciences* (Paris, 1708), which documented the society's meetings.

The genre Fontenelle chooses is important. *Discovery* is a dialogue between a philosopher and a noble woman, which allows for "Liberty of natural Conversation" between them (90).⁵⁷ The dialogue's dialectic quality enacts the process of learning: making mistakes is part of learning, not an occasion to abandon the inquiry, and the precedent of Fontenelle made the genre popular.⁵⁸ The French salon culture, in which powerful women were active leaders, was especially amenable to philosophical and scientific conversations.⁵⁹ Fontenelle's was a world organized by elaborate rules of social etiquette, practices that reflected the ideals of *politesse*, gallantry, and *bonnêteté*.⁶⁰ These "social norms" "shaped some of the earliest representations of enlightened philosophers."⁶¹ In Britain, with its masculinized coffee house culture, eighteenth-century scientific dialogues often cast a sister learning from her brother within the domestic sphere. Benjamin Martin's two-volume educational treatise, *The Young Gentleman and Lady's Philosophy, in a Continued Survey of the Works of Nature and Art; By Way of dialogue* (1759–1763), and James Ferguson's *Easy Introduction to Astronomy, for Young Gentlemen and Ladies* (1768) both depict a scientific dialogue between an enthusiastic university-trained brother and his sister at home. Later scientific texts published by women regularly adopted the genre, a practice that suggests the dialogue's effectiveness, flexibility, and availability.⁶²

Fontenelle uses his dialogue to challenge heliocentrism: this is the belief held by the marchioness when she first meets the philosopher. Fontenelle's lady is of a superior rank to her tutor, an example Algarotti follows.⁶³ Throughout the pages of *Discovery*, the philosopher teaches the marchioness about Copernican cosmology and Cartesian physics, specifically the theory of vortices. In the Cartesian understanding, particles are always in motion and always in contact with each other, each spinning like a planet. Descartes's vortices, or *tourbillions*, were disproved by Newton's theory of gravity the year after Fontenelle published *Discovery*, but Cartesian physics remained intellectually plausible for the next fifty years.⁶⁴ Fontenelle expresses admiration in *Eloge de Newton* (1727), but he was not convinced by Newton's theories (88).

For Fontenelle, natural philosophy traverses the known world and, in so doing, opens up a window to unknown worlds. He aspires "to know how this World which we inhabit, is made, and that there are other Worlds that resemble it, and that are inhabited as well as this" (88). The promise of discovery, of course, is laced through scientific texts, but in *Discovery*, Fontenelle takes the possibility of exploration to a cosmological level, a trajectory that simultaneously introduces pathways to reconfigure the authority grounded in the heliocentric model. The frontispieces of the original 1686 Paris edition and a 1737 English translation (see Figures 3.1 and 3.2) graphically communicate the cosmological plentitude that inspires Fontenelle. In the 1686 engraving, concentric circles represent the universe. The image communicates two messages: the concentric circles evoke a vestigial heliocentrism as a way of situating this cosmology within a familiar worldview while also accommodating an expanded universe of multiple worlds. The circles are punctuated with planets, only six of them identified ("1. Mercure 2. Venus 3. La Terre 4. Mars 5. Jupiter 6. Saturne").[65] In the center, Mercury floats, surrounded by concentric circles of cloud-like shapes that seem to mushroom off the page. These puffs are unnamed and unmarked yet feature the radial and spoke lines of dissection that imply their eventual knowability. The concentric circles and the graphic units of other worlds combine to impart the fundamental possibilities that Copernican cosmology implements. The image denotes and connotes: it schematizes current planetary knowledge while also graphically representing the yet unknown. The frontispiece of the 1737 translation replicates this cosmological view and supplements it with a second image that depicts the philosopher and the marchioness animatedly talking in a garden.

For Fontenelle, the literary imagination is central to the dialogue's educational project of replacing the traditional understanding of cosmology with Copernican and Cartesian cosmology. Although the earth's rotation is not an observable phenomenon, Fontenelle's philosopher assembles an imaginative scenario to explain how one might visualize the planet's movement: "Sometimes I fancy I am hanging in the Air, and that I stay there without moving, while the Earth turns round under me in four and twenty Hours time, and that I see beneath me all those different Faces" (107). Imagining himself stationary and suspended above the globe, he can witness the earth's entirety over the course of a day, from sun-up to sundown. The succeeding description lists "all those different Faces"—"some white, some black, some tawny, others of an Olive-colour; first I see Hants, then Turbants, there Hands cover'd with Wool, there shav'd Heads" (107)—and the built landscapes they occupy: "sometimes Towns with Steeples, some with their long small-pointed Pyramids, and Half-moons on their tops; sometimes Towns with Porcelane Towers" (107–108). All told, the philosopher imaginatively views "all the Variety that is to be seen upon the Face of the Earth" (108). Of course, "all the Variety" cannot fully be conveyed in Fontenelle's truncated description, particularly with its reliance on the words *some*, *others*, and *sometimes* that refuse adjectival specificity. Yet this same language of generalization allows the reader to hang in space with the philosopher in a second act of imagination, inserting into those generic terms whatever particularity comes to the reader's mind.

The philosopher's imaginative scene prompts the marchioness to counter with her own. Rather than being suspended above the earth, she envisages remaining grounded on the earth's surface, physically moving through the air that blankets the earth while the planet rotates: "the same place where we now are (I do not mean this Park, but that space of Air which our Bodies fill) several other Nations must successively pass, and we return hither, in twenty four hours, to our own place again" (108). The marchioness's depiction alludes to travel narratives such as Thévenot's *Relations de divers voyages curieux* (1664), *La Chine illustrée* (1667; the account of two Jesuits, Dorville and Greuber, who visited China in 1661), and *Les six Voyages de J.-B. Tavernier* (1676) (108, note). As the globe turns, various groups move through the same pocket of air: the English "discoursing . . . upon some politick Design," a few ships spotted in "a vast Ocean," "Canibals" (Behn deviates from Fontenelle's original "Iroquois"), "women of the Country of *Jesso*," the "Tartars" and the "Little Tartars," and the philosopher and the marchioness, at the conclusion of twenty-four hours, "perhaps talking as we do now" (108). The earth's air becomes a shared tactile experience. Playfully underscoring the physicality of such a possibility—the idea that one could *feel* the earth moving and its air with it—the philosopher asks the marchioness the next morning "how she had slept the Night in turning around" (111). Her witty response acknowledges the element of imagination involved in such a hypothesis and also proves her position within a learned community: "Now she was pretty well accustom'd to the Motion of the Earth, and that *Copernicus* himself cou'd not have rested better that Night than she did" (111).

In both of these forms of imaginative viewing, Fontenelle's text extracts the literary figuration inherent to scientific observation discussed in Chapter 1. In the first description, the philosopher dreams he hangs in the air; in the second, the marchioness remains stationary on a rotating globe, feeling her body pass

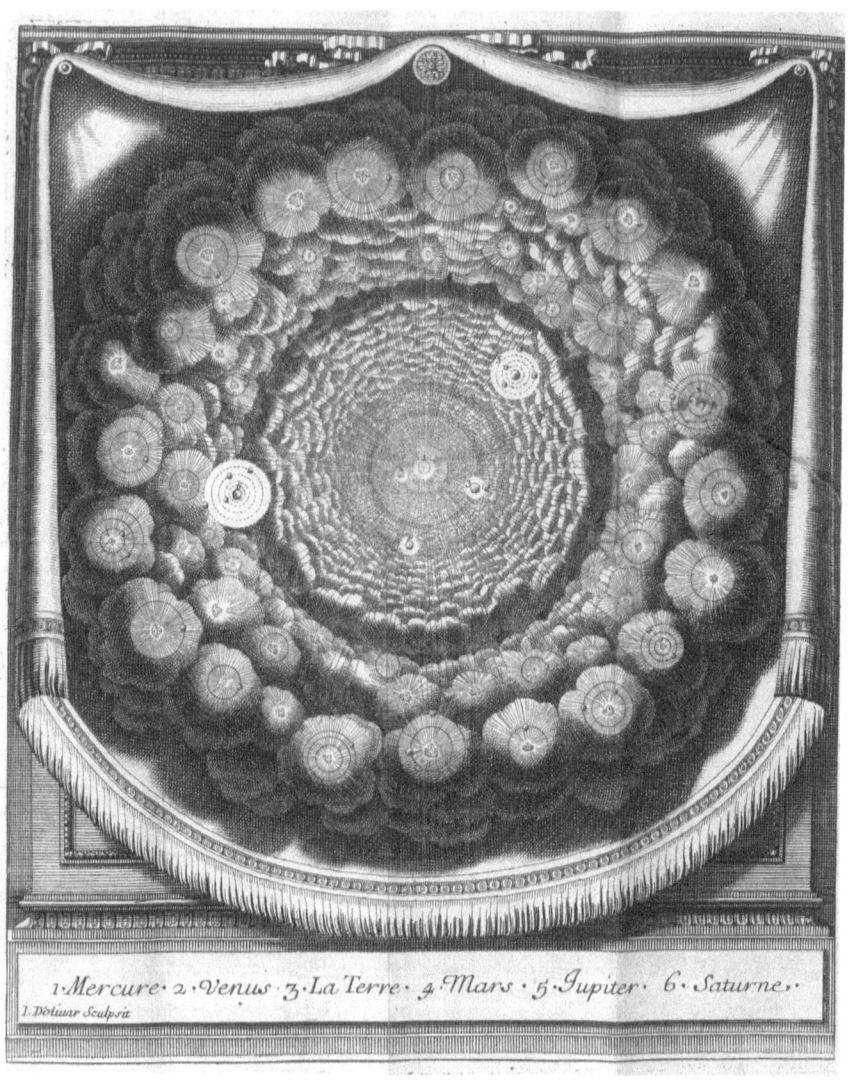

FIGURE 3.1. M. de Fontenelle, *Entretiens sur la Pluralité des Mondes* (Paris, 1686). Folger 228-339q. Used by permission of the Folger Shakespeare Library under a Creative Commons Attribution-ShareAlike 4.0 International License.

FIGURE 3.2. Monsieur de Fontenelle, *A Week's Conversation on the Plurality of Worlds* (London, 1737). Folger 213161. Used by permission of the Folger Shakespeare Library under a Creative Commons Attribution-ShareAlike 4.0 International License.

through the air. Either option suggests a model of observation physically untenable but imaginatively possible. For Fontenelle, the experimental imagination is equally central to technologies associated with scientific practice. Telescopes, for example, promise visual apprehension of the moon, though the experience is based on both empirical and imaginative vision: natural philosophers "travel daily thither [to the moon] by the help of long Telescopes" (117). Seeing a place is like being there.

The observer Fontenelle constructs shares qualities with both modest and immodest witnesses. Scientific education requires the literary acts of figuration that shape the idealized modest witness, yet it also discloses that this too is incomplete. Even if a prosthetic such as the telescope facilitates a virtual experience that can acquire the epistemological certainty of an observed particular in natural philosophical terms, the philosopher contends, we are always subject to "misfortune, still to be plac'd in a false Light: Wou'd we judge of our selves, we are too near; if of others, we are too far off: Coul'd one be plac'd between the Moon and the Earth, that wou'd be a true Station to consider both well: To this End, we ought only to be Spectators of the World, and not Inhabitants" (113). The marchioness concurs: "There are errors and mistakes everywhere" (114). At this moment, the philosopher argues that the subject position of the natural philosopher is inherently biased because we cannot but be "inhabitants" with only a partial, immodest view.

For Fontenelle, scientific facts are mediated and textual; they are forms of literary knowledge.[66] *Discovery* alludes to established forms of literariness to make different scientific points—to Ariosto's *Orlando Furioso*, an epic that some call an epic romance, during a discussion of life on the moon (118–120) and to the natural world as an opera stage (97). The metaphors of the theater and opera promote the notion of natural philosophy as a wonder and spectacle to be discovered.[67]

Yet the most striking turn to literariness as a category of knowledge is Fontenelle's allusion to the genre of romance, a reference that has the effect of easing the dialogue's conjunction of science and seduction. In the Author's Preface, Fontenelle explains:

It is not to penetrate by force of Meditation, into a thing that is obscure in it self, or any thing that is obscurely explained; 'tis only to read, and to represent to your selves at the same what you read, and to form some Image of it that may be clear and free from perplexing Difficulties. I ask of the Ladies (for this System) but the same Attention that they must give the Princess of *Cleve*, if they would follow the Intrigue, and find out the

Beauties of it; though the truth is, that the *Idea's* of this Book are not so familiar to the most part of Ladies, as those of the Princess of *Cleve*; but they are not more obscure, than those of that Novel, and yet they need not think above twice at most, and they will be capable of taking a true Measure, and having a just Sense of the whole. (89)

Commentators have unfairly dismissed Fontenelle's allusion to Lafayette as evidence that the text is easy to read—as easy as reading a romance.[68] Such a response misses the intellectual complexity Fontenelle evokes with the comparison and also forgets the doubled audience of scholars and amateurs Fontenelle envisages. He calls on the example of Cicero to have "those who were not Philosophers . . . be tempted to the Reading of it . . . [and] those who were Philosophers . . . be curious enough to see how well it had been turned" (87). He writes for specialists and casual enthusiasts, all of whom would have their curiosity heightened by Copernican and Cartesian cosmology. As Behn explains, Fontenelle's design "*is to treat this part of a Natural Philosophy in a more familiar Way than any other hath done, and to make every body understand him*" (77). In Fontenelle's words, he brings natural philosophy "to a Point not too rough and harsh for the Capacity of the *Numbers*, nor too light and trivial for the *Learned*" (87). The aspiration of cultivating a broad readership that includes natural philosophers legitimizes Fontenelle's scientific explications; for if he is willing and eager to have experts read *Discovery*, the implied logic goes, then his account must be accurate. From our vantage, Fontenelle's innovation resides in the understanding of his audience as both learned and amateur, practitioners devoted to natural philosophy and its advancement, as well as the elite of the salon culture.[69] Fontenelle's configuration of the scientific community represents an important historical alternative possibility that deviated from the masculinist intellectual ethos that preceded and succeeded his vision.[70] Unsurprisingly, *Discovery* inspired a generation of scientific works produced for a wide audience.[71] Even if it never developed into the status quo, Fontenelle's version of scientific discussion includes scholar and enthusiast, elite and professional, men and women.

With the reference to Lafayette, Fontenelle enjoins readers to interpret *Discovery* as though they were attending to the detailed nuances and turns of a seduction narrative set in the sixteenth-century French court. Such reading is an active engagement in the process of representation; one is called "to represent to your selves at the same time what you read" (89). Near the conclusion of *Discovery*, the marchioness relates the effect of this scientific education to her sense of self: "I find the Worlds, the Heavens and the Celestial Bodies so subject to change, that

I am altogether returned to my self" (165). This "return to my self" is not an attempt to reject or renounce the self's subjective bias but to welcome it. Learning requires the ability "to represent to your selves at the same what you read, and to form some Image of it that may be clear and free from perplexing Difficulties." In the Lockean lexicon, this is the imagination, which fiction writers in the eighteenth century understood as enabling learning through fiction and feeling.[72] Fontenelle insists that a good reader—a good learner—actively engages the imagination to apprehend new ideas, concepts, and materials. Anyone conversant in the language of romance such as *La Princesse de Clèves* is equally capable of using her careful attention and imagination to understand Copernicus and Descartes.

The genre of romance has long been associated with absorptive reading. In Congreve's 1692 preface to *Incognita*, he declares that romance "elevate[s] and surprise[s] the Reader into a giddy Delight, which leaves him flat upon the Ground whenever he gives of, and vexes him to think how he has suffer'd himself to be pleased and transported, concernd and afflicted at the several Passages which he has Read."[73] Scholars often oppose the romance to the novel, stipulating that the former is infatuated with the extraordinary, the latter with the real.[74] Within this critical tradition, romance pertains to things that are unobservable, a class of description that refuses experimental verification.[75]

None other than Robert Boyle challenged the perception that romance exclusively applies to unverifiable experience. Among his many intellectual pursuits, Boyle pondered the intellectual coincidences of romance and natural philosophy, the purportedly antithetical realms of the imaginative and the observable. He authored the now-lost "Apology for Romances" and published his own romance, which he penned as a young man, *The Martyrdom of Theodora and Didymus* (London, 1687).[76] In *The Excellency of Theology Compar'd with Natural Philosophy* (1671), Boyle makes a comparison similar to Fontenelle's. The experience of nature and romances, Boyle argues, is analogical: "In the Book of Nature, as in a well contriv'd Romance, the parts have such a connection and relation to one another, and the things we would discover are so darkly or incompleatly knowable by those that precede them, that the mind is never satisfied till it comes to the end of the Book."[77] The intricacy of the natural world correlates to that of the romance world; the connection supposes, though does not fully depict, a philosopher and a reader who share the skill of careful observation. Romance may induce an absorptive reader, but it also primes that reader to perceive the meaningful data of the natural world.

Fontenelle's choice of *La Princesse de Clèves* as an intellectual model also establishes an early link in *Discovery* to the seduction plot. *La Princesse de Clèves* is a seduction story that follows the affective tangle of a married woman and a nobleman. The narrative trajectory and educational imperative in *Discovery* require a conversion to Copernican and Cartesian principles, and Fontenelle understands this process as a seduction story.

Seduction allows Fontenelle to take a literary plot and use it to narrate how one learns and comes to believe natural philosophy. The hallmarks of seduction appear throughout the dialogue. The philosopher and the marchioness are impatient to spend time alone together (e.g., 111) and the philosopher concludes with the plea of a lover to be remembered: now that the marchioness is "learned," he asks for "this as a Recompence for my pains, that you will never look on the Heavens, Sun, Moon or Stars, without thinking of me" (165). In the first dialogue, the marchioness and the philosopher enjoy a walk in the garden after supper as they discuss the beauty of the night sky. It is, they determine, an ambience most amenable to lovers. The philosopher's description is luxurious: the moon shining through the trees "checker'd the Paths beneath with a most resplendent white upon the green"; the stars "lookt all like pure polish Gold, whose Luster was extreamly heightened by the deep Azure Field on which they were placed" (93). When the philosopher praises the beauty of daytime, the marchioness turns to metaphor—day and night as fair and dark ladies, the latter of whom are superior. She also insists that the philosopher agree with her. Nighttime and dark-haired women produce "soft Effects" that lead to romance: "How comes it, that Lovers who are the best Judges of what is pleasing and touching, do always address themselves to the Night, in all their Songs and Elegies?" (94). They both become diverted by how daylight obscures the stars. The star-filled night sky facilitates "our roving Fancies" about the universe in a way that daylight cannot; enlightenment occurs in the absence of the sun. The marchioness has "always felt those effects of Night you tell me of, I love the Stars, and could be heartily angry with the Sun for taking them from my sight" (95). Her sentiment prompts the philosopher to exclaim, "I cannot forgive his [the sun's] taking from me the sight of all those Worlds that are there" (95). With that, the marchioness's curiosity is piqued and insatiable.

"Worlds, she said, what Worlds?" is the question that forms the provocation for the ensuing scientific dialogue. The philosopher immediately sees this swerve to cosmology as the loss of an opportunity for sexual seduction, for which he will be faulted: "Ah, Madam, cry'd I, I shall never indure to be reproach'd with that neglect of my own happiness, that in a Grove at ten a Clock of the Night, I talk'd of nothing but Philosophy, to the greatest Beauty in the World; no, Madam, search for Philosophy some where else" (95). He resists, she insists, and the moment for seduction seems to be lost. Astronomy displaces eroticism.

However, rather than abandon the seductive framework, Fontenelle instead recalibrates it. The garden bathed in moonlight allows the philosopher to articulate his own doubled seduction: he is seduced by the prospect of other worlds, and he is also seduced by the intellectual desires of the marchioness. The text explicitly characterizes the philosopher as succumbing to the marchioness: "But 'twas in vain to put her off by Excuses, from a Novelty she was already but too much prepossest with: There was a necessity of yielding, and all I could do was to prevail with her to be secret, for the saving of my Honour" (95–96). Cosmology and the marchioness are both alluring—they both seduce the philosopher. The philosopher capitulates to these desires with the language of surrender: "I found my self engaged past retreat" (96). Such enjoinders and resignation could easily be transported from the voice of a desperate heroine in a seduction narrative.

Even if one is tempted to dismiss this inaugural scene of seduction as merely a contrivance to provide a narrative framing for their scientific dialogues, Fontenelle returns on the fifth night to the same process of seduction. At this point, the marchioness and philosopher are discussing Cartesian vortices, which they call *tourbillions*. The topic supplies fanciful and humorous asides; for example, the marchioness says, "Let my Brains turn round, said she, laughing, if they will" (143). Amid this conversation, the philosopher confesses that his one "distemper" is love, "wherein the Tourbillions are not concern'd at all. The infinite Multitude of other Worlds may render this little in your Esteem, but they do not spoil fine Eyes, a pretty Mouth, or make the Charms of Wit ever the less: These will still have their true Value, still bear a price in spight of all the Worlds in the Universe" (155). All of the astronomical discoveries that he might encounter and that fundamentally change one's worldview, the philosopher argues, will not challenge his ideas about love. The marchioness laughs that "Love saves himself from all Dangers, and there is no Systeme or Opinion can hurt him" (155).

The scientific dialogue's turn to love does more than offer the philosopher and the marchioness an excuse for repartee. Falling in love—that is, giving oneself over to the possibilities of seduction—acts as a model for knowledge acquisition. Scientific education requires that a learner be seduced:

Since we are always in the humour of mixing some little Gallantries with our most serious Discourses, give me leave to tell you, that Mathematical reasoning is in some things near a-kin to Love; and you cannot allow the smallest Favour to a Lover, but he will soon perswade you to yield another, and after that a little more, and in the end prevails entirely; so if you grant the least Principles to a Mathematician, he will instantly draw a consequence from it, which you must yield also, and from that another, and then a third, and maugre all your Resistance, in a short time, he will lead you so far, that you cannot retreat. These two sorts of Men, the Lover and Philosopher, always take more than is given 'em. (156)

Persuasion is seduction. Here, Fontenelle's philosopher recounts the step-by-step process wherein one figure inculcates another into a new worldview, whether it concerns amatory relations or cosmology. The process of seduction is inherently social, whether embodied between two lovers or virtual between a learned text and a reader. And it relies on the lure of feeling, as one finds oneself swept up on a rushing current of proposition after proposition. Believing cosmology results from a series of actions enacted by another. Those actions transport an individual from one set of beliefs to another, a dynamic that mimics the narrative structure of seduction stories. The conclusion, whether in intellectual or amatory terms, is submission. While the philosopher in the opening pages positions himself as succumbing to the marchioness's ardent desire to know about cosmology, he here turns to the marchioness to tell her that "you are too far engag'd to retire; and therefore you must generously yield" (156). Submission confirms consent and agreement: "I yield and confess, you have over-charg'd me with Worlds and *Tourbillions*," she announces, confessing "I am extreamly in love . . . with these *Idea's* you give me" (157, 160).

In *Discovery*, we see the delineation of scientific education that evokes and, in so doing, revises the trope of seduction so often associated with sexual coercion. The setting of nighttime, bathed by moonlight, could be seen as anticipating an erotic encounter, but it is an equally appropriate environment for a discussion of cosmology. Of course, sex and the cosmos are never far from each other. The subject position that Fontenelle imagines for his marchioness depends on careful observation and learning. It also depends on her willingness and ability to be seduced into the Copernican and Cartesian imaginary.

NEWTONIAN SEDUCTION: ALGAROTTI

Francesco Algarotti published *Il Newtonianismo per le dame, ovvero, dialoghi sopra la luce e i colori* in 1737; the title page names Naples as the place of publication, though it was printed in Milan under somewhat covert circumstances.[78] *Il Newtonianismo* went through six Italian editions in the six years after its original publication, with ten more editions by 1812; it also was translated quickly into English, French, Russian, Swedish, German, and Portuguese.[79] *Il Newtonianismo*, just like *Discovery* earlier, does not denounce Copernicanism and was placed on the Catholic Church's *Index of Forbidden Books*.[80] Also like his predecessor, Algarotti uses the genre of the scientific dialogue.

Algarotti was a natural philosopher and a poet. In 1728, as a student and at the request of the Royal Society in Britain, he repeated the Newtonian *experimentum crusis* on the immutability of light, the main experiments illustrated in the *Opticks*, at the Istituto delle Scienze of Bologna; many others attempted but had imperfect prisms.[81] In 1732, he penned a Newtonian canzone to the academic Laura Bassi.[82] In Florence, he became acquainted with Martin Folkes, the vice president of the Royal Society, and befriended the Newtonian John Theophilous Desaguliers while he lived in London in 1736.[83] Shortly after he arrived in England, Algarotti was invited to attend a meeting of the Royal Society. The following week, he was nominated to become a fellow, and six weeks later he was elected to the Society of Antiquaries.[84] For a spell, he was a favorite of Voltaire and Emilie du Châtelet, spending six weeks with them at her estate Circey in fall 1735.[85] While in their company, he worked on *Il Newtonianismo* and continued to do so in London, where he met Lord Hervey on the recommendation of Voltaire, and through Hervey, he met Lady Mary Wortley Montagu. Algarotti asked both for editorial advice on the Newton manuscript.[86] As Wortley Montagu's biographer notes, "In less than two weeks Lady Mary was wildly in love."[87] He was twenty-three, she, forty-seven.[88] Hervey also fell for Algarotti, though he likely was under fewer illusions as to the viability of any long-term relationship.[89] When Lady Mary moved to Italy in 1739—in no small part to meet with Algarotti again (*"Je pars pour vous chercher"*)—she packed his Italian original and Elizabeth Carter's translation.[90] Algarotti's reputation among the London elite was at once learned and amatory. He was a scientific Lothario, with equal interest in ideas, men, and women.

Algarotti's appropriation of the seduction plot demonstrates its persistence as a means to enact scientific education. Although the science he teaches is different, Algarotti models his scientific dialogue on Fontenelle's. At the moment the noblewoman insists on an education in Newton's theories of light and color, Algarotti evokes his predecessor: in response to the noblewoman, the philosopher "begged she would at least have Patience till Evening, telling her that the Night had always been the Time consecrated to philosophical Affairs," explaining that "the most polite Philosopher in *France* had made use of it in a Circumstance resembling mine, and made no Scruple of entertaining a fine Lady with philosophical Discourses in a Wood at Mid-Night" (1:16–17). Yet Algarotti's marchioness is impatient: "She spoke this with an Air of Authority that inforced her Commands in the most amiable Manner, and made it a Pleasure to obey" (1:17). The marchioness's refusal to accede to the philosopher's desire for a nighttime tête-à-tête reflects her agency and also has the effect of increasing the philosopher's desire to be seduced by her intellectual curiosity. The philosopher fails to seduce the marchioness sexually and finds himself instead seduced by her epistemological desires. Philosophers are no different from mistresses, argues the philosopher, for both have the obligation "to make good" on their promises: a mistress must accede to enter into a sexual relation, a philosopher into an intellectual one (1:33).

But the pathway of seduction works both ways: if the marchioness seduces the philosopher with her desire to learn, then Newtonianism, presented by the philosopher, in turn seduces her. As in Fontenelle, mathematicians are like lovers: "If what you grant them at first be ever so little, they know how to make so good an Advantage of it, as to lead you insensibly farther than you ever imagined" (1:48). Even though the marchioness demurs, "I have as little Skill in the Artifices of Love . . . as in those of Philosophy and Mathematics" (1:48–49), she is enchanted—and ultimately seduced—by the principles of Newtonianism. Her epistemological craving returns throughout their dialogues. She "felt the utmost Impatience to be more learned than *Huygens*. She was not for losing a Moment's Time, but would have continued our Discourses upon Vision the next Morning as soon as ever we were up. . . . This was all the Optics she could get from me in the Morning" (2:148–149). Following an extensive discussion concerning the refrangibility of light, the philosopher responds to the marchioness in terms that point to the structure of desire and to the plot of seduction: "'Tis in Philosophy as in all other human Affairs, where the Accomplishment of one Desire often gives Birth to another" (2:70).

For all of the similarities with Fontenelle's precedent, Algarotti envisages a markedly different reader. For Algarotti, his audience is exclusively female rather than the variety of readers available through the salon model. And Algarotti's female reader does not have the intelligence that Fontenelle recognizes in his. Algarotti narrows women's intellectual potential in three ways. He invokes metaphors of cosmetic self-fashioning to describe the process for women learning Newtonianism and insists on the metaphor of "softening" to characterize his own acumen in doing so. And then he delimits women's capacity for understanding as merely affect.

The metaphoric relation between cosmetics and intellectual beautification recurs throughout the eighteenth century as a way for writers to endorse or critique female learning.[91] With a description that echoes Mr. Spectator's claims for his own periodical, Algarotti explains, "Your [Fontenelle's] *Plurality of Worlds* first softened the savage Nature of Philosophy, and called it from the solitary Closets and Libraries of the Learned, to introduce it into the Circles and Toilets of Ladies" (1:ii). *Sir Isaac Newton's Philosophy* continues this project. When the philosopher observes, "The most simple Things are generally discovered the latest, and with the greatest Difficulty," the marchioness responds with her own allusion to cosmetics: "This Aphorism is too well verified in the Toilet, where an elegant, but simple Disposition of our Hair or our Patches, often costs great Trouble, and the utmost Anxiety of Mind" (2:38). The philosopher even congratulates himself when suggesting that, regardless of whether the text is a success, women ought to thank him if they enjoy this "new kind of amusement; a new Mode of cultivating the Mind, rather than the present momentary Fashion of adjusting their Head-dress" (1:xiii) and if he has "brought into *Italy* a new Mode of cultivating the Mind, rather than the present momentary Fashion of adjusting their Head-dress and placing their curls" (1:xiii–xiv). Rather than subject themselves merely to the sartorial and cosmetic strictures of the dressing room, women—thanks to Algarotti—may now beautify their minds. The language of fashion assists this undertaking, as the philosopher declares in response to the marchioness's request to learn about Newton; his activity will be "propagating Sir *Isaac Newton's* Philosophy and bringing it into Fashion" (1:15).

If Algarotti sees his purpose in bringing scientific thinking into the "Circles and Toilets of Ladies" as his predecessor did, then he does so through simplification, expressed through a metaphor of softening. Here Algarotti emphasizes the difference between Copernican and Cartesian natural philosophy and Newtonianism. The former is easier to understand than the latter, which is a "savage Philosophy" with "the most abstruse *Geometry*" and "Austerity": "You [Fontenelle] have embellished the *Cartesian* Philosophy; and I have endeavoured to soften the *Newtonian*, and render its very Severities agreeable" (1:v–vi). One form of this softening is the omission of mathematical equations. Though Algarotti's philosopher tells his companion that in Fontenelle, "there you will see a Marchioness, who exactly resembles you in every Accomplishment of Mind" (1:62), Algarotti steps back from Fontenelle's insistence that the science he presents in *A Discovery* withstands the scrutiny from specialists. Algarotti instead emphasizes the intellectual translation he exerts to bring Newton's theories on light and color into language that women could understand. Algarotti may claim that *Il Newtonianismo* is "a complete Treatise of the Newtonian Philosophy," but his own metaphors consistently undercut this assertion: "The Sanctuary of the Temple will always be reserved for the Priests and Favourites of the Deity; but the Entrance and its other less retired Parts will be open to the profane" (1:viii). Whereas Fontenelle imagines a mixed audience of learned and elite, men and women, and offers Copernican and Cartesian cosmology in a way that does not lessen its difficulty or significance, Algarotti insists that his is a simpler version of Newtonianism, a popularization wherein readers gain access only to the temple's entrance and "its other less retired Parts."

The metaphors of fashion and softening synchronize with Algarotti's estimation of women's minds. In Carter's translation, Algarotti states, "I have endeavoured to set Truth, accompanied with all that is necessary to demonstrate it, in a pleasing Light, and to render it agreeable to that Sex, which had rather *perceive* than *understand*" (1:vi–vii). This statement has served as evidence that Algarotti believed women were intellectual inferiors to men.[92] This may well be the case, but Algarotti's conceptualization depends on a particular reading of female minds in which affect—arguably the mode most appropriate to the seduction plot—serves a central role. Carter's translation slightly adjusts the original, with her rendering of *sentire*: the Italian version reads, "*Io ô intrapreso di far piacere la Verità accompagnata datutto ciò, che necessario è per dimostrarla, e di farla piacere a quell sesso, che ama più tosto di sentire, che di sapere.*"[93] Mirella Agorni suggests that Carter uses *perceive* rather than *feel* (which is the closer translation) "to smooth down the masculine discourse of gallantry," but *perceive* in the eighteenth century does not eschew this meaning.[94] A stronger example of Agorni's thesis is Carter's exclusion of Algarotti's quip about a blind sculptor who uses only his touch to produce resemblances of his models—such a man would never sculpt a lady without adding her breasts.

Carter's use of *perceive* for *sentire* suggests an important emphasis: *perceive* encompasses intellectual or sensory perception along with apprehension; they are not two separate activities. According to the *Oxford English Dictionary*, the primary definition of *perceive* is "to take in or apprehend with the mind or senses" (I). Samuel Johnson's central definition of the word in *A Dictionary of the English Language* likewise acknowledges the relation between perception and understanding, particularly in the second definition: "to know; to observe." The third illustrative quotation he provides is from Locke: " 'Till we ourselves see it with our own eyes, and perceive it by our own understanding, we are still in the dark." "Understand," according to Johnson, means "to comprehend fully; to have knowledge of," "to conceive," "to have use of intellectual faculties; to be an intelligent or conscious being," and "to be informed." But Carter's choice to translate *sentire* as *perceive* relies on two less frequent usages of the term: "to be affected by" (Johnson, 3) and the now obsolete, though available up through the mid-eighteenth century definition, "to receive, take in; to get obtain" (*OED* II.8.b.). Carter's *perceive* conveys an emphasis on feeling and also introduces another possibility wherein feeling is a form of sensory perception that correlates to knowledge acquisition.

Carter's translation points to the reconfiguration that resides at the heart of Algarotti's project: women, his imagined audience, are characterized as players in a seduction narrative, one in which they are *affected by* and *receive* the learning of Newton. In this way, then, the female reader of Algarotti's text is portrayed as an eager, if passive, recipient, ready to be swayed by the seductive allure of Newtonian science. She is an affective being. The plot of seduction is appropriate because it concerns affect—a subject's heart rather than her mind. Algarotti writes, "The *marvelous*, of which the Heart always desirous of being affected is so fond, happily arises in true Philosophy of itself, without the help of Machines," and queries, "Is there any Thing (especially where Ladies are concerned) in which a Writer should omit any Endeavours to move the Heart?" (1:viii, 1:vii). The role of affect in seduction introduces the possibility that the conversion to Newtonianism may not succeed. Because she perceives rather than understands—that is, she is "affected by" and "receives" Newtonianism—the marchioness second-guesses herself. When they discuss the refrangibility of light, the marchioness panics, asking, "Have I acted wrong in suffering myself to be too easily convinced?" (2:39). The philosopher assures her that "a Lady cannot err in this Point" (2:39). Uncertainty does not derail the conversion process. "Let me entreat you," she declares, "to make me a compleat Newtonian. I plainly see that by my Conversion I shall acquire the Knowledge of Truth without losing that Pleasure which I found in being deceived" (2:40). The end of their six dialogues accomplishes her desire for conversion—to be seduced into the belief of Newtonianism.

If the marchioness is seduced by Newtonianism, then she provokes the philosopher by placing Newton within such a plot as well: "You seem ... to represent Nature as a Coquet, and Sir *Isaac Newton* as a jealous Lover, who never thinks he has Proof enough of the Fidelity of his Mistress" (2:39–40). The marchioness's portrait of Newton recalls the scientific and erotic legacy of masculinized intellectual mastery commonly found in Bacon and his followers. The process of acquiring natural philosophical knowledge that then can be distributed to acolytes requires endless experimentation and pursuit; a single experiment does "not satisfy a Philosopher resolved to try Nature a thousand Ways, and put her to a thousand Proofs, in order to establish his Belief on a sure Foundation" (2:39). The philosopher's answer, "This ... was the only Object of his love," confirms the legitimacy of the comparison, suggesting that Newton's rightful posture was of a jealous lover, driven to distraction to find out any and all secrets of the natural world (2:40). Newton as a natural philosopher embodies the suspicion of a controlling lover. However, Algarotti's philosopher presses for a key difference.

Newton exhibits "philosophical Jealousy," a phrase that vividly binds the seduction rubric to scientific discovery (2:40). Undergirding the process of seduction the philosopher and the marchioness undergo is a superstructure that understands seduction as a relation of power and control. Newton's knowledge acquisition does not reside in a static realm; it forcibly encounters nature, its subject, and bends nature to the practitioner's intellectual will. The philosopher also qualifies the admission that Newton too has the desires of a seducer. At the text's conclusion, he distinguishes the marchioness's passion from Newton's "Moderation": "The Moderation of our Philosophers, in never affirming any Thing to be true which was not demonstrated by Observation, may serve for an Example to the most rash Asserters" (2:243). In spite of the marchioness's enthusiastic response, Newton's findings, insists the philosopher, are sober and reasoned. They are not assertions. They are discoveries.

In Algarotti's text, we witness the multivalent nature of the seduction paradigm in ways that accord with and differ from the precedent of Fontenelle. As in the earlier text, the philosopher reports that the marchioness seduces him, and the marchioness admits that she is seduced by her scientific education, in this instance, Newtonianism. These are moments of learning, especially for the marchioness. But Algarotti privileges a woman's power of perception over her understanding, a form of cognition that eschews Fontenelle's celebration of the imagination and presents feeling as a mode of learning. Algarotti's text also highlights the imperative for seduction built into the project of natural philosophy as a practice, a view in which practitioners of natural philosophy pursue nature until she concedes. In this final seduction, the producer of knowledge seduces a vulnerable and feminized nature, in the process revealing the gender and sexual politics of knowing and being known.

For Fontenelle, the possibility of other worlds inherent to Copernican and Cartesian cosmology makes available other ways of thinking and imagining, occasions that render the participating subject attentive and also willing to make an intellectual leap of faith. For Algarotti, Newtonianism requires a more controlled subject that has the inclination to open herself to the persuasiveness of the teacher, whether in the form of the male philosopher or in the practice of natural philosophy itself. For both, these are facts most forcefully learned in the affective imaginings available through the literary imagination. Scientific education is a process of being seduced. The seduction takes these imaginings and directs them into a narrative arc that charts the transformation from ignorant or poorly educated to knowledgeable. In both of these influential texts, women are the paradigmatic learners, in mind and body. And in response, prominent intellectual women of the period—Aphra Behn and Elizabeth Carter—recognized the significance of women learning science and, in their own learned translations, laid claim to the scientific discoveries of Descartes, Copernicus, and Newton through their ability to translate them (and in the case of Carter, translate *back*) for an English audience.

Through their evocation and adaptation of the seduction plot, these scientific dialogues and their English translations demonstrate that believing in science is not merely a matter of rational understanding. The "virtual witnessing" of Boyle and others, as analyzed in Chapter 1, establishes textual mediation as a vital technology of scientific inquiry, which ultimately depends on readers reading and imagining, and thus corroborating, the accuracy of reported findings. But the seduction plot exposes another technology, as deeply literary as textual mediation. Understood as a transformative process, seduction plots move an individual from one circumstance or set of beliefs to another. Seduction acts on the individuals who experience it. It pushes one beyond the limits of rational disbelief or belief, and it exacts submission. To use the seduction plot as a model for scientific education spells out the conversion one must undergo—the conversion to which one must be subjected—to become a modern, enlightened subject. And to use a literary paradigm to teach a scientific one testifies to the profound indebtedness of the latter on the former. New scientific insights require new imaginings. Knowing the world, understanding the world, perceiving the world—these all depend on a subject with the imaginative capability to picture what might be in order to see what is.

4 POLITICAL SCIENCE

The seduction plot narrates the process of acquiring scientific education: an individual, imagined female in the cases of Fontenelle and Algarotti, moves from ignorance to wisdom, from epistemological naiveté to experience, from old ways of understanding the natural world to modern discoveries. The conversion a learner undergoes is both rational and affective. Mathematicians, for Fontenelle and Algarotti, are like lovers: when they exhaust rational argument, they change registers and demand affective allegiance. Coming to understand science is a process wherein one moves from subscribing to outdated principles to believing their modern replacements. Scientific redactors and educators conceive of that transformation as possible through the literary plot and language of seduction. And as I have argued throughout this book, literary knowledge enables the formulation of what scientific practice might be—its objects of study and its practitioners, whether modest or immodest witnesses.

When we adjust the scale from an individual practitioner to a collective body, representations of natural philosophy in the British Enlightenment seem inevitably to involve theories of government. Science provides a metaphor and a topic to understand, assess, and even manage the political realm. There is historical precedent for this affiliation. Late seventeenth-century Royal Society natural philosophers looked back to Francis Bacon as their intellectual model, and they inherited the conjunction of politics and science at the core of Bacon's experimental project.[1] Bacon, who became lord chancellor in 1618 under James I, viewed his natural philosophy as of and for the state. An ardent supporter of the divine and absolute rights of the monarch, Bacon advised James as the monarch mounted claims of legal absolutism.[2] For example, Parliament, according to Bacon, was best understood not as an independent legal entity but as "Council to the King and Kingdom."[3] Scholars disagree about the extent to which Bacon's role as a statesman shaped his natural philosophical work, but Bacon himself identified natural philosophy as an instrument of state power; structures of knowledge were also simultaneously structures of power and authority.[4] Baconianism ensured "royal control of the machinery of governance."[5]

The epistemological work at the heart of natural philosophy's emergence could not be separated from the political institutions that allowed it to flourish. Although Bacon had vocal opponents such as Henry Stubbe, early experimental practice was irrevocably bound up with politics.⁶

Historians of science, most notably Steven Shapin and Simon Schaffer, have trod a well-worn path on this topic. As I posit in Chapter 1, the experimental method depended on regulating protocols of facticity and modest witnessing; Boyle and his acolytes actively defended the plausibility and accuracy of such knowledge, but they did so through recourse to literariness. With the issue of science and politics, Shapin and Shaffer situate Boyle's story in relation to Thomas Hobbes's skepticism. Hobbes insisted that experimental practices were logically incoherent (he was particularly doubtful of the vacuum at the center of Boyle's air pump) and that they would produce dangerous social upheaval and discord.⁷ Studying the differences between Boyle and Hobbes communicates an important message: problems of knowledge and social order are mutually constitutive.⁸ Both Hobbes and Boyle, along with their supporters, were keenly aware of the pressing need to develop a "means of guaranteeing assent" to establish an "indefeasible civil order."⁹ However, Bruno Latour has shown that Boyle and Hobbes did not represent merely the articulation of science (in the case of Boyle) and politics (in the case of Hobbes), but also a process through which both discourses emerge as repressions of the other.¹⁰ Latour's critique of Shapin and Schaffer is specific: they leave the language of politics and power unquestioned.¹¹ As Sandra Harding astutely notes, Latour's own reimagining of democracy refuses to acknowledge the identities and politics of those subjects already marginalized by the traditionally celebratory history of Western science. The lessons of feminism and postcolonialism are incidental to Latour, and the models of difference they reveal cannot be fully accommodated in his thinking: Who, she asks, is the "we" in his foundational question, "We have never been modern"?¹²

I respond to the pressing question of who "we" might be by expanding the archive beyond a consideration of Boyle and Hobbes to British Enlightenment writers across the political spectrum, writers who variously voiced the gendered and colonial implications of such a conjunction. I read three writers who were at turns fascinated and troubled by the implications of science and politics: Thomas Sprat, Margaret Cavendish, and Jonathan Swift. Through the genres of manifesto, romance, and satire, respectively, they all insist that natural philosophy cannot be understood apart from the political institutions enabling and enabled by its practice and promulgation.¹³ They also use the conventions of literary knowledge to articulate their critique. Sprat's vision in *The History of the Royal Society* is a step in the history of scientific triumphalism and a model for schooling gentlemen away from factionalism and into political consensus. For Cavendish in *The Blazing World*, the institutionalization of experimental philosophy threatens the control necessary for an absolutist monarch, but its practice is necessary to the embodied display of such absolutism. Science becomes spectacle, and spectacle is power. And for Swift in *Gulliver's Travels*, the underlying literalization of experimental philosophy expands to its fundamentally imperialist, colonial agenda: Swift warns that natural philosophy inevitably generates a dystopian, brutal world that instrumentalizes reason and denies subjects their existence. Swift's perspective upends the compensatory gestures in both Sprat and Cavendish by insisting that science and politics are not only inextricable but also self-serving, blinding, and imperialistic.

SPRAT'S CIVIL GOVERNMENT

Shortly after its founding, Thomas Sprat, later bishop of Rochester and dean of Westminster, wrote *The History of the Royal Society*. He began in 1663 and finished in 1667 after delays due to the plague and the fire of 1666. *The History of the Royal Society* is a scientific manifesto, and contemporary reaction was both supportive and critical, as evident in the publication of a range of attacks and defenses.[14]

The historical circumstances of its composition have led scholars to question *The History*'s veracity and reliability. Although the Royal Society commissioned the book, no one supervised its production.[15] Historians conclude that Sprat's text presents a sharper view of the ideological and social effects of natural philosophy than founders believed, with some suggesting that *The History* does not even provide an accurate view of the society's activities.[16] Michael Hunter describes it as "little short of a disaster."[17] Samuel Johnson's observation that "*The History of the Royal Society* is now read not with the wish to know what they were then doing, but how their transactions are exhibited by Sprat" supports this view.[18] However, other scholars have challenged the idea that Sprat's *History* is solely propaganda, suggesting instead that it was aligned with the mission and principles of the Royal Society at the time of its publication.[19]

Discussions concerning the composition or reception of Sprat's *History* distract us from its significance. The text is both descriptive and prescriptive, and it had a strong association with the Royal Society for decades after its publication (it was ninety years before another official volume was published), in no small part because of its primary intellectual purpose: to explicate and defend the experimental method that shaped the Royal Society's every endeavor.[20] As I contend in Chapter 1, Sprat promotes the Royal Society as naturally forward thinking. Although *The History* includes over a dozen experiments reprinted from *Philosophical Transactions*, Sprat's advocacy goes far beyond reproducing the journal. The political agenda of *The History* is to position the Royal Society as a model institution for the functioning of a "civil Government," even if such an emphasis, after Sprat, was not considered a central preoccupation.[21] The practice of natural philosophy gives Sprat a blueprint for a well-regulated government, mobilizing in turn an analogy between epistemology and politics. Sprat imagines the Royal Society to represent an idealized polis and its obedient subjects: the Royal Society produces an idealized civil sphere, characterized by social improvement, sober debate, and gentlemen who enact "a just and a manly Submission" (428).

To establish his ideal social formation, Sprat first dismisses others, which include the monarchy, the church, and the commonwealth. In each instance, Sprat links a political model to its own quality of literariness, a conjunction that brings out the oppressive nature of each system. Although Sprat vigorously supported Charles II, he claims that court culture exhibits an inappropriate preoccupation with poetry and other forms of aesthetic refinement. Sprat calls these things "the Ornament of Language, and *Poetry*, and such more delicate Arts" (19). Court subjects run the risk of becoming enthralled by the pleasures of literary language to such an extent that a centralized monarchical power becomes untenable—a position in stark opposition to John Dryden's celebration of eloquence in court culture and language as a basis for a polite national culture.[22] The church, for Sprat, renders its subjects equally unseeing, in this instance by the purely imaginative. Monastic isolation produces only one sort of response: "melancholy Contemplations, or ... *Devotion*, and the Thoughts of another World" (19). The church as a social model forestalls interaction and perpetuates self-absorption.

Yet the court and the church are not Sprat's primary concern. The threat of political upheaval experienced in the all-too-recent past of Sprat's audience shadows *The History*, as it does many of his earlier writings.[23] The Interregnum constituted "twenty years of Melancholy ... confusion and slavery," which only the return of the Stuart king in 1660 could end (58). Even so, England in the 1660s was restored "yet not settled," with the circulation of antiroyalist and nonconformist pamphlets, the failed Farnley Wood Plot to overthrow the monarchy in 1663, and the second Anglo-Dutch War (1665–1667).[24] The primary threat Sprat imagines within the pages of *The History* is the formation of another commonwealth. His definition is revealing: a commonwealth is the "violence of popular assemblies" (19). It is also associated with the "Danger of a Civil War" (56). The singularly damning quality of a commonwealth is its promotion of eloquence, or the art of persuasive speaking. Eloquence catalyzes a chaotic social framework, with individuals driven by their passions rather than their reason: "So much Sweetness there is, in leading Parties: so much Pride, in following a Faction; such various Artifices there are, to ensnare Men's *Passions*, and soon after their *Understandings*" (70). This is a vision of confusion and irrationality. The individual subject of the commonwealth is vulnerable to the temptations of factionalism, wrapped up as they are in the allure of eloquence: "sweetness" and "pride" blind individuals just as they yoke them to "parties" and "factions." Eloquence arouses the public's "passions" and "understandings" rather than their sober enlightenment.

In this description of the commonwealth, Sprat opposes eloquence to truth, but he makes this case through an intermediary reference to politeness. Eloquence is "a Weapon, which may be as easily procur'd by *bad* men as good"; since its use for ill or positive ends cannot be regulated, Sprat recommends that eloquence "ought to be banish'd out of all *civil Societies*, as a thing fatal to Peace and good Manners" (111). Eloquence accrues a specious connotation: listeners are swayed by the lure of rhetoric rather than by the veracity of truth. As a consequence, these same listeners forget the ethics of polite behavior, that is, "Peace and good Manners." Even if Sprat recuperates Ciceronian rhetoric and elsewhere defends English eloquence, *The History* identifies the Interregnum as a political failure because of the commonwealth's promotion of eloquence over facticity.[25]

The authority Sprat imagines in *The History* is at once hierarchical (the king) and distributive (the Royal Society and society at large).[26] While royal authority is assumed throughout, the social body under the king's rule needs to modify its tone and tenor: factionalism and dissent must be rejected, consensus and civil discourse promoted.

To imagine this future, Sprat turns back to the social cohesion experimentalists sought during the Interregnum. He describes these meetings not in terms of their scientific discussions, but as having been occasions for each participant to imagine himself as a civil political subject. Nostalgia fuels Sprat's conception of political life possible through the Royal Society. Gatherings that ultimately coalesced into the Royal Society once Charles II ascended to the throne, the meetings in Oxford offered members a respite from the political, religious, and cultural tumult of Cromwell's rule; these sessions gave them "the satisfaction of breathing a freer air, and of conversing in quiet one with another, without being ingag'd in the passions, and madness of that dismal Age" (53). The early meetings inculcated attendees in the merits of "*sober* and *generous knowledge*," which "arm'd [them] against all the inchantments of *Enthusiasm*" (53). The term *enthusiasm*, of course, pointed to Puritan oratorical practice, and throughout the long eighteenth century, it was used to describe various religious dissenters— and Sprat's usage reminds readers of this association between a commonwealth and religious zeal.[27] In contrast, the early meetings provided "candid and unpassionate Company" (55). "*Nature* alone" saves men from themselves: "The Contemplation of that, draws our Minds off from past, or present Misfortunes . . . [it] never separates us into moral Factions; . . . and permits us to raise contrary Imaginations upon it, without any Danger of a *Civil War*" (55–56).

The talismanic effect of the natural world seems to ensure the creation and regulation of a proper civil society, one impervious to the vicissitudes of factionalism and animosity. Yet it is not merely nature but the proper study of nature that produces these ameliorative effects.

The experiments at Oxford provide a template for the larger political transformation that Sprat conjures through the pages of *The History*. Sprat aligns the royalism embodied by Charles II with the intellectual and social goals of the Royal Society: "Methinks there is an Agreement, between the Growth of *Learning*, and of *Civil Government*" (29).[28] Evoking the metaphor of the body politic, Sprat argues that "the present *Temper* of our *Nation*" is suited to natural philosophy (362). This is the moment to embrace natural philosophy as a means to ensure the health of the kingdom. In making this argument, Sprat uses metaphors of illumination to visualize the future: "It is now the fittest Season for *Experiments* to arise, to teach us Wisdom, which springs from the depths of *Knowledge*, to shake off the Shadows, and to scatter the Mists" (362). This is at once a rebirth and a rejection; gone are the "*Omens* or *Praedictions* that pass'd about amongst [men in the recent past], on little or no Foundations" (362). Experimentalists find social cohesion because "they only deal in Matters of *Fact* [as well as the] Security of the Inclinations of the greatest part of the *Members* of the *Society* it self" (70). The "gentle and easy *Method*" of experimental philosophy diffuses balkanization because "our several *Interests*, and *Sects* may come to suffer one another, with the same Peaceableness of Men of different *Trades* live one by another in the same *Street*" (426–427). Sprat turns to an image of commerce between merchants and artisans—not gentlemen—to project how this society of gentlemen might cohere. The Royal Society models a future society where "Men of disagreeing Parties ... have forgotten to hate" (427). The darkness and discord of the commonwealth cannot withstand the bright harmony of civility. The "Peace, and good Manners" that the meetings in Oxford provided during the Interregnum are an example of this "lucky Tide of *Civility*" (111, 389).

Sprat's emphasis on civility accords with Robert Boyle's affirmation of the civility at the heart of scientific discourse. Boyle fashions himself a "Christian philosopher" to be free from the social demands of a gentleman, but he uses the language of sociability to describe his methodology.[29] Moderation and civility, even in disagreements, are de rigeur: "I love to speak of persons with civility, though of things with freedom. Nor do I think it reasonable, either that any man's reputation should protect his errors, or that the truth should fare the worse for his sake, that delivers it."[30] Boyle's formulation distances the individual from the phenomena, the modest witness from the observed particulars. To scrutinize the latter does not constitute an attack the former.

Sprat's *History* expressly delineates who these individual modest witnesses, the appropriate subjects of a "civil Government," might be. At times, he insists on a vision that draws from various strata of social, commercial, and political life: "There the *Soldier*, the *Tradesman*, the *Merchant*, the *Scholar*, the *Gentleman*, the *Courtier*, the *Divine*, the *Presbyterian*, the *Papist*, the *Independent*, and those of *Orthodox Judgment*, have laid aside their Names of Distinction, and calmly conspir'd in a mutual Agreement of *Labours* and *Desires*" (427). Rather than upholding the "Retirements of *Schools*," the corporate body of the Royal Society resembles the dynamism of a city "compounded of all Sorts of Men, of the *Gown*, of the *Sword*, of the *Shop*, of the *Field*, of the *Court*, of the *Sea*; all mutually assisting each other" (76). Indeed social leveling was a fundamental value of natural philosophy, even if this was not the case in practice.[31] The expense of membership alone would have excluded most artisans and mathematical practitioners.[32]

In spite of such gestures to inclusivity and diversity, the primary subject position conceived through Sprat's model of "civil Government" is that of a gentleman, a specification that locates his political plan safely within the status quo of traditional social order.³³ The ideal experimentalist is the ideal citizen and the Royal Society the ideal institution.³⁴ The civic benefits of the Royal Society and its method support Sprat's defense against accusations that it is worthless and even corrosive—that the Royal Society threatens "our public Duties and civil Actions" (342). Sprat's attitude reflects the ethos of the Royal Society more generally as a group with "no interest in undermining the social hierarchy" and "sensitive to the need to attract support from the Restoration elite."³⁵

Sprat claims that the Royal Society's experimental philosophy already has the support of the powerful. But for Sprat, this coterie includes tradesmen, suggesting a more inclusive civil society than a Royalist such as Dryden. By emphasizing its acceptance rather than ridicule and by expanding the centers of power to include trade, Sprat may subsequently contend that he is descriptive rather than prescriptive. He does not "exhort" but "confirm[s] the *Gentlemen* of our *Nation*, in the prosecution of this *Art*, to which their *Purses* and their *generous Labours* are most necessary" (404). The self-conscious distinction between the terms *exhort* and *confirm* points to the terrain that Sprat navigates: although *The History* is a work of exhortation, its language attempts to render these conclusions a fait accompli. The inherent tension between the prescriptive and descriptive modes sharpens when Sprat turns to the potentially conflicting interests of the commercial and noble classes. He hastens to add that the improvements and growth of commerce do not threaten the current social hierarchies; instead they "have given Mankind a higher Degree than any Title of *Nobility*, even that of *Civility* and *Humanity* itself," and they strengthen the political empire (408). If the specific subjectivity Sprat devises is that of a gentleman, then he concludes by expanding that category to include all of those who engage in the ennobling study of natural philosophy—but only fictionally.

Within this identity of gentlemanliness available through the practice of experimental philosophy, Sprat inserts a final safeguard: he claims that experimental philosophical work produces obedient subjects. These gentlemen are reasonable and civil, and they also know their place. Sprat lodges the obedience argument in response to criticism that increased knowledge "renders Men mutinous, arrogant, and incapable of *Superiors*" (427), a condition that threatens the social hierarchy of the world he inhabits. Sprat agrees insofar as "a little *Knowledge* is subject to make Men headstrong, insolent, and untractable; but a great deal has a quite contrary Effect, inclining them to be submissive to their *Betters*, and obedient to the *Sovereign Power*" (429). Writing to garner the approval from the elite who would buy *The History* and more generally support the Royal Society, Sprat assures his readers that natural philosophy does not "undermine his *Authority* [the *Prince*] whose Aid it implores" (429). The most striking advantage of experimental philosophy from this perspective is that "the influence of Experiments" produces "*Obedience to the Civil Government*" and "a just and a manly Submission" (427, 428). To the end, *The History* imagines a collective that is genteel and peaceful and that subjects itself to the corporate power of the Royal Society and, ultimately, the civil government of Charles II. And for Sprat, experimental philosophy is the best and natural engine of that political community.

CAVENDISH'S ROMANCE OF "ABSOLUTE POWER"

Margaret Cavendish, the duchess of Newcastle, found little to admire in the work of the experimental philosophers. Provoked by the appearance of Robert Hooke's *Micrographia* (1665), Cavendish responded with her own treatise, *Observations upon Experimental Philosophy* (1666), which was bound together with a utopian fiction, *The Description of a New World, called the Blazing World* (1666).[36] Cavendish's *Observations* primarily feature a point-by-point refutation of Hooke's findings, along with thorough critiques of Henry Power's *Experimental Philosophy in Three Books* (1664) and Robert Boyle's *Experiments and Considerations Touching Colours* (1664). Soon thereafter, Cavendish was formally invited to visit the Royal Society, which she did on May 30, 1667. Her visit is quietly recorded in Birch's *The History of the Royal Society*. She was the only woman to visit officially until the twentieth century.[37] As Londa Schiebinger notes, "Cavendish's visit indeed appears to have set a precedent—a negative one."[38]

Responding to these public and popular texts printed under the auspices of the Royal Society, Cavendish rejects their mechanical philosophy and promotes vitalistic materialism, according to which all things in nature are composed of animate matter.[39] Cavendish's main complaint concerns her doubt that sensory perception is a valid means to acquire knowledge, much less "absolute knowledge of nature."[40] While exiled in Antwerp with her husband, Cavendish wrote to Christiaan Huygens about his microscope, skeptical that the instrument could produce legitimate knowledge.[41] In *Observations*, she explains that the study of objects' surfaces, arguably the primary focus of experiments utilizing optical instrumentation, fails to produce any useful information: "The truth is, most of these arts are fallacies, rather than discoveries of truth; for sense deludes more than it gives a true information, and an exterior inspection through an optic glass, is so deceiving, that it cannot be relied upon."[42] Sense misleads, and her distrust is redoubled in the chapter "Of Art, and Experimental Philosophy":

How can a fool order his understanding by art, if nature has made it defective? Or, how can a wise man trust his senses, if either the objects be not truly presented according to their natural figure and shape, or if the senses be defective, either through age, sickness, or other accidents, which do alter the natural motions proper to each sense?[43]

Cavendish's allusion to art explicitly answers Hooke's argument that "Artificial Instruments" will correct the errors of human sensory perception.[44] Hers is a two-pronged rebuttal: even the most reliable sensory perception will not improve a stupid mind, and sensory perception itself can never be reliable. For Hooke, at least in theory, sensory perception is the only true way to acquire knowledge, and any physical limitations are themselves merely idiosyncratic and local. For Cavendish, the fact that sensory perception is not standard or universal impugns its reliability; all perceptions, therefore, are characterized by delusion and error. Instead, "regular reason" divorced from the senses "is the best guide to all arts."[45]

Yet the privileging of "regular reason" in *Observations* does not suffice; rather it must be elaborated and explicated through literary representation. Cavendish publishes *Observations* in tandem with the romance, *The Description of the New World, called the Blazing World*. This remarkable conjunction enables Cavendish to use the genre of romance and the literary imagination to express her intellectual argument concerning the unreliability—and even danger—of sensory perception and experimental knowledge. These forms of knowledge production are unreliable because they depend on embodied observers who cannot be objective, and they are dangerous because they threaten the political status quo of royalism. And the inculcation of these insights requires that Cavendish produce literary knowledge.

The quality of *fancy* is fundamental in Cavendish's deployment of literary knowledge: reason "requires sometimes the help of Fancy, to recreate the Mind, and withdraw it from its more serious contemplations."[46] The world of discoveries mandates that one be able to think anew to recognize them, and fancy has the productive and necessary cognitive effects: it allows reason to find truth through the imagination. One might argue that "Regular reason" and "Fancy" work together in Cavendish's natural philosophy as epistemological partners, "dual expositors of her philosophy."[47] Yet in practice "Fancy" does not require

"Regular reason." The relationship between the two is unidirectional. Cavendish's injunction, "To recreate the Mind," points to the efficacy of literary knowledge and its explanatory function: "And this is the reason," Cavendish writes, "why I added this Piece of Fancy to my Philosophical Observations, and joined them as two Worlds at the ends of their Poles" (153). Cavendish celebrates the imaginative possibilities some advocates of experimental philosophy labored to suppress.

But Cavendish's texts are more than a "fiction of the mind."[48] Her image of experimental philosophy and romance as two worlds conjoined "at the ends of their Poles" converts genre into epistemology: the fanciful text enables the scientific text. This inaugural spatialization of genre and epistemology in the Preface reverberates in the landscape of *The Blazing World*'s narrative in which worlds are linked by entryway-like poles that allow movement from one to another, a landscape that has been read as hermaphroditic.[49] *The Blazing World* begins with the abduction of a lady. Movement through this topography proves dangerous and harrowing, and the difficulty of the passage from one world to another is matched by its inevitability—the boat "was forced into another World" (155). The transition from reason to fancy—that is, from experimental knowledge to literary knowledge—is fraught, precarious, and inevitable. The two-part structure of Cavendish's volume, as a treatise on experimental philosophy bound with a romance, positions literary knowledge as enabling experimental knowledge.

Politically, the Blazing World is an absolute monarchy; intellectually, it features scientific practitioners who embody what they study, a literalization that renders them blind and self-interested. First, its politics. The kingdom is peaceful; indeed, there is no room for anything *but* peacefulness: they speak only one language and have "one Emperor, to whom they all submitted with the greatest duty and obedience" (160). The Blazing World does not suffer from internecine nation-states or partisan politics. All of its subjects are exemplary in their devotion and obedience. In terms of the body politic metaphor, the statesmen of the Blazing World view a commonwealth "like a Monster of many heads" (164). In contrast, "a Monarchy is a divine form of Government, and agrees most with our Religion; for as there is but one God, whom we all unanimously worship and adore with one Faith, so we are resolved to have but one Emperor, to whom we all submit with one obedience" (164). And this same Emperor falls in love with the Lady, marries her, makes her Empress, and fades from the narrative, leaving the Empress to rule singlehandedly.

Analogical thinking supports the connection between god and king. *Duty*, *obedience, submission*—these terms underscore the constitutive elements of a monarchical government. This is divine rule, which ensures that its predominant characteristic is cohesion, a quality possible only through a communal understanding of the social and political fabric as serving a monarch appointed by God. Theirs is a "continued peace and happiness" (160), an existence impossible in the multiheaded, discordant commonwealth model of Cavendish's recent memory. Later in the narrative, the Duchess—Cavendish's persona who enters the fiction—endorses absolutism, arguing that the ideal is "to have but one Sovereign, one Religion, one Law, one Language, so that all the World might be but as one united Family, without divisions" (229).

The celebratory representation of the divine right of kings places Cavendish's text securely in the royalist sphere. As we know from her autobiography, Cavendish was on the side of the royalist cause, having served in Henrietta Maria's court, and she lived abroad in France during the Interregnum, where she met and married her husband, the duke of Newcastle.[50] Emma Rees reads the trope of exile as an expression of powerlessness that shapes Cavendish's writings, particularly in the 1650s.[51] Yet the political philosophy of *The Blazing World* is not forged from an experience of powerlessness and alienation, but correlates to the patriarchalism espoused by Robert Filmer in *Patriarcha* (1680). By the early 1660s, aligning herself with Charles II's insistence on royal prerogatives, Cavendish was invested in royal power.[52] Cavendish's key difference from traditional royalist arguments hangs on gender. For Filmer, kings are fathers, rulers of nations and families, upholding the analogy between natural and political bodies (an analogy Swift later parodies) as an "authoritative instrument of knowledge."[53] For Cavendish, rulers are rulers, a view that derives its rationale from the claims of rank and status.[54] Cavendish herself traded on her status as duchess (not her gender) to distinguish her natural philosophy as superior to that of professional experimenters such as Robert Hooke.[55]

One of the Empress's first acts as an absolute monarch in the Blazing World is to harness her subjects' abilities by forming learned societies. Cavendish's literary imagination elaborates a vision of scientific practitioners as hybrids, "men of several different sorts, shapes, figures, dispositions, and humors" (163). Their specializations reflect their corporeality; their embodiments endow them with insight into particular topics: "The Bear-men were to be her Experimental Philosophers, the Bird-men her Astronomers, the Fly- Worm- and Fish-men her Natural Philosophers, the Ape-men her Chymists, the Satyrs her Galenick

Physicians, the Fox-men her Politicians, the Spider- and Lice-men her Mathematicians, the Jackdaw- Magpie- and Parrot-men her Orators and Logicians, the Gyants her Architects" (163). In Cavendish's satire, each discipline is to be furthered by those who have the closest affinity to it, a likeness understood in material rather than intellectual terms.

The schools and societies that populate *The Blazing World* satirize both Bacon's idealized scientific society in *The New Atlantis* (1627) and the Royal Society in London.[56] The hybridity of the inhabitants confuses the division between observer and observed at the core of the modest witness ideal. Objectivity and distance are fictions.[57] The Bird-men are astronomers who admit they cannot explain what air is, to which the Empress responds, "If you can give no account of the Air, said she, you will hardly be able to inform me how Wind is made" (167). Her allusion could be to Boyle's air pump and Bacon's "The History of Winds." But Cavendish's derision extends beyond a particular allusion. Unsatisfied with the Bird-men's incomplete and contradictory answers concerning thunder and lightning, and "to avoid hereafter tedious disputes, and have the truth of the Phaenomena's of Celestial bodies more exactly known," the Empress calls for the Bear-men, the experimental philosophers, to use their telescopes (169). The Bear-men's findings result in conflicting perspectives that lead to dissension: "These Telescopes caused more differences and divisions amongst them, then ever they had before ... some fell into a great dispute ... [and] they could not agree" (169–170). When the microscopists proudly show the Empress a flea and a louse under the microscope, she swoons at the magnified sight. But they rebuff her suggestion that microscopes ought to stop fleas from biting—that is, the assumption that their endeavors ought to have a practical application, in this instance, to alleviate pain and discomfort—declaring that "such Arts [are] mechanical and below that noble study of Microscopical observations" (174).[58]

Through the characterization of these scientists, *The Blazing World* satirizes the notion that natural philosophy produces any useful knowledge and also warns of the political dangers of such futility and self-interest. After listening to the Ape-Men (the chemists), the Empress commands her subjects to devote themselves to utilitarian practice. If, as Lisa T. Sarasohn has argued, Cavendish distinguishes herself as a philosopher with claims to civility and honor, then she underscores this distinction by questioning those qualities of her learned subjects.[59] All of their discussions result in misinformation, infighting, and futility. The Empress tells the Bear-men to destroy their telescopes; she also angrily reprimands her subjects and cuts the learned societies off from the general public: "Confine your disputations to your Schools, lest besides the Commonwealth of Learning, they disturb also Divinity and Policy, Religion and Laws, and by that means draw an utter ruine and destruction both upon Church and State" (191). Cavendish's repudiation condemns scientific practice as merely a mechanism for crass and destructive self-interest. The natural philosopher's underlying self-interest, from Cavendish's point of view, leads to an unstable, fractious body politic. The practices of natural philosophy are inextricable from "the civil wars' destructions."[60] The image of the commonwealth as "a Monster of many heads" resonates. In Cavendish's royalism, Sprat's and other royalists' support for the institutionalization of science in the Royal Society is foolhardy and can lead only to political crises.

Yet quarantining the learned societies does not eradicate the political danger they pose. The Empress worries that the Blazing World is becoming riven with "continual contentions and divisions"; she even "fear[s] they'l break out into an open Rebellion, and cause a greater disorder and ruine of the Government" (229). The Duchess concurs and urges the Empress to eradicate the societies altogether because their fights "breed factions in their Schools, which at last break out into open Wars, and draw sometimes an utter ruine upon a State or Government" (230). Intellectual dissension opens the way to political dissension. The learned societies foment social unrest that fundamentally threatens the power and authority of the monarch. The phrases "open Rebellion," "disorder and ruine of the Government," and "utter ruine upon a State or Government" all signal political danger, particularly in the context of Cavendish's Restoration England (229, 229, 230). The Duchess's advice to dissolve the societies is radical but decisive. In sharp contrast to advocates such as Sprat, Cavendish insists that learned societies lead to political upheaval.

To establish the learned societies is one of the Empress's first acts as absolutist monarch of the Blazing World. The way forward that the text imagines is backward—eliminate them to ensure that monarchical power remains intact and absolute. The Second Part of *The Blazing World* soberly opens with a brief assertion of renewed political harmony: "The Emperess having now ordered and setled her Government to the best advantage and quiet of her *Blazing-world*" (231). The institutionalization of experimental philosophy is too deeply associated with the politics of discord and dissension, all too reminiscent of a commonwealth, to survive in Cavendish's absolutist utopia.

Even with these cautions, *The Blazing World* enacts a seemingly contradictory view of experimental philosophy: the text rejects its independent institutionalization but values its practice under the control of absolutist politics. The central work of an absolutist monarch is maintaining control of her subjects. Although one might read what results as "trickery and superstition," the image of the Empress as an absolutist specifically depends on the work of her scientists.[61] In two key episodes of *The Blazing World*, Cavendish envisages displays of power that utilize the expertise and materials of the natural philosophers, those hybrids who, left to their own devices, sow the seeds of discord. Under the unbending authority of the Empress, their experimentalism produces alluring effects that promote her authority and keep her subjects obedient.

When establishing a new church in the Blazing World, the Empress musters the analogical relationship between religion and politics. She preaches with great skill and conviction, and her subjects become devoted and passionate followers. The hallmark of her church is its inclusion of women. Yet the Empress soon begins to worry that the sway of religious fervor will dissipate because of "the inconstant nature of Mankind" (191). The danger to her religious leadership, like the danger to her political rule, is the unpredictability of individual desire and self-interest. Establishing a church and serving as its charismatic leader are not enough. The Empress understands that her devoted followers always have the option of self-rule. The political problem the Empress faces is also one of figuration: she must capture her followers' "fancies," or else they will "follow their own" (191). That is, she must command their imaginative lives if she is also to govern their experiential lives. To safeguard against the degradation of her power, the Empress calls on the expertise and knowledge of those whom she later comes to denounce, the astronomer Bird-men and the natural philosophy Worm-men, to create a spectacle of her power. She commands them to bring star-stone and fire-stone to build chapels representative of heaven and hell—the first will be all light and the other all fire. The Empress has a star cannibalized for a supply of star-stone; the fire-stone flames when it touches water. The chapels also rotate in opposite directions. Within these spaces devoted to artifice and stagecraft, an obvious renunciation of Puritan starkness and implicitly Roman Catholic in their extravagance, the Empress preaches.

These marvels of construction must be a secret, but they also produce a metaphor of power: all that her subjects may perceive is an awe-inspiring Empress proclaiming the merits of virtue and the evils of sin, emblazoned in light and then in fire as she does so. Her performance is designed to keep these subjects in awe of all she represents, a point the narrative underscores: "not onely [did she] convert the Blazing-world to her own Religion, but kept them in a constant belief, without inforcement or blood-shed; for she knew well, that belief was a thing not to be forced or pressed upon the people, but to be instilled into their minds by gentle perswasions" (193). The Empress astutely understands how to exercise her absolutist authority, and the narrative claims that such spectacles of power convince subjects rather than compel them: "for Fear, though it makes people obey, yet does not last so long, nor is it so sure a means to keep them to their duties, as Love" (193). The Empress draws on affect, particularly a feeling of awe and submission, which seems to convince but in fact compels her congregants. The chapels are designed purposefully to overwhelm viewers with a metaphorically laden spectacle and to keep them in a state of "constant belief."

When the Empress assumes a military role, she again deploys the figurative potential of experimental philosophy. She travels home to protect her country from invasion and "become Mistress of all that World [she] came from" (233). The Empress brings all of the Blazing World's scientific innovations to establish absolute rule over her home: the Fish-men pull submarines through the pole to transport Bird-, Worm-, Bear-, and Fish-men, as well as an ample supply of firestone, which, with its chemical dependence on water to flame, will burn enemy ships. The Empress's fleet is made from gold and painted black, and impervious to the optics of telescopes.

With this experimental retinue, the Empress arrives home. The Bird-men fly with damp Fire-stones, the Fish-men raise them flaming above the water, and the Empress's forces "made a terrible shew; for it appear'd as if all the Air and Sea had been of a flaming Fire; and all that were upon the Sea, or near it, did verily believe, the time of Judgment, or the Last Day was come, which made them all fall down, and Pray" (236). This terrifying barrage of otherworldly blazes seems like the end of days, leaving the Empress's enemies fearful and weakened. Even when the Empress approaches her own country, she wants them to see her ravishing splendor only, and only from afar. The narrative describes the awesomeness: she "appeared onely in her Garments of Light, like an Angel, or some Deity, and all kneeled down before her, and worshipped her with all submission and reverence: But the Empress would not come nearer then at such a distance where her voice might be generally heard, by reason she would not have that of her Accoutrements any thing else should be perceived, but the splendor thereof" (237). Just as with the chapels of good and evil, the spectacle of the Empress in state obscures the technological contrivances that make it possible. All one can perceive, therefore, is "the splendor thereof."

The Empress's spectacle makes absolutist power visible, serving the immediate purpose of vanquishing those who have threatened her country. The aim of the campaign to save her homeland quickly transitions to the larger goal of forcing "all the rest of that World to submit to that same Nation," installing her country's monarch as the leader of this world (239). As the Empress moves to attack her opponents' trading routes, she also resolves to destroy cities with the fire-stone, which she commands be placed beneath all structures so that the towns go up in a blaze when it rains. There is one city that resists, for it rarely gets rain, though it quickly succumbs when the annual tide arrives and sparks the fire-stones, which destroy houses and leave the countryside barren. The Empress's brutal campaign is successful. She saves her home country and "made it the absolute Monarchy of all that World" (241). Cavendish's royalism seems to take its inspiration from the English view of a "Universal Monarchy" associated with the absolutist French, the Dutch Republic, and the imperial Ottomans.[62]

Yet the text is not content to leave the Empress's effect on the other leaders undocumented. She rises like a deity; they submit to her. Cavendish's emphasis is on the continued metaphorics of the Empress's image: "both the effects of her Power and her Beauty did kindle a great desire in all the greatest Princes to see her" (241). She agrees to their request for an audience, but only insofar as she condescends to provide yet another spectacle of her power. With all the other ships forming a circle to honor her, her own enters, as though she were Cleopatra on the barge: "The Emperess appeared upon the face of the Water in her Imperial Robes; . . . she had placed some of the Star-Stone, near her face . . . all that were present . . . believed her to be some Celestial Creature, or rather an uncreated Goddess, and they all had a desire to worship her" (242).

Before delivering a departing speech, she commands her subjects to provide entertainment that features, among other things, the Empress being spirited as if flying (though carried by the Bird-men) and singing as if the sea and the sky were themselves singing (when it is the Fish-men and the Bird-men). Unsurprisingly, the Empress's departure involves more dramatic staging: all of the ships sink "immediately into the bottom of the Seas, and left all the Spectators in a deep amazement" (243). She stipulates that none of the ships might rise to the surface of the water until they returned to the Blazing World. To the end, the Empress is keenly aware of her image.

While *The Blazing World*, in the context of science, is best known for its satiric critique of learned societies' contradictory and useless findings, the text endorses such technology and praxis when they serve an absolute royalist ideology and, in so doing, provides a template for the production of figurative knowledge. The Empress's power is certainly real, but its perpetuation depends on the effects of metaphoric meaning. Cavendish may well be drawing on the precedent of Charles II's return to London in 1660 and his coronation in 1662, events filled with theatrical grandeur and pageantry.[63] But the literary lesson of *The Blazing World* is clear: a light on her face, the awesomeness of fire, and all such pyrotechnics connote the Empress's power rather than denote it. The discoveries of the Bird-, Bear-, and Fish-men do not improve the social health of the subjects—remember, they may study fleas and lice, but cannot eradicate them—but they do facilitate another version of social health, the Empress's absolutist rule. Within the politics of Cavendish's world, the commonwealth is a multiheaded monster and the absolute monarch is the singular, imaginatively alluring alternative. However, if *The Blazing World* documents the manufacture of the Empress's absolute monarchy through the production of science as a system of metaphorics, then it does so in a way that potentially calls that absolutism into question. In a text that presumes the existence and superiority of absolutism, we are given access to its construction and, by implication, its vulnerability. Throughout, the Empress's governing practices are explicit: her absolutism is not naturally self-perpetuating, but depends on overt cultivation. Without the assistance she receives and without eradicating dissension, the Empress would not have the ability to subject those who come under her figurative spell. As a result, the text implicitly demystifies the Empress's absolutism and alerts us to the contingency of absolutism as a political model.

Recalling Cavendish's explicit evocation of "the help of Fancy" in the Preface, we can see that the author signals not only an endorsement of literary knowledge as a way of explicating reason but also, through the narrative's plot, the centrality of figuration to imagining and instituting political order. Cavendish's evocation of fancy, a specifically literary form of knowledge, heralds a system of signification wherein the materials of experimental philosophy accrue meaning and value through their effects and metaphoric connotations. It is no wonder, then, that Cavendish concludes the volume by invoking a desire for political power alongside her status as a literary writer: in the "Epilogue to the Reader," Cavendish declares, "My ambition is not only to be Empress, but Authoress of a whole world" ("Epilogue").

SATIRE, IMPERIALISM, SWIFT

Swift's satire of science in *Gulliver's Travels* is legion. In two chapters devoted to the scientific experiments and experimenters in the Academy of Lagado, Swift parodies the learned societies that were coming to populate the European landscape, including the University of Leiden (where Gulliver attended), the Dublin Philosophical Society, and—most closely—the Royal Society. The Academy of Lagado chapters in Voyage III are layered with Swift's borrowings from *Philosophical Transactions*. Swift also likely consulted *The Philosophical Works of the Honourable Robert Boyle, Esq, Abridged, Methodized and Disposed*, published in 1725.[64] The satire's evocation of early scientific practice has been noted since its publication, beginning with the earl of Orrery's claim that Voyage III was "in general written against chymists, mathematicians, mechanics, and projectors of all kinds."[65]

Gulliver describes a number of experimentalists myopically engrossed in various projects: the manufacture of ice bullets; architectural plans that begin construction of a house with its roof and build down from there; paint colors chosen and mixed by a blind man; a method of plowing a field by burying food that hogs will dig up; a sundial that registers the effects of the wind; and a treatment for "Cholick" that sucks air from the anus or, if that fails to produce the desired effect, blows it back.[66] Even "*the universal Artist*," who employs fifty men working on projects for the "Improvement of human Life," is devoted to projects that promise to produce the opposite (265). Gulliver, although partially identifying with the projectors, admits confusion: when an investigator explains the desirability of "sow[ing] Land with Chaff," Gulliver explains that such a claim is based on "several Experiments which I was not skilful enough to comprehend" (265). Gulliver's bewilderment underscores the yawning gap between an idea and material objects. Various bodies are mined not for their beneficial properties but for something altogether worthless—such as a breed of sheep that does not grow wool. Swift's satiric leveling highlights foolishness, always in implicit contrast to the commonsensical. For practitioners who devote themselves to experiential learning, they concoct notions that are the opposite. Gulliver's torrential inventory uses the logic of reductio ad absurdum. Each practitioner is satirized for deluded views that obfuscate any commonsensical, much less beneficial, approach to studying and experimenting with the natural world. In *Gulliver's Travels*, one is tempted to dismiss the projectors in the Academy of Lagado as futile and impotent. They are comic, and this can lead one to conclude that they do not represent any real threat with their silly and self-interested experiments. The conception that material transformation can ameliorate the wrongs and injustices of the world not only fails; as we shall see, it also produces even more wrongs and injustices.

Yet to describe Swift's accomplishment as only a satiric leveling is inadequate. Satire, as Fredric V. Bogel points out, creates the difference that it proclaims to describe.[67] This creation of difference—of inferiority, of degradation, of danger—emerges through Swift's manipulation of the logic of figuration: throughout *Gulliver's Travels*, and especially in the treatment of scientific discourse and practice, Swift literalizes metaphors. When Gulliver recounts with disgust the cancerous breast of a Brobdingnagian wet nurse, he sees as though he were a microscope, a transformation that literalizes the views made possible by optical instruments (just as Locke warned).[68]

Swift takes natural philosophers at their word. He transforms the vehicles of scientific metaphors into their tenors: the metaphor of the body politic becomes the body of a politician. Gulliver's account of the "School of Political Projectors" examines and satirizes natural philosophical practice, but within an explicitly political context that raises questions of society and morality.[69] Opening with a skeptical account of reasonable and just government, Gulliver embraces a "most ingenious Doctor" who views the metaphor of the body politic in literal terms (275). The body politic is only as healthy as its leaders are—and these politicians are afflicted by innumerable "Diseases of the Head, and more of the Heart," as well as "Spleen, Flatus, Vertigoes, and Deliriums" (276). Therefore, each is treated with a robust menu of medicines before any political gathering. Treating the senators and councilors not only ensures their health, but also that of the body politic they represent.

When Swift turns to contemplate political factionalism and the potential for civil war, the metaphor of the body politic receives an even more rigorous and violent literalization. Dissection and surgery, the tools of experimental practice, provide an evocative vehicle to imagine political compromise. "When Parties in a State are violent," a doctor argues, brain surgery can fuse the minds of political opponents: "The two half Brains being left to debate the Matter between themselves within the Space of one Scull, would soon come to a good Understanding" (278). By confining political debate into a single human body, the doctor's surgical solution contains the tension and its commensurate potential for civil unrest. Of course, the good doctor imagines one hundred leaders from each party will be treated, a number that admits the necessity of instituting forced reconciliation repeatedly. The solace of a single resolution is too tenuous. And the surgical violence to the individual bodies, reputedly in the service of promoting political harmony? Gulliver merely looks away from the inherent contradiction.

Swift's literalization of the body politic metaphor intermingles experimental philosophy and political order. In the "School of Political Projectors," Swift's language signals the quality and seriousness of such political problems: the statement, "When Parties in a State are violent," does not present a minor conundrum. This is not about a new way of mixing paint colors. Swift's reconfiguration of a metaphor's tenor and vehicle exposes the animating relationship between the politics of science and the science of politics.

Swift's understanding of the effect of experimental philosophy on political life corresponds to Cavendish's: experimentalism is ridiculous until it spreads into the polis.[70] Gulliver's tour of the city of Balnibarbi focuses on the devastating effects of natural philosophers' meddling in affairs of daily life. Buildings fall down and farming techniques fail. Projectors dismantle a perfectly functioning mill and move it up a mountain because they insist that water pumped up to a higher elevation produces more energy. These instances prove that experimental philosophy fails to provide meaningful, productive technical innovation, precisely the promise that advocates reiterate.[71] And the effects on citizens subject to such "improvements" warrant particular note: "I never knew . . . a People whose Countenances and Habit expressed so much Misery and Want" (251–252). Swift's practitioners make literal what natural philosophical discourse conveys metaphorically. When the metaphor becomes material, their science results in real-life suffering. No wonder that Laputa is a "kingdom of natural violence and acceptable suffering": this is a world in which state institutions bolster policies and practices that lead to "Misery and Want."[72] These are not merely excesses of experimental philosophy but the cruel imperial politics at its core. While Voyage III has not often been considered within the text's larger colonial and imperial ideology, in no small part because it focuses on European institutions and vices, and although few scholars have attended to the relationship between colonialism and science in Book III, Swift's point is clear.[73] Science is never inextricable from politics—and neither offers relief for anyone out of power.

The government overseeing this literalization and its concomitant misery is Laputa, the Flying Island, "(quite literally) π in the sky."[74] The court literalizes the elite's devotion to theoretical mathematics and music. They adorn their clothing with astronomical figures and musical instruments, and their bodies contour themselves for their subjects of study: "their Heads were all reclined either to the Right or the Left; one of their Eyes turned inward, and the other directly up to the Zenith" (226). The Laputan's obsession with mathematics and music takes them out of their already contorted bodies such that they require the aid of "Flappers," servants who physically poke them to bring them back to their sensory selves (227). Without the Flappers, the Laputans would remain in their speculative reveries and forget to converse with one another. Or they would trip and fall over. Gulliver complains that they are terrible company, "so abstracted and involved in Speculation" (249). The Laputans are not Projectors, slavishly devoted to experiments, but they share a similar self-preoccupation associated with scientists throughout the long eighteenth century.[75] They are also in a constant state of panic, as they worry about various apocalyptic scenarios. These men are terrified by something that they cannot perceive, much less do anything to mitigate.

The male ruling elite on Laputa embody how speculative thinking, in the hands of the powerful, has real-world and practical effects. The married women of Laputa enjoy sexual freedom. They may take lovers so long as their husbands "be but provided with Paper and Implements, and without [their] *Flapper[s]* at [their] side" (237–238). However, women are not allowed to leave the island because the men fear that they would never return, an admission of the unappealing nature of this society. One woman who left now lives in an "obscure Eating-House in all rags" with a "deformed" footman who beats her; even in such misery, she refuses to return (238). Gulliver attributes this to women's "Caprices," but the text makes clear that the women of Laputa bear the costs of their husbands' imperial power (238). Their choice is the nonchoice of patriarchy: for women, living in a tavern in rags and being physically abused is preferable to living on the Flying Island.

Laputa has been understood allegorically as a figure for English economic oppression of the Irish, especially evident in the resistance of the city Lindalino as a vehicle for Dublin.[76] Indeed, analyzing the colonial politics of *Gulliver's*

Travels has been a fruitful topic, providing interpretations that attend to the text's persistent and uncomfortable reckoning of imperial and racist practices that are dramatized with particular virulence in Book IV.[77] In Book III, if state-sponsored projectors ruin commerce and daily living in the communities on terra firma, then the Flying Island symbolically and functionally acts out state power. The Loadstone, controlled by a scientist, enables the island to fly, but it can be manipulated for authoritarian ends. It can be directed to hover over a dominion "to bring [it] under [the Prince's] Obedience" (244). In such a position, the island can cause natural devastation below, cutting off a community's sunlight and water "if any Town should engage in Rebellion or Mutiny, fall into violent Factions, or refuse to pay the usual Tribute" (246). The king of Laputa holds a final solution: collapsing the island onto the rebellious community below, destroying all. Swift uses figuration to demonstrate that the work of scientists benefits rulers. Scientific innovation in the service of political coercion echoes the practices of Cavendish's Empress. For Cavendish, the appropriation of science for absolutism is acceptable; for Swift, it is not.

Swift's distrust of mathematics as a scientific practice permeates Voyage III. He responded, perhaps in part, to Bernard de Fontenelle's defense of mathematics in *Histoire du renouvellement de l'Académie Royale* (Paris, 1708), a copy of which Swift owned.[78] *Philosophical Transactions* also likely provided Swift comical and satiric fodder.[79] But Swift's primary object of satiric bile was unequivocally Isaac Newton. For Swift, the connection between the power elite in Laputa and Newtonian mathematical thinking exposes the interconnections and interdependencies of the Newtonian Whigs and the Hanoverian court, all frequent objects of Swift's animus.[80]

By the time Swift published *Gulliver's Travels* in 1726, Newton was an old man—still nominally president of the Royal Society, living in Winchester, dying in London in 1727. However, Newton's influence intellectually and institutionally rendered him a metonymy for British natural philosophy.[81] His importance was evident in the work of the Royal Society and other learned circles, and also in the consumer and fashionable set of London and the countryside. "Scientific Entrepreneurs," including Benjamin Martin, James Hodgson (who was assistant to the Astronomer Royal of Flamsteed, later working as a mathematics teacher and experimental lecturer), William Whiston, and John Theophilus Desaguliers, marketed Newton's science in popular publications, lectures, and courses.[82] Mechanical demonstrations of Newton's physics gave a vivid sense of the economic potential of natural philosophy.[83] The financial implications of Newtonianism corresponded to a larger civic sense (for some) that Newton's natural philosophy modeled and promoted an idealized social harmony, in the spirit of Sprat's "civil Government."[84] In a 1702 sermon, Samuel Clarke linked social and theological orders in language that drew on Newtonian science.[85] The Boyle lectures, which began in 1692 with an endowment from Robert Boyle's will, integrated Newtonian natural philosophy with liberal Protestant social ideology; they were also read far more frequently than Newton's own work.[86] Newton's *Philosophiæ Naturalis Principia Mathematica* (*Mathematical Principles of Natural Philosophy*, 1687) developed principles of bodies in movement, such as the theory of gravity, based on mathematical calculations, a science that enabled a "new geo-political imagination," a "planetary consciousness" that used scientific language to support a Eurocentric worldview.[87] During Swift's lifetime, the effect of Newton's thinking on English politics was widespread and profound, allowing, for instance, Whiston and Edmund Halley to explain astronomy as supporting the Hanoverian succession in 1715.[88] Newtonian natural philosophy helped to shore up British political stability.[89]

These affiliations between natural philosophy and politics left Swift skeptical of, and often even enraged at, the imperialistic and colonial agendas undergirding this putative stability. Newton's association with the Hanoverian government particularly raised Swift's ire. As warden of the mint, Newton authorized the assay of William Wood's copper coinage.[90] Wood's patent used copper, rather than silver, for the halfpence coins, and the change in material authorized £100,000 of money with a metallic value of £30,000.[91] Wood was also permitted to ship the Irish coins without having them regulated or even inspected.[92] The Wood coinage and Newton's involvement quite likely substantiated Swift's fear that natural philosophy served the interests of capital accumulation and imperialist government, while further subjugating everyone else, especially the Irish.[93] Wood's halfpence institutionalized the continued financial oppression of the Irish; they would receive debased currency and have no means to redress the exploitation.

The affair of Wood's halfpence placed Newton firmly in Swift's crosshairs, and Swift did not contain his fury. He broke off writing *Gulliver's Travels* to pamphleteer against it. *A Modest Proposal* vividly expresses Swift's rage at the English's colonialization of Ireland, as he force-feeds the reader with the image of Irish babies as culinary delicacies.[94] And Swift condemns Newton as responsible for the assay in the *Bickerstaff Papers* (1738). Newton is a "Conjurer, because he knew how to draw Lines and Circles upon a Slate, which no Body could understand."[95] The image of "Lines and Circles" reduces mathematics to a semiotics with no referent: in terms of metaphor, this is a vehicle with no tenor. Newton's claim for mathematical plainness is, for Swift, drivel. In *Gulliver's Travels*, Swift even has Aristotle announce that Newtonianism is just a fad.

Newtonianism is a critical flashpoint for Swift; it represents not only bad science but also a politics of imperial power. How else could Newton authorize Wood's coin? In Voyage III of *Gulliver's Travels*, composed in the aftermath of the halfpence affair, the idea that mathematicians fancy themselves politicians is laughable, if not in fact terribly dangerous.[96] Swift marshals his favorite literary technique, the literalization of metaphors. By suggesting a spatial affinity between circles and globes, Swift skewers the presumption that mathematics and politics have anything to do with each other. As Gulliver explains, "Most of the Mathematicians I have known in *Europe* . . . suppose, that because the smallest Circle hath as many Degrees as the largest, therefore the Regulation and Management of the World require no more Abilities than the handling and turning of a Globe" (235–236). The gentle reorientation of "in *Europe*" turns the reader's mind to the contemporary context. Swift sabotages the purported similitude between mathematics and political theory: mathematicians mistakenly assume a correspondence and similarity between spinning a globe and governing. Mathematicians are deluded and dangerous because they view governance as computational and, for Swift, devoid of morality. The text's understanding of mathematicians and governing needs to be understood through the context of Newton's assay of Wood's halfpence. The indictment articulated in *Gulliver's Travels* impugns imperialistic principles that, Swift suggests through these allusions, Newton, the Whigs, and George I represent. The Flying Island's devotion to natural philosophy renders its imperialism a form of geometry and calculus, an association that Swift vehemently satirizes. Natural philosophy is not merely a scientific structure for governance. It also bears the means for an oppressive political system to thrive. Not coincidently, once Gulliver's experience with the Laputans concludes, he visits other communities equally devoted to social control and degradation, particularly Luggnagg and Japan.

Reading beyond the Academy of Lagado and its environs more fully exposes the troubling connections between imperial governance and scientific practice that preoccupy Swift. These linkages reappear—transformed and abstracted—in the imperialistic and colonial government of Voyage IV. While Swift's horse-like creatures have often been read through the tradition of Stoicism, I argue that Voyage IV transports the principles of natural philosophy and political theory into a dystopia that instrumentalizes reason.[97] Swift presents in narrative form the political theory made possible by natural philosophy: the rationality of Voyage IV produces an even more terrifying form of authoritarian government.[98]

Swift's use of the word *thing* links Books III and IV through the epistemology of natural philosophy, as the experimentalism and mathematics of the former fade into the rationality of the latter. Consider its presence among the Houyhnhnms. In Book IV, Gulliver encounters the word *thing* when he butts against what he perceives to be the limitations of the Houyhnhnm language: "They have no Word in their Language to express Lying or Falshood" (349). The only way the Houyhnhnms can conceptualize a lie is through the phrase "*the thing which was not*" (349). This famous coinage demonstrates an apparent unwillingness to think imaginatively. It also reveals an effort to cordon off the discursive and ontological realm in which things are. The metaphorics of the Houyhnhnm language require literalization, and literalization demands plausibility. Gulliver first hears "*the thing which was not*" after narrating his journey to Houyhnhnmland. From the Houyhnhnm perspective, Gulliver utters "*the thing which was not*" because "it was impossible that there could be a Country beyond the Sea, or that a Parcel of Brutes could move a wooden Vessel wither they pleased upon Water" (349). In the narrow sense to which it is applied here, "*the thing which was not*" refers to the possibilities of a world across the ocean, the manufacture and use of ships, and human sailors.

Given their stated lack of imagination and, comically, their hooves (although they do sew), it is not surprising that the Houyhnhnms have no written literary tradition. But they do have poetry. Gulliver praises the "Justness of their Similes, and the Minuteness, as well as Exactness of their Descriptions, [which] are indeed inimitable" (412). Similes require figuration, of course, the deployment of a vehicle and tenor. Yet when Gulliver's Houyhnhnm Master uses a simile to indict human rationality, he expresses a fundamental distrust of representation more generally. After listening to Gulliver's various descriptions of English society and politics, the Houyhnhnm Master concludes that humans "were only possessed of some Quality fitted to our natural Vices; as the Reflection from a troubled Stream returns the Image of an ill-shapen Body, not only *larger*, but more *distorted*" (367). According to the Houyhnhnm Master, humans converse in figuration, which is irrational and founded on lying. The mimesis simile is likely the Houyhnhnm Master's, though there is enough syntactical ambiguity that it might be Gulliver's. Regardless, it utilizes an image of the representational effects of reflection. According to this logic, perception and reflection are distinct: the original is best known through perception, for reflection has the potential to distort it. As we shall see, Houyhnhnms believe that their reason is merely a matter of accurate perception.

The Houyhnhnm understanding of links between language and reality echoes the language experiments in Voyage III. At the Academy of Lagado, things dominate, a parodic celebration of the principle undergirding natural philosophy and the Royal Society's motto, "*nullius in verba.*"[99] As I demonstrated in Chapter 1, natural philosophy's *observed particulars* acquire their legitimacy through literary knowledge. But Swift's experimental philosophers view language experiments as relying on denotative rather than figurative meaning.[100] They miss the need for figuration and claim things can replace words because they (mistakenly) assume a fixity to language that repudiates figuration entirely. In a parody of the great principle of natural philosophy, "since Words are only Names for *Things,*" Gulliver explains, "It would be more convenient for all Men to carry ... *Things* ... necessary to express the particular Business they are to discourse on" (271). The crowning example of the Academy's repudiation of figuration is a language machine. When a professor and his pupils turn its levers, the language machine spits out sentences and reduces the process of writing to bodily labor. It might be an early computer or a satire of the Royal Society's myriad language schemes, such as John Wilkins's *Essay Towards a Real Character and a Philosophical Language* (1668).[101] However, Swift's satiric representation is more pointed than mere allusion. Turning the levers of a machine to generate language means that language is instrumental. To such believers, language is insistently nonfigurative.

To return to the vexing phrase in Voyage IV, "*the thing which was not*" is an expression of disbelief, as well as an assertion of nonexistence. "*The thing which was not*" is irrational and does not exist. The Houyhnhnms's language institutes a division between "things" and "being," on the one hand, and "not" and "nonbeing," on the other. Truth exists; its opposite does not. At the moment Gulliver tells his history—he comes from England and traveled by ship—he is denied the subjectivity that makes that history possible because it would require the Houyhnhnms to use the imagination, the realm of figuration. Try as he might to trot like a horse, Gulliver will never be one. Within the world of the

Houyhnhnms, Gulliver not only has no place; he has no subject position. He cannot be a non-Yahoo Yahoo.[102]

"*The thing which was not*," of course, is an example of Houyhnhnm epistemology: their "grand Maxim is, to cultivate *Reason*, and to be wholly governed by it.... [it] strikes you with immediate Conviction; as it must needs do where it is not mingled, obscured, or discoloured by Passion and Interest" (401–402). Theirs is an embodiment of Lockean intuitive knowledge.[103] The Houyhnhnms's view of reason is tautological: they have "no Conception of how a rational Creature can be *compelled*, but only advised, or *exhorted*; because no Person can disobey Reason, without giving up his Claim to be a rational Creature" (422). One cannot be considered a reasonable person if one is not reasonable.

However, given Voyage III, it is important to recall that Swift's critique of Houyhnhnm reason is first articulated through the term *thing*. Swift refuses to separate this word from its central role in natural philosophy, a connection that signals his deep skepticism about the use of scientific principles to advance authoritarianism. Not coincidently, Gulliver turns to the topic of natural philosophy shortly after his explication of the Houyhnhnms's rationality. His Master's response? Laughter. Ironically, Gulliver's Houyhnhnm Master inspects him as if he were a scientific specimen, with Gulliver registering the sense of powerlessness and objectification this process induces.[104]

Gulliver operates as an uneasy Yahoo, desirous of being a non-Yahoo Yahoo and exhilarated that the Houyhnhnms "would condescend to distinguish me from the rest of my Species" (420). Erin Mackie suggests that Gulliver's desire for happiness in Voyage IV unravels the hope for a "good life"; Swift rejects imagining a path beyond Gulliver's conflicted self.[105] Gulliver's uneasy existence as a non-Yahoo Yahoo also manifests itself in his relation to the Yahoos. He sees himself in the Yahoos, loathes this about himself, and desperately wants to be accepted by the Houyhnhnms as one of them instead.

Within this Houyhnhnm schema that Gulliver adopts, the Yahoos are the debased antithesis that confirms the integrity and superiority of the Houyhnhnm. Yet the difference that the Houyhnhnms institute is vividly unsettled in a discussion that unwittingly turns to figurative language. In a rather offhand way, Gulliver observes,

I know not whether it may be worth observing, that the *Houyhnhnms* have no Word in their Language to express any thing that is *evil*, except what they borrow from the Deformities or ill Qualities of the *Yahoos*. Thus they denote the Folly of a Servant, an

Omission of a Child, a Stone that cuts their Feet, a Continuance of foul or unseasonable Weather, and the like, by adding to each the Epithet of *Yahoo*. For Instance, *Hhnm Yahoo, Whnaholm Yahoo, Ynlhmnawihlma Yahoo*, and an ill contrived House *Ynholmhnmrohlnw Yahoo*. (414–415)

This observation—something he is not sure is "worth observing"—comes as Gulliver concludes his description of the "Manners and Virtues of this excellent People" (415). The absence of written language in Houyhnhnmland, a common colonial conceit of English missionaries, for example, takes the joke of Voyage III's language experiments a treacherous step further.[106]

Not having a word for evil evokes the Houyhnhnm principle of "*the thing which was not*." However, the Houyhnhnms use the occasion of not having a word to make one up: they convert the noun *Yahoo* into an adjective. The Yahoos become metaphors. The thing that was not, at least syntactically, becomes a thing that is through its association with Yahoos. In the process of this figuration, Yahoos become intertwined with the term *evil*, just as a thing that is not as a category of being comes to be linked to Yahoos. The Yahoos are the logical incoherence generated by Houyhnhnm reason.

The discourse of the Yahoos in *Gulliver's Travels* can be read as a Latourian purification in which the Houyhnhnms attempt to reduce politics to a science, with Swift powerfully showing the irrationality of their logic. The Houyhnhnms are, in fact, subject to the "Passion and Interest" they claim to eschew, and their Grand Assembly exemplifies what reason looks like when it instead promotes its opposite. The only topic the Grand Assembly ever takes up is whether to perpetrate genocide on the Yahoos. In the Houyhnhnms's treatment and representation of the Yahoos, eradicating the figurative from language does not merely unearth a "moral relativity"; it evacuates morality and ethics altogether.[107] One advocate for genocide evokes "tradition": the origin story the Houyhnhnms tell themselves about the Yahoos, which is compelling because, striking the eager listener like reason, "there seemed to be much Truth in this Tradition" (409). Voyage IV exposes the ideological and ethical dangers of believing that reason is perception. The repetition of a debate about genocide, in a purportedly civil society that insists things just are, reveals the imperialist politics at the core of instrumentalized reason. This so-called debate pivots to tradition, recounted with unacknowledged though fierce passion, and bears no marks of empathy. In a polis that professes to privilege sober observation and facticity, this Member of the Grand Assembly voices a brutal imperialism, irrationality, and prejudice masquerading as rational political argumentation. Voyage IV may well be designed to vex the reader by replicating the colonial dialect to critique it.[108] Yet by the time Gulliver opines that he has attempted to produce scientific objectivity in his own writing, Swift has thoroughly refuted Gulliver's aspiration and aligned it instead with a punitive, imperialistic political structure that refuses to acknowledge the imperatives of self-interest and power built into it. Through their shared investment in the imperialism enabled by natural philosophical thinking, the Houyhnhnms and Gulliver, their human acolyte, together receive the full bite of Swift's satiric ire.

The seventeenth-century institutionalization of natural philosophy offered some a template for political governance. For Sprat, the Royal Society as a collective provided safeguards against the animosity and disputes of the previous generation, though for Cavendish and Swift, learned societies ensured the proliferation of those same qualities. Even among writers with such distinct visions for social order, the interlacing of natural philosophy and political theory in these texts reflects a symbiosis and more. Ways of knowing are bound up with ways of governing, with the promise of experimentalism gaining unqualified support from Sprat, equivocal advocacy from Cavendish, and thorough contempt from Swift. Writing in the 1660s, Sprat and Cavendish share a deep concern about the return to the disruption of the Interregnum but diverge in how science might safeguard the polis. For Swift, in the following century, the threat of civil war is dim, displaced by the looming horror of imperialism writ large. These writers also disclose the profundity of literariness to the articulation of what science might mean politically: through purposeful concentration on genre as well as on the possibilities and limitations of metaphor, Sprat, Cavendish, and Swift teach that even the most instrumental of sociopolitical orders depend on the literary imagination.

In the following chapter, I move from the political possibilities enabled by and associated with natural philosophy as a form of literary knowledge to my grandest claim of all. Literariness does not merely facilitate the practice and conceptualization of natural philosophy but also contains within it a hidden reciprocity with science: experimentalism's logic and structure are an unacknowledged core of eighteenth-century aesthetics. In this story of the British Enlightenment, literary knowledge lays claim to being the most reliable and most authoritative mode to apprehend the world around us.

5 WHEN SCIENCE BECOMES LITERATURE

I argue in this book that literariness enables writing about science as well as thinking about science, its practitioners and objects, its pedagogy and politics. Modest and immodest witnesses, observed particulars and things, the processes of learning science and governing—these subjects, objects, and institutions tell the story of British modernity with its fitful possibilities and limitations. The quality of literariness that inheres to natural philosophy as a practice, theme, and metaphor authorizes writers to imagine new definitions of evidence and new modes of authority. The figuration at the heart of literariness contains a simultaneous gesture to referent and sign that produces a way of knowing to reconcile the material and the imaginative. Science operates as such a productive and provocative metaphor in the British Enlightenment because it introduces the occasion to foreground this doubleness. Natural philosophy as a principle looks to the natural world for answers and information, and literary knowledge sees insight and wisdom beyond the material.

In this final chapter, I contend that the literary becomes an epistemological project through its relationship with natural philosophy. The development of scientific concepts and processes reciprocally provides a hidden structure for the epistemological claims of eighteenth-century aesthetics. Poetic texts that fully exploit the figurative potential of the scientific mode do so to propose the epistemological superiority of literary knowledge. This is the experimental imagination.

Within the Enlightenment context, how do natural philosophers view poetry? As we have seen throughout this book, individuals whom we would now call scientists wrote self-consciously literary texts. Robert Boyle penned his romance, and Henry Baker, poetry, reminding us that this was not a world divided into disciplinary silos. Natural philosophy, Thomas Sprat argues, is good for verse: "The *Wit* that is founded on the *Arts* of mens hands is masculine and durable."[1] For Sprat, "masculine and durable" literary art emerges from a close observation of the things the experimental method unearths.

Abraham Cowley's prefatory ode to *The History of the Royal Society* accepts

Sprat's invitation and discusses the aesthetics of such poetry.² In line with the masculinization of the experimental project, Cowley's poem converts the gender of philosophy, renouncing the feminine *Sophia*: "Philosophy, I say, and call it, He,/For whatsoe're the Painters Fancy be,/It a Male Virtu seems to me."³ The poem tells a story of intellectual liberation, moving from the imprisonment of scholastic thinking to the freedom of natural philosophy. Scholastic epistemology clouds and even perverts true thinking, claims that Cowley's language amplifies through its metaphors: "the sports of wanton Wit," "the Desserts of Poetry," and the "pleasant Labyrinths of ever-fresh Discourse" all fail to provide substantive nutrition.⁴ Sporting, sweets, labyrinths—these are the aesthetic allures that trap men into unenlightened ways of thinking.

For Cowley, art is a mimetic form requiring the substance of the material world. Representation *must* come out of a careful and sustained engagement with the findings of experimental philosophy. Such attention produces clarity of vision and accuracy of perception, qualities that lead to good art. Sweeping aside the Flemish pictorial arts, especially the portraiture that profoundly influenced English painting in the early seventeenth century, Cowley promotes an aesthetic that requires the artist to have an experimental-like eye.⁵ True art—valuable art—is possible only if the artist behaves as a natural philosopher:

> No, he before his sight must place
> The Natural and Living Face;
> The real Object must command
> Each Judgment of his Eye, and Motion of his Hand.⁶

Cowley's conjunction of the artist's optics and graphia shares fundamental qualities with Hooke's "sincere Hand and a faithful Eye" metaphor for the modest witness that produces microscopy.⁷

Cowley's theory of mimesis favors the object over the poet's "Ideas" and "Images" "In his own Fancy, or his Memory," emphasizing scrupulous ocular examination and faithful rendering rather than the imaginative potential of literariness.⁸ Yet those "real Object[s]" have already been determined and discovered by natural philosophers; it is up to the poet to follow the experimentalists' lead, as difficult as this may be. Cowley proclaims that *The History of the Royal Society* "has all the Beauties Nature can impart/And all the comely Dress without the paint of Art."⁹ Ironically, within this *poem*, natural philosophy takes precedence in revealing beautiful things and doing so without any aestheticization. There is no "paint of Art" in experimental philosophy's beautiful things. Cowley's renunciation sets up an aesthetic hierarchy, raising natural philosophy above poetry. The charge inherent in Cowley's and Sprat's imaginings concerns more than mere admiration for natural philosophy. They forge an aesthetic model that utilizes the protocols and exigencies of natural philosophy thematically and formally.

A lesson of Cowley's *Ode* is that poetry devoted to natural philosophy opens up space for debates about aesthetics. Poets regularly use the theme and metaphor of natural philosophy to make the case for aesthetics as a form of knowledge, expressing an early distinction between (albeit with considerable overlap and tension) what we now consider the sciences and the arts. Science in seventeenth- and eighteenth-century poetry often occasions a self-consciously framed rivalry between the two forms of knowledge, a sort of recalibration of the sister-arts antipathy. Aesthetics, of course, as a term was not coined until 1735, but the ideas cohered decades earlier. For the earl of Shaftesbury and Francis Hutcheson, the interrelated notions of the disinterested observer and the internal sense are pivotal. Aesthetic disinterestedness imagines a stable, unbiased observer with an enlightened and exclusive ability for sensory perception. Aesthetic theory shares qualities with the modest witness at the core of experimental practice, though the end result is the production of aesthetic, rather than scientific, knowledge.

This chapter studies aesthetic mediations of natural philosophy. These poems use an expressly aesthetic mode to imagine beyond the limits of experimental knowledge—to see beyond its confines, to take up where science leaves off, even though eighteenth-century aesthetics takes shape through unacknowledged appropriation of scientific structures and processes. With this reciprocity obscured, natural philosophy may well disclose sights unseen, but poetry does more. Alexander Pope's *The Rape of the Lock* heeds the imaginative possibilities introduced by the experimental method, drawing on but also explicitly moving beyond the technological limitations of practice to inculcate a new vision of the material world of things and the individual who has access to it. Queen Caroline's Hermitage, dedicated to accomplishments of theologians and natural philosophers, honors these British worthies with landscape, architecture, and statuary, a monument that in turn generates a poetry contest held by the *Gentleman's Magazine* and appeals for even more poetry. James Thomson's Georgic poem, *The Seasons*, inaugurates aesthetic disinterestedness characterized by insight and exclusivity, not terribly dissimilar from natural philosophy's modest witness, though Thomson's subject position results in an unexpected celebration of difference.

Each of my poetic examples aestheticizes science, that is, represents science as a literary object. But these are not merely aestheticizations. They are aesthetic mediations. What is the difference? The former is the rendering of something into art. But the latter, the aesthetic mediation, produces a self-conscious discourse about art as art. I use the term *mediation* to insist on the epistemological claims that the process of aestheticizing may produce. The association with processes of legal resolutions suggests that mediation displays the relationship between potentially adversarial domains.[10] Mediation is "everything that intervenes, enables, supplements, or is simply in between."[11] Aesthetics as an act of mediation does not merely suggest an instrumental transformation of natural philosophy but also the framework—the tool, the medium—through which an understanding of art emerges. In these poems, science becomes literature: aesthetic mediations of natural philosophy draw on but also challenge the intellectual processes of science, reimagine subjectivity, and mount a case for the superiority of the literary.

First, a discussion of eighteenth-century aesthetics.

AESTHETIC SUBJECTS

In 1735, a young philosopher, Alexander Gottlieb Baumgarten, conceived the term *aesthetics*. According to Baumgarten, *aesthetics* first meant a "science of how things are to be known by means of the senses"; later it included the "logic of the lower cognitive faculty, the philosophy of the graces and the muses, lower gnoseology, the art of thinking beautifully, the art of the analogue of reason"; and finally it combined the two earlier definitions: "Aesthetics (the theory of the liberal arts, lower gnoseology, the art of beautiful thinking, the art of the analogue of reason) is the science of sensitive cognition."[12] Baumgarten's definitions situate the discourses of arts and beauty in relation to theories of sensory perception, opening the way to considering experimental philosophy and art. His definitions also codify a strand of thinking that had been emerging with particular resonance in Britain in the 1710s and 1720s in the writings of Anthony Ashley Cooper, third earl of Shaftesbury, and Francis Hutcheson.

For Shaftsbury, a disinterested observer is at the heart of the aesthetic experience, a subject position that necessitates acts of self-effacement not too dissimilar from natural philosophy's modest witness. While there is critical debate about the uses of disinterestedness in eighteenth-century aesthetic theory, its emergence is generally agreed upon.[13] To inculcate disinterestedness in *The*

Moralists, a Philosophical Rhapsody (1709), Shaftesbury presents beautiful objects scaled from the grand to the small. The first is a prospect of the open sea. Theocles explains to his interlocutor Philocles, "Imagine . . . if being taken with the beauty of the ocean, which you see yonder at a distance, it should come into your head to seek how to command it and, like some mighty admiral, ride master of the seas."[14] To react to the distant, beautiful ocean with one's own fantasy of control and mastery, Theocles argues, would "be a little absurd."[15] The next example, "nearer home," is a beautiful tract of land.[16] If one "should, for the enjoyment of the prospect, require the property or possession of the land," this would be a "covetous fancy . . . as absurd altogether as that other ambitious one."[17] A third example defines possession as consumption: if one sees beautiful trees and subsequently desires to eat their fruit, "the fancy of this kind . . . would be as sordidly luxurious and as absurd, in my opinion, as either of the former."[18] In each case, Shaftesbury presents the pleasures of seeing a beautiful object to insist that the proper mode of aesthetic appreciation is *not* to imagine oneself in a possessive relation to it. Instead, aesthetic responses require that the spectator stave off the self and imagine only a form of enjoyment in which the observer has no investment and no stake in the object. A truly aesthetic process imagines a firm border between subject and object, a division that simultaneously ensures the integrity and truthfulness of aesthetic objects, as well as those who appreciate them. For Shaftesbury, as for Hutcheson after him, the aesthetic is moral, eschewing the "luxurious" and the "absurd." The experience of beauty, for Shaftesbury, is possible only in the absence of possession and use, for those reflect mere self-interested desire.

Francis Hutcheson's 1725 preface to *An Inquiry into the Original of our Ideas of Beauty and Virtue* praises Shaftesbury and specifically evokes his standard of disinterestedness.[19] Hutcheson refutes the egoistic models promoted by Thomas Hobbes and Bernard Mandeville, in which an aesthetic experience is characterized by the perceiver's self-interested pleasure.[20] The pleasure one feels from a beautiful object, Hutcheson argues, is a result of sensory perception that does not have a constitutive effect on the object itself. Even if it is, in Mandeville's sense, self-pleasure, Hutcheson labors to distinguish the observer's integrity and self-effacement.[21] The beautiful object is a separate and distinct entity, impervious to any modification from the processes of observation. Since the beautiful does not exist in relation to the observer, at least theoretically, the pleasure it instills is universal. Hutcheson explains: "The Ideas of Beauty and Harmony, like other sensible Ideas, are necessarily pleasant to us, as well as immediately so; neither can any Resolution of our own, nor any Prospect of Advantage or Disadvantage, vary the Beauty or Deformity of an Object."[22] Hutcheson's claim accords with the natural philosophical overt insistence that the object under view exists separate from the modest witness who views it. In both instances, the object is not a product of the imagination, whether that act of imagination concerns an individual's desire to do something with the object (as in the case of Shaftesbury or Hutcheson) or to create that object (as in the case of experimental philosophers). The same model of knowing defines both aesthetic theory and experimental philosophy.

Hutcheson's argument hinges on an understanding of aesthetic response as sensory perception. Beauty is a secondary quality, just as Locke would classify sound and color: "There is nothing like our ideas, existing in the bodies themselves."[23] The possibility of an internal sense organ that perceives without reflection emerged in the seventeenth century, and Hutcheson uses Lockean empiricism to elaborate Shaftesbury's internal sense.[24] Beautiful things produce pleasure not from "any Knowledge of Principles, Proportions, Causes, or of the Usefulness of the Object," even "the most accurate Knowledge." They instead "strike us at first with the Idea of Beauty."[25]

However, if the perception of beauty is sensory, then it is accomplished through an internal sense that functions slightly differently from the five external senses. There is no guarantee that an individual will be able to perceive the beautiful and its pleasures. Even if the disinterested spectator is separate from the object and does not imagine himself into that object, aesthetic perception still necessitates action.[26] The perception of the aesthetic requires discrimination. Just as some people have better external sensory perception than others, so too do others have superior perception through their internal sense, though there is no promise of the remediation available through scientific instrumentation. Hutcheson finds this distinction first in ordinary sensory perception, for an individual "of a good Taste" may feel "Pleasure of Beauty or Harmony" from an external sense. As he moves to define the internal sense of aesthetic perception, the possibility narrows. Hutcheson creates the notion of internal sense by eliminating what the aesthetic is *not*: it is neither cognition nor volition, so it is therefore sensory.[27] The aesthetic concerns "higher, and more delightful Perceptions," and this is implicitly an experiential realm available to those who can access this sense, namely, the disinterested spectator who has the "Power of receiving such Impressions."[28]

Hutcheson's aesthetics "offers a model of 'knowing' without knowledge";[29] it is "abstract, without being cerebral."[30] Later in the century, as Peter de Bolla has demonstrated, aesthetic experience came to be understood through, alternately, a regime of the eye or that of the picture, a distinction that points to the contrast between seeing the ideal viewer as either untrained or schooled.[31]

Aesthetics is simultaneously an intellectual category and a mediation of beauty, but its dependence on sensory perception requires that the ideal observer be imagined as well. Disinterestedness removes sensory perception from the vagaries of the subject's desires by renouncing any claim to possession. The aesthetic response is one that admires but does not desire; it positions the observer at a distance from the object under consideration, a process that simultaneously ensures and reflects the observer's integrity and detachment. The disinterested spectator endeavors to be active insofar as this internal sense must be recognized, acknowledged, and cultivated as a source of legitimate information. But as a form of sensory perception, the internal sense joins the other senses—the external senses of Hutcheson's analysis—as a conduit to receive knowledge, in its ideal form, without the disruptive effects of cognition.

To circle back to Sprat's and Cowley's visions, natural philosophy ensures superior aesthetic perception of the natural world because the observer will apprehend "the real Object."[32] Sprat and Cowley do not pause to consider aesthetics as sensory perception, only the production of aesthetic objects that, from their perspective, inevitably give viewers pleasure. One hundred years later, Edmund Burke and Immanuel Kant focus the aesthetic on mental imagines, as Frances Ferguson has shown.[33] Yet the seventeenth-century insistence on "the real Object" and the commensurate subject able to perceive according to this dictum reveals a profound, if unexpected, alliance between the modest witness of natural philosophy and the disinterested spectator of aesthetics. This affinity, moreover, illuminates the twinned conceptual work of discrimination and repudiation inherent to both forms of knowledge.

The internal sensory perception of aesthetics may supply individuals a way to recognize beauty, but this is a restricted possibility. In Jacques Rancière's "distribution of the sensible," the aesthetic is always political, for each medium enacts a "delimitation of spaces and times, of the visible and the invisible, of speech and noise."[34] As we have seen in Shaftesbury and Hutcheson, early eighteenth-century aesthetics actively delimits; it can be understood as an act of classification, but it also needs to be understood as policing what art is and is not, as well as who may or may not apprehend it. Rancière reminds us, "Politics revolves around what is seen and what can be said about it, around who has the ability to see and the talent to speak, around the properties of spaces and the possibilities of time."[35] Within the specific context of early eighteenth-century Britain, those who are able to tell the difference, moreover, are endowed with the virtue of aesthetic disinterestedness and refined sociability. To perceive the aesthetic meant to fashion oneself a member of a particular community, a move that by necessity needed to be obscured. As we shall see, the possibilities of the aesthetic in poems grappling with scientific tropes and figures foretell a reconfiguration of subject, object, and process.

POPE'S THINGS

Alexander Pope's *The Rape of the Lock* is indisputably concerned with aesthetics, and articulates this concern by representing myriad forms of beauty—Belinda's, the beau monde's, the poem's. The mock epic charts the cosmetic construction of the main character in the famous dressing table scene, details the richness of various luxury objects available to the urban elite of London, and self-consciously reflects on the beauty of its own poetic form, the heroic couplet.

Yet among the many items lost to the "Lunar Sphere" in the final canto are objects associated with experimental philosophy: "Cages for Gnats, and Chains to Yoak a Flea;/Dry'd Butterflies, and Tomes of Casuistry."[36] These are the possessions of a virtuoso. They appear alongside various affects of the beau monde, such as beaux's wits "in *Snuff-boxes* and *Tweezer-Cases*," "broken Vows," "The Courtier's Promises," "The Smiles of Harlots, and the Tears of Heirs" (5.116, 117, 119, 120). Belinda's lock too rises up into the Lunar Sphere by the poem's end. The collection of items Pope groups together suggests a relation among them that hinges on a shared quality of ephemerality. Experimental philosophy shows up in *The Rape of the Lock* as evidence that it had infiltrated modern, fashionable life and served as yet another fashionable accoutrement of the urban beau monde.[37]

Pope's evocation of experimental philosophy in *The Rape of the Lock* accomplishes far more than a thematic indictment of the frivolity of both science and society, however. Epistemologically, experimental philosophy equips Pope with the tools to model imagining sights unseen. As I discuss in Chapter 1, accurate observation of previously unknown worlds is a mainstay of experimental philosophy, and descriptions of these findings use language that often focuses on wonder and aesthetic refinement. The instrument maker and lecturer Benjamin

Martin, for instance, is in awe of the "World of Miniature," "the curious Forms, the particular Structure of Parts, and the rich Colours that adorn most of the invisible Tribes of Animals!"[38] Pope's own language draws on such figurative models; the otherworldly entities in *The Rape of the Lock* are arguably possible to imagine because of the optical instruments and practices integral to experimental philosophy, especially microscopy.[39] The sylphs, sylphids, fays, fairies, genies, elves, and demons added to the five-canto version are likewise members of such "invisible Tribes of Animals," notable for their curious forms, particular structures, and rich colors: they are "Transparent Forms, too fine for mortal Sight," with "fluid bodies half dissolv'd in Light" and "Dipt in the richest Tincture of the Skies" (2.61, 2.62, 2.64). They even have "silken wings" and a "thin Essence" (2.130, 2.132), properties visible only through a microscope's magnifying lens.

What inaugurates the poem's rapid and cluttered miniaturization? The provocatively banal phrase, "trivial Things" (1.2). The poem's preoccupation with things refers in part to contemporary consumer culture. *The Rape of the Lock* is a mock-epic chock-full of things from consumer culture.[40] The Twickenham Pope editor wryly observes that "the epic is thing-less beside Pope's poem with its close-packed material objects"; Helen Deutsch suggests that Pope's is a miniaturized epic, a "curiosity cabinet" of a poem; and Jonathan Lamb reads Belinda and her world not merely as objects but as surfaces like still lives, stripped of their inherited meanings.[41] These are the now *describable* objects that began to populate the novelistic tradition with Defoe.[42] In the poem's first description of Belinda, we visually enter her chamber along with the sun's beams, but Belinda is only metonymically evoked as a pair of eyes blinking awake. The poem provides much more detailed focus on accessories of a fashionable woman, such as a bell to call for the maid, a slipper, a silver watch, and a "downy Pillow" (1.19).

But Pope's *things* also allude to experimental philosophy's *things*. As we have seen, the term *things* is an important keyword for experimental philosophers; it connotes the observed particular that is simultaneously empirical and literary. While Swift's attention to *things* in *Gulliver's Travels* serves an explicitly political critique of instrumental reason, Pope's elaboration challenges the notion of aesthetic and scientific disinterest by exposing the instability of material objects. In *The Rape of the Lock,* the repeated reference to "unnumber'd" objects—all of those things that include the "unnumber'd Spirits" who fly around Belinda, the "Unnumber'd Treasures" of Belinda's toilette, and the "Unnumber'd Throngs" swarming the Cave of Spleen (1.41, 3.129, and 4.47)—reveals that *things* are uneasy composites of material and theory that only seem to be solely observed particulars. Within a self-consciously aesthetic production, Pope meditates on observation and things. Literary knowledge in *The Rape of the Lock* introduces a more expansive mode of observation than is possible in experimental philosophy and, as a result, exposes things as existing over a temporal plane. Those "quick poetic eyes" at the poem's conclusion unveil a form of ocular apprehension that can perceive the transformation of a thing over time. *The Rape of the Lock* trains us to see the history of a thing within its formal embodiment; any single thing is the accumulation of its material existence, even if that materiality is no longer necessarily visible to an untrained eye. This is how literary knowledge provides a fuller and more accurate view of the world.

The Cave of Spleen vividly enacts the doubled nature of Pope's *things* as at once embodying an object's present and past. With an excursion to this ephemeral and peculiar world, Pope's poem displays the plasticity and historicity of matter and, as a consequence, trains readers in the protocols of accurate observation. Following the hard edges of the scissors that conclude canto 3, the Cave of Spleen takes us far away from the social spaces of Hampton Court: "A constant *Vapour* o'er the Palace flies;/Strange Phantoms rising as the Mists arise" (4.39–40). Pope's Cave of Spleen is a netherworld characterized by mists similar to the "Airy Substance" of the sylphs themselves (3.152), and the term *vapour* even appears twice more (4.18, 4.59). When Umbriel arrives, "Unnumber'd Throngs on ev'ry side are seen/Of Bodies chang'd to various Forms by *Spleen*" (4.47–48). Here, bodies have transformed into hybrids, new forms of embodiment that maintain elements and features of their original shape. The poem's language leisurely underscores their seeming discordance:

> Here living *Teapots* stand, one Arm held out,
> One bent; the Handle this, and that the Spout;
> A Pipkin there like *Homer's Tripod* walks;
> Here sighs a Jar, and there a Goose-pye talks;
> Men prove with Child, as pow'rful Fancy works,
> And Maids turn'd Bottels, call aloud for Corks. (4.49–54)

To imagine the various bodies in the Cave of Spleen, Pope alludes to Dryden's translation of Ovid's *Metamorphoses* and Anne Finch's "Ode to Spleen." With the Gnome's descent, he also parodies the epic hero's journey to the underworld. Confining our understanding of the various bodies in the Cave of Spleen only to these influences, though, blinds us to the ways in which these figures invoke—and transform—experimental philosophy's language of things. In the Cave of Spleen, present participles animate inert objects, suggesting a vividly organic place where the objects and people of ordinary life actively acquire new forms and new meanings. With its lifelike things and thing-like lives, the Cave of Spleen contains sights that are beyond normal apprehension, giving free play to a basic premise of experimental philosophy: the natural world has innumerable wonders, if one only knows where and how to look. This is the lesson of attentiveness that Robert Boyle teaches in *A Proemial Essay*.[43] But it is more than that: one must also recognize that matter contains traces of its own history. Pope teaches us that things do not solely exist in space; they also exist in time.

The bodies in the Cave of Spleen could be read as merely transformed in a hodgepodge manner. Yet Pope eliminates this possibility by linking these bodies to the spleen as an affliction, a type of melancholia. The ailments represented in these fanciful bodies are common to splenetics (4.47–54, note), and Pope included his own gloss of the talking goose-pye to draw the connection, claiming that it "alludes to a real fact, a Lady of distinction imagin'd herself in this condition" (4.52, note). For most eighteenth-century contemporaries, both men and women can suffer from the spleen, but Pope restricts the condition to women, save for the single line about pregnant men (4.59–62, note). The gendering of the spleen accords with how these bodies refer to something beyond their own physical selves and how they function as interpretive clues. The spleen is a physical condition that is also a *sign* of something else, in this case a psychological disorder. Given the proto-psychoanalytic discourse of the spleen, Freud's famous *Fragment of an Analysis of a Case of Hysteria* is instructive. Freud reads "Dora's" symptoms, which included "dyspnoea, *tussis nervosa*, aphonia, and possibly migraines, together with depression, hysterical unsociability and a *taedium vitae*," as signifying "the representation—the realization—of a phantasy with a sexual content, that is to say, it signifies a sexual situation." Each symptom has behind it "a number of secrets" to be detected by the analyst. Symptoms are particular forms imbued with theoretical significance; in Freud's case, that theoretical significance concerns his theory of female sexuality.[44]

These physical symptoms are *things*—the observed particular filtered through a theoretical apparatus, although those observations seem to represent specific objects empirically. Splenetic symptoms appear to be physical entities in their own right, while they also stand in metonymically for something else. Pope literalizes the metaphor, as does Swift, but he also twists the literalized metaphor into another figure. In the Cave of Spleen, Pope extends the logic of the thing to the extreme by turning bodies into symptoms altogether: the living teapots, the pregnant men, the women as bottles calling for their corks have all become only the symptom of the disease that the symptom represents. They are reduced to interpretive clues—paradoxically, to bodies of theory. These bodies are embodied metaphors, but they are also metaphors for something else altogether.

Pope plays with such transformations throughout *The Rape of the Lock*, often using metonymic logic. Peers and dukes are "Garters, Stars and Coronets" (1.85), and beaux are "Wigs" and "Sword-knots" (1.101). However, the poem does not go to the same lengths as in the Cave of Spleen to insist that these material transformations are literal; peers, dukes, and beaus are not transformed into their accoutrements. The metonyms reduce their subjects, of course, to critique the beau monde's emphasis on appearance, and Pope's metonymic and satiric usage obscures the referent to make the satiric point. The difference with the Cave of Spleen is important to remember: there, Pope attenuates such figurative transformations by representing them as literal. The insight the poem grants is an illustration of the process that observation assumes but also attempts to erase. As readers, we are instructed in the transformation of observed particulars that *seem* to be only and exclusively particular substances, even though they are not. The bodies in the Cave of Spleen not only contain traces of their previous forms, but they also function as signs of a disorder well beyond bodily impairment. Popean things have histories. Popean things also function, paradoxically, as embodiments of abstractions.

Reading the splenetic forms of the Cave of Spleen clarifies *The Rape of the Lock*'s other great scene of transformation, Belinda's toilette. The dressing table scene is a moment at which Belinda's physical appearance emerges through the sylphs' magical cosmetic powers, metonymically represented by objects that appear to mutate mystically. "Th'inferior Priestess," Belinda's maid, Betty, "begins the sacred Rites of Pride," and the materials of the toilette are thrust into motion, active in their peculiar agency:

> Unnumber'd Treasures ope at once, and here
> The various Off'rings of the World appear;
> From each she nicely culls with curious Toil,
> And decks the Goddess with the glitt'ring Spoil.
> This Casket *India's* glowing Gems unlocks,
> And all *Arabia* breathes from yonder Box.

> The Tortoise here and Elephant unite,
> Transform'd to *Combs*, the speckled and the white. (2.127–136)

I have argued elsewhere that this scene writes out the physical figure of Belinda, displacing her through an ekphrastic rendering of her cosmetics. The effect of this strategy is to evoke and erase the female subject to promote one aesthetic ideology (ekphrasis) over another (cosmetics).[45] Concurrent with this earlier argument about aesthetics is my focus on Pope's things as a form of literary knowledge. While the objects on Belinda's dressing table are not refigured into symptoms of a nervous disorder as the splenetic forms in the Cave of Spleen are, they certainly are signs of the commercial networks that undergird the early eighteenth-century mercantilist economy and furnish London consumers access to such "glitt'ring Spoil." As Laura Brown has astutely argued, Belinda's beauty, whether "created or awakened is attributed to the products of trade and defined through a catalogue of commodities for female consumption"; as such, "female adornment becomes the main cultural emblem of commodity fetishism."[46]

Brown's reading continues to be so persuasive because the things that fashion Belinda carry with them the traces of their own transformations. These objects strike one as resoundingly inert bodies—they are gems, perfume, and combs, after all—and in this way, they are unlike the mixture of lifelike things and thing-like beings that organically populate the Cave of Spleen. But the items from Belinda's dressing table are explicitly animated and evoke—in some ways, even revert to—the forms that they had *before* they were converted into commodities and traded in the global marketplace. The dressing table presents things that, given the symptomatic renderings to come in the Cave of Spleen, are infused with animation because they continue to embody their original forms. The text insists, in particular, that the combs adorning Belinda's hair overtly refer to the tortoise shell and elephant tusk that they originally were. The things on Belinda's dressing table are Popean things because they gesture to two forms at once and thereby demonstrate the lingering presence of a substance's original form even when it undergoes the transformative effects of commodification. What results is a mode of observation that demands the reader see both things at once—an object's past and its present. Pope's vision of aesthetic observation contrasts with scientific observation because his allows for a temporally expansive view that sees an object's history within its current material presence.

Pope repeats his theory of things and observation in miniature in the final canto when an enraged Belinda draws her "deadly *Bodkin*" (5.88). It is hardly deadly, much less a weapon—the bodkin here is a hairpin, after all—but the irony proliferates nonetheless. Pope presents a parenthetical genealogy to chart the bodkin's material and symbolic degradation from a sign of a paternal ancestor's political power to an ornamental buckle to a child's whistle to its current form, a lady's adornment:

> (The same, his ancient Personage to deck,
> Her great great Grandsire wore about his Neck
> In three *Seal-Rings*; which after, melted down,
> Form'd a vast *Buckle* for his Widow's Gown:
> Her infant Grandame's *Whistle* next it grew,
> The *Bells* she gingled, and the *Whistle* blew;
> Then in a *Bodkin* grac'd her Mother's Hairs,
> Which long she wore, and now *Belinda* wears.) (5.89–96)

By canto 5, the reader is accustomed to viewing objects as existing on a temporal plane. Here the message indicates the allure of adornment. But the satire also emerges in the sentence's punctuation and its effects. Pope delivers this history of the bodkin within parentheses, which serve the purpose of deferring—and belittling—Belinda's angry speech. Just as her bodkin was once an embodiment of political power and now is merely a cosmetic accessory, so too is Belinda's ability to threaten devoid of power and reduced to parody. Her rage is genuine; her capacity to act meaningfully on that rage is eviscerated.

Belinda's hair is the object that most profoundly changes form in *The Rape of the Lock*. This transformation is, after all, the narrative premise of the poem. In the spirit of the various mutations enacted elsewhere, the poem explicitly indicates that hair can take on any number of forms. A hair might be a slight substance, but its effects are incommensurately grand. The power of hair includes effects on hearts "held in slender Chains," birds snared in "hairy Sprindges," fish caught by "Slight Lines of Hair," and "Man's Imperial Race" lured by "Fair Tresses" (2.23–27). As the poet concludes, "Beauty draws us with a single Hair" (2. 28). We are told that Belinda's locks will have a similar effect, though on a much grander scale—"the Destruction of Mankind" (2.19). Her hair follows a specific trajectory of transformation through the course of the poem: it morphs from hair to a pair of matching curls to a single snipped curl to the tail of a star to a poem, "This *Lock*" (5.149). The toilette scene interestingly refrains from describing how Belinda's hair changes form initially, except to indicate that the sylphs work busily, and so our introduction to the curls comes in canto 2. Belinda, we learn, "Nourish'd two Locks, which graceful hung behind/In equal Curls, and well conspir'd to deck/With shining Ringlets the smooth Iv'ry Neck" (2.20–22). Clarissa later lectures Belinda that "Curl'd or uncurl'd" "Locks will turn to grey" (5.26), but the idea that Belinda's hair is subject to art—that its substance is molded into an aesthetic form—is clear from the beginning of the poem. The verbs *nourish'd* and *conspir'd* associate the process of molding hair into an aesthetic form with a savvy, knowing subject, one who views beauty as a means of acquiring social power.

Although hair can grow back, the poet's language ("thy ravish'd Hair!" [4.10]) and Belinda's lament ("any Hairs but these" [4.176]) together indicate that hers is what Joseph Roach calls "social hair," a performance "with all its magic and its risks."[47] In this case, Belinda's curls are stunningly beautiful, profoundly fragile, and metonymies for her chastity. When Ariel warns that a dire event will take place, whether "some frail *China* Jar receive a Flaw,/Or stain her Honour, or her new Brocade" (2.106–107), the poem famously forces an equivalence among the snipped curl, cracked china, stained fabric, and sexual experience, a similarity that also reinforces a commensurate loss of value. The parodic tension of the poem, of course, depends on these confusions, just as the rape refuses to be settled as literal or figurative.[48]

In the face of Belinda's blinding fury, the poet insists that the apotheosis of Belinda's hair is visible, if only to the figures of the "Muse" and the poet. Pope famously writes, "But trust the Muse—she saw it upward rise,/Tho' mark'd by none but quick Poetic eyes" (5.123–124). Do the "quick Poetic eyes" of *The Rape of the Lock* evoke experimental philosophy's modest witness? Or the aesthetic disinterestedness imagined by Shaftesbury and Hutcheson? No one in the poem's beau monde has the qualities to be a perceptive observer. Almost by poem's end, the curl is visible and comprehensible only to the knowing viewer, who is credentialed to discern the aesthetics and epistemology of things. In the first instance, this can only be those "quick Poetic eyes," but in the second, it is the reader of the poem. The model of ocular apprehension imagined in *The Rape of the Lock* is at once exclusive and expansive. Readers of the poem, equipped with the insights of literary knowledge, may figuratively see the conversion of Belinda's hair into an astrological figure.

Once Belinda has risked all with her "social hair," and lost, the poet explicitly enters the poem to insist that she is amply compensated by the curl's apotheosis and the publication of "*This Lock*" (5.149). After the final transformation of the curl into a poem, *The Rape of the Lock*, Pope assures Belinda, will bring her much more fame—and much more *lasting* fame—than a lock on her head ever could. Repeating Clarissa's earlier warning about the transience of physical beauty, Pope promises Belinda that even after "your self shall die," "*This Lock,* the Muse shall consecrate to Fame,/And mid'st the Stars inscribe *Belinda's* Name!" (5.149–150). Because of the Baron, Belinda is left with the "Sister-Lock," which she says "now sits uncouth, alone," for curls—like couplets—come in pairs (4.171). Imagined as an ultimately compensatory move, the poet takes the fact of the snipped curl and produces couplets in its ironic honor.

Pope's transformation of a piece of hair into so many other things is perhaps the most ambitious and banal of the poem's effects, a coincidence of figuration that uneasily elevates and trivializes its subject. That Belinda's hair changes form several times is clearly a central conceit of the poem, but my previous analysis has demonstrated that these transformations cannot be interpreted in isolation. Taken together, the sylphs, the Cave of Spleen, the bodkin, and the dressing table instead anchor the poem's preoccupation with the epistemology of things, of which the transformation of a curl into couplets is the most significant example. These moments require a mode of representation that emphasizes an observed particular's theoretical significance and gives cluelike traces to its material history. The model of apprehension available through the experimental method offers some insight into this form of knowledge, but the poem presents the alternative of aesthetic observation and literary knowledge as the more appropriate mode.

Things may well change in *The Rape of the Lock*, but as they do, they carry within them various aesthetic hierarchies, material and theoretical indices, and ideological imperatives. The couplets that ultimately make up *The Rape of the Lock* need to be understood in relation to the poem's representation of its things. If Pope's couplets as a form work toward "refinement," as J. Paul Hunter suggests, then the transformation of curl to couplet is a key example of that process of refinement.[49] As much as the fantasy of the poem labors to eradicate Belinda's curl from "This *Lock*," replacing one with the other and leaving it at that, such a transformation is profoundly and necessarily incomplete. Even with the abstracting powers of refinement at work in the poem, disembodying Belinda and leaving only words on a page, the movement from an adorned and sexualized female body to a poem powerfully indicates that the form of the poem is inextricably linked and indebted to that body. Belinda's curl thereby exposes the process by which a thing—as a simultaneously aesthetic, epistemological, and ideological category—is valued according to its theoretical status, though it can never be extricated from the material conditions that gave rise to it.

QUEEN CAROLINE'S HERMITAGE

The apotheosis of Belinda's lock into a star and then into *The Rape of the Lock* hallmarks the imaginative potential Pope identifies with poetic observational practice: the act of observing makes visible the traces of historical transformation that the material bodies of the diurnal world have undergone. The transformations I have discussed are even more remarkable because they seem to be agentless: the reader observes them virtually through the mediation of the text, but they occur within the mystified logic of the poem. Belinda's lock carries meaning, but it does not connote agency. It is an object. It is a trophy.

Belinda's lock is first objectified by the Baron: he views Belinda's curl as another trophy to add to his "Altar of Love." Yet the Baron is not singular in this desire; indeed, the ownership and possession of Belinda's hair animates the poem's conflict among the beau monde and, ultimately, its transformation into a poetic figure. The Baron cannot hold onto the aesthetic object—Belinda's lock—because he misunderstands the social contract of aesthetic theory that Shaftesbury and Hutcheson espouse. The narrative of *The Rape of the Lock* insists that the Baron fails because he does not recognize that Belinda's beauty is to be admired rather than possessed.

Aesthetic mediation helps us to apprehend the moral errors that Pope identifies in *The Rape of the Lock*; it also supplies an important heuristic to understand the relationship among trophies, aesthetics, and natural philosophy. This triangulation, implicit in *The Rape of the Lock*, appears in the context of a sculptural monument to natural philosophy that was also commemorated in poetry—a poetic mediation of an aesthetic trophy. In the early 1730s, Queen Caroline commissioned William Kent to design a monument to celebrate natural philosophy and physico-theology. The result was the Hermitage in the royal gardens at Richmond Lodge, her favorite retreat.[50] Celebrated as "A Temple from vain glories free,/Whose Goddess is Philosophy," Caroline's Hermitage explicitly framed these accomplishments as innovations heralding "*Britannia's ... classic age.*"[51] Rather than feature the "spoils of martial fields," Caroline's Hermitage displayed "more noble trophies."[52] And those trophies? They were busts of Isaac

Newton, John Locke, William Wollaston, Samuel Clarke, and—the Hermitage's "presiding deity"—Robert Boyle.[53]

Why did Caroline build a monument to religion and science, imagined as "trophies"? There are biographical hints we can gather. The queen's interest in natural philosophy was deep: she attended lectures at the Royal Society with her husband, George Augustus, and she also facilitated scientific debates between Leibniz and Samuel Clarke about Newtonian calculus.[54] She amassed a formidable library and maintained a cabinet of curiosities, which included a lodestone, an ivory tusk, and scientific instruments.[55] In 1736, Voltaire praised Caroline as Émilie du Châtelet's intellectual equal—both princesses of the Enlightenment.[56]

The construction of the Hermitage transformed Caroline's interests into a built landscape and statuary for royal consumption; its name, of course, evokes solitude, even though the retreat was also available to a wider public. Caroline's Hermitage moved natural philosophy from the laboratory, parlor, and shop into an explicitly aesthetic space. Built in 1732–1733, it resembled a hermit's cell and sat in the park's woodlands at the end of a long walkway, nestled into a hillside covered with bushes and fir trees.[57] To some, it evoked "*Calypso's* fabled cell," a Homeric allusion to subversive female power.[58] The exterior of the Hermitage was designed to appear indistinguishable from nature, an effect—as Jill H. Casid notes of imperial landscapes more generally—that obscures the process and history of its own construction.[59] But commentators also viewed it as a simulacrum: the Hermitage "very much resembles Antiquity," though it was "lately done, (within these three Years)."[60] And while its natural, rustic exterior seemed "just like a shallow cave by nature made," the interior was adorned with stalactites, suggesting the encroachment of nature and the passage of time, and arranged according to neoclassical design, with a central domed octagon about sixteen feet in diameter, flanked by two rectangular wings (one a bedroom and the other a library), and extended by an exedra with an altar.[61]

The arrangement of the Hermitage's sculptures conveyed the structure's intellectual argument. On the left were busts of Newton and Locke, on the right of Wollaston and Clarke. The center, the honorific space of the exedra's altar, was reserved for Boyle's bust, framed by a sunburst painted on the wall. Boyle was a fitting centerpiece: in his will, the author of *The Christian Virtuoso* (1690) endowed a lecture series devoted to discussing the existence of God. As the *Gentleman's Magazine* recounts, the Hermitage's design privileged Boyle's contributions and significance: "the Bust of Mr *Boyle* stands higher than these, on a Pedestal, in the inmost, and, as it were, the most sacred Recess of the Place; behind his Head a large Golden Sun, darting his wide spreading Beams all about and towards the others, to whom his Aspect is directed."[62] The image of Boyle struck the viewer immediately: "Upon entering, you behold, elevated on high, a very curious busto of the Honourable, and justly celebrated, Robert Boyle, Esq; incompassed with rays of gold."[63] Whether the light emanates from Boyle or encases him, the image visualizes enlightenment.

The Hermitage presented natural philosophy as an aesthetic experience in a second, mediated fashion. The arrival of the Boyle bust (months after the others were installed) not only garnered significant attention in the press but also occasioned the first literary contest in an English journal.[64] In April 1733, the *Gentleman's Magazine* announced a competition for works commemorating the Hermitage, explaining that a panel of five judges would select the first- and second-prize winners and that, if the contest were popular, the periodical would hold a contest on another topic the following year. The editor invited submissions from both men and women, from England or Ireland.[65] Poems that did not win a ranked place were published in a book, *The Contest: Being Poetical Essays on the Queen's Grotto*.

The literary record presented by this poetry contest associates the Hermitage with natural philosophy, rather than with physico-theology, and especially foregrounds Boyle and Newton. Stephen Duck, for example, asks the muse to take him "to the sequester'd Cell,/Where Boyle and Newton, mighty Sages! dwell."[66] Another poet describes Boyle as having a "happy genius, [and] piercing mind" that together "did science clear,/Philosophy from rust refin'd."[67] A poem devoted entirely to honoring Boyle (the only of the group to have a single figure as its subject, "Ode on the Bust of the Hon. Robert Boyle, Esq; in her Majesty's Grotto") opens with a characteristic apostrophe: "Nature, O Boyle! tho' hid in night,/Her laws, to Thee, were clear as light."[68] He is commended for the "coy pow'r" of his observations, which enable him to view "the secret springs of nature," and for "his *all discovering ray*."[69] Poems embody Boyle's "enlighten'd science," which "Solves all our doubts, and ignorance disarms," by alluding to the placement of his bust in the Hermitage's exedra, framed by radiating sunbeams.[70] According to the logic of similitude, Boyle himself is a source of light in a poem that reflects and reflects on an aesthetic monument to him. In Jane Brereton's "On the Bustoes in the Royal Hermitage," "*Wisdom*, and *Piety*, their Beams unite/To shine in *Boyle*, with strong, convictive Light."[71] The author of "On the Queen's

Grotto" makes the link between Boyle's illuminating power and his pursuit of experimental knowledge explicit:

> Boyle first arose, and, like the morning star,
> Gave joyful promise of the *day's* approach:
> With *patient search* he from the *plain effect*
> Trac'd the *remoter cause*; and, with success,
> Into the secret springs of nature div'd.[72]

Although Boyle repeatedly declined to speculate about the causes of phenomena (which he called "medling"), claiming only to record the observation, the poet admires Boyle for unlocking nature's mysteries by determining origins, or "the remoter cause."[73] In the context of occasional poetry, the particulars of Boyle's methodology matter less than his popular reputation as a natural philosopher, devoted to the "patient search."[74]

Praise for Newton uses similar metaphors to cite and commend his observational acumen. Like Boyle, Newton is represented through figures of illumination. As the "ornament and wonder of his age," "sagacious" Newton "Sublimely, on the Wings of Knowledge, soars."[75] He is praised for casting light on the shadows of earlier generations' mistakes—"The system never was from errors free/Till Newton rose and said, *Let darkness flee*"—and for bringing the mysteries of the natural world into clear focus ("The works of nature, that in embryo lay,/Dawn into life, and in a flood of day/Newton's great genius to the world convey"[76]). He is also admired for improving all bodies of knowledge that he considered: "Whate're he touch'd, howe'er abstruse his theme,/He clear'd the rubbish, and refin'd the scheme."[77] Lauded for discovering "the laws" governing "the *shining orbs*," Newton is imagined to be "Enraptur'd" while studiously observing the sky as he "track[ed] the planets wand'ring way,/And orbits where excentrick comets stray."[78] Such is the magnificence of his insight that his name is presented as a synonym for the natural world itself: "Nature and Newton mean the very same."[79]

The poems in the *Gentleman's Magazine*'s contest collectively glorify the skills of insight and innovation that Boyle and Newton exemplify by figuring them as beacons (often literally) for the advancement of knowledge. However, while the poems imagine the figures of Boyle and Newton as objects of admiration, they do not propose that readers ought to emulate them or even attempt to replicate their experiments.

The purpose of these poems differs markedly from the educational texts widely available in the marketplace: the Hermitage poems foreground their literary transformation of natural philosophy to encourage a reader's reflection and, in particular, a reader's admiration. The aesthetic mediation of natural philosophy results in poetry designed to make readers ruminate. Caroline herself actively cultivated the role of reader: according to *An Essay towards the character of Her late Majesty Caroline, queen-consort of Great Britain*, Caroline "was frequently engaged in reading such Books as are rarely attempted but by persons of much leisure and retirement."[80] The site of the British worthies, nestled preciously within the Hermitage, was not a laboratory for followers to reproduce experiments or to make their own discoveries; this was not the virtual witnessing of experimental philosophy. It was, instead, a site for the meditative postures that the poets imagine the queen and other visitors would strike. Some represent the collection of busts as "for contemplation form'd."[81] Others claim that "solemn silence guards the place."[82] The model for contemplation is Caroline, portrayed in deep repose in the Hermitage. With the busts in her view, she "feeds on thoughts sublime, which raise the mind/Above the trifling cares of humankind"; she "loves that solitary scene/To converse with the learned dead"; and "Hither at chosen hours,/The royal Hermit takes her lonely way,/Indulging thoughts which lift the raptur'd soul/Above mortality."[83] She is, in all of these instances, an example of the reflection that one is expected to assume in the vicinity of the Hermitage.

The subjectivity imagined through the Hermitage poems refuses a desire for possession. The queen's engagement with the substance of the work extends only to admiration, "These are the studies which a Queen admires."[84] Of course, this statement willfully ignores the royal privilege and wealth that make such a space possible. But in aesthetic terms, the appropriate response to an aesthetically mediated science is admiration, not possession. Just as the busts are "in stone profoundly grave, as, when alive, in thought," so, too, are the queen and anyone else who visits the Hermitage drawn to contemplate its statuary.[85] When she turns away from the fleeting pleasures of a fashionable life, those "splendid scenes which females most admire," "the Solitary Queen . . . seeks her humble *Cell*."[86] The author of "To her Majesty, on her Grotto" likewise imagines the queen stealing away from "the splendid court's admiring train" to spend time by herself in the Hermitage.[87] Converting from direct address—the poet first wishes to "obtain the secret power/To trace thee in thy calm sequester'd hour"—the poet paints a picture of the Queen in third person.[88] The reader is enjoined to witness the queen's quiet occupancy of the Hermitage, during which she might look on "each *reverend bust* with *earnest gaze*" or "read th' *immortal labours* of their mind."[89] In the former instance, the poet imagines an affective response; on viewing the busts, "*dewy tears* her *tender conflict* tell."[90] The poet likewise imagines that the queen, when reading, pauses for "An *intervening glance* her thought relieves/And the *lov'd form* her *silent praise* receives," a look that arguably could be imagined to lead to the same affective response.[91] As a relatively singular example, this poem positions the queen as reading, but even then she quickly turns to thinking about the material and presumably its implications. These poems do not adhere to the protocols of observation and description that Boyle, Hooke, and others promulgated, but instead imagine activating the beholder's internal sense, perceiving science as aesthetic pleasure.

The Hermitage poems demand the production of more poetry. If, within this local context, the poems most vividly imagine visitors to the Hermitage or the queen herself admiring and gaining pleasure from the intellectual contributions of Boyle et al. because they can gaze at these sculptures, then these same poems also encourage others to write their own. The queen's oft-repeated and oft-admired contemplation prompts one poet to urge others to praise her (as the vast majority of the poems related to the Hermitage do), but the call is specific: the appropriate form of praise is presented as poetry, an aesthetic mediation that not only expresses but also reproduces admiration: "String to her praise, ye bards, your sounding lyres,/In ev'ry clime repeat her honor'd name,/And spread thro' hers your own immortal fame."[92] The fruits of quiet contemplation and the pleasure of learning extend the possibilities for new kinds of vision available. This is a vision of the imagination, sparked by figurative imagery and the aesthetic contract of admiration. That these implications are borne out by poetry suggests that aesthetic mediation registers possibilities natural philosophy cannot.

THOMSON'S WINTER; OR, DIFFERENCE

James Thomson's *The Seasons* (1730, 1744, 1746) is a poem famous for its celebration of Newtonianism. Drawing out the epistemological possibilities inherent in literariness, Thomson's poem presents a model of observation and understanding exceeding that which natural philosophy provides, but which the experimental imagination advances.

To begin, the poem's observational practices cannot be separated from its politics. *The Seasons* has long been understood as a celebration of Whiggish politics. Its Georgic—and Georgian—scope imagines the ideal viewer as a property owner who both embodies and asserts principles of British nationalism that locate England at the center of a global trade network, reimagined by Thomson as a mechanism for promulgating political liberty worldwide. Indeed, as Suvir Kaul wryly notes, Thomson's poem is "an encyclopedia of nationalist desire."[93] The poem's partisan attitudes are well documented and well debated. A particular critical preoccupation is whether the poem coheres in an idealistic vision of Britishness, even if that unity is the ideological product of an aristocratic subject position.[94] The prospect view in landscape poetry structurally replicates and mystifies the property owner's view and, by extension, his political and economic authority. By naturalizing this perspective, landscape poetry such as Thomson's aesthetically conveys legibility and authorization for imperial political structures.[95]

The Seasons legitimizes a simultaneously national and imperial ideology through its strong reading of a centralized poetic eye. The ocular potential of Thomson's poetry caught Wordsworth's attention, who praised Thomson for teaching "the art of seeing."[96] And what, precisely, did Thomson's "art of seeing" produce? According to Joseph Warton, *The Seasons* reflects a "minute and particular enumeration of circumstances" and a "close and faithful representation of nature."[97] Seeing and the world are bound together in Thomson's poetic vision—how one sees determines what one sees, in other words, a principle that itself cannot be extricated from the poem's engagement with and embodiment of Newtonian philosophy. Thomson's fascination with optics was evident from the time he published *The Seasons*: while teaching at Watts, an academy renowned for its embrace of Newtonian philosophy, Thomson dedicated *Winter* (1726) to Newton.[98]

Much like Caroline's Hermitage and the corpus of poetry celebrating it, *The Seasons* intermingles nationalistic ambition with the principles and effects of natural philosophy. In *Summer*, "Happy Britannia!" gives birth to Bacon, Boyle, Locke, and Newton.[99] Natural philosophy ensures modern enlightenment and, Thomson promises, a host of commensurate social benefits—the party line for advocates. "Without thee [natural philosophy] what were unenlightened man?/A savage, roaming through the woods and wilds," with "Nothing, save rapine, indolence, and guile,/And woes on woes, a still-revolving train" (*Summer*, 1758–1759, 1771–1772). "Taught by thee"—natural philosophy—"Ours are the plans of policy and peace;/To live like brothers" (*Summer*, 1774–1776), a dream of national progress that attributes British greatness to the epistemology and ideology of science. Natural philosophy exists as an all-pervasive, if invisible, force in the world: "like the liberal breath/Of potent heaven, invisible, the sail [natural philosophy]/Swells out, and bears the inferior world along" (*Summer*, 1780–1781). The all-encompassing influence of natural philosophy underscores the poem's celebratory narrative of progress and serves as evidence of its Whiggish politics.[100] But natural philosophy is also "invisible," perceivable only in its effects. And those effects are most easily apprehended through the modes of vision Thomson imagines in *The Seasons*.

The politics of the poem can be read as a straightforward and homogeneous Whiggish platform plank, but this downplays Thomson's commitment to "Patriot Opposition," which censured Walpole's domestic and foreign policy.[101] The political dissent that Thomson renders, even if provisionally, finds a stronger corollary in his critical embrace of science. If Thomson celebrates Newtonian optics, he likewise registers unease with the instrumentalization of natural philosophy. In a poem that overtly lauds social, aesthetic, and ideological divisions, instrument-aided vision challenges such boundaries. Thomson's caution is evident in his most graphic example of the natural philosophical method, the famous instance of the "microscopic eye," which he originally drafted for *Spring* but ultimately incorporated into *Summer* (*Summer*, 288). Thomson's choice of the microscope turns to one of the two instruments most regularly associated with the foundation of the Royal Society; the other was Boyle's air pump.[102] Thomson's evocation of microscopy does not portray an individual peering through a microscope but instead collapses the instrument with the eye. Thomson's image harks back to Locke's warning that microscopy blinds individuals to anything but the most minute—and the most trivial—of things, leaving such people unable to function within a commercial society. Thomson's image also evokes Cavendish's hybridization of scientific practice and physicality, the scientists in *The Blazing World* who embody their objects of study.

Why does Thomson introduce a microscopic eye? Its primary purpose is to document that "Full Nature swarms with life" (*Summer*, 289). Microscopy as a mode of ocularity makes visible organic material previously imperceptible. How one sees determines what one sees. This is the "art of seeing" in action. Thomson's phrase "Full Nature swarms with life" also echoes experimental accounts of microscopy, as do the poem's descriptions of various liquids: "Amid the floating verdure millions stray" and "Each liquid . . . /With various forms abounds" (*Summer*, 305, 306–308). Thomson here repeats the standard natural philosophic view that endorses optical instrumentation.[103] Multitudinous entities may be discovered through the instrument's powers of magnification, in effect transforming what seem to be smooth substances—"one transparent vacancy"—into "various forms" (*Summer*, 310, 308).

In Thomson's literary imagination, microscopy, and visual perception more generally, activate other senses, potentially creating a tidal wave of sensory perception. The organic bodies under the view of the microscopic eye are knowable through the mediating technology of the microscopic glass, but that instrument does not inoculate the viewer against an unmanageable influx of perceptions. Thomson's sharp warning addresses the figurative, epistemological, and even ontological implications of magnifying one's view, pointing to the limits and dangers of experimental knowledge acquisition. As anticipated in the evocation of "millions stray," the microscope cannot contain the minute wonders it reveals; close observation of them results only in their proliferation, a process that has the effect of leaving the viewer, as it turns out, "stunned with noise" (*Summer*, 317). Thomson's idea of the senses being interconnected finds an interesting precedent in Newton's *Opticks*, which uses simile to bind sight and sound: "May not the harmony and discord of Colours arise from the proportions of the vibrations propagated through the Fibres of the Optick Nerves into the Brain, as the harmony and discord of Sounds arise from the proportions of the Vibrations of the Air?"[104] Moreover, in the microscopic description of "liquid," Thomson includes the word *taste* (*Summer*, 308). The term may well indicate the cultural and aesthetic category, but in the context of Thomson's amplified sensory processes, it simultaneously introduces the possibility of the sense of taste. Kevis Goodman's insights are helpful: Thomson's microscopic eye sees the vegetation of a global landscape through an insistent, though incomplete, erasure of "unseen people" (*Summer*, 311). Thomson's microscopic eye paradoxically "reverses direction and opens out to an influx of the historical world," leaving the observer overwhelmed and stunned.[105] With this possibility of an optical instrument turning its magnification and surveillance on the observer, *Summer* shortly thereafter imagines a global tour to the "torrid zones" of Africa, South America, and India (*Summer*, 632ff.). The microscopic eye in *Summer* challenges what might be considered a safely confident imperial account with the reimagined power of the microscopic eye. Thomson's vignette uses experimental philosophical protocols to illuminate the vulnerability of visual perception.

The microscopic eye of *Summer* shows Thomson's interest in alternative modes of ocular perception, as well as a sustained interest in exploring their limits and implications. In *Summer*, Thomson contemplates the theoretical implications of these instruments, even if these effects might be well beyond the technological capability possible at the moment; scientific observation introduces only the possibility that the decaying object under view can leave the viewer similarly decayed. If microscopy promises mastery—and aspires to an imperial gaze—then it likewise contains the short-circuiting effect of its antithesis, which simultaneously opens up profound unease and anxiety as the observer is subjected to the onslaught of the spectacle.[106] Scenes of microscopic discovery threaten to infect not only the observer's senses but also the detached, genteel subjectivity advocates wished to associate with the praxis of scientific observation more generally. Magnification promises insight, yet it also implies the ontology of similitude and, by extension, infection. Bluntly stated, if the scenes under a microscope can turn back on the viewer, then that same viewer "would abhorrent turn," "stunned with noise" (*Summer*, 316, 317). The logic of infection embedded in "putrid steams" and "the living cloud/Of pestilence" means that the boundary between two bodies, that of the object and that of the observer, is porous (*Summer*, 292–294). This entanglement evokes both the doubled form of putrefaction and the subject of experimental philosophical project more generally.[107] While the replacement of vision with sound registers the fluidity of sensory perception, the threat of infection brings these connections between subjects and objects—between ways of seeing and ways of being seen—into focus.[108]

If summer's rotten energy threatens to infect both landscape and observer, then one might presume that the opposite season shuts down such boundary crossings. Winter blankets the landscape and the viewer, seemingly suspending nature and its infectious decay in the process. In winter, all is dreary and grim: "joyless rains" turn fields into an "unsightly plain" with a "brown deluge" (*Winter*, 73, 76, 77). "Reeling clouds/Stagger with dizzy poise" (*Winter*, 121–122). This is a wasteland, as Vittoria Di Palma would claim, defined not by what it has but what it lacks. As a lack, a wasteland serves as a productive figure of otherness, and Thomson's brutal and unforgiving winterscape appears to accomplish such othering.[109] The snow and ice are a "wintry waste," a "smothering ruin," a "glittery waste," a "solitary vast," a "frozen main," a "white abyss," a "boundless frost," or a "bleak expanse" (*Winter*, 419, 423, 798, 804, 805, 819, 915, 917). The snowstorm is a "whitening shower," "dimming the day"; the fields are covered in "their winter-robe of purest white./'Tis brightness all" (*Winter*, 229, 231, 233–234). Thomson's winter thwarts visual examination with its blinding optics of "brightness all."

Thomson introduces slight tonal differences that hint at a variegated landscape underneath, a difference that can exist only briefly when the fresh snow melts on the small creeks and streams that are not yet frozen: that is, "'Tis brightness all; save where the new snow melts/Along the mazy current" (*Winter*, 234–235). This one subtle sign of a boundary is an index of the landscape's difference, but even that is too fragile to remain: it is quickly subsumed by the all-encompassing storm. By dusk, "Earth's universal face, deep-hid and chill,/Is one wild dazzling waste, that buries wide/The works of man" (*Winter*, 238–240). Scrutiny and attention are the observational modes associated with landscape poetry.[110] But no matter how much an observer applies to this landscape, it cannot be differentiated. It cannot be read.

Thomson is not unique in representing snow as a case limit for observational work. The idea of snow producing an impenetrable topography is also expressed in Ambrose Philips's "A Winter-Piece" (1709), which wearily responds to a drawn-out winter in Copenhagen. The snow-covered landscape hinders ocular apprehension:

> The Hills and Dales, and the delightful Woods,
> The Flowry Plains, and Silver Streaming Floods,
> By Snow disguis'd, in bright Confusion lye,
> And with one dazzling Waste fatigue the Eye.[111]

If wintertime erases anything worth representing in poetry, then Philips conveys this principle (without seeming irony) within a poem whose subject is winter. Beyond this contradiction, Philips registers the difficulty a winter landscape produces for the perceiving body. The spectator's vision is overwhelmed by the bright uniformity of the snow-covered land; the sort of thinking that emerges from such optical confusion is both unclear and distracting.[112] To view a snow-covered prospect is to be induced into "fatigue," the human eye's skills for discrimination outmatched by the relenting similitude of a frozen horizon that looks to be "one dazzling Waste."

Thomson's *Winter* clearly participates in the literary tradition of topographical poetry that Philips represents, one that imagines the isolated individual beset by an overwhelming nature. Yet Thomson's language suggests a second allusion, Newtonianism, evident in the verbal echoes between *Winter* and Thomson's figuration of Newton's optics. In *A Poem Sacred to the Memory of Sir Isaac Newton* (London, 1727), Thomson returns to the language of *Winter* when he describes

Newton's prism. Thomson implies an affinity between the blanketing of white snow and that of light:

> Even *Light itself*, which every thing displays,
> Shone undiscover'd, till his brighter Mind
> Untwisted all the shining Robe of Day;
> And from the whitening, undistinguish'd Blaze,
> Collecting every Ray into his Kind,
> To the charm'd Eye educ'd the gorgeous Train
> Of *Parent-Colours*.[113]

As a "whitening, undistinguish'd Blaze," light introduces the effect of similitude on objects. Light passes this effect of similitude off as clarity, when it more accurately is the introduction of specific physical properties to the objects under consideration. As an optical instrument, the prism makes visible the difference of light, in contrast to the trope of reflection, which, as Karen Barad suggests, "reflects the themes of mirroring and sameness."[114] Optical instruments are a technology of mediation; so too is light.

Light is a medium on which all observation depends; Newton has taken that technology and applied another to it—the prism—to reveal that light is in fact an effect of various colors, a revelation that "charm'd" the observer's eye. Thomson's poem evokes the opening of Newton's famous first letter to the Royal Society dated February 6, 1672, recounting his early prismatic experiments. Setting up his room to function like a camera obscura, himself bathed in darkness, Newton placed a prism in a small beam of light coming through the shutter. His first reaction is illustrative: "It was at first a very pleasing divertissement to view the vivid and intense colours produced thereby."[115] Close observation of light through the prismatic technology produces pleasure in the observer.

Thomson's elaborate characterization of "light" shares properties with snow in *Winter*, as we recall, the poet views a "winter-robe of purest white./'Tis brightness all" (*Winter*, 233–234). Yet the resonance is more than incidental, for it points to a deeper epistemological connection between light and snow in Thomson's poetry. If the prism discloses the "*Parent-Colours*" that make up light, then light's similitude is in fact an effect of an invisible and unperceivable (without an optical instrument) difference. For all of its illuminating properties and associations with clarity and insight, light is most powerfully understood as the absence of difference. The poem's language emphasizes not similitude, but an absence of difference, and this is articulated most vividly through the gerund *whitening* and the negative prefix in *undistinguish'd*.

Thomson figures snow as overwhelming and as a sign of the absence of difference he associates with light. He also conveys particularly tragic consequences for specific bodies within that landscape. A swain enters the scene from the repository of Georgic convention, a poetic type vulnerable to winter's blinding and undifferentiated snowscape. While the storm develops, the swain "his own loose-revolving fields . . . /Disastered stands," lost and stranded (*Winter*, 278–279). As a swain, he is familiar with the land around him; he knows what should be where, but in the whiteness of winter, he mistakes a "dusky spot" (*Winter*, 290) for "His tufted cottage" (*Winter*, 291) and "wanders on/From hill to dale, still more and more astray—" (*Winter*, 283–284). The swain loses his way in a strong winter snowstorm, a dire circumstance that is directly attributable to his inability to see. Scientific observation promises to survey and render the landscape knowable; its failure here unveils the limits of ocular apprehension. The swain

> sees other hills ascend,
> Of unknown joyless brow; and other scenes,
> Of horrid prospect, shag the trackless plain;
> Nor finds the river nor the forest, hid
> Beneath the formless wild. (*Winter*, 279–283)

The preponderance of words in their negative formulation—*unknown, joyless, trackless, formless*, and, later, *shapeless drift* (*Winter*, 306)—in combination with the swain's stated failure to find either river or forest because they are hidden from view, create a scene in which a familiar landscape exists only as a trace of his mind's eye. The menace is physical, for the swain does not know where it is safe to step. In their material absence, the swain imaginatively sees the boundaries and contours constitutive of the ground, but this vision haunts him.

The snow-covered fields and hills contain only hints of what is not there, a repeated and insistent absence that has the effect of evoking its positive presence. The threat is underscored by the poem's refusal to imagine the snow through the trope of similitude. As a scene under erasure, the "wild dazzling waste" consumes the swain, materially transforming his body into a frozen waste. More than merely a tragic Georgic episode or an intellectual meditation on a negative epistemology, the "formless wild" of *Winter* is unreadable, almost unobservable. All that it allows the observer to apprehend is its "less"-ness—and this exacts a substantially greater cost than the fatigued eye that Ambrose Philips laments.

The swain weakens as "night resistless closes fast" (*Winter*, 294) and, shortly after, he dies from exposure. The landscape seems to absorb the swain, Alastor-like, as he is transformed from a living being to a corpse bleached as white as the snow-covered fields and hills (*Winter*, 317–321).

The swain's experience recalls—though with great tragedy—Anne Finch's "A Nocturnal Reverie," a single-sentence poem (and favorite of William Wordsworth) that dramatizes what happens when visual perception is thwarted at night. The natural world surrounding the poet shimmers in a series of gray shadows, images, and reflections that produce a more profound and true illumination than "fierce Light [that] disturbs, whilst it reveals."[116] The quality of light that allows for experimental practice, Finch suggests, introduces its own form of disruption, a contention that Thomson's description of the prism also explores. Light does not operate neutrally: there is a commensurate loss of vision that Finch associates with its presence. As a result, Finch's poem is interested in exploring a substitute form of observation, the imaginative observation, "When a sedate Content the Spirit feels," that is, when one is at peace.[117] At this moment, and presumably only in these circumstances of quiet and contented blindness, one cannot see but can still perceive: "silent Musings urge the Mind to seek/Something, too high for Syllables to speak."[118] That "Something" points to an object that has a material quality, even if it is indescribable and even if it is in excess of discourse.

The difference with Thomson's swain, of course, is that his silent musing occurs in a moment of despair and trauma. To enforce the tragedy, Thomson redoubles the perceptual complications under consideration: his swain is blinded not only by the snow but also by nightfall. Therefore, in a slightly different vein, though consonant with the notion of the materialism of thinking, the poem depicts pictorially the things that the swain *thinks* about as though they are visually and materially in his mind. Just as the prism exposes the difference in light that the eye cannot see on its own, here the swain's imagination perceives the differences that the snow obliterates. As a result, his imaginative vision activates and catalogs:

> Then throng the busy shapes into his mind
> Of covered pits, unfathomably deep,
> A dire descent! beyond the power of frost;
> Of faithless bogs; of precipices huge,
> Smoothed up with snow; and (what is land unknown,
> What water) of the still unfrozen spring,

> In the loose marsh or solitary lake,
> Where the fresh fountain from the bottom boils. (*Winter*, 297–304)

These specific topographical descriptions, accompanied by a recurring anxiety expressed adjectively ("dire," "faithless"), may well be represented here in the swain's imagination, but they accrue a material presence at the moment of their introduction in the poem. The words *throng* and *shapes* connote a material quality to these imaginative things, and suggest that they are, in fact, things in the experimental philosophical sense. What results is seeing that exceeds the limits of empirical observation.

Within the narrative of the observing body succumbing to the unintelligibility of the difference-less landscape, the swain's crisis mobilizes an important observational alternative that Thomson elaborates in the rest of *Winter*. Those same nerves that eventually cease are, for the period he is lost, the only means through which the swain can perceive the outside world. Yet the failure of these perceptions to accord with his experience produces an alternative mode of seeing. When empirical observation produces only a scene of "less"-ness, the swain turns to its alternative, the imaginative eye. Thomson elaborates this potential in the voice of the poem's "I," a spectator with significantly greater privilege than the swain. The "I" of *Winter* luxuriates in a fantasy of retirement unavailable to the tragic, pastoral swain; this fantasy of retirement is a space of comfort exclusive to the poet and his ilk. Nor is this "I" vulnerable to the inundating reversal of the microscopic eye, whether through the threat of sound or infection. Instead, a 150-line encomium to "my retreat" (*Winter*, 426), modeled on *Il Penseroso*, imagines a train of ghosts of ancient sages beginning with Socrates, who appear one after another to allow the poet to "hold high converse with the mighty dead—/Sages of ancient time" (*Winter*, 431–432). Without the previous example of the swain, the pantheon of dead sages would be solely a turn to the ancient epistemology, a renunciation of the modern mode. However, these paradoxically embodied spectral and phantasmagoric entities proffer an alternative to the empirical observation of the natural world in which the poem has been engaged and been critiquing.

If detailed description of the natural world is a symbol of the modern gesture as well as the foundation on which the principles of experimental philosophy are built, then the poet's mingling with the ancient sages registers a nostalgic, ancient turn in both form (the imagined scene) and content (inherited wisdom). The pleasures for the poet are reminiscent of the swain's visualized imagination but with decidedly lower risks. The inequity of who has access to this subject position is striking: the nostalgic mode of seeing is available comfortably to the "I" of the poem in his privileged retirement. If, the poet muses, those "larger prospects" fail to materialize, then the imagination would supply ample material: it "would play the shapes/Of frolic fancy; and incessant form/Those rapid pictures, that assembled train/Of fleet ideas, never joined before" (*Winter*, 610–613). In contrast, when the swain's visual apprehension fails, he freezes in a snowdrift.

The seemingly hopeful possibility of the poet in retirement contrasts sharply with the inevitable oblivion of the swain. The contrast between seeing and blindness activates the optical possibilities that the poem moves to imagine in *Winter*'s excursion to the frigid zone, presented in opposition to *Summer*'s journey to the torrid zone. This environment seems, at first glance, to present more examples of a menacing landscape that is impossible to detail visually. The snowy Alps and the clouds merge and mount in an increasingly overwhelming scene for an increasingly panicky spectator: "Snows swell on snows," "icy mountains high on mountains piled," and "Alps frown on Alps" convey an observer's inability to distinguish visually between landscape and weather (*Winter*, 905, 906, 910). Snow, mountains, and clouds intermingle, generating an ever more overpowering spectacle. There is no chance for scrutiny and no hope of disambiguation. Here is a moment that encapsulates what later emerges as a characteristic scene of the sublime, deeply imbricated in the experience of an individual in the Alps.

Yet alongside such moments of the frightening failure of vision is a sign that an alternative mode of optical apprehension might be possible. The conditions of winter weather prompt Thomson to stage a counterpart to *Summer*'s microscope. Thomson adopts the prism to demonstrate its imaginative potential for visual apprehension. The poem explicitly views northern geography through a lens of difference that is imaginable because of the logic of the prism. Thomson announces that in the frigid zone, "All nature feels the renovating force/Of Winter—only to the thoughtless eye/In ruin seen" (*Winter*, 704–706). The thoughtful, rather than the thoughtless, eye is prismatic: it is trained to see difference. The prismatic eye accurately apprehends that the "icy horrors" of Russia are not an undistinguished, undifferentiated mass (*Winter*, 805). The frozen expanse instead accommodates living organisms, perceivable to that thoughtful, prismatic eye: "Yet there life glows;/Yet, cherished there, beneath the shining waste/The furry nations harbor" (*Winter*, 809–811). The example of a hibernating bear that "Hardens his heart against assailing want" (*Winter*, 833) represents not only an embodied resilience possible in winter, but also the demarcation of the boundary between life and death, warmth and cold, organic and inorganic. This is the difference available to Thomson's reader.

Within the seemingly frozen wasteland of the frigid zone, Thomson provides a specific counterpart to the forsaken swain, he whose nervous system slowly succumbs to the numbing effects of the wintry cold. In the frigid zone, the "I" pauses to commemorate a ship of British explorers, iced into their frozen ship. The adventurer and his crew are not subsumed into a blanket of snow. They instead stand as aesthetic monuments, converted into statues attesting to their (former) vigor: "Each full exerted at his several task,/Froze into statues" (*Winter*, 933–934). The explicit aestheticization of the sailors into statuary is possible because of Thomson's perceiving "I," a subject position that not only apprehends difference but also does so within an explicitly aesthetic framework. The sailors are not more evidence of a horrific wasteland. Their frozen, dead bodies transform a naval failure into an aesthetic tribute to British nationalism and scientific ingenuity.

To not see in detail is the unfortunate truth that *Winter* teaches. The landscape challenges conventional modes of visual apprehension: the naked eye fails to perceive such an environment. The failure of vision here has uneven effects; for the vulnerable, such blindness leads to oblivion. With this alternate mode of seeing as imaginative observation, *Winter* presents specific epistemological and ontological payoffs. The model of prismatic vision, extended to a figurative possibility unavailable in its physical form, emerges as profoundly productive. Only with prismatic visual perception in place is what the editor, James Sambrook, identifies as "the intention of *The Seasons*" possible.[119] For such readers, *The Seasons* explicitly refigures the traditional opposition between particulars and generalizations, pointing a way to reconcile them. In the wake of the swain's imagination of materialism, the "I" of *Winter* is equipped to see more, and to see it figuratively as a whole, even though this is practically or, that is to say, empirically, impossible:

> Hence larger prospects of the beauteous whole
> Would gradual open on our opening minds;
> And each diffusive harmony unite
> In full perfection to the astonished eye. (*Winter*, 579–82)

Thomson imagines the possibility that natural philosophy cannot accommodate: the eye and the mind, working as mutual alibis, produce material insight and, to adapt a phrase from Bruce Robbins, the difficult generalization.[120] The idealization of experimental philosophy's observed particular also forecloses the experiential and intellectual value of contemplating its epistemological and ontological opposite—what Thomson optimistically calls "the beauteous whole."

In *Winter,* Thomson stages an appropriation of the logic and epistemology of the prism, in large part by disentangling its potential from its practical applications. Therefore, as much emphasis as there has been on the microscopic eye that absorbs present history as a noisy imperial landscape and as much as that microscopic eye precipitates a global journey that animates the literary trope of taking that seeing body around the world to reimagine a visual alternative to empirical observation, Thomson's *Winter* foregrounds a deep skepticism about the possibility of empirical observation and draws on the epistemology of the prism to compensate for those limitations. In the process, he articulates a model of imaginative vision that evokes the material and figurative simultaneously in order to perceive difference. As a counterpoint to the flight to the torrid zone in *Summer,* the winter journey to the frigid zone puts into action a prismatic vision, enabling the viewer to see the difference that winter regularly obscures. This visual subjectivity attentive to difference thus allows Thomson to imagine a world in which both observed particulars and difficult generalizations cohere, if only in the imaginative space of the prism-like eye.

The self-conscious rendering of art as art operates as a form of knowledge production in the eighteenth century. The notion of "aesthetic" leans on the notion of a detached observer whose sensory perceptions produce a metacritical understanding of art as a separate domain. At the core of eighteenth-century aesthetics resides a debt, easily obscured, to the epistemological structures and protocols of natural philosophy. When poets take up art through science, they produce a theory of knowledge. To render a thing, a grotto, a landscape poetically is to make claims about the world. Pope's *The Rape of the Lock* challenges us to reconsider the limits and possibilities of the objects we view. A poem preoccupied with things, Pope's mock epic uses the revelatory power of close observation to reveal the uneasy balance between material and theory that constitutes the observed particular in natural philosophy. If Hooke needs to take multiple views of a single object to produce a composite that is, in fact, presented as a singular instance, then Pope pulls out the narrative implications of this process: the poetic eye of *The Rape of the Lock* sees things in their present and past states at one and the same time. Things in Pope's imagination are mutable—they have always been and always will be—and this quality of changefulness requires a mode of apprehension available only to the aesthetic observer. The lesson Pope teaches is that the material world, that is, the phenomena under the scrutiny of natural philosophers, always has a past, present, and future.

The potential for things to function as trophies—as symbols of conquest, as signs of mastery—inspires Pope's narrative as well as the construction of Queen Caroline's Hermitage. Considered as an experiential site, the Hermitage demands that one situate oneself within it: the movement from exterior to interior and from one British worthy to another requires that the spectator be a participant in this paean to native thinking. Imagined as a sacred place of retirement, where one—namely, the queen herself—might repose to contemplate the brilliance of Boyle, Newton, et al., the Hermitage presents natural philosophy not as a practice to be emulated but as a mode to produce an aesthetic experience. The Hermitage and the poems commemorating it do not inculcate the techniques of natural philosophy as, for example, a lecture or course at Benjamin Martin's instrument shop would. Instead, these monuments, both architectural and textual, function as calls to produce art—and, once produced, to produce more art. The proliferation of poems, galvanized around the occasion of the *Gentleman's Magazine*'s poetry contest, provide varied and variable aesthetic mediations of natural philosophy.

If some poets celebrate British intellectual innovation as the means to produce an aesthetic experience, then others imagine beyond the limits of what close observation of the world uncovers. Taking the idea of scientific instrumentation as a founding conceit, James Thomson positions the poet—the stand-in for a modest/immodest witness—as the observational eye subject to sensory perception of the world. The microscope in *The Seasons* proves horrific, pulling the viewer into an unfiltered mass of sensory stimulation that correlates to a disembodied yet imperial account of the globe. Thomson adapts the logic of the prism as a scientific instrument that perceives difference the naked eye cannot, applying its optics to a world far beyond one's ordinary view. *Winter*, as a season and a state of (at best) stasis or (at worst) decimation, absorbs the vulnerable into its unrelenting sameness. But Thomson's homage to Newton's prismatic logic reveals that aesthetics allows one to perceive and acknowledge difference, a move that uncovers ideological fissures endangering some individuals and protecting others.

When science becomes literature—that is, in aesthetic mediations of natural philosophy—we see the limits of science and the truths of the literary, a revelation possible through the experimental imagination.

NOTES

INTRODUCTION

1. Hasok Chang takes a similar approach but from the vantage of a scientist by "dredging up exactly those parts of past science that scientists themselves tend not to notice or remember because they do not fit nicely into current conceptions or customs." In Hasok Chang, "Practicing Eighteenth-Century Science Today," in *Nature Engaged: Science in Practice from Renaissance to the Present*, ed. Mario Biagioli and Jessica Riskin (New York: Palgrave Macmillan, 2012), 41, 55.

2. "Experiment," Samuel Johnson, *A Dictionary of the English Language* (London, 1755).

3. As Julian Martin explains, "Bacon used the single term 'experiment' to describe very different sorts of activity by the natural historian: the passive reporting both of observed craft practices and techniques, and of particular inquiries conducted by other men; the 'artificial' investigations he carried out himself; and any subsequent, 'more subtle,' investigations." In Julian Martin, *Francis Bacon, the State and the Reform of Natural Philosophy* (Cambridge: Cambridge University Press, 1992), 155. See the extended discussion of the post-Baconian seventeenth-century experiment as an early scientific practice in Steven Shapin and Simon Schaffer, *Leviathan and the Air-Pump: Hobbes, Boyle, and the Experimental Life* (Princeton, NJ: Princeton University Press, 1985), 3–21. The connection between "experiment" and "observation" emerged in the eighteenth century. See Lorraine Daston, "The Empire of Observation, 1600–1800," in *Histories of Scientific Observation*, ed. Lorraine Daston and Elizabeth Lunbeck (Chicago: University of Chicago Press, 2011), 81–113. See also Marie Boas Hall, *Promoting Experimental Learning: Experiment and the Royal Society, 1660–1727* (Cambridge: Cambridge University Press, 1991).

4. Ian Hacking, *Representing and Intervening: Introductory Topics in the Philosophy of Natural Science* (Cambridge: Cambridge University Press, 1983), 173; see also 191.

5. Experiments were absolutely central to the acceptance of (and familiarity with) Newtonianism in the early eighteenth century. See Simon Schaffer, "Glass Works: Newton's Prisms and the Uses of Experiment," in *The Uses of Experiment: Studies in Natural Sciences*, ed. David Gooding, Trevor Pinch, and Simon Schaffer (Cambridge: Cambridge University Press, 1989), 95–96.

6. For Mitchell, the adjectival use of *experimental* is a key modifier for his use of *vitalism* because it refers to the practices developed and promulgated in the late seventeenth century. See Robert Mitchell, *Experimental Life: Vitalism in Romantic Science and Literature* (Baltimore, MD: Johns Hopkins University Press, 2013), 3, 7.

7. Robin Valenza, *Literature, Language, and the Rise of the Intellectual Disciplines in Britain, 1680–1820* (Cambridge: Cambridge University Press, 2009), 139–72.

8. A complete bibliography of the history of science is too large to list here, but important books from the last thirty years that attend to literary and aesthetic culture

include Michael Hunter, *Science and Society in Restoration England* (Cambridge: Cambridge University Press, 1981); Margaret C. Jacob, *The Cultural Meaning of the Scientific Revolution* (Philadelphia: Temple University Press, 1988); Barbara Maria Stafford, *Body Criticism: Imaging the Unseen in Enlightenment Art and Medicine* (Cambridge, MA: MIT Press, 1991); Larry Stewart, *The Rise of Public Science: Rhetoric, Technology, and Natural Philosophy in Newtonian Britain, 1660–1750* (Cambridge: Cambridge University Press, 1992); Londa Schiebinger, *Nature's Body: Gender in the Making of Modern Science* (Boston: Beacon Press, 1993); Peter Dear, *Discipline and Experience: The Mathematical Way in the Scientific Revolution* (Chicago: University of Chicago Press, 1995) and *Revolutionizing the Sciences: European Knowledge and Its Ambitions, 1500–1700* (Princeton, NJ: Princeton University Press, 2001); Lorraine Daston and Katharine Park, *Wonders and the Order of Nature, 1150–1750* (New York: Zone Books, 1998); Lorraine Daston, ed., *Biographies of Scientific Objects* (Chicago: University of Chicago Press, 2000); Lorraine Daston and Peter Galison, *Objectivity* (New York: Zone Books, 2007); and Lorraine Daston and Elizabeth Lunbeck, ed., *Histories of Scientific Observation* (Chicago: University of Chicago Press, 2011).

9. Shapin and Schaffer, *Leviathan and the Air-Pump*, 80–154.

10. Ibid., 15.

11. Ibid., 283.

12. Ibid., 60–65.

13. See, for example, Margaret C. Jacob, *The Newtonians and the English Revolution, 1689–1720* (Ithaca, NY: Cornell University Press, 1976) and *The Cultural Meaning*; Kenneth J. Knoespel, "The Narrative Matter of Mathematics: John Dee's Preface to the Elements of Euclid of Megara (1570)," *Philological Quarterly* 66, no. 1 (1987): 27–46, and "The Mythological Transformations of Renaissance Science," in *Literature and Science as Modes of Expression*, ed. Frederick Amrine and Stephen J. Weininger (Dordrecht: Kluwer Academic, 1989), 99–112; James J. Bono, *The Word of God and the Languages of Man: Interpreting Nature in Early Modern Science and Medicine* (Madison: University of Wisconsin Press, 1995); Anita Guerrini, *Obesity and Depression in the Enlightenment: The Life and Times of George Cheyne* (Norman: University of Oklahoma Press, 2000) and *Experimenting with Humans and Animals: From Galen to Animal Rights* (Baltimore, MD: Johns Hopkins University Press, 2003); Lissa Roberts, "An Arcadian Apparatus: Steam Engines and Landscapes in the History of Dutch Culture," *Technology and Culture* 45, no. 2 (April 2004): 251–276; and William R. Newman and Lawrence M. Principe, *Alchemy Tried in the Fire: Starkey, Boyle, and the Fate of the Helmontian Chymistry* (Chicago: University of Chicago Press, 2002).

14. Ian Watt, *The Rise of the Novel: Studies in Defoe, Richardson, and Fielding* (Berkeley: University of California Press, 1957).

15. See, for example, John Bender, *Ends of Enlightenment* (Stanford, CA: Stanford University Press, 2012), 38–56; and Michael McKeon, *The Origins of the English Novel, 1600–1740* (Baltimore, MD: Johns Hopkins University Press, 1987), 65–73; Susan Stewart, *On Longing: Narratives of the Miniature, the Gigantic, the Souvenir, the Collection* (Durham, NC: Duke University Press, 1992), 44; and Mary Baine Campbell, *Wonder and Science: Imagining Worlds in Early Modern Europe* (Ithaca, NY: Cornell University Press, 1999), 201, 186–187.

My initial interest in literature and science concerned novelistic details and experimentalism's minute particulars. See "Minute Particulars: Microscopy and Eighteenth-

Century Narrative," *Mosaic: A Journal for the Interdisciplinary Study of Literature* 39, no. 2 (2006): 143–161; "'the More I Write, the More I Shall Have to Write': The Many Beginnings of *Tristram Shandy*," in *Narrative Beginnings: Theories and Practices*, ed. Brian Richardson (Lincoln: University of Nebraska Press, 2008), 83–95; and "Details and Frankness: Affective Relations in *Sir Charles Grandison*," *Studies in Eighteenth-Century Culture* 38 (2009): 45–68.

16. Helen Thompson, *Fictional Matter: Empiricism, Corpuscles, and the Novel* (Philadelphia: University of Pennsylvania Press, 2017), 16–21.

17. Rajani Sudan, *The Alchemy of Empire: Abject Materials and the Technologies of Colonialism* (NY: Fordham University Press, 2016); Lucinda Cole, *Imperfect Creatures: Vermin, Literature, and the Sciences of Life, 1600–1740* (Ann Arbor, MI: University of Michigan Press, 2016); and Al Coppola, *The Theater of Experiment: Staging Natural Philosophy in Eighteenth-Century Britain* (Oxford: Oxford University Press, 2016).

18. Jonathan Kramnick, *Actions and Objects from Hobbes to Richardson* (Stanford, CA: Stanford University Press, 2010); Jayne Elizabeth Lewis, *Air's Appearance: Literary Atmosphere in British Fiction, 1660–1794* (Chicago: University of Chicago Press, 2012); Wolfram Schmidgen, *Exquisite Mixture: The Virtues of Impurity in Early Modern England* (Philadelphia: University of Pennsylvania Press, 2013); and Thompson, *Fictional Matter*. Courtney Weiss Smith focuses on poetry in *Empiricist Devotions: Science, Religion, and Poetry in Early Eighteenth-Century England* (Charlottesville: University of Virginia Press, 2016).

19. Raymond Williams, *Keywords: A Vocabulary of Culture and Society* (New York: Oxford University Press, 1976), 13.

20. "Science," *Oxford English Dictionary*, n. 1a: "The state or fact of knowing; knowledge or cognizance *of* something; knowledge as a personal attribute." n. 3b: "A branch of study that deals with a connected body of demonstrated truths or with observed facts systematically classified and more or less comprehended by general laws, and incorporating trustworthy methods (now esp. those involving the scientific method and which incorporate falsifiable hypotheses) for the discovery of new truth in its own domain." On the terms *science* and *natural philosophy*, see Andrew Cunningham, "Getting the Game Right: Some Plain Words on the Identity and Invention of Science," *Studies in History and Philosophy of Science* 19, no. 3 (1988): 365–389; and Peter Dear, "Religion, Science and Natural Philosophy: Thoughts on Cunningham's Thesis," *Studies in History and Philosophy of Science* 32, no. 2 (2001): 377–386.

21. Johann Karl Möhsen, "What Is to Be Done toward the Enlightenment of the Citizenry?" (1783); Moses Mendelssohn, "On the Question: What Is Enlightenment?" (1784); Immanuel Kant, "An Answer to the Question: What Is Enlightenment?" (1784); and Karl Leonhard Reinhold, "Thoughts on Enlightenment" (1784). The bibliography on the Enlightenment is vast, but Peter Hulme and Ludmilla Jordanova give an illustrative account of how the term came to function in historiography. "Introduction," in *The Enlightenment and Its Shadows*, ed. Peter Hulme and Ludmilla Jordanova (London: Routledge, 1990), 1–15; see esp. 1–4.

22. I refer to Geoffrey Galt Harpham's reading of the Spanish Inquisition as a form of Enlightenment. In Geoffrey Galt Harpham, "So . . . What Is Enlightenment? An Inquisition into Modernity," *Critical Inquiry* 20, no. 3 (1994): 524–564. See also Max Horkheimer and Theodor W. Adorno, *Dialectic of Enlightenment*, trans. John Cumming (New York: Herder and Herder, 1972); Michel Foucault, "What Is Enlightenment?" from *The Foucault Reader*,

ed. P. Rabinow (New York: Pantheon Books, 1984), 32–50; Jürgen Habermas, "The Unity of Reason in the Diversity of Its Voices," in *Postmetaphysical Thinking: Philosophical Essays*, trans. William Mark Hohengarten (Cambridge, MA: MIT Press, 1992), 115–148; Max Horkheimer, "Reason Against Itself: Some Remarks on Enlightenment," *Theory, Culture & Society* 10 (1993): 79–88; and Richard Rorty, "The Continuity between the Enlightenment and 'Postmodernism,'" in *What's Left of Enlightenment? A Postmodern Question*, ed. Keith Michael Baker and Peter Hanns Reill (Stanford, CA: Stanford University Press, 2001), 19–36. Clifford Siskin and William Warner's *This Is Enlightenment* contends that the Enlightenment is an event in what they describe as the history of mediation. See Siskin and Warner, "This Is Enlightenment: An Invitation in the Form of an Argument," in *This Is Enlightenment*, ed. Clifford Siskin and William Warner (Chicago: University of Chicago Press, 2010), 1–33.

23. Richard Foster Jones, *Ancients and Moderns: A Study of the Rise of the Scientific Movement in Seventeenth-Century England*, 2nd ed. (St. Louis, MO: Washington University Press, 1961); and Joseph M. Levine, *The Battle of the Books: History and Literature in the Augustan Age* (Ithaca, NY: Cornell University Press, 1991).

24. Particularly fine examples include Robert Mitchell's study of vitalism, *Experimental Life*; Catherine Packham's *Eighteenth-Century Vitalism: Bodies, Culture, Politics* (Basingstoke, Hampshire: Palgrave Macmillan, 2012); and Helen Thompson's work on chemistry in *Fictional Matter*.

25. The scientific allusions and themes in *Gulliver's Travels* have been well documented, beginning with Marjorie Hope Nicolson's *Science and Imagination* (Ithaca, NY: Cornell University Press, 1956). More recent contributions include Fredrick N. Smith, "Scientific Discourse: *Gulliver's Travels* and the *Philosophical Transactions*," in *Genres of Gulliver's Travels*, ed. Fredrick N. Smith (Newark: University of Delaware Press, 1990), 139–162; Deborah Needleman Armintor *The Little Everyman: Stature and Masculinity in Eighteenth-Century English Literature* (Seattle: University of Washington Press, 2011), 56–79; and Kristin M. Girten, "Mingling with Matter: Tactile Microscopy and the Philosophic Mind in Brobdingnag and Beyond," *The Eighteenth Century: Theory and Interpretation* 54, no. 4 (2013): 497–520. For editorial practice, see, for example, Jonathan Swift, *Gulliver's Travels*, ed. Albert J. Rivero (New York: Norton, 2002), 28, n. 3; 40, notes 1, 2, 4; 45, n. 7; 56, n. 6; 60, n. 2; and 61, n. 4; and Jonathan Swift, *Gulliver's Travels*, ed. with an introduction by Claude Rawson and notes by Ian Higgins, new edition (Oxford: Oxford University Press, 2005), 292, n. 34; 292–93, n. 36; 294, n. 48.

26. Marjorie Hope Nicolson's foundational scholarship in the field from the mid-twentieth century onward assumes that science produces an innovation that literary writers then lambaste or celebrate. Nicolson's understanding is that there is a model of influence at work—science on literature. Science is the modernizing impulse, and literature is an arena of conservative reaction, a trajectory that expedites the epistemic shift to science as the dominant source of truth. See Marjorie Hope Nicolson, *Newton Demands the Muse: Newton's Opticks and the Eighteenth Century Poets* (Princeton, NJ: Princeton University Press, 1966); *Science and Imagination*; *Pepys' Diary and the New Science* (Charlottesville: University of Virginia Press, 1965); and, with G. S. Rousseau, *"This Long Disease, My Life": Alexander Pope and the Sciences* (Princeton, NJ: Princeton University Press, 1968). For more recent examples of the "influence" model, see Ilse Vickers, *Defoe and the New Sci-*

ences (Cambridge: Cambridge University Press, 1996), and Stuart Peterfreund, *William Blake in a Newtonian World: Essays on Literature as Art and Science* (Norman: University of Oklahoma Press, 1998).

27. Hayden White, "Literature and Social Action: Reflections on the Reflection Theory of Literary Art," *New Literary History* 11, no. 2 (1980): 363–380.

28. Fredric V. Bogel, *The Difference Satire Makes: Rhetoric and Reading from Jonson to Byron* (Ithaca, NY: Cornell University Press, 2001), 11; see also 5–6. Dustin Griffin suggests that "the historical particulars in satire always have a curious in-between status, neither wholly fact nor wholly fiction." In *Satire: A Critical Reintroduction* (Lexington: University Press of Kentucky, 1995), 123; see also 115–132.

29. Tita Chico, *Designing Women: The Dressing Room in Eighteenth-Century English Literature and Culture* (Lewisburg, PA: Bucknell University Press, 2005).

30. C. P. Snow, *The Two Cultures and the Scientific Revolution* (Cambridge: Cambridge University Press, 1959). See also Erwin Schrödinger's lectures, *"Nature and the Greeks" and "Science and Humanism"* (Cambridge: Cambridge University Press, 2014).

31. L. J. Jordanova, "Introduction," in *Languages of Nature: Critical Essays on Science and Literature*, ed. L. J. Jordanova (London: Free Association Books, 1986), 15–16.

32. The popular accounts of the privileging of STEM are ubiquitous in the modern press. In spring 2016, President Obama's proposed budget included $4.1 billion for STEM education in primary and secondary education. See, for example, Mikhail Zinshteyn, "The Reality of Coding Classes," in *The Atlantic*, February 1, 2016.

33. See G. S. Rousseau, *Enlightenment Borders: Pre- and Post-modern Discourses: Medical, Scientific* (Manchester: Manchester University Press, 1991), 217–218; and Judith Hawley, "General Introduction," in *Literature and Science, 1660–1834*, gen. ed. Judith Hawley, 8 vols. (London: Pickering & Chatto, 2003–2004), 1:xii.

34. Gillian Beer, *Open Fields: Science in Cultural Encounter* (Oxford: Oxford University Press, 1996), 177.

35. Peter Galison, *Image and Logic: A Material Culture of Microphysics* (Chicago: University of Chicago Press, 1997).

36. In the Romantic period, for example, natural history, neither fully science nor fully literature, provides a venue for their interplay. See Noah Heringman, "The Commerce of Literature and Natural History," in *Romantic Science: The Literary Forms of Natural History*, ed. Noah Heringman (Albany: State University of New York Press, 2003), 1–19; esp. 1–11; and *Romantic Rocks, Aesthetic Geology* (Ithaca, NY: Cornell University Press, 2004), 7–19.

37. Jacques Derrida, *Of Grammatology*, trans. Gayatri Chakravorty Spivak (Baltimore, MD: Johns Hopkins University Press, 1998).

38. Robert Boyle, *The Excellency of Theology Compar'd with Natural Philosophy, (as both are Objects of Men's Study)* (London, 1674), 121.

39. Robert Markley, *Fallen Languages: Crises of Representation in Newtonian England, 1660–1740* (Ithaca, NY: Cornell University Press, 1993), 7.

40. Ibid., 8; and Joanna Picciotto, *Labors of Innocence in Early Modern England* (Cambridge, MA: Harvard University Press, 2010), 1–4.

41. Boyle, *The Excellency of Theology*, 117.

42. Ibid., 118–119.

43. To debunk the Enlightenment legacy of scientific objectivity, Gerald Holton uses

firsthand accounts from Albert Einstein, Enrico Fermi, and Robert Andrews Millikan to argue that the "scientific imagination" is central to the discipline today. See Gerald Holton, *The Scientific Imagination* (Cambridge, MA: Harvard University Press, 1998), 3–24.

44. Sharyn Clough makes the persuasive case that matters of epistemology in feminist science studies rely on "representationalism," defined as "a philosophical model that . . . invoke[s] an image of knowers as interpreters, collecting data about the empirical world without themselves being part of that world. . . . On this model we are the uninterpreted interpreters examining the empirical data as they have been filtered and presented to us." The effect is a recapitulation of normative patriarchy. See Sharyn Clough, *Beyond Epistemology: A Pragmatist Approach to Feminist Science Studies* (Lanham, MD: Rowman & Littlefield, 2003), 12.

My understanding of trope draws on Karen Barad's theory of agential realism, which contends that the reflective model of representation—one undergirding poststructuralist and, implicitly, structuralist theory—inadequately imagines a sharp, optically infused division between subject and object or even between and among objects, no matter their epistemological, ontological, or ideological positionings. Barad offers a new optical model based on diffraction, the fundamental understanding borne out of quantum physics, to theorize relations of difference anew, developing what she calls "a diffractive mode of analysis." Reflection and diffraction are both optical metaphors, but "whereas the metaphor of reflection reflects the themes of mirroring and sameness, diffraction is marked by patterns of difference." A diffractive model focuses on the entanglements that make difference seem ontological and a priori, though such boundaries are produced only through the convergence of that which they seem to separate. These "agential cuts" emerge at the moment of entanglement and have the effect of retrospective being. This is more than being mutually constitutive. They produce what they purport merely to reflect, and they also produce these differences as if they always existed. The work of the critic, therefore, is to "refuse the idea of a natural (or, for that matter, a purely cultural) division between nature and culture" and provide "an accounting of how this boundary is actively configured and reconfigured." Diffraction acknowledges that boundaries, as markers of difference, seem stable until we look closely enough to see that the looking produces those boundaries as if they were ontological. See Karen Barad, *Meeting the University Halfway: Quantum Physics and the Entanglement of Matter and Meaning* (Durham, NC: Duke University Press, 2007), 73, 71, 72, 136.

45. "Trope," *Oxford English Dictionary*, n. I.1.a.

46. Eliza Haywood, *The Adventures of Eovaai, Princess of Ijaveo: a Pre-Adamitical History*, ed. Earla Wilputte (Peterborough, ONT: Broadview Press, 1999), 94.

47. Ibid., 94.

48. My reading of *Eovaai* is inspired by Natasha Myers's work on protein modelings that present the biological body as known best by an emphatically embodied scientist. Myers demonstrates that researchers use "their bodies kinesthetically to manipulate and learn protein structures." These are forms of "body-work" "intrinsic to the work of mechanistic modeling." In Natasha Myers, *Rendering Life Molecular: Models, Modelers, and Excitable Matter* (Durham, NC: Duke University Press, 2015), 6. For related and important discussions of feminism and science studies, see the essays in Barbara Laslett, Sally Gregory Kohlstedt, Helen Longino, and Evelynn Hammonds, eds., *Gender and Scientific Author-*

ity (Chicago: University of Chicago Press, 1996); and Londa Schiebinger, *Has Feminism Changed Science?* (Cambridge, MA: Harvard University Press, 1999).

CHAPTER 1

1. Peter Dear, *Revolutionizing the Sciences: European Knowledge and Its Ambitions, 1500–1700* (Princeton, NJ: Princeton University Press, 2001), 132.

2. Julie Robin Solomon, *Objectivity in the Making: Francis Bacon and the Politics of Inquiry* (Baltimore, MD: Johns Hopkins University Press, 1998), 28. See also R. W. Newell, *Objectivity, Empiricism, and Truth* (London: Routledge, 1986), 16–38. Lorraine Daston and Peter Galison locate the emergence of objectivity later in the nineteenth century. See Lorraine Daston and Peter Galison, *Objectivity* (New York: Zone Books, 2007), 55–113.

3. Charles Webster, *The Great Instauration: Science, Medicine, and Reform, 1626–1660* (London: Duckworth, 1975); Steven Shapin and Simon Schaffer, *Leviathan and the Air-Pump: Hobbes, Boyle, and the Experimental Life* (Princeton, NJ: Princeton University Press, 1985); Daston and Galison, *Objectivity*; and Dear, *Revolutionizing the Sciences*, 131–148.

4. Dear, *Revolutionizing the Sciences*, 147–148.

5. Nancy Leys Stepan, "Race and Gender: The Role of Analogy in Science," *Isis* 77, no. 2 (1986): 261.

6. Shapin and Schaffer, *Leviathan and the Air-Pump*, 18.

7. Ibid., 17–18.

8. Ibid., 60.

9. See A. R. Hall and M. B. Hall, "The Intellectual Origins of the Royal Society: London and Oxford," *Notes and Records of the Royal Society* 23 (1969): 157–168.

10. R. G. Frank, Jr. *Harvey and the Oxford Physiologists: A Study of Scientific Ideas* (Berkeley: University of California Press, 1980), 44.

11. Lorrain Daston, "The Empire of Observation, 1600–1800," in *Histories of Scientific Observation*, ed. Lorraine Daston and Elizabeth Lunbeck (Chicago: University of Chicago Press, 2011), 81. For a recent discussion of observation in German science and literature, see the special issue of *Monatshefte*, "Observation in Science and Literature," 105, no. 3 (2013): 371–488.

12. Michael Hunter, *Establishing the New Science: The Experience of the Early Royal Society* (Woodbridge, Suffolk: Boydell Press, 1989), and Marie Boas Hall, *Henry Oldenburg: Shaping the Royal Society* (Oxford: Oxford University Press, 2002).

13. For this final point, I am inspired by Richard Kroll's claim that empiricism can function "as a way of thinking, *as a way of behaving* . . . [that] could likewise prove subversive." In Richard Kroll, "Instituting Empiricism: Hobbes's *Leviathan* and Dryden's *Marriage à la Mode*," in *Cultural Readings of Restoration and Eighteenth-Century English Theater*, ed. J. Douglas Canfield and Deborah C. Payne (Athens: University of Georgia Press, 1995), 41.

14. *The Diary of Samuel Pepys*, ed. Robert Latham and William Mathews, 11 vols. (London: Bell & Hyman Limited, 1985), 7.239 (Wednesday, August 8, 1666).

15. A. D. C. Simpson, "Robert Hooke and Practical Optics: Technical Support at a Scientific Frontier," in *Robert Hooke: New Studies*, ed. Michael Hunter and Simon Schaffer (Woodbridge, Suffolk: Boydell Press, 1989), 36–41. Reeve's son helped Pepys at home, *The Diary of Samuel Pepys*, 7.254 (August 19, 1666).

16. Quoted in Simpson, "Robert Hooke and Practical Optics," 37, note 15.

17. Ellen Tan Drake, *Restless Genius: Robert Hooke and His Earthly Thoughts* (New York: Oxford University Press, 1996), 16-23; and Lisa Jardine, *Ingenious Pursuits: Building the Scientific Revolution* (New York: Anchor, 2000), 49.

18. *The Diary of Samuel Pepys*, 7.240 (Wednesday, August 8, 1666).

19. Gerard L'E. Turner, "Decorative Tooling on 17th- and 18th-Century Microscopes and Telescopes," in *Essays on the History of the Microscope*, ed. G. L'E. Turner (Oxford: Senecio Publishing Company, 1980), 70-108; and Marc Olivier, "Binding the Book of Nature: Microscopy as Literature," *History of European Ideas* 31 (2005): 173–191.

20. *The Diary of Samuel Pepys*, 5.240 (August 13, 1664).

21. Ibid., 5.241 (August 13, 1664, August 14, 1664).

22. Ibid., 5.241 (August 14, 1664).

23. Ibid., 6.2, 6.17 (January 2, 1664/1665, January 20, 1664/1665).

24. My argument and terminology contrast sharply with Joanna Pioccioto's claims that what she calls the "experimental text" of the seventeenth century "offered itself as an instrument to *escape* fiction, to purge perception of the false images generated by custom, idols of the mind, and the fallen body itself," enabling these writers to "align themselves against literature conceived of as fiction." *The Experimental Imagination* counters that such "experimental texts" looked not to the past but to the future, a future bound up with the literary imagination. In Joanna Picciotto, *Labors of Innocence in Early Modern England* (Cambridge, MA: Harvard University Press, 2010), 15–16.

25. Thomas Sprat, *The History of the Royal Society of London, For the Improving of Natural Knowledge*, 3rd ed. (London, 1722), 338.

26. Ibid.

27. James Fortescue, *Science: An Epistle on Its Decline and Revival* (London, 1750).

28. Jeremy Black, *Eighteenth-Century Britain, 1688–1783*, 2nd ed. (London: Palgrave, 2008), 159. See also Michael Hunter, *Science and Society in Restoration England* (Cambridge: Cambridge University Press, 1981), 22, 55–56, 75, 84–86, 96, 97, 191–192, 195, 216; Larry Stewart, *The Rise of Public Science: Rhetoric, Technology, and Natural Philosophy in Newtonian Britain, 1660–1750* (Cambridge: Cambridge University Press, 1992), xxiv–xxv; Jan Golinski, *Science as Public Culture: Chemistry and Enlightenment in Britain, 1760–1820* (Cambridge: Cambridge University Press, 1992); Robert Markley, *Fallen Languages: Crises of Representation in Newtonian England, 1660–1740* (Ithaca, NY: Cornell University Press, 1993), 208; and Patricia Fara, *Sympathetic Attractions: Magnetic Practices, Beliefs, and Symbolism in Eighteenth-Century England* (Princeton, NJ: Princeton University Press, 1996), 37. For scientific consumer goods, see Simon Schaffer, "The Consuming Flame: Electrical Showmen and Tory Mystics in the World of Goods," in *Consumption and the World of Goods*, ed. John Brewer and Roy Porter (London York: Routledge, 1993), 489–526; and Larry Stewart, "Seeing through the Scholium: Religion and Reading Newton in the Eighteenth Century," *History of Science* 34 (1996): 123–165. By the end of the eighteenth century, children were increasingly educated in science, according to James Secord, "Newton in the Nursery: Tom Telescope and the Philosophy of Tops and Balls, 1761–1838," *History of Science* 23 (1985): 127–151.

29. Larry Stewart, "Other Centres of Calculation, or, Where the Royal Society Didn't Count: Commerce, Coffee-Houses and Natural Philosophy in Early Modern London," *The British Journal for the History of Science* 32, no. 2 (1999): 133–153. A 1750 text dedicated

to discussing "Royal Societies" in France (where "every thing here was Irregularity and Confusion") and England concludes with a long account of the coffeehouse gathering that took place following the English Royal Society's official meeting. See *A Dissertation on Royal Societies. In Three Letters* (London, 1750), 9, 32–35.

30. Margaret C. Jacob and Larry Stewart, *Practical Matter: Newton's Science in the Service of Industry and Empire, 1687–1851* (Cambridge, MA: Harvard University Press, 2004), 15; and Sprat, *The History of the Royal Society*, 421, 64.

31. English instrument makers belonged to either the Clockmaker's Company, founded in 1631, or the Spectaclemaker's Company, neither of which had particularly dogmatic regulations (e.g., the right to search a workshop was abandoned by 1735). They became firmly established in the early eighteenth century and greatly expanded their production and commercial presence from 1750 to 1790; they also shared their manufacturing techniques and materials with one another, keeping these innovations from Europeans, particularly the French. Moreover, optical instrument makers could make microscopes and telescopes without belonging to the Spectaclemaker's Company. Comparing the availability and quality of optical instruments in England and France, Maurice Daumas argues that the comparative weakness of the English guild system (as compared to that of France up until the Revolution) paired with English trade monopolies created a culture where "English scientific and technical circles, more broadminded in their outlook, showed also a certain solidarity, and the success of the more gifted constructors helped to raise the standard of work among the artisans." See Maurice Daumas, *Scientific Instruments of the Seventeenth and Eighteenth Centuries,* trans. and ed. Mary Holbrook (New York: Praeger, 1972), 91–93, 104. Later in the century, Martin observes that the microscope uses sophisticated glass-making technology: "the Glasses in each Sort are the largest and best that can be made, and therefore the Perfection of these Microscopes the greatest that possibly can be." See Benjamin Martin, *Micrographia Nova* (Reading, 1742), vii.

32. Edward G. Ruestow, *The Microscope in the Dutch Republic: The Shaping of Discovery* (Cambridge: Cambridge University Press, 1996), 6–24.

33. Leeuwenhoek was a minor city official in the Dutch town of Delft who, for fifty years beginning in 1673, wrote long, detailed letters to the Royal Society describing observations through his homemade single-lens microscope; he was elected a fellow of the Royal Society in 1680. Henry Oldenburg (born in Germany and fluent in French and Dutch) and Hooke (who taught himself Dutch) translated Leeuwenhoek's letters, and the Royal Society commissioned Hooke and Nehemiah Grew, a botanist who was also appointed secretary, to replicate Leeuwenhoek's experiments. See A. Schierbeek, *Measuring the Invisible World: The Life and Works of Antoni van Leeuwenhoek* (London: Abelard-Schuman, 1959), 60, 34; Ruestow, *The Microscope in the Dutch Republic*, 146–200; Catherine Wilson, *The Invisible World: Early Modern Philosophy and the Invention of the Microscope* (Princeton, NJ: Princeton University Press, 1995), 88–90; and Marian Fournier, *The Fabric of Life: Microscopy in the Seventeenth Century* (Baltimore, MD: Johns Hopkins University Press, 1996), 75, 97.

34. Robert Hooke, "Discourse concerning Telescopes and Microscopes," in *Philosophical Experiments and Observations* (1726), ed. W. Derham, facsimile reprint (London: Cass, 1967), 261. Natural philosophers and instrument makers such as Henry Baker and George Adams worried that consumers would discard it after only a few uses. See Henry

Baker, *The Microscope Made Easy* (London, 1742), 51, and George Adams, *Essays on the Microscope* (London, 1787), 127.

35. Martin, *Micrographia Nova*, vii; and Jutta Schickore, *The Microscope and the Eye: A History of Reflection, 1740–1870* (Chicago: University of Chicago Press, 2007), 17.

36. Daumas, *Scientific Instruments*, 136, 142.

37. Ibid., 239.

38. See, for example, *A Plain and Familiar Introduction to the Newtonian Experimental Philosophy*, 5th ed. (London, 1765).

39. Stewart, *The Rise of Public Science*, 108.

40. Benjamin Martin, *The Young Gentleman and Lady's Philosophy*, 2 vols. (London, 1759–1763), 1:2. In the section of their dialogue in which Cleonicus outlines the benefits to women of the pocket microscope and the "Parlour-Microscope," Euphrosyne says that her brother has brought examples "of the newest Fashion and Taste." When Martin endorses a specific kind of "Parlour-Microscope" for women, it is not only for two technical features that make the microscope easier to use in a variety of conditions (it can be used either perpendicularly or horizontally and has a circular stage that allows the viewer to rotate the specimen with ease). But Martin also recommends this "Parlour-Microscope" because "the Lightness, Air, and elegance of the Form, render it, in my Opinion, most proper for a *Lady's Use*." He continues: "To which may be added, it being contained in a neat *Shagreen* Case, with a complete Apparatus, renders it much more portable than those of the unusual Forms kept in wooden Boxes" (Martin, *The Young Gentleman*, 2:181). For a discussion of women and the pocket microscope, see Deborah Needleman Armintor, *The Little Everyman: Stature and Masculinity in Eighteenth-Century English Literature* (Seattle: University of Washington Press, 2011), 62–66.

Scientific practice was ever more available, conceptually and historically, to women. See Patricia Phillips, *The Scientific Lady: A Social History of Woman's Scientific Interests, 1520–1918* (London: Weidenfeld and Nicolson, 1990), 57–188; Gerald Dennis Meyer, *The Scientific Lady in England, 1650–1760: An Account of Her Rise, with Emphasis on the Major Roles of the Telescope and Microscope* (Los Angeles: University of California Press, 1955); and the essays in *Men, Women, and the Birthing of Modern Science*, ed. Judith P. Zinsser (DeKalb: Northern Illinois University Press, 2005).

41. Martin, *The Young Gentleman*, 2:175.

42. Ibid., 2:163.

43. Jonathan Swift, *Journal to Stella: Letters to Esther Johnson and Rebecca Dingley, 1710–1713*, ed. Abigail Williams, vol. 9 of *The Cambridge Edition of the Works of Jonathan Swift*, general eds. Claude Rawson, Ian Higgins, David Womersley, and Ian Gadd, 17 vols. (Cambridge: Cambridge University Press, 2013), 68–69 (November 15, 1710) and 96 (December 22, 1710).

44. *The Record of the Royal Society of London for the Promotion of Natural Knowledge*, 4th ed. (London: Morrison & Gibb, 1940), 290.

45. See William T. Lynch's discussion of "things" in *Solomon's Child: Method in the Early Royal Society of London* (Stanford, CA: Stanford University Press, 2001), 21–25: "Bacon's view of 'things' served as a metaphorical ontology enabling nature to speak once the interference of the idols had been checked" (21). See also A. C. Howell, "*Res et verba:* Words and Things," *ELH: English Literary History* 13 (1946): 131–141; and Martin Elsky,

"Bacon's Hieroglyphs and the Separation of Words and Things," *Philological Quarterly* 63 (1984): 449–460.

46. Abraham Cowley, "To the Royal Society," in *The History of the Royal Society*, 3rd ed. (London, 1722), iv.

47. Robert Hooke, *Micrographia: or Some Physiological Descriptions of Minute Bodies* (London, 1665), Preface.

48. Ibid.

49. Sprat, *The History of the Royal Society*, 426.

50. Jonathan Lamb, "Locke's Wild Fancies: Empiricism, Personhood, and Fictionality," *The Eighteenth Century: Theory and Interpretation* 48, no. 3 (2007): 192.

51. Cynthia Sundberg Wall, *The Prose of Things: Transformations of Description in the Eighteenth Century* (Chicago: University of Chicago Press, 2006), 72; Lynch, *Solomon's Child*, 21.

52. Robert Boyle, *A Proemial Essay* (London, 1661), 2:16.

53. Shapin and Schaffer, *Leviathan and the Air-Pump*, 22–79.

54. Jan V. Golinski, "Robert Boyle: Scepticism and Authority in Seventeenth-Century Chemical Discourse," in *The Figural and the Literal: Problems of Language in the History of Science and Philosophy, 1630–1800*, ed. Andrew E. Benjamin, G. N. Cantor, and J. R. R. Christie (Manchester, England: Manchester University Press, 1987), 68; and Laura Baudot, "An Air of History: Joseph Wright's and Robert Boyle's Air Pump Narratives," *Eighteenth-Century Studies* 46, no. 1 (2012): 15–18.

55. Boyle, *A Proemial Essay*, 2:16.

56. Ibid..

57. Samuel Butler, "The Elephant in the Moon," *The Genuine Remains in Verse and Prose of Mr. Samuel Butler* (London, 1749), 1, note.

58. Barbara Maria Stafford, *Body Criticism: Imaging the Unseen in Enlightenment Art and Medicine* (Cambridge, MA: MIT Press, 1993), 346. See also Introduction.

59. Cowley, "To the Royal Society," IX.

60. Ibid.

61. Robert Boyle, *The Christian Virtuoso Shewing that by Being Addicted to Experimental Philosophy, a Man is Rather Assisted than Indisposed to be a Good Christian* (1690), in *The Works of Robert Boyle*, ed. Michael Hunter and Edward B. Davis (London: Pickering & Chatto, 1999), 11:11 ("The Preface").

In his will, Boyle endowed a lecture series devoted to discussing the existence of God. The Boyle lectures ran from 1692 to 1732, and Richard Bentley delivered the first, "A Confutation of Atheism." See Henry Guerlac and M. C. Jacob, "Bentley, Newton, and Providence: The Boyle Lectures Once More," *Journal of the History of Ideas* 30, no. 3 (1969): 307–318.

62. Boyle, *The Christian Virtuoso*, 11. "The Preface."

63. Ibid.

64. Ibid.

65. Ibid.

66. Jayne Elizabeth Lewis, *Air's Appearance: Literary Atmosphere in British Fiction, 1660–1794* (Chicago: University of Chicago Press, 2012), 47. See also 43–58.

67. Ibid., 51.

68. Ibid., 52.

69. Boyle, *New Experiments*, 165, 170

70. Ibid., 165.

71. Ibid., 169.

72. Ibid.

73. Dear, *Revolutionizing the Sciences*, 137.

74. Daniel Defoe, *A tour thro' the whole island of Great Britain* (London, 1724–1727).

75. Henry Power, *Experimental Philosophy in Three Books* (London, 1664), 1:6–7.

76. Christa Knellwolf, "Robert Hooke's *Micrographia* and the Aesthetics of Empiricism," *The Seventeenth Century* 16 (2001): 196, 198.

77. James A. W. Heffernan, *Museum of Words: The Poetics of Ekphrasis from Homer to Ashbery* (Chicago: University of Chicago Press, 1993), 3. See also Frédérique Aït-Touati, *Fictions of the Cosmos: Science and Literature in the Seventeenth Century*, trans. Susan Emanuel (Chicago: University of Chicago Press, 2011), 149–51.

78. Bruno Latour, *We Have Never Been Modern*, trans. Catherine Porter (Cambridge, MA: Harvard University Press, 1993), 23, 28.

79. Christiane Frey, "The Art of Observing the Small: On the Borders of the subvisibilia (from Hooke to Brockes)," *Monatshefte* 105, no. 3 (Fall 2013): 377; and Aït-Touati, *Fictions of the Cosmos*, 143.

80. Hooke, *Micrographia*, Preface.

81. Ibid.

82. Mary Poovey, *A History of the Modern Fact: Problems of Knowledge in the Sciences of Wealth and Society* (Chicago: University of Chicago Press, 1998), 100.

83. Hooke, *Micrographia*, Preface.

84. Ibid.

85. Ibid.

86. Ibid.

87. Ibid.

88. Hooke, "Discourse concerning Telescopes and Microscopes," 262.

89. Brian W. Ogilvie understands observation as a process in *The Science of Describing: Natural History in Renaissance Europe* (Chicago: University of Chicago Press, 2006), 140–141.

90. Shapin and Schaffer, *Leviathan and the Air-Pump*, 60–65; Lynch, *Solomon's Child*, 76–77; and Michael Aaron Dennis, "Graphic Understanding: Instruments and Interpretation in Robert Hooke's *Micrographia*," *Science in Context* 3 (1989): 309–364, esp. 319.

91. Anna Battigelli, *Margaret Cavendish and the Exiles of the Mind* (Lexington: University Press of Kentucky, 1998), 92.

92. Robert Hooke, "A General Scheme, or Idea of the Present State of Natural Philosophy, and How its Defects may be Remedied by a Methodological Proceeding in the making Experiments and Collecting Observations," in *The Posthumous Works of Robert Hooke*, ed. Richard Waller (London, 1705), 1–70.

93. Hooke, *Micrographia*, Preface.

94. Ibid.

95. G. L'E. Turner, "Micrographia Historica: The Study of the History of the Microscope," in *Essays on the History of the Microscope*, ed. G. L'E. Turner (Oxford: Senecio, 1980), 20.

96. Matthew C. Hunter, *Wicked Intelligence: Visual Art and the Science of Experiment in Restoration London* (Chicago: University of Chicago Press, 2013), 28–67.

97. Turner, "Micrographia Historica," 20; and G. L'E. Turner, "Microscopical Communication," in *Essays on the History of the Microscope*, ed. G. L'E. Turner (Oxford: Senecio, 1980), 216.

98. Robert Boyle, *Some Considerations Touching the Usefulness of Experimental Natural Philosophy* (London, 1663), 1:89–90.

99. Peter de Bolla, *The Education of the Eye: Painting, Landscape, and Architecture in Eighteenth-Century Britain* (Stanford, CA: Stanford University Press, 2003), 9, 25–26.

100. Boyle, *Some Considerations*, 1:89–90.

101. Boyle, *A Proemial Essay*, 2:18.

102. Ibid., 2:33, 2:12–13.

103. Daston, "The Empire of Observation," 99–100.

104. Power, *Experimental Philosophy*, 3:192.

105. Ibid.

106. Ibid.

107. Shapin and Schaffer, *Leviathan and the Air-Pump*, 59.

108. Ibid. 65-69; and Donna J. Haraway, *Modest_Witness@Second_Millennium. FemaleMan©Meets_OncoMouse™: Feminism and Technoscience* (New York: Routledge, 1997), 23–30.

109. Stephen Shapin, *The Social History of Truth: Civility and Science in Seventeenth-Century England* (Chicago: University of Chicago Press, 1994), xxvi. For a discussion of "believability" and visual displays, see Ian Hacking, *Representing and Intervening: Introductory Topics in the Philosophy of Natural Science* (Cambridge: Cambridge University Press, 1983), 199. Jonathan Crary makes a similar argument about the eighteenth-century observer based on the technology of the camera obscura in *Techniques of the Observer: On Vision and Modernity in the Nineteenth Century* (Cambridge, MA: MIT Press, 1992), 24, 9.

110. Hooke wrote, "Many other things I long to be at, but I do extremely want time." Robert Boyle, *The Correspondence of Robert Boyle*, ed. Michael Hunter, Antonio Clericuzio and Lawrence Principe (London: Pickering & Chatto, 2001), 3:332 (September 5, 1667).

111. Stephen Inwood, *The Man Who Knew Too Much: The Strange and Inventive Life of Robert Hooke, 1635–1703* (London: Macmillan, 2002), 5, 167, 228–230, 438–39; and Lisa Jardine, *The Curious Life of Robert Hooke: The Man Who Measured London* (New York: Harper Perennial, 2003), 1–15.

112. Jacob and Stewart, *Practical Matter*, 14; and Stephen Pumfrey, "Who Did the Work? Experimental Philosophers and Public Demonstrators in Augustan England," *The British Journal for the History of Science* 28, no. 2 (1995): 131–156.

113. Shapin and Schaffer, *Leviathan and the Air-Pump*, 59. See also Peter Dear, "From Truth to Disinterestedness in the Seventeenth Century," *Social Studies of Science* 22 (1992): 619–631; and Picciotto, *Labors of Innocence*, 193.

114. Shapin and Schaffer, *Leviathan and the Air-Pump*, 65.

115. Steven Shapin, "Pump and Circumstance: Boyle's Literary Technology," *Social Studies of Science* 14 (1984): 481–520.

116. Hooke, *Micrographia*, Preface.

117. Haraway, *Modest_Witness@Second_Millennium*, 23.

118. Ibid., 30. The dominant meaning of the term *modesty* for women in this period was sexual modesty and appeared with great frequency in conduct books and pedagogical texts. Richard Allestree's *The Ladies Calling* (1676) defines female modesty primarily in terms of

its violation, not in any specifically definitional terms. The closest that Allestree comes to defining it is to suggest that it is opposed to "Boldness and Indecency" as well as "to Lightness and Wantonness." See Richard Allestree, *The Ladies Calling*, 4th ed. (London, 1676), 1–27, esp. 5. Richard Steele copies Allestree's language in *The Ladies Library* (London, 1714), 179.

119. Marie Boas Hall, *Robert Boyle and Seventeenth-Century Chemistry* (Cambridge: Cambridge University Press, 1956), 185.

120. Alpers alludes to Hooke's disembodied witness to characterize the representational protocols emerging in pictorial regimes, titling a key chapter, "'With a Sincere Hand and a Faithful Eye,'" in *The Art of Describing: Dutch Art in the Seventeenth Century* (London: John Murray, 1983).

121. Hooke, *Micrographia*, Preface.

122. Ibid.

123. John Locke, *An Essay Concerning Human Understanding*, ed. Peter H. Nidditch (Oxford: Oxford University Press, 1975), 2.23.12.

124. Ibid.

125. Hooke, *Micrographia*, Preface.

126. Ibid.

127. Sprat, *The History of the Royal Society*, 85.

128. Robert Boyle, *New Experiments Physico-Mechanicall, Touching the Spring of the Air, and its Effects* (1660), in vol. 1 of *The Works of Robert Boyle*, ed. Michael Hunter and Edward B. Davis (London: Pickering & Chatto, 1999), 1:164.

129. Richard Holmes characterizes the late eighteenth and early nineteenth centuries as "the age of wonder" in which science became popularized. See *The Age of Wonder: How the Romantic Generation Discovered the Beauty and Terror of Science* (New York: HarperPress, 2008). For Sarah Tindal Kareem, *wonder* is both affect and noun: wonder sustains incredulity and ambivalence. In *Eighteenth-Century Fiction and the Reinvention of Wonder* (Oxford: Oxford University Press, 2014).

130. Michael Hunter, "Robert Hooke: The Natural Philosopher," in *London's Leonardo: The Life and Work of Robert Hooke*, ed. Jim Bennett (Oxford: Oxford University Press, 2003), 149. Aït-Touati reads *Micrographia* in the tradition of wonder books. See *Fictions of the Cosmos*, 144–148.

131. Baker also published a companion piece, *Employment for the Microscope* (London, 1753), which includes seventy-seven observations and instructions for readers to replicate.

132. "Henry Baker," *Biographia Britannica: Or, the Lives of the Most Eminent Persons Who Have Flourished in Great Britain and Ireland*, 2nd ed. (London, 1778), 1:525, 1:526.

133. Baker, *The Microscope Made Easy*, 135.

134. Ibid., 51.

135. Lorraine Daston, "Enlightenment Fears, Fears of Enlightenment," in *What's Left of Enlightenment? A Postmodern Question*, ed. Keith Michael Baker and Peter Hanns Reill (Stanford, CA: Stanford University Press, 2001), 118, 120.

136. Sprat, *The History of the Royal Society*, 331.

137. Ibid., 335.

138. Ibid. Matthew L. Jones argues that Descartes, Pascal, and Leibniz similarly opened up the space for scientific practitioners to be—and to become—virtuous, in contrast to the notion that natural philosophy would lead an individual into dangerous moral territory. In Matthew L. Jones, *The Good Life in the Scientific Revolution: Descartes, Pascal, Leibniz, and the Cultivation of Virtue* (Chicago: University of Chicago Press, 2006).

139. Henry Baker, A*n Attempt towards a Natural History of the Polype: In a Letter to Martin Folkes, Esq; President of the Royal Society* (London, 1743), 215–216.

140. Ibid.

141. Barbara M. Benedict, *Curiosity: A Cultural History of Early Modern Inquiry* (Chicago: University of Chicago Press, 2002).

142. Baker, *Natural History of the Polype*, 207.

143. Ibid.

CHAPTER 2

1. Lisa A. Freeman, *Character's Theater: Genre and Identity on the Eighteenth-Century Stage* (Philadelphia: University of Pennsylvania Press, 2002), 11–46; and Manushag N. Powell, *Performing Authorship in Eighteenth-Century English Periodicals* (Lewisburg, PA: Bucknell University Press, 2012), 13–48.

2. Donna J. Haraway, *Modest_Witness@Second_Millennium. FemaleMan©Meets_Onco-Mouse™: Feminism and Technoscience* (New York: Routledge, 1997), 29; John Shanahan, "Theatrical Space and Scientific Space in Thomas Shadwell's Virtuoso," *SEL: Studies in English Literature, 1500–1900*, 49, no. 3 (2009): 549–71; esp. 549–50; Joanna Picciotto, *Labors of Innocence in Early Modern England* (Cambridge, MA: Harvard University Press, 2010), 285; and Al Coppola, *The Theater of Experiment: Staging Natural Philosophy in Eighteenth-Century Britain* (Oxford: Oxford University Press, 2016), 6–10.

3. Michael Hunter, *Science and Society in Restoration England* (Cambridge: Cambridge University Press, 1981), 67; and William T. Lynch, *Solomon's Child: Method in the Early Royal Society of London* (Stanford, CA: Stanford University Press, 2001), 6.

4. Walter E. Houghton, Jr. "The English Virtuoso in the Seventeenth Century: Part I," *Journal of the History of Ideas* 3, no. 1 (1942): 66, 71–72; and Craig Ashley Hanson, *The English Virtuoso: Art, Medicine, and Antiquarianism in the Age of Empiricism* (Chicago: University of Chicago Press, 2009), 2–8.

5. Robert Boyle, *New Experiments Physico-Mechanicall, Touching the Spring of the Air, and its Effects* (1660), in vol. 1 of *The Works of Robert Boyle,* ed. Michael Hunter and Edward B. Davis (London: Pickering & Chatto, 1999), 1:169.

6. Houghton, "The English Virtuoso: Part I," 53.

7. *OED* and David Walton, "Copernicus or Cheesecake? Faultlines and Unjust Des(s)erts: Notes towards the Cultural Significance of the Virtuosa," *Cuardernos de Filogia Inglesa* 9, no. 2 (2001): 48.

8. Walter E. Houghton, Jr. "The English Virtuoso in the Seventeenth Century: Part II," *Journal of the History of Ideas* 3, no. 1 (1942): 204, 211; and Houghton, "The English Virtuoso in the Seventeenth Century: Part I," 63.

9. Mary Astell, *An Essay in Defence of the Female Sex* (London, 1696), 103.

10. John Dryden, *Sir Martin Marr-All: or, the Feigned Innocence* (1668), vol. 9 of *The Works of John Dryden,* ed. John Loftis (Berkeley: University of California Press, 1966), III.i.60–61.

11. Samuel Johnson, *The Idler and The Adventurer,* ed. W. J. Bate, John M. Bullitt, L. F. Powell, vol. 2 of *The Yale Edition of the Works of Samuel Johnson* (New Haven, CT: Yale University Press, 1963), 199 (no. 64; Saturday, July 7, 1759).

12. Tipping Silvester, "The Microscope. A Poem," *Original Poems and Translations* (London, 1733), 47.

13. Ibid., 48.

14. "The Microscope," in *Female Inconstancy Display'd in three Diverting Histories... To which is added, Several Diverting Tales and Merry Jokes* (London, 1732), 41.

15. Lorraine Daston, "The Empire of Observation, 1600–1800," in *Histories of Scientific Observation*, ed. Lorraine Daston and Elizabeth Lunbeck (Chicago: University of Chicago Press, 2011), 102. This figure also provides material for the "mad scientist" character. See Barbara M. Benedict, "The Mad Scientist: The Creation of a Literary Stereotype," in *Imagining the Sciences: Expressions of New Knowledge in the "Long" Eighteenth Century*, ed. Robert C. Leitz, III and Kevin L. Cope (New York: AMS Press, 2004), 59–107.

16. "The Microscope," 42.

17. Ibid., 41.

18. Deborah Needleman Armintor, *The Little Everyman: Stature and Masculinity in Eighteenth-Century English Literature* (Seattle: University of Washington Press, 2011), 56–79.

19. Edward G. Ruestow, *The Microscope in the Dutch Republic: The Shaping of Discovery* (Cambridge: Cambridge University Press, 1996), 23–26.

20. Alexander Pope, *The Correspondence of Alexander Pope*, ed. George Sherburn (Oxford: Clarendon Press, 1956): 1:465 (February 18, 1718).

21. Henry Baker, *The Microscope Made Easy* (London, 1742), 152–167.

22. *The Diary of Robert Hooke*, ed. Henry W. Robinson and Walter Adams (London: Taylor & Francis, 1935), 235.

23. Marie Boas Hall, *Promoting Experimental Learning: Experiment and the Royal Society, 1660–1727* (Cambridge: Cambridge University Press, 1991), 3, 22.

24. Lisa Jardine, *The Curious Life of Robert Hooke: The Man Who Measured London* (New York: HarperCollins, 2004), 1–15.

25. Marjorie Hope Nicolson, *Science and Imagination* (Ithaca, NY: Cornell University Press, 1956), 113, 142; Claude Lloyd, "Shadwell and the Virtuosi," *PMLA* 44, no. 2 (1929): 472–494; Joseph M. Glide, "Shadwell and the Royal Society: Satire in *The Virtuoso*," *SEL: Studies in English Literature, 1500–1900*, 10, no. 3 (1970): 469–490; and Peter Anstey, "Literary Responses to Robert Boyle's Natural Philosophy," in *Science, Literature and Rhetoric in Early Modern England*, ed. Juliet Cummins and David Burchell (Aldershot, Hampshire: Ashgate, 2007), 147.

26. David A. Brewer, *The Afterlife of Character, 1726–1825* (Philadelphia: University of Pennsylvania Press, 2005), 6.

27. William Wotton, *Reflections upon Ancient and Modern Learning* (London, 1697), 418.

28. William Congreve, "Prologue to Pyrrhus King of Epirus," in *The Works of Mr. William Congreve*, 4th ed. (London, 1725), 3:277; Joseph Addison, *The Tatler*, ed. Donald F. Bond (Oxford: Clarendon Press, 1987), 3:133–135 (no. 216; August 26, 1710); and John Hildrop, *A Modest Apology for the Ancient and Honourable Family of the Wrongheads* (London, 1744), 22.

29. Thomas Shadwell, *The Virtuoso*, ed. Marjorie Hope Nicolson and David Stuart Rodes (Lincoln: University of Nebraska Press, 1966), II.ii.298–300. Subsequent citations will be noted parenthetically within the text.

30. Stephen Shapin, "The House of Experiment in Seventeenth-Century England," *Isis* 79 (1988): 373–404.

31. Jean I. Marsden, "Ideology, Sex, and Satire: The Case of Thomas Shadwell," in *Cutting Edges: Postmodern Critical Essays on Eighteenth-Century Satire*, ed. James E. Gill (Knoxville: University of Tennessee Press, 1995), 47–48.

32. Judith B. Slagle, "'A Great Rabble of People': The Ribbon-Weavers in Thomas Shadwell's *The Virtuoso*," *Notes and Queries* 36 (September 1989): 353–354.

33. Piccotto, *Labors of Innocence*, 244.

34. James Miller, *The Humours of* Oxford (London, 1730), 13. Subsequent citations will be noted parenthetically within the text.

35. Tita Chico, *Designing Women: The Dressing Room in Eighteenth-Century English Literature and Culture* (Lewisburg, PA: Bucknell University Press, 2005).

36. Susanna Centlivre, *The Basset-Table*, vol. 3 of *The Works of the Celebrated Mrs. Centlivre* (London, 1760–1761), 222, 220. Subsequent citations will be noted parenthetically within the text.

37. Chico, *Designing Women*, 25–45.

38. Beth Kowaleski Wallace, "A Modest Defense of Gaming Women," *Studies in Eighteenth-Century Culture* 31 (2002): 21–39.

39. Katharine M. Rogers, *Feminism in Eighteenth-Century England* (Urbana: University of Illinois Press, 1982), 100; Patsy S. Fowler, "Rejecting the Status Quo: The Attempts of Mary Pix and Susanna Centlivre to Reform Society's Patriarchal Attitudes," *Restoration and 18th-Century Theatre Research* 11, no. 2 (1996): 52; and Eleanor Mattes, "The 'Female Virtuoso' in Early Eighteenth-Century English Drama," *Women and Literature* 3, no. 2 (1975): 8.

40. Laura J. Rosenthal, *Playwrights and Plagiarists in Early Modern England: Gender, Authorship, Literary Property* (Ithaca, NY: Cornell University Press, 1996), 206.

41. For a discussion of this relationship between empire and the domestic in the period's drama, see Bridget Orr, *Empire on the English Stage, 1660–1714* (Cambridge: Cambridge University Press, 2001), 1–27.

42. Ruth Perry, *Novel Relations: The Transformation of Kinship in English Literature and Culture, 1748–1818* (Cambridge: Cambridge University Press, 2004), 19–20.

43. Steele, *The Tatler*, 1:154 (no. 19; 24 May 1709).

44. Douglas R. Butler, "Plot and Politics in Susanna Centlivre's *A Bold Stroke for a Wife*," in *Curtain Calls: British and American Women and the Theater, 1660–1820*, ed. Mary Anne Schofield and Cecilia Macheski (Athens: Ohio University Press, 1991), 362, 370.

45. John O'Brien, "Busy Bodies: The Plots of Susanna Centlivre," in *Eighteenth-Century Genre and Culture: Serious Reflections on Occasional Forms. Essays in Honor of J. Paul Hunter*, ed. Dennis Todd and Cynthia Wall (Newark: University of Delaware Press, 2001), 166.

46. Eliza Haywood, *The History of Miss Betsy Thoughtless*, ed. Christine Blouch (Peterborough, ONT: Broadview Press, 1998), 142.

47. Ibid., 176.

48. Juliette Merritt, "Reforming the Coquette: Eliza Haywood's Vision of Female Epistemology," in *Fair Philosopher: Eliza Haywood and the Female Spectator*, ed. Lynn Marie Write and Donald J. Newman (Lewisburg, PA: Bucknell University Press, 2006), 180–181.

49. Ibid., 180.

50. See Shelley King and Yaël Schlick, eds., *Refiguring the Coquette* (Lewisburg, PA: Bucknell University Press, 2008), and Theresa Braunschneider, *Our Coquettes: Capacious Desire in the Eighteenth Century* (Charlottesville: University of Virginia Press, 2009).

51. On Mr. Spectator's characterization, see Scott Paul Gordon, "Voyeuristic Dreams: Mr. Spectator and the Power of Spectacle," *The Eighteenth Century: Theory and Interpre-*

tation 36, no. 1 (1995): 3; Anthony Pollock, *Gender and the Fictions of the Public Sphere, 1690–1755* (New York: Routledge, 2009), 55–74; and Joanna Picciotto, *Labors of Innocence in Early Modern England* (Cambridge, MA: Harvard University Press, 2010), 566–583.

52. Joseph Addison and Richard Steele, *The Spectator*, ed. Donald F. Bond (Oxford: Clarendon Press, 1987), 1:519 (no. 262; December 31, 1711). All subsequent citations will be included in the text.

53. Barbara Maria Stafford, *Body Criticism: Imaging the Unseen in Enlightenment Art and Medicine* (Cambridge, MA: MIT Press, 1993), 346.

54. Erin Mackie, *Market á la Mode: Fashion, Commodity, and Gender in* The Tatler *and* The Spectator (Baltimore, MD: Johns Hopkins University Press, 1997), 1–29.

55. Juliette Merritt, *Beyond Spectacle: Eliza Haywood's Female Spectators* (Toronto: University of Toronto Press, 2004), 11; and Iona Italia, *The Rise of Literary Journalism in the Eighteenth Century: Anxious Employment* (London: Routledge, 2005), 123–129. More recently, Manushag N. Powell has read the Female Spectator as a spinster (*Performing Authorship in Eighteenth-Century English Periodicals*, 154).

56. For a discussion of the relation between the *Spectator* and the *Female Spectator*, see Deborah J. Nestor, "Representing Domestic Difficulties: Eliza Haywood and the Critique of Bourgeois Ideology," *Prose Studies* 16, no. 2 (1993): 3; Shawn Lisa Maurer, *Proposing Men: Dialectics of Gender and Class in the Eighteenth-Century Periodical* (Stanford, CA: Stanford University Press, 1998), 204–231; Eve Tavor Bannet, "Haywood's Spectator and the Female World," in *Fair Philosopher: Eliza Haywood and* The Female Spectator, ed. Lynn Marie Wright and Donald J. Newman (Lewisburg, PA: Bucknell University Press, 2006), 82–103; Lynn Marie Wright and Donald J. Newman, "Introduction," in *Fair Philosopher: Eliza Haywood and* The Female Spectator, ed. Lynn Marie Wright and Donald J. Newman (Lewisburg, PA: Bucknell University Press, 2006), 13–17; and Pollock, *Gender and the Fictions of the Public Sphere*, 147–84.

57. Eliza Haywood, *The Female Spectator* (London, 1746), 17:291. Subsequent citations are noted parenthetically within the text.

58. Leon Battista Alberti, *On the Art of Building in Ten Books,* trans. Joseph Rykwert, Neil Leach, and Robert Tavernor (Cambridge, MA: MIT Press, 1994), 144; Orest Ranum, "The Refuges of Intimacy," in *Passions of the Renaissance,* ed. Roger Chartier, vol. 3 of *A History of Private Life*, ed. Philippe Ariès and Georges Duby (Cambridge, MA: Harvard University Press, 1989), 210–229; and Alan Stewart, "The Early Modern Closet Discovered," *Representations* 50 (1995): 76–100.

59. Richard Steele, *The Ladies Diary* (London, 1714), 1:59–66

60. Kristin M. Girten, "Unsexed Souls: Natural Philosophy as Transformation in Eliza Haywood's Female Spectator," *Eighteenth-Century Studies* 43, no. 1 (2009): 57.

61. Celia Fiennes, "To the Reader," in *The Illustrated Journeys of Celia Fiennes*, 1685-c. 1712, ed. Christopher Morris (London: Macdonald, 1982), 32.

62. Mackie, *Market á la Mode*, 20; and James Noggle, *The Temporality of Taste in Eighteenth-Century British Writing* (Oxford: Oxford University Press, 2012), 1–39.

63. Ricardo Miguel-Alfonso, "Social Conservatism, Aesthetic Education and the Essay Genre in Eliza Haywood's *Female Spectator*," in *Fair Philosopher: Eliza Haywood and* The Female Spectator, ed. Lynn Marie Wright and Donald J. Newman (Lewisburg, PA: Bucknell University Press, 2006), 79. Robert W. Jones, "Eliza Haywood and the Discourse of Taste," in *Authorship, Commerce and the Public: Scenes of Writing,*

1750–1850, ed. E. J. Clery, Caroline Franklin, and Peter Garside (New York: Palgrave Macmillan, 2002), 103.

64. Simon Gikandi, *Slavery and the Culture of Taste* (Princeton, NJ: Princeton University Press, 2011), 17.

65. Dabney Townsend, *Hume's Aesthetic Theory: Taste and Sentiment* (London: Routledge, 2001), 86–136.

66. David Hume, "Of the Standard of Taste," in *Essays: Moral, Political, and Literary*, ed. Eugene F. Miller (Indianapolis, IN: Liberty Classics, 1985), 241.

67. Hume, "Of the Delicacy of Taste and Passion," in *Essays: Moral, Political, and Literary*, ed. Eugene F. Miller (Indianapolis, IN: Liberty Classics, 1985), 4.

68. Denise Gigante, *Taste: A Literary History* (New Haven, CT: Yale University Press, 2005), 1–21.

69. Hume, "Of the Standard of Taste," 242.

70. Ibid., 243.

71. Ralph Cohen, "David Hume's Experimental Method and the Theory of Taste," *ELH: English Literary History* 25 (1958): 288; Redding S. Sugg, Jr., "Hume's Search for the Key with the Leathern Tongs," *Journal of Aesthetics and Art Criticism* 16 (1957): 101; and Ernest Campbell Mossner, "Hume's 'Of Criticism,'" in *Studies in Criticism and Aesthetics, 1600–1800*, ed. Howard Anderson and John S. Shea (Minneapolis: University of Minnesota Press, 1967), 239.

72. David Marshall, *The Frame of Art: Fictions of Aesthetic Experience* (Baltimore, MD: Johns Hopkins University Press, 2005), 187.

CHAPTER 3

1. Eliza Haywood, *Love in Excess*, ed. David Oakleaf, 2nd ed. (Peterborough, ONT: Broadview Press, 2000), 86.

2. Ibid., 99.

3. Ibid.,100.

4. Ibid.

5. Ibid.

6. Ibid.

7. Ibid., n. 1.

8. See Toni Bowers, *Force or Fraud: British Seduction Stories and the Problem of Resistance, 1660–1760* (Oxford: Oxford University Press, 2011), 228–237. As Bowers notes, Melliora exercises "virtue *within*, not only *against*, apparently transgressive sexual desire" (232).

9. Francis Bacon, *Novum Organum*, in *The Works of Francis Bacon*, ed. James Spedding, Robert Leslie Ellis, and Douglas Denon Heath, facsimile edition (Stuttgart-Bad Cannstatt: F. Frommann Verl. G. Holzboog, 1963), 8:71, 8:63.

10. Francis Bacon, "Plan of the Work," in *The Works of Francis Bacon*, ed. James Spedding, Robert Leslie Ellis, and Douglas Denon Heath, facsimile edition (Stuttgart-Bad Cannstatt: F. Frommann Verl. G. Holzboog, 1963), 8:47.

11. Desiree Hellegers, *Handmaid to Divinity: Natural Philosophy, Poetry, and Gender in Seventeenth-Century England* (Norman: University of Oklahoma Press, 2000), 52; see also 43–54. See also Carolyn Merchant, *The Death of Nature: Women, Ecology, and the Scientific Revolution* (San Francisco: Harper and Row, 1980), 164–91; Evelyn Fox Keller,

Reflections on Gender and Science (New Haven, CT: Yale University Press, 1985), 33–42; and Brian Easlea, *Science and Sexual Oppression: Patriarchy's Confrontation with Women and Nature* (London: Weidenfeld and Nicolson, 1981). In a seeming contradiction, Bacon also links experiment to respectable marriage, yet even this association draws on the prototypical logic of the seduction plot.

12. Alan Bewell, "A Passion that Transforms: Picturing the Early Natural History Collector," in *Figuring It Out: Science, Gender, and Visual Culture*, ed. Ann B. Shteir and Bernard Lightman (Hanover, NH: Dartmouth College Press, 2006), 28–53.

13. Abraham Cowley, "Ode. Upon Dr. *Harvey*," in *Verses, Written Upon Several Occasions* (London, 1663), 18.

14. Mary Baine Campbell, *Wonder and Science: Imagining Worlds in Early Modern Europe* (Ithaca, NY: Cornell University Press, 1999), 186–187, 189, 201.

15. James Grantham Turner, *Schooling Sex: Libertine Literature and Erotic Education in Italy, France, and England, 1543–1685* (Oxford: Oxford University Press, 2003), 316. My thanks to Kathy Lubey for pointing to this connection.

16. On epistemological and sexual desire, see Scott Black, "Trading Sex for Secrets in Haywood's Love in Excess," *Eighteenth-Century Fiction* 15, no. 2 (January 2003): 207–226; and Katherine Binhammer, *The Seduction Narrative in Britain, 1747–1800* (Cambridge: Cambridge University Press, 2009), 9.

17. Bowers, *Force or Fraud*, 3. See also Jonathan Kramnick, *Actions and Objects from Hobbes to Richardson* (Stanford, CA: Stanford University Press, 2010), 177.

18. Bowers, *Force or Fraud*, 9.

19. Ibid.

20. The dynamic I describe counters Lisa Anscomb's claim that both Fontenelle and Algarotti sexualize the philosopher's female companions as a way of denigrating women and proving masculine virility. In Lisa Anscomb, "'As Far as a Woman's Reasoning Can Go': Scientific Dialogue and Sexploitation," *History of European Ideas* 31 (2005): 193–208.

21. Stuart Gillespie and Penelope Wilson, "The Publishing and Readership of Translation," in *The Oxford History of Literary Translation in English: 1660–1790*, ed. Stuart Gillespie and David Hopkins (Oxford: Oxford University Press, 2005), 39.

22. See David Hopkins and Pat Rogers, "The Translator's Trade," in *The Oxford History of Literary Translation in English: 1660–1790*, ed. Stuart Gillespie and David Hopkins (Oxford: Oxford University Press, 2005), 82–83.

23. Mary Helen McMurran, *The Spread of Novels: Translation and Prose Fiction in the Eighteenth Century* (Princeton, NJ: Princeton University Press, 2010), 7.

24. Peter France, "Moralists and Philosophers," in *The Oxford History of Literary Translation in English: 1660–1790*, ed. Stuart Gillespie and David Hopkins (Oxford: Oxford University Press, 2005), 369–370.

25. *A Discourse of the Plurality of Worlds*, trans. Sir W. D. Knight (Dublin, 1687), dedication. Knight dedicates his volume, *A Discourse of the Plurality of Worlds* (which was never reissued), to William Molyneux, a member of Parliament, fellow of the Royal Society, founder of the Dublin Philosophical Society, and translator of Descartes, who in turn pens the address "To the Bookseller" (France, "Moralists and Philosophers," 368). Knight praises Molyneux for introducing him to Fontenelle: the text, Knight argues, was Fontenelle's "Diversion in the Country, so I made them mind" (Knight, *A Discourse*, dedication).

26. Knight, *A Discourse*, dedication.

27. Ibid. Molyneux's epistle to the Bookseller opposes Knight's view of women (Knight, *A Discourse*, "To the Bookseller").

28. Glanvill's enthusiasm to promote and defend the Royal Society in his published work likely led to his election as a fellow in 1664. See Marie Boas Hall, *Promoting Experimental Learning: Experiment and the Royal Society, 1660–1727* (Cambridge: Cambridge University Press, 1991), 52–53.

29. See Sarah Annes Brown, "Women Translators," in *The Oxford History of Literary Translation in English: 1660–1790*, ed. Stuart Gillespie and David Hopkins (Oxford: Oxford University Press, 2005), 115; Sherry Simon, *Gender in Translation: Cultural Identity and the Politics of Transmission* (London: Routledge, 1996), 52–58; and Elizabeth Spearing, "Aphra Behn: The Politics of Translation," in *Aphra Behn Studies*, ed. Janet Todd (Cambridge: Cambridge University Press, 1996), 154–177.

30. France, "Moralists and Philosophers," 368.

31. Aphra Behn, *A Discovery of New Worlds*, in *The Works of Aphra Behn*, ed. Janet Todd (London: William Pickering, 1996), 4:86. Subsequent references are cited parenthetically within the text.

32. Robert Markley, "Global Analogies: Cosmology, Geosymmetry, and Skepticism in some Works of Aphra Behn," in *Science, Literature and Rhetoric in Early Modern England*, ed. Juliet Cummins and David Burchell (Aldershot, Hampshire: Ashgate, 2007), 201.

33. Ibid.

34. Ibid., 190.

35. E. J. Clery, *The Feminization Debate in Eighteenth-Century England: Literature, Commerce and Luxury* (London: Palgrave Macmillan, 2004), 76.

36. Melanie Bigold, *Women of Letters, Manuscript Circulation, and Print Afterlives in the Eighteenth Century: Elizabeth Rowe, Catharine Cockburn, and Elizabeth Carter* (New York: Palgrave Macmillan, 2013), 170. See esp. "Elizabeth Carter: 'a very extraordinary Phaenomenon in the Republic of Letters,'" 169–212. Carter was also known to have tutored her younger brother and nephew for entry into Cambridge and Oxford, according to Melanie Bigold, "Letters and Learning," in *The History of British Women's Writing, 1690–1750*, ed. Ros Ballaster, vol. 4 of *The History of British Women's Writing*, ed. Jennie Batchelor and Cora Kaplan (Basingstoke: Palgrave Macmillan, 2010), 181. See also Clery, *The Feminization Debate*, 76–77.

37. Clery, *The Feminization Debate*, 76.

38. *Memoirs of the Life of Mrs. Elizabeth Carter with A New Edition of her Poems*, ed. Montagu Pennington (London, 1807), 9. See Robert DeMaria, Jr., *The Life of Samuel Johnson: A Critical Biography* (Oxford: Blackwell, 1994); Anthony W. Lee, "Who's Mentoring Whom? Mentorship, Alliance, and Rivalry in the Carter-Johnson Relationship," in *Mentoring in Eighteenth-Century British Literature and Culture*, ed. Anthony W. Lee (Surrey: Ashgate, 2010), 191–210; and Bigold, *Women of Letters*, 185–193.

39. Thomas Birch, *History of the Works of the Learned*, Art. 31 (June 1, 1739), 392.

40. For the description of Carter as a "university," see Elizabeth Carter and Catherine Talbot, *A Series of Letters between Mrs. Elizabeth Carter and Miss Catherine Talbot, from the year 1741 to 1770*, facsimile edition, (New York: AMS Press, 1975), 2:186 (November 26, 1754), 2:351 (Lambeth, September 17, 1760). Although Carter's name does not appear on the title page of either volume, contemporaries knew that she was the translator of

both. See Sylvia Harcstark Myers, *The Bluestocking Circle: Women, Friendship, and the Life of the Mind in Eighteenth-Century England* (Oxford: Clarendon Press, 1990), 52–54.

41. For example, Carter visited William Haley in 1738 and engaged in a lengthy correspondence about mathematics with the astronomer and mathematician Thomas Wright of Durham. The Algarotti and the Crousaz translations both required substantial knowledge of Newton's theories. See Gwen I. Hampshire, "An Edition of Some Unpublished Letters of Elizabeth Carter, 1717–1806, and a Calendar of Her Correspondence" (B.Litt. dissertation, Oxford University, 1972), xlvi, and Carter, *Memoirs of the Life*, 16. Hampshire's edition of Carter's letters is published as *Elizabeth Carter, 1717–1806: An Edition of Some Unpublished Letters*, ed. Gwen Hampshire (Newark: University of Delaware Press, 2005).

42. Bigold, "Letters and Learning," 181; Claudia Thomas, " 'Th'instructive Moral, and Important Thought": Elizabeth Carter reads Pope, Johnson and Epictetus," *The Age of Johnson* 4 (1991): 137–169; and Myers, *The Bluestocking Circle*.

43. Myers, *The Bluestocking Circle*, 169; and Judith Hawley, "Elizabeth Carter and Modes of Knowledge," in *Woman to Woman: Female Negotiations during the Long Eighteenth Century*, ed. Carolyn D. Williams, Angela Escott, and Louise Duckling (Newark: University of Delaware Press, 2010), 157.

44. Margaret C. Jacob and Larry Stewart, *Practical Matter: Newton's Science in the Service of Industry and Empire, 1687–1851* (Cambridge, MA: Harvard University Press, 2004), 14–15.

45. Patricia Fara, *Newton: The Making of Genius* (London: Picador, 2003), 66.

46. Clery, *The Feminization Debate*, 77.

47. Paula Findlen, "A Forgotten Newtonian: Women and Science in the Italian Provinces," in *The Sciences in Enlightened Europe*, ed. William Clark, Jan Golinski, and Simon Schaffer (Chicago: University of Chicago Press, 1999), 316. See also Paula Findlen, "Translating the New Science: Translating the New Science: Women and the Circulation of Knowledge in Enlightenment Italy," *Configurations* 2 (1995): 167–206; and Mary Fissell and Roger Cooter, "Exploring Natural Knowledge: Science and the Popular," in *Eighteenth-Century Science*, ed. Roy Porter, vol. 4 of *The Cambridge History of Science* (Cambridge: Cambridge University Press, 2003), 138.

48. To Lady Bute, October 10, 1753, *The Complete Letters of Lady Mary Wortley Montagu*, ed. Robert Halsband (Oxford: Clarendon Press, 1967), 3:39.

49. Ibid., 3:40.

50. Francesco Algarotti, *Sir Isaac Newton's Philosophy Explain'd for the Use of the Ladies*, [trans. Elizabeth Carter], (London, 1737), 1:22, 1:24, 1:72. Subsequent references are cited parenthetically within the text.

51. Spearing, "Aphra Behn: The Politics of Translation," 166–167.

52. Leonard M. Marsak, "Bernard de Fontenelle: The Idea of Science in the French Enlightenment," *Transactions of the American Philosophical Society*, n.s. 49, pt. 7 (1959): 3–64; Leonard M. Marsak, "Cartesianism in Fontenelle and French Science, 1686–1752," *Isis* 50 (1959): 51–60; and Steven J. Dick, *Plurality of Worlds: The Origins of the Extraterrestrial Life Debate from Democritus to Kant* (Cambridge: Cambridge University Press, 1982), 123–128.

53. In my discussion of Fontenelle, I use Behn's translation, including its English title.

54. Nina Rattner Gelbart, "Introduction," to Bernard le Bovier de Fontenelle, *Conversations on the Plurality of Worlds*, trans. H. A. Hargreaves (Berkeley: University of California Press, 1990), vii; and J. B. Shank, "Neither Natural Philosophy, Nor Science, Nor Literature:

Gender Writing, and the Pursuit of Nature in Fontenelle's *Entretiens sur la pluralité des mondes habités*," in *Men, Women, and the Birthing of Modern Science*, ed. Judith P. Zinsser (DeKalb: Northern Illinois University Press, 2005), Table 2, note b.

55. Gelbart, "Introduction," xxiv.

56. J. B. Shank reminds us that Fontenelle's appointment was "based, it should be remembered, on almost no other scientific credentials than his authorship of *Les mondes*" (Shank, "Neither Natural Philosophy," 99).

57. The genre of the dialogue also provided a medium for female voices, particularly in the seventeenth century. See Jane Donawerth, *Conversational Rhetoric: The Rise and Fall of a Woman's Tradition, 1600–1900* (Carbondale: Southern Illinois University Press, 2012), 17.

58. Robert Niklaus, "Fontenelle as a Model for the Transmission and Vulgarization of Ideas in the Enlightenment," in *Voltaire and His World: Studies Presented to W. H. Barber*, ed. R. J. Howells, A. Mason, H. T. Mason, and D. Williams (Oxford: Voltaire Foundation, 1985), 176; and Londa Schiebinger, *The Mind Has No Sex? Women in the Origins of Modern Science* (Cambridge, MA: Harvard University Press, 1989), 37–44. For a discussion of Fontenelle's use of the dialogue in *The Dialogues of the Dead*, see John W. Cosentini, *Fontenelle's Art of Dialogue* (New York: King's Crown Press, 1952).

59. See Erica Harth, *Cartesian Women: Versions and Subversions of Rational Discourse in the Old Regime* (Ithaca, NY: Cornell University Press, 1992); Dena Goodman, *The Republic of Letters: A Cultural History of the French Enlightenment* (Ithaca, NY: Cornell University Press, 1994) and "Enlightenment Salons: The Convergence of Female and Philosophic Ambitions," *Eighteenth-Century Studies* 22 (1988–1989): 329–350; Geoffrey Sutton, *Science for a Polite Society: Gender, Culture, and the Demonstration of Enlightenment* (Boulder, CO: Westview Press, 1995); and Mary Terrall, "Gendered Spaces, Gendered Audiences: Inside and Outside the Paris Academy of Sciences," *Configurations* 3, no. 2 (1995): 207–232.

60. See Emmanuel Bury, *Littérature et politesse: L'invention de l'honnête home, 1580–1750* (Paris: Presses Universitaires de France, 1996), 195–203; Norbert Elias, *The Civilizing Process: Sociogenetic and Psychogenetic Investigations*, trans. Edmund Jephcott (Oxford: Blackwell, 2000); Carolyn Lougee Chappell, *Le Paradis des Femmes: Women, Salons, and Social Stratification in Seventeenth-Century France* (Princeton, NJ: Princeton University Press, 1976); Joan DeJean, *Tender Geographies: Women and the Origins of the Novel in France* (New York: Columbia University Press, 1991); Benedetta Craveri, *The Age of Conversation*, trans. Teresa Waugh (New York: New York Review of Books, 2005); and Dan Edelstein, *The Enlightenment: A Genealogy* (Chicago: University of Chicago Press, 2010), 34–35.

61. Edelstein, *The Enlightenment*, 35; and Niklaus, "Fontenelle as a Model," 168.

62. See, for example, *Mental Improvement, or the Beauties and Wonders of Nature and Art* (1794–1797), and Jane Marcet's *Conversations on Chemistry* (1806) and *Conversations on Natural Philosophy* (1819).

63. The roles of the powerful noblewoman and her socially inferior instructor correlate to the historical record. Princess Elisabeth of Bohemia corresponded with Descartes about subtle and sophisticated philosophical topics. Galileo published *Letter to the Grand Duchess Christina* (1615), which purportedly reproduced scientific arguments from a gathering at the duchess's. See Peter Dear, "A Philosophical Duchess: Understanding Margaret Cavendish and the Royal Society," in *Science, Literature and Rhetoric in Early Modern England*, ed. Juliet Cummins and David Burchell, (Aldershot, Hampshire: Ashgate, 2007), 126.

Life and art combined to generate a literary convention: following Fontenelle's portrayal of a marchioness in *Les mondes*, women appeared with increasing frequency as interlocutors in scientific texts. See Findlen, "Translating the New Science," 167–206.

64. Srinivas Aravamudan, *Enlightenment Orientalism: Resisting the Rise of the Novel* (Chicago: University of Chicago Press, 2012), 117. See also Dick, *Plurality of Worlds*, 123–128; Gelbart, "Introduction," xi; and Bernard Cohen, "Introduction," in Isaac Newton, *The Principia. Mathematical Principles of Natural Philosophy*, trans. Bernard Cohen and Anne Whitman (Berkeley: University of California Press, 1999), 1:43–49.

65. Frontispiece to French edition, 1686.

66. Frédérique Aït-Touati explains that Fontenelle's "mode of discourse permits a curious and refined audience to access an elegant and figurative scientific discourse." Frédérique Aït-Touati, *Fictions of the Cosmos: Science and Literature in the Seventeenth Century*, trans. Susan Emanuel (Chicago: University of Chicago Press, 2011), 83.

67. Ibid., 88–89; and Srinivas Aravamudan, *Enlightenment Orientalism*, 119.

68. A representative example is Steven J. Dick's claim that "Fontenelle suggested that his work be read with no more concentration than one reads a romance or a novel." Dick, *Plurality of Worlds*, 123.

69. Gelbart, "Introduction," xix.

70. Shank, "Neither Natural Philosophy," 87–88.

71. Aileen Douglas, "Popular Science and the Representation of Women: Fontenelle and After," *Eighteenth-Century Life* 18 (1994): 1–14.

72. Kathleen Lubey, *Excitable Imaginations: Eroticism and Reading in Britain, 1660–1760* (Lewisburg, PA: Bucknell University Press, 2012), 1–33.

73. William Congreve, "The Preface to the Reader," in *Incognita: Or, Love and Duty Reconcil'd* (London, 1692), *The Works of William Congreve*, ed. D. F. McKenzie (Oxford: Oxford University Press, 2011), 3:4 (ll. 11–15).

74. Michael McKeon, *The Origins of the English Novel, 1600–1740* (Baltimore, MD: Johns Hopkins University Press, 1987), 15; Scott Black, "Romance Redivivus," in *The Cambridge History of the English Novel*, ed. Robert L. Caserio and Clement Hawes (Cambridge: Cambridge University Press, 2012), 246–248. See also Scott Black, "Quixotic Realism and the Romance of the Novel," *Novel* 42, no. 2 (2009): 239–244.

75. Rebecca Tierney-Hynes, *Novel Minds: Philosophers and Romance Readers, 1680–1740* (Basingstoke, Hampshire: Palgrave Macmillan, 2012), 6.

76. See Lawrence M. Principe, "Newly Discovered Boyle Documents," *Notes and Records of the Royal Society of London* 49 (1995): 57.

77. Boyle continues, "Till when all that is discover'd in the progress, is unable to keep the mind from being molested with Impatience to find that yet conceal'd, which will not be known till one does at least make a further progress." Robert Boyle, *The Excellency of Theology Compar'd with Natural Philosophy, (as both are Objects of Men's Study.) Discours'd of In a Letter to a Friend* (London, 1671), 118.

78. Maria Teresa Marcialis, "Francesco Algarotti's Worldly Newtonianism," *Memorie della Società astronomica italiana* 60, no. 4 (1989): 806.

79. Marta Féher, "The Triumphal March of a Paradigm: A Case Study of the Popularization of Newtonian Science," *Tractrix* 2 (1990): 100. For a comparison of Algarotti's editions, see Marcialis, "Francesco Algarotti's Worldly Newtonianism," 806–821. For the

publication history of Algarotti's English translations, see Laura Miller, "Publishers and Gendered Readership in English-Language Editions of *Il Newtonianismo per le Dame*," *Studies in Eighteenth-Century Culture* 42 (2013): 191–214. On the French translation of Algarotti, see Claudio Giovanardi, "Note su Algarotti tradotto in Francese," *Nuovi annali della Facoltà di magistero dell'Università di Messina* (1988): 91–125.

80. Franco Arato, "Minerva and Venus: Algarotti's *Newton's Philosophy for the Ladies*," in *Men, Women, and the Birthing of Modern Science*, ed. Judith Zinsser (De Kalb: Illinois University Press, 2005), 114.

81. *De Bononiensi Scientiarum et Artium Instituto atque Academia Commentarii* (Bologna: Dalla Volpe, 1731), 1:200–201; and Franco Arato, *Il secolo delle cose. Scienza e storia en Francesco Algarotti* (Genova: Marietti, 1991), 17–40.

82. Arato, "Minerva and Venus," 112. On Bassi and Algarotti, see Marta Cavazza, *Settecento inquieto. Alle origini dell'Istituto delle Scienze di Bologna* (Bologna: Il Mulino, 1990), 237–256.

83. Mauro De Zan, "*La messa all'Indice del* Newtonianism per la dame," in *Scienza e letteratura nella cultura italiana del Settecento*, ed. R. Cremante and W. Tega (Bologna: Il Mulino, 1984), 133–147.

84. Isobel Grundy, *Lady Mary Wortley Montagu* (Oxford: Oxford University Press, 1999), 357.

85. For Algarotti's friendship with Voltaire and du Châtelet, including a comparison of *Il Newtonianismo* and Voltaire's *Éléments de la philosophie de Newton* (1738), see Arato, "Minerva and Venus," 111–120. For an account of du Châtelet's intellectual accomplishments, see Judith P. Zinsser, "Emilie du Chatelet: Genius, Gender, and Intellectual Authority," in *Women Writers and the Early Modern British Political Tradition*, ed. Hilda L. Smith (Cambridge: Cambridge University Press, 1998), 168–190.

86. Grundy, *Lady Mary Wortley Montagu*, 359.

87. Ibid.

88. Their correspondence suggests that she supported him financially. Ibid., 360, n. 22.

89. Ibid., 360.

90. To Francesco Algarotti, July 16, 1739, *The Complete Letters*, 2:139; and Robert Halsband, *The Life of Lady Mary Wortley* (Oxford: Clarendon Press, 1956), 180. Lady Mary and Algarotti were still corresponding as late as 1758. In *The Complete Letters*, the last letter she wrote to him dates from May 1758 (3:149–150).

91. See Tita Chico, *Designing Women: The Dressing Room in Eighteenth-Century British Literature and Culture* (Lewisburg, PA: Bucknell University Press, 2005).

92. Moira R. Rogers, *Newtonianism for the Ladies and Other Uneducated Souls: The Popularization of Science in Leipzig, 1687–1750* (New York: P. Lang, 2003), 100, 102.

93. Francesco Algarotti, *Il Newtonianism per le dame ovvero Dialoghi sopra la luce e I colori* (Napoli, 1737), v.

94. Mirella Agorni, "Women Manipulating Translation in the Eighteenth Century: The Case of Elizabeth Carter," in *The Knowledges of the Translator: From Literary Interpretation to Machine Classification,* ed. Malcolm Coulthard and Patricia Anne Odber de Baubeta (Lewiston: Edwin Mellen Press, 1996), 137.

CHAPTER 4

1. William T. Lynch, *Solomon's Child: Method in the Early Royal Society of London* (Stanford: Stanford University Press, 2001), 7–33.

2. Margaret Judson, *Crisis of the Constitution: An Essay in Constitutional and Political Thought in England, 1603–1645* (Rutgers, NJ: Rutgers University Press, 1949), 142.

3. *The Letters and Life of Francis Bacon*, ed. James Spedding (London, 1861–1874), 6:38.

4. Julian Martin, *Francis Bacon, the State and the Reform of Natural Philosophy* (Cambridge: Cambridge University Press, 1992), 2–3, 164–165; Desiree Hellegers, *Handmaid to Divinity: Natural Philosophy, Poetry, and Gender in Seventeenth-Century England* (Norman: University of Oklahoma Press, 2000), 23; and Julie Robin Solomon, *Objectivity in the Making: Francis Bacon and the Politics of Inquiry* (Baltimore, MD: Johns Hopkins University Press, 1998), xv–xvi.

5. Martin, *Francis Bacon*, 131–132. See also Charles Whitney, *Francis Bacon and Modernity* (New Haven, CT: Yale University Press, 1986), 14; see also 16–17, 99–100. On Baconianism and republicanism, see Adrian Johns, *The Nature of the Book: Print and Knowledge in the Making* (Chicago: University of Chicago Press, 1998).

6. See, for example, Henry Stubbe, *The Lord Bacons Relation to the Sweating-Sickness Examined* (London, 1671).

7. Steven Shapin and Simon Schaffer, *Leviathan and the Air-Pump: Hobbes, Boyle, and the Experimental Life* (Princeton, NJ: Princeton University Press, 1985), 80–154.

8. Ibid., 15.

9. Ibid., 283.

10. Bruno Latour, *We Have Never Been Modern*, trans. Catherine Porter (Cambridge, MA: Harvard University Press, 1993), 27.

11. Ibid., 26.

12. Sandra Harding, *Sciences from Below: Feminisms, Postcolonialities, and Modernities* (Durham, NC: Duke University Press, 2008), 36–48.

13. Jessica Riskin's account of late eighteenth-century French culture suggests an analogous preoccupation. See *Science in the Age of Sensibility: The Sentimental Empiricists of the French Enlightenment* (Chicago: University of Chicago Press, 2002), 227–282.

14. See, for example, *A Censure upon Certaine Passages Contained in the History of the Royal Society, As being Destructive to the Established Religion and Church of England* (London, 1670); Henry Stubbe's *Campanella Revived, Or an Enquiry into the History of the Royal Society, Whether the Virtuosi there do not pursue the Projects of Campanella for the reducing England unto Popery* (London, 1670); and *A Reply unto The Letter Written to Henry Stubbe in Defense of the royal Society* (Oxford, 1671).

15. Michael Hunter, *Establishing the New Science: The Experience of the Early Royal Society* (Woodbridge: Boydell Press, 1989), 45–72.

16. Michael Hunter, "Latitudinarianism and the 'Ideology' of the Early Royal Society: Thomas Sprat's *History of the Royal Society* (1667) Reconsidered," in *Philosophy, Science, and Religion in England, 1640–1700*, ed. Richard Kroll, Richard Ashcraft, and Perez Zagorin (Cambridge: Cambridge University Press, 1992), 200. See also P. B. Wood, "Methodology and Apologetics: Thomas Sprat's 'History of the Royal Society,'" *The British Society for the History of Science* 13, no. 1 (1980): 1–26. On the composition of the *History*, see Hunter, "Latitudinarianism," 203–5.

17. Hunter, "Latitudinarianism," 215, 216. Hunter continues, "The Society felt obliged to stick by the *History* as an 'official' statement, although embarrassed by the reaction it had inspired" (215).

18. Samuel Johnson, "Sprat," *The Lives of the Poets*, vols. 21–23 of *The Yale Edition of the Works of Samuel Johnson*, ed. John H. Middendorf (New Haven, CT: Yale University Press, 2010), 22:547.

19. See John Morgan, "Science, England's 'Interest' and Universal Monarchy: The Making of Thomas Sprat's *History of the Royal Society*," *History of Science* 47 (2009): 27–28; and J. Ereck Jarvis, "Thomas Sprat's 'Mixt Assembly': Association and Authority in *The History of the Royal Society*," *Restoration: Studies in English Literary Culture, 1660–1700* 37, no. 2 (2013): 55–77.

20. In 1756, Thomas Birch published *The History of the Royal Society* as an explicit continuation of Sprat's work, even though the generic difference is striking. Birch's *History* serves less as a narrative sequel to Sprat's *History* and more as an accounting ledger of the society. He scrupulously lists full historical data drawn from the society's official records beginning in 1660. See Thomas Birch, *The History of the Royal Society* (London, 1756), 1.

21. Thomas Sprat, *The History of the Royal Society of London, For the Improving of Natural Knowledge*, 3rd ed. (London, 1722), 29. Subsequent references are cited parenthetically within the text. Hunter, "Latitudinarianism," 217. William T. Lynch characterizes Sprat's goal as to engage in "imaginative nation-building" in *Solomon's Child*, 160; see also 159–161, 167–170.

22. John Dryden, *Essay on Dramatic Poesy* appended to *The Conquest of Granada Part II*, vol. 11 of *The Works of John Dryden*, ed. John Loftis, David Stuart Rodes, and Vinton A. Dearing (Berkeley: University of California Press, 1978). My thanks to Suvir Kaul for drawing this contrast to my attention.

23. Morgan, "Science, England's 'Interest' and Universal Monarchy," 28–30.

24. Ibid., 27.

25. In *Observations on Monsieur de Sorbière's Voyage into England*, Sprat champions English eloquence, particularly defending the lord chancellor's. See Thomas Sprat, *Observations on Monsieur de Sorbière's Voyage into England* (London, 1665), 196–203. For a discussion of Sprat's use of rhetoric, see Tina Skouen, "Science versus Rhetoric? Sprat's *History of the Royal Society* Reconsidered," *Rhetorica: A Journal of the History of Rhetoric* 29, no. 1 (2011): 23–52.

26. For a discussion of the forms of authority imagined through the *History*, see Jarvis, "Thomas Sprat's 'Mixt Assembly,'" 56.

27. The Protestant attack on enthusiastic religious movements began with Martin Luther's derision of the Münster Anabaptists. During the Interregnum, key texts on enthusiasm included Méric Casaubon's *Treatise Concerning Enthusiasme* (1654) and Henry More's *Enthusiasmus Triumphatus; or, A Discourse of the Nature, Causes, Kinds, and Cure of Enthusiasme* (1656). See Jeffrey S. Shoulson, "Milton and Enthusiasm: Radical Religion and the Poetics of *Paradise Regained*," *Milton Studies* 47 (2008): 219–257, and Jonathan Gil Harris, *Foreign Bodies and the Body Politic: Discourses of Social Pathology in Early Modern England* (Cambridge: Cambridge University Press, 1998).

28. Jarvis, "Thomas Sprat's 'Mixt Assembly,'" 61.

29. Steven Shapin, "The House of Experiment in Seventeenth-Century England," *Isis* 79 (1988): 373–404, esp. 387–388.

30. Robert Boyle, *A Proemial Essay* (London, 1661), 2:26.

31. The membership of the Royal Society from 1660 to 1664 included aristocrats (14 percent), courtiers and politicians (24 percent), gentlemen (12 percent), lawyers (6 percent), clergy (8 percent), doctors (16 percent), scholars and writers (7 percent), civil servants (5 percent), and merchants and tradesmen (4 percent). See Michael Hunter, *The Royal Society and Its Fellows, 1660–1700: The Morphology of an Early Scientific Institution* (Chalfont St. Giles: British Society for the History of Science, 1982), 116, table 6.

32. Hunter, *The Royal Society and Its Fellows*, 8. That said, Barbara Shapiro's point is worth remembering: the Royal Society brought together people who would not have ordinarily interacted socially. See Barbara Shapiro, "Natural Philosophy and Political Periodization: Interregnum, Restoration and Revolution," in *A Nation Transformed: England after the Restoration*, ed. Alan Houston and Steve Pincus (Cambridge: Cambridge University Press, 2001), 309.

33. Michael Hunter, *Science and the Shape of Orthodoxy: Studies of Intellectual Change in Late Seventeenth-Century Britain* (Woodbridge: Boydell Press, 1995), 111.

34. Lynch, *Solomon's Child*, 168–70.

35. Shapiro, "Natural Philosophy and Political Periodization," 309, 305.

36. Although few women published on natural philosophy in the seventeenth century, Cavendish is not unique. For example, Anne Conway published *The Principles of the Most Ancient and Modern Philosophy*, first in Latin (1690) and then translated into English (1692).

37. Birch, *History of the Royal Society*, 2:177–178. The first women to be elected to full membership were Kathleen Lonsdale and Marjory Stephenson in 1945. See Ruth Watts, *Women in Science: A Social and Cultural History* (London: Routledge, 2007), 50; and Londa Schiebinger, *The Mind Has No Sex? Women in the Origins of Modern Science* (Cambridge, MA: Harvard University Press, 1989), 26.

38. Schiebinger, *The Mind Has No Sex?* 26.

39. Eileen O'Neill, "Introduction," Margaret Cavendish, *Observations upon Experimental Philosophy* (Cambridge: Cambridge University Press, 2001), xvii–xxxv. From 1645 to 1648, Cavendish, her husband, and her brother-in-law formed a group, the Newcastle Circle, of thinkers influenced by the mechanical philosophy, including Hobbes, Digy, and Charleton (O'Neill, "Introduction," xiii). Cavendish discussed her natural philosophy with her brother-in-law, Charles Cavendish, Constantijn Huygens, and Joseph Glanvill (O'Neill, "Introduction," xviii).

40. Lisa T. Sarasohn, *The Natural Philosophy of Margaret Cavendish: Reason and Fancy during the Scientific Revolution* (Baltimore, MD: Johns Hopkins University Press, 2010), 16–17. See also Evelyn Fox Keller, "Producing Petty Gods: Margaret Cavendish's Critique of Experimental Science," *English Literary History* 64 (1997): 447–471; Rebecca Merrens, "A Nature of 'Infinite Sense and Reason': Margaret Cavendish's Natural Philosophy and the 'Noise' of a Feminized Nature," *Women's Studies* 25 (1996): 421–438; John Rogers, *The Matter of Revolution: Science, Poetry, and Politics in the Age of Milton* (Ithaca, NY: Cornell University Press, 1996), 177–211; and Emma Wilkins, "Margaret Cavendish and the Royal Society," *Notes and Records: The Royal Society Journal of the History of Science* 68 (2014): 247–249. For a discussion of Cavendish's rhetorical approach to writing natural philosophy, see Stephen Clucas, "Variation, Irregularity and Probabilism: Margaret Cavendish and Natural Philosophy as Rhetoric," in *A Princely*

Brave Woman: Essays on Margaret Cavendish, Duchess of Newcastle, ed. Stephen Clucas (Aldershot: Ashgate, 2003), 199–209.

41. The letter is reproduced in Hilda L. Smith, "Margaret Cavendish and the Microscope as Play," in *Men, Women, and the Birthing of Modern Science*, ed. Judith P. Zinsser (DeKalb: Northern Illinois University Press, 2005), 41.

42. Cavendish, *Observations*, 9.

43. Ibid., 49.

44. Robert Hooke, *Micrographia* (London, 1665), Preface.

45. Cavendish, *Observations*, 9.

46. Margaret Cavendish, *The Description of a New World, Called the Blazing World*, in *Paper Bodies: A Margaret Cavendish Reader*, ed. Sylvia Bowerbank and Sara Mendelson (Peterborough, ONT: Broadview Press, 2000), 152–153. Subsequent references are cited parenthetically within the text.

47. Sarasohn, *The Natural Philosophy of Margaret Cavendish*, 18.

48. Emma L. E. Rees, *Margaret Cavendish: Gender, Genre, Exile* (Manchester: Manchester University Press, 2003), 179.

49. Nichole Pohl, "'Of Mixt Natures': Questions of Genre in Margaret Cavendish's *The Blazing World*," in *A Princely Brave Woman: Essays on Margaret Cavendish, Duchess of Newcastle*, ed. Stephen Clucas (Aldershot: Ashgate, 2003), 51. See also William R. Newman, *Promethean Ambitions: Alchemy and the Quest to Perfect Nature* (Chicago: University of Chicago Press, 2004), 283–288.

50. Margaret Cavendish, "A True Relation of my Birth, Breeding, and Life," in *Natures Pictures Drawn by Fancies Pencil to the Life* (London, 1656), 373–377.

51. Rees, *Margaret Cavendish*, 5.

52. Sarasohn, *The Natural Philosophy of Margaret Cavendish*, 106.

53. Wolfram Schmidgen, *Exquisite Mixture: The Virtues of Impurity in Early Modern England* (Philadelphia: University of Pennsylvania Press, 2013), 184, n. 1.

54. More commonly, scholars read Cavendish's politics in terms of gender exclusively rather than gender and rank. See, for example, Pohl, "'Of Mixt Natures,'" 51.

55. Peter Dear, "A Philosophical Duchess: Understanding Margaret Cavendish and the Royal Society," in *Science, Literature and Rhetoric in Early Modern England*, ed. Juliet Cummins and David Burchell (Aldershot, Hampshire: Ashgate, 2007), 125–144. For a discussion of Cavendish's visual self-presentation in her frontispieces, see also James Fitzmaurice, "Fancy and the Family: Self-Characterizations of Margaret Cavendish," *Huntington Library Quarterly* 53 (1990): 198–209.

56. On Cavendish's satire, see Sarah Hutton, "Science and Satire: The Lucianic Voice of Margaret Cavendish's *Description of a New World Called the Blazing World*," in *Authorial Conquests. Essays on Genre in the Writings of Margaret Cavendish*, ed. Line Cottegnies and Nancy Weitz (Madison, NJ: Fairleigh Dickinson University Press, 2003), 161–178; and Sandrine Parageau, "La satire des sciences dans *Observations upon Experimental Philosophy* et *The Blazing World* de Margaret Cavendish," *Études Épistémè* 10 (2006): 75–97.

57. See Anna Battigelli, *Margaret Cavendish and the Exiles of the Mind* (Lexington: University Press of Kentucky, 1998), 107; Keller, "Producing Petty Gods," 460; and Cristina Malcolmson, *Studies of Skin Color in the Early Royal Society: Boyle, Cavendish, Swift* (Farnham, Surrey: Ashgate, 2013), 114.

58. Mary Baine Campbell provides a bravura reading of Cavendish's rebuttal to Hooke's account of the dead eye of a gray drone-fly magnified to the point that he can see 140,000 hemispheres in it. Cavendish, according to Campbell, imagines her Empress as a surrogate for the drone-fly, covered with pearls and diamonds that thwart any perception of her interior. Mary Baine Campbell, *Wonder and Science: Imagining Worlds in Early Modern Europe* (Ithaca, NY: Cornell University Press, 1999), 213–218.

59. Sarasohn, *The Natural Philosophy of Margaret Cavendish*, 149–152.

60. Frédérique Aït-Touati, *Fictions of the Cosmos: Science and Literature in the Seventeenth Century*, trans. Susan Emanuel (Chicago: University of Chicago Press, 2011), 177.

61. Christopher F. Loar, *Political Magic: British Fictions of Savagery and Sovereignty, 1650–1750* (New York: Fordham University Press, 2014), 35, 62–65.

62. See Steven C. A. Pincus, "Republicanism, Absolutism, and Universal Monarchy: English Popular Sentiment during the Third Dutch War," in *Culture and Society in the Stuart Restoration*, ed. Gerald MacLean (Cambridge: Cambridge University Press, 1995), 242–243; and Matthew Birchwood, "Vindicating the Prophet: Universal Monarchy and Henry Stubbe's Biography of Mohammed," *Prose Studies* 29, no. 1 (2007): 63.

63. See *London's Glory Represented by Time, Truth and Fame* (London, 1660); Samuel Pepys, *The Diary of Samuel Pepys*, ed. Robert Latham and William Matthews (London: Bell & Hyman Limited, 1970–1976), 3:175; and John Evelyn, *The Diary of John Evelyn*, ed. E. S. de Beer, 6 vols. (Oxford: Clarendon Press, 1955), 3:333. See also Matthew Jenkinson, *Culture and Politics at the Court of Charles II* (Woodbridge: Boydell Press, 2010), 73–74.

64. Nicolson, *Science and Imagination*, 114–115, n. 10.

65. John Boyle, Earl of Orrery, *Remarks on the Life and Writings of Dr. Jonathan Swift* (London, 1752), 147. See also Marjorie Hope Nicolson and with N. M. Mohler, "The Scientific Background of Swift's Voyage to Laputa," in Marjorie Hope Nicolson, *Science and Imagination* (Ithaca, NY: Cornell University Press, 1956), 117–152; Colin Kiernan, "Swift and Science," *The Historical Journal* 14, no. 4 (1974): 709–722; Dennis Todd, "Laputa, the Whore of Babylon, and the Idols of Science," *Studies in Philology* 75 (1978): 93–120; John R. Christie, "Laputa Revisited," in *Nature Transfigured: Science and Literature, 1700–1900*, ed. John Christie and Sally Shuttleworth (Manchester: Manchester University Press, 1989), 45–60; Frank T. Boyle, *Swift as Nemesis: Modernity and Its Satirist* (Stanford, CA: Stanford University Press, 2000). For Swift's views of Bacon, see Brian Vicker's "Swift and the Baconian Idol," in *The World of Jonathan Swift: Essays for the Tercentenary*, ed. Brian Vickers (Cambridge, MA: Harvard University Press, 1968), 87–128; Alan D. Chalmers, *Jonathan Swift and the Burden of the Future* (Newark: University of Delaware Press, 1995); Brean Hammond, "Swift's Reading," in *The Cambridge Companion to Jonathan Swift*, ed. Christopher Fox (Cambridge: Cambridge University Press, 2003), 73–86; and John Shanahan, "'In the Mean Time': Jonathan Swift, Francis Bacon, and Georgic Struggle," in *Swift as Priest and Satirist*, ed. Todd C. Parker (Newark: University of Delaware Press, 2009), 193–214.

66. Jonathan Swift, *Gulliver's Travels*, ed. David Womersley, vol. 16 of *The Cambridge Edition of the Works of Jonathan Swift*, ed. Claude Rawson, Ian Higgins, David Womersley, and Ian Gadd (Cambridge: Cambridge University Press, 2013), 259–264. Subsequent references are cited parenthetically within the text.

67. Fredric V. Bogel, *The Difference Satire Makes: Rhetoric and Reading from Jonson to Byron* (Ithaca, NY: Cornell University Press, 2001), 12.

68. Deborah Needleman Armintor, *The Little Everyman: Stature and Masculinity in Eighteenth-Century English Literature* (Seattle: University of Washington Press, 2011), 56–79.

69. Gregory Lynall, *Swift and Science: The Satire, Politics, and Theology of Natural Knowledge, 1690–1730* (Basingstoke, Hampshire: Palgrave Macmillan, 2012), 109.

70. Cristina Malcolmson argues that Swift read and was influenced by Cavendish's work. Malcomson, *Studies of Skin Color*, 195–203.

71. See Sprat, *History,* 423; and James Fortescue, *Science: An Epistle on Its Decline and Revival* (London, 1750), 11–12.

72. Neil Chudgar, "Swift's Gentleness," *ELH: English Literary History* 78, no. 1 (2011): 146.

73. Pace Robert Markley, "Gulliver and the Japanese: The Limits of the Postcolonial Past," *Modern Language Quarterly* 65, no. 3 (2004): 457; and Bruce McLeod, *The Geography of Empire in English Literature, 1580–1745* (Cambridge: Cambridge University Press, 1999), 188; Danielle Sprat, "Gulliver's Economized Body: Colonial Projects and the Lusus Naturae in the Travels," *Studies in Eighteenth-Century Culture* 41 (2012): 137–159; and Malcolmson, *Studies of Skin Color*, 169–187.

74. David Rosen and Aaron Santesso, "Swiftian Satire and the Afterlife of Allegory," in *Swift's Travels: Eighteenth-Century British Satire and Its Legacy*, ed. Nicholas Hudson and Aaron Santesso (Cambridge: Cambridge University Press, 2008), 21.

75. Lorraine Daston, "The Empire of Observation, 1600–1800," in *Histories of Scientific Observation,* ed. Lorrain Daston and Elizabeth Lunbeck (Chicago: University of Chicago Press, 2011), 102.

76. McLeod, *The Geography of Empire,* 189. See also Carole Fabricant, *Swift's Landscape* (Notre Dame: University of Notre Dame Press, 1995); Marie Mulvey Roberts, "Science, Magic and Masonry: Swift's Secret Texts," in *Secret Texts: The Literature of Secret Societies*, ed. Marie Mulvey Roberts and Hugh Ormsby-Lennon (New York: AMS Press, 1995), 104; and Sean D. Moore, *Swift, the Book, and the Irish Financial Revolution: Satire and Sovereignty in Colonial Ireland* (Baltimore, MD: Johns Hopkins University Press, 2010).

77. Laura Brown, *The Ends of Empire: Women and Ideology in Early Eighteenth-Century English Literature* (Ithaca, NY: Cornell University Press, 1993), 170—200, esp. 182–99; Anna Neill, *British Discovery Literature and the Rise of Global Commerce* (Basingstoke, Hampshire: Palgrave, 2002), 104–115; and Ann Cline Kelly, "Gulliver as Pet and Pet Owner: Conversations with Animals in Book 4," *ELH: English Literary History* 74, no. 2 (2007): 323–349.

78. *A Catalogue of Books: The Library of the late Rev. Dr. Swift* (Dublin, 1745), 4, n. 137. In the preface to *Memoirs of the Royal Academy at Paris,* republished as a preface to *Miscellenea Curiosa* (1707), Fontenelle defends the moderns.

79. For example, "The Theory of Musick reduced to Arithmetical and Geometrical Progressions, by the Reverend Mr Tho. Salmon," Royal Society of London, *Philosophical Transactions for the Month of August* 1705, in vol. 24, "for the Years 1704 and 1705" of *Philosophical Transactions* (London, 1705), 2072–2077.

80. For parallels between Laputa and the Whigs and the Hanoverian court, see Ian Higgins, *Swift's Politics: A Study in Disaffection* (Cambridge: Cambridge University Press, 1994), 177.

81. G. S. Rousseau, *Enlightenment Borders: Pre- and Post-Modern Discourses: Medical, Scientific* (Manchester: Manchester University Press, 1991), 282. For Newton's philosophi-

cal reception, see Margaret C. Jacob, *The Radical Enlightenment: Pantheists, Freemasons and Republicans* (London: George Allen & Unwin, 1981), 87–108.

82. Margaret C. Jacob and Larry Stewart, *Practical Matter: Newton's Science in the Service of Industry and Empire, 1687–1851* (Cambridge, MA: Harvard University Press, 2004), 65–69. See also my Chapter 1.

83. Jacob and Stewart, *Practical Matter*, 15.

84. Ibid., 71.

85. Ibid., 20–21.

86. Margaret C. Jacob, *The Newtonians and the English Revolution, 1689–1720* (Hassocks, Sussex: Harvester Press, 1976), 162–200.

87. My thanks to Ralph Bauer for this observation. Ralph Bauer, *The Cultural Geography of Colonial American Literatures: Empire, Travel, Modernity* (Cambridge: Cambridge University Press, 2003), 180; and Mary Louise Pratt, *Imperial Eyes: Travel Writing and Transculturation* (London: Routledge, 1992), 9–10, 15–37.

88. Jacob and Stewart, *Practical Matter*, 21–22.

89. Ibid., 75; and Colin Kiernan, "Swift and Science," *The Historical Journal* 14, no. 4 (1971): 712.

90. Kiernan, "Swift and Science," 710–711.

91. Joseph Johnston, "Irish Currency in the Eighteenth Century," *Hermathena* 27, no. 52 (1938): 18.

92. Irvin Ehrenpreis, *Swift: The Man, His Works, and the Age* (London: Methuen, 1983), 3:192, 3:187–197. See also Higgins, *Swift's Politics*, 22.

93. Lynall, *Swift and Science*, 101.

94. Griffin, *Satire*, 194.

95. Jonathan Swift, *A Treatise on Polite Conversation*, in *Parodies, Hoaxes, Mock Treatises*, ed. Valerie Rumbold, vol. 2 of *The Cambridge Edition of the Works of Jonathan Swift*, ed. Claude Rawson, Ian Higgins, David Womersley, and Ian Gadd (Cambridge: Cambridge University Press, 2013), 299–300.

96. On the composition of *Gulliver's Travels*, see Ehrenpreis, *Swift*, 3:442–447.

97. See J. A. Downie, *Jonathan Swift: Political Writer* (London: Routledge & Kegan Paul, 1984), 284–287; and Chudgar, "Swift's Gentleness," 155. On Swift and horses, see Donna Landry, *Noble Brutes: How Eastern Horses Transformed English Culture* (Baltimore, MD: Johns Hopkins University Press, 2008), 123–132, 139–146.

98. William Bowman Piper, "Gulliver's Account of Houyhnhnmland as a Philosophical Treatise," in *The Genres of Gulliver's Travels*, ed. Frederik N. Smith (Newark: University of Delaware Press, 1990), 179–202.

99. Clive Sutton argues that the motto has been misread as "nothing but words." Clive Sutton, "'Nullius in Verba' and 'Nihil in Verbis': Public Understanding of the Role of Language in Science," *The British Journal for the History of Science* 27, no. 1 (1994): 55–64.

100. Barbara M. Benedict, "Self, Stuff, and Surface: The Rhetoric of Things in Swift's Satire," in *Swift's Travels: Eighteenth-Century British Satire and Its Legacy*, ed. Nicholas Hudson and Aaron Santesso (Cambridge: Cambridge University Press, 2008), 95.

101. Martin Gierl, "Science, Projects, Computers, and the State: Swift's Lagadian and Leibniz's Prussian Academy," in *The Age of Projects*, ed. Maximillian E. Novak (Toronto: University of Toronto Press, 2008), 297–317; and Denise Tillery, "Engendering the Lan-

guage of the New Science: The Subject of John Wilkins's Language Project," *The Eighteenth Century: Theory and Interpretation* 46, no. 1 (2005): 59–79.

102. Srinivas Aravamudan reads Gulliver's impossibility in terms of the genres of utopia and oriental romance. Srinivas Aravamudan, *Enlightenment Orientalism: Resisting the Rise of the Novel* (Chicago: University of Chicago Press, 2012), 149–50.

103. John Locke, *An Essay Concerning Human Understanding*, ed. Peter H. Nidditch (Oxford: Oxford University Press, 1975), 4.2.1.

104. Frederik N. Smith, "Scientific Discourse: *Gulliver's Travels* and the *Philosophical Transactions*," in *The Genres of* Gulliver's Travels, ed. Frederik N. Smith (Newark: University of Delaware Press, 1990), 157–158.

105. Erin Mackie, "Gulliver and the Houyhnhnm Good Life," *The Eighteenth Century: Theory and Interpretation* 55, no. 1 (2015): 109–115.

106. Sarah Rivett, "The Algonquian Word and the Spirit of Divine Truth: John Eliot's Indian Library and the Atlantic Quest for a Universal Language," in *Colonial Mediascapes: Sensory Worlds of the Early Americas*, ed. Matt Cohen and Jeff Glover (Lincoln: University of Nebraska Press, 2014), 380.

107. Benedict, "Self, Stuff, and Surface," 95.

108. Clement Hawes, *The British Enlightenment and Global Critique* (New York: Palgrave Macmillan, 2005), 152, 140.

CHAPTER 5

1. Thomas Sprat, *The History of the Royal Society of London, For the Improving of Natural Knowledge*, 3rd ed. (London, 1722), 415.

2. See Frank T. Boyle, *Swift as Nemesis: Modernity and Its Satirist* (Stanford, CA: Stanford University Press, 2000), 83–85.

3. Abraham Cowley, "To the Royal Society," in *The History of the Royal Society, For the Improving of Natural Knowledge*, 3rd ed. (London, 1722), I.

4. Ibid., II.

5. Ellis Waterhouse, *Painting in Britain, 1530–1790*, 4th ed. (New Haven, CT: Yale University Press, 1978), 70–77.

6. Cowley, "To the Royal Society," IV.

7. Robert Hooke, *Micrographia: or Some Physiological Descriptions of Minute Bodies* (London, 1665), "Preface."

8. Cowley, "To the Royal Society," IV.

9. Ibid., IX.

10. John Guillory, "Enlightening Mediation," in *This Is Enlightenment*, ed. Clifford Siskin and William Warner (Chicago: University of Chicago Press, 2010), 37–63, esp. 52–56.

11. Clifford Siskin and William Warner, "Introduction," in *This Is Enlightenment*, 5–19.

12. Gottlieb Baumgarten, *Meditations philosophicae de nonnulis ad poem pertinentibus*, §§ cxv-cxvi; *Metaphysica*, §533; *Aesthetica*, §1. Quoted in Paul Guyer, *Values of Beauty: Historical Essays in Aesthetics* (Cambridge: Cambridge University Press, 2005), 3.

13. See Jerome Stolnitz, "On the Origins of 'Aesthetic Disinterest,'" *Journal of Aesthetics and Art Criticism* 20, no. 2 (1961): 131–143; George Dickie, *Art and the Aesthetic: An Institutional Analysis* (Ithaca, NY: Cornell University Press, 1974), 53–77; Elizabeth A. Bohls, "Disinterestedness and the Denial of the Particular: Locke, Adam Smith, and the

Subject of Aesthetics," in *Eighteenth-Century Aesthetics and the Reconstruction of Art*, ed. Paul Mattick, Jr. (Cambridge: Cambridge University Press, 1993), 16–51; Miles Rind, "The Concept of Disinterestedness in Eighteenth-Century British Aesthetics," *Journal of the History of Philosophy* 4, no. 1 (2002): 67–87; and Jane Kneller, "Disinterestedness," in *Encyclopedia of Aesthetics*, gen. ed. Michael Kelly, 2nd ed. (Oxford: Oxford University Press, 2014), 2:421–426.

14. Anthony Ashley Cooper, 3rd Earl of Shaftesbury, *The Moralists, a Philosophical Rhapsody* in *Characteristics of Men, Manners, Opinions, Times*, ed. Philip Ayres (Oxford: Clarendon Press, 1999), 2:318.

15. Ibid.

16. Ibid., 2:318–319.

17. Ibid., 2:319.

18. Ibid.

19. Francis Hutcheson, "1725 Preface," in *An Inquiry into the Original of Our Ideas of Beauty and Virtue in Two Treatises*, ed. Wolfgang Leidhold (Indianapolis: Liberty Fund, 2008), 12.

20. Carolyn Wilker Korsmeyer, "Relativism and Hutcheson's Aesthetic Theory," *Journal of the History of Ideas* 36, no. 2 (1975): 320.

21. See David Paxman, "Aesthetics as Epistemology; Or Knowledge Without Certainty," *Eighteenth-Century Studies* 26, no.2 (1992–1993): 298.

22. Hutcheson, *An Inquiry*, 25 [I.§xiv].

23. Ibid.,, 15 [II.viii].

24. Peter Kivy, *The Seventh Sense: A Study of Francis Hutcheson's Aesthetics and Its Influence in Eighteenth-Century Britain* (New York: Burt Franklin, 1976), 1–4.

25. Hutcheson, *An Inquiry*, 25 [I.§xiii].

26. Paxman, "Aesthetics as Epistemology," 295.

27. Guyer, *Values of Beauty*, 13–14.

28. Hutcheson, *An Inquiry*, 24 [I.§xii].

29. Paxman, "Aesthetics as Epistemology," 295.

30. Bohls, "Disinterestedness and Denial of the Particular," 27.

31. Peter de Bolla, *The Education of the Eye: Painting, Landscape and Architecture in Eighteenth-Century Britain* (Stanford, CA: Stanford University Press, 2003), 1–71, 218–234.

32. Cowley, "To the Royal Society," IV.

33. Frances Ferguson, *Solitude and the Sublime: Romanticism and the Aesthetics of Individuation* (New York: Routledge, 1992), 3–4.

34. Jacques Rancière, *The Politics of Aesthetics*, trans. Gabriel Rockhill (New York: Continuum, 2006), 17, 13.

35. Ibid., 13.

36. Alexander Pope, *The Rape of the Lock* in *The Rape of the Lock and Other Poems*, ed. Geoffrey Tillotson, vol. 2 of *The Twickenham Edition of the Poems of Alexander Pope*, gen. ed. John Butt. (New Haven, CT: Yale University Press, 1964), 5.122–123. Subsequent quotations from this work are cited parenthetically in the text.

37. Jayne Elizabeth Lewis takes a scientific approach to the poem, but to argue that it coincides with the emergent discourse of pneumatics, and Elizabeth Kowaleski-Wallace uses vitalism to read the poem. In Jayne Elizabeth Lewis, *Air's Appearance: Literary Atmo-*

sphere in British Fiction, 1660–1794 (Chicago: University of Chicago Press, 2012), 61–91; and Elizabeth Kowaleski-Wallace, "The Things Things Don't Say: *The Rape of the Lock*, Vitalism, and New Materialism," *The Eighteenth Century: Theory and Interpretation*, forthcoming.

38. Benjamin Martin, *A New and Compendious System of Optics* (London, 1740), xii.

39. Marjorie Nicolson and G. S. Rousseau imply this point in *"This Long Disease, My Life": Alexander Pope and the Sciences* (Princeton, NJ: Princeton University Press, 1968), 247; and Robert W. Williams, "Pope and the 'Microscopic Eye,'" *Sydney Studies in English* 14 (1988–1989): 21–37.

40. See Maxine Berg, *Luxury and Pleasure in Eighteenth-Century Britain* (Oxford: Oxford University Press, 2005).

41. Geoffrey Tillotson, "Introduction," *The Rape of the Lock and Other Poems*, 118; Helen Deutsch, *Resemblance and Disgrace: Alexander Pope and the Deformation of Culture* (Cambridge, MA: Harvard University Press, 1996), 61, 41; and Jonathan Lamb, *The Things Things Say* (Princeton, NJ: Princeton University Press, 2011), 99.

42. Cynthia Sundberg Wall, *The Prose of Things: Transformations of Description in the Eighteenth Century* (Chicago: University of Chicago Press, 2006).

43. Robert Boyle, *A Proemial Essay* (London, 1661), 2:18.

44. Sigmund Freud, *Dora: An Analysis of a Case of Hysteria*, ed. Philip Rieff (New York: Simon & Schuster, 1963), 17, 39; Neil Hertz, "Dora's Secrets, Freud's Techniques," in *In Dora's Case: Freud—Hysteria—Feminism*, ed. Charles Bernheimer and Claire Kahane, 2nd ed. (New York: Columbia University Press, 1990), 227. See also Jacqueline Rose, "Introduction II," in *Feminine Sexuality: Jacques Lacan and the Ecole Freudienne*, ed. Juliet Mitchell and Jacqueline Rose, trans. Jacqueline Rose (New York: Norton and Pantheon 1985), 48.

45. Tita Chico, *Designing Women: The Dressing Room in Eighteenth-Century English Literature and Culture* (Lewisburg, PA: Bucknell University Press, 2005), 107–131.

46. Laura Brown, *The Ends of Empire: Women and Ideology in Early Eighteenth-Century English Literature* (Ithaca, NY: Cornell University Press, 1993), 113, 119. See also Laura Mandell, *Misogynous Economies: The Business of Literature in Eighteenth-Century Britain* (Lexington: University Press of Kentucky, 1999), 21–36.

47. Joseph Roach, *It* (Ann Arbor: University of Michigan Press, 2007), 127.

48. Robert Markley, "Beyond Consensus: *The Rape of the Lock* and the Fate of Reading Eighteenth-Century Literature," *New Orleans Review* 15 (1998): 68; Christopher Norris, "Pope among the Formalists: Textual Politics and 'The Rape of the Lock,'" in *Post-Structuralist Readings of English Poetry*, ed. Richard Machin and Christopher Norris (Cambridge: Cambridge University Press, 1987), 142.

49. J. Paul Hunter, "Formalism and History: Binarism and the Anglophone Couplet," *MLQ* 61 (2000): 119.

50. The Hermitage was sometimes called a "grotto" by contemporaries and, along with Merlin's Cave, eventually came under the care of the "thresher poet," Stephen Duck. Queen Caroline later commissioned Kent to design and build "Merlin's Cave" in the Richmond gardens.

51. [Matthew Green], *The Grotto, A Poem. Written by Peter Drake, Fisherman of Brentford* (London, 1733), 4.

52. "Essay I. On the Five Bustoes in the Queen's Grotto," in *The Contest: Being Poetical Essays on the Queen's Grotto* (London, 1734), 2.

53. Judith Colton, "Kent's Hermitage for Queen Caroline at Richmond," *Architectura* 4, no. 2 (1974): 186. The busts were designed and carved by the Italian sculptor Giovanni Battista Guelfi, though scholars earlier believed that Michael Rysbrack was the artist. See Gordon Balderston, "Giovanni Battista Guelfi: Five Busts for Queen Caroline's Hermitage in Richmond," *Sculpture Garden* 17, no. 1 (2003): 83–88.

54. Joanna Marschner, *Queen Caroline: Cultural Politics in the Early Eighteenth-Century Court* (New Haven, CT: Yale University Press, 2014), 149–169.

55. María Luisa López-Vidriero, *The Polished Cornerstone of the Temple: Queenly Libraries of the Enlightenment* (London: British Library, 2005), 7–10; and Marschner, *Queen Caroline*, 154–163.

56. López-Vidriero, *The Polished Cornerstone*, 23.

57. Colton, "Kent's Hermitage," 182; Cinzia Maria Sicca, "Like a Shallow Cave by Nature Made: William Kent's 'Natural' Architecture at Richmond," *Architectura* 16, no. 1 (1986): 68; and Balderston, "Giovanni Battista Guelfi," 83–84.

58. "Essay V. On the Royal Grotto," *The Contest*, 6, l. 14.

59. Jill H. Casid, *Sowing Empire: Landscape and Colonization* (Minneapolis: University of Minnesota Press, 2005), 105.

60. *A Description of the Royal Gardens at Richmond in Surry, the Village, and Places Adjacent* (London, n.d. [circa 1736?]), 21.

61. "Richmond Gardens," *London Magazine: and Monthly Chronologer* 6 (1738): 38–39. The stalactites are visible in John Vardy's engraving, "William Kent, Section of Queen Caroline's Hermitage at Richmond," in *Some Designs of Mr. Inigo Jones and Mr. William Kent* (London, 1744), pl. 33; see also Colton, "Kent's Hermitage," 183.

62. *Gentleman's Magazine* 3 (April 1733), 208, Note.

63. Edmund Curll, *The Rarities of Richmond: being Exact Descriptions of the Royal Hermitage and Merlin's Cave with his Life and Prophecies. The Second Edition* (London, 1736), 11–12.

64. F. N. L. Poynter, "Rysbrack's Bust of Robert Boyle," *Journal of the History of Medicine and Allied Sciences* 24, no. 4 (1969): 475; and Judith Colton, "Merlin's Cave and Queen Caroline: Garden Art as Political Propaganda," *Eighteenth-Century Studies* 10, no. 1 (1976): 3.

65. Editor's note, *Gentleman's Magazine* 3 (April 1733): 208.

66. Stephen Duck, "On Richmond Park, and Royal Gardens," in *Poems on Several Occasions* (London, 1736), 79.

67. "Essay IX. On the Bustoes in Her Majesty's *Hermitage*," in *The Contest*, 16.

68. "Essay II. Ode on the Bust of the Hon. Robert Boyle, Esq; in her Majesty's Grotto," in *The Contest*, 3, ll. 1–2.

69. "Essay VI. On the Queen and the Bustoes plac'd in her Grotto," in *The Contest*, 8, ll. 36, 35; and "Essay VIII. To her Majesty, on her Grotto," in *The Contest*, 13.

70. "Essay X. To the Queen on her Grotto," in *The Contest*, 17.

71. Jane Brereton, "On the Bustoes in the Royal Hermitage," in *Poems on Several Occasions* (London, 1735), 175.

72. "Essay IV. On the Queen's Grotto," in *The Contest*, 5, ll. 12–16.

73. Robert Boyle, *New Experiments Physico-Mechanicall, Touching the Spring of the Air, and its Effects* (1660), in vol. 1 of *The Works of Robert Boyle*, ed. Michael Hunter and Edward B. Davis (London: Pickering & Chatto, 1999), 1:166. See also Steven Shapin,

"Pump and Circumstance: Boyle's Literary Technology," *Social Studies of Science* 14 (1984): 481–520.

74. Boyle's theology does not receive as much literary attention in the commendatory poems as his natural philosophy; one of the rare examples is when a poet directly addresses Boyle, explaining that "Seraphic Boyle, thy search in nature's store,/Was but to learn t'admire thy maker more!" "Essay VII. On the Queen's Grotto," in *The Contest*, 10.

75. Ibid., 11; "Essay IX. On the Bustoes in her Majesty's Hermitage," in *The Contest*, 16; and Brereton, "On the Bustoes," 175.

76. "Essay VII. On the Queen's Grotto," in *The Contest*, 11; and "Essay X. To the Queen on her Grotto," in *The Contest*, 17.

77. "Essay VII. On the Queen's Grotto," in *The Contest*, 11.

78. "Essay IV. On the Queen's Grotto," in *The Contest*, 5, ll. 23; and "Essay VI. On the Queen and the Bustoes plac'd in her Grotto," in *The Contest*, 8, ll. 49–50.

79. "Essay VII. On the Queen's Grotto," in *The Contest*, 11.

80. Alfred Clarke, *An Essay towards the character of Her late Majesty Caroline, queen-consort of Great Britain* (London, 1738), 19.

81. "Essay IV. On the Queen's Grotto," in *The Contest*, 5, l. 9.

82. "Essay III. On the Queen's Grotto. An Ode," in *The Contest*, 4, l.12.

83. "Essay VI. On the Queen and the Bustoes plac'd in her Grotto," in *The Contest*, 8, ll. 33–34; "Essay IX. On the Bustoes in her Majesty's Hermitage," in *The Contest*, 15; and "Essay XI. On her Majesty and the Bustoes in the royal Grotto," in *The Contest*, 19.

84. "Essay VI. On the Queen and the Bustoes plac'd in her Grotto," in *The Contest*, 9, l. 55.

85. "Essay VII. On the Queen's Grotto," in *The Contest*, 9.

86. "Essay VI. On the Queen and the Bustoes plac'd in her Grotto," in *The Contest*, 8, l. 29; and "Essay VI. On the Queen and the Bustoes plac'd in her Grotto," in *The Contest*, 8, ll.30- 31.

87. "Essay VIII. To her Majesty, on her Grotto," in *The Contest*, 13.

88. Ibid.

89. Ibid.

90. Ibid.

91. Ibid.

92. "Essay VI. On the Queen and the Bustoes plac'd in her Grotto," in *The Contest*, 9, ll. 56–58.

93. Suvir Kaul, *Poems of Nation, Anthems of Empire: English Verse in the Long Eighteenth Century* (Charlottesville: University Press of Virginia, 2000), 147.

94. See Ralph Cohen, *The Unfolding of* The Seasons (Baltimore, MD: Johns Hopkins University Press, 1970), 7; John Barrell, *English Literature in History, 1730–1780: An Equal, Wide Survey* (New York: St. Martin's Press, 1983); John Barrell and Harriet Guest, "On the Use of Contradiction: Economics and Morality in the Eighteenth-Century Long Poem," in *The New Eighteenth Century: Theory, Politics, English Literature*, ed. Felicity Nussbaum and Laura Brown (New York: Routledge, 1987), 121–143.

95. Tim Fulford, *Landscape, Liberty, and Authority: Poetry, Criticism, and Politics from Thomson to Wordsworth* (Cambridge: Cambridge University Press, 1996), 3; see also 1–17. John Barrell, *The Idea of the Landscape and the Sense of Place, 1730–1840: An Approach to the Poetry of John Clare* (Cambridge: Cambridge University Press, 1972); W. J. T. Mitchell,

"Imperial Landscape," in *Landscape and Power*, ed. W. J. T. Mitchell, 2nd ed. (Chicago: University of Chicago Press, 2002), 5–34; Karen O'Brien, "Imperial Georgic, 1660–1789," in *The Country and the City Revisited: England and the Politics of Culture 1550–1850*, ed. Gerald MacLean, Donna Landry, and Joseph P. Ward (Cambridge: Cambridge University Press, 1999), 160–179; Kaul, *Poems of Nation, Anthems of Empire*, 147–167; Kevis Goodman, *Georgic Modernity and British Romanticism: Poetry and the Mediation of History* (Cambridge: Cambridge University Press, 2004); and Casid, *Sowing Empire*.

96. William Wordsworth, "Essay, Supplementary to the Preface," in *The Poetical Works of William Wordsworth*, ed. Edward Dowden (London: George Bell & Sons, 1893), 5:265–266. See also Sandro Jung, "Visual Interpretations, Print, and Illustrations of Thomson's *The Seasons*, 1730–1797," *Eighteenth-Century Life* 34, no. 2 (2010): 23–64; and "Print Culture, High-Cultural Consumption, and Thomson's *The Seasons*, 1780–1797," *Eighteenth-Century Studies* 44, no. 4 (2011): 495–514.

97. Joseph Warton, *Essay on the Genius and Writings of Pope* (London, 1756), 4.

98. See Herbert Drennon, "Scientific Rationalism and James Thomson's Poetic Art," *Studies in Philology* 31 (1934): 453–471; Marjorie Hope Nicolson, *Newton Demands the Muse: Newton's Opticks and the Eighteenth Century Poets* (Princeton, NJ: Princeton University Press, 1946); William Powell Jones, *The Rhetoric of Science: A Study of Scientific Ideas and Imagery in Eighteenth-Century English Poetry* (Berkeley: University of California Press, 1966), 106–120; Patricia Fara and David Money, "Isaac Newton and Augustan Anglo-Latin Poetry," *Studies in the History and Philosophy of Science* 35 (2004): 549–571; and Philip Connell, "Newtonian Physico-Theology and the Varieties of Whiggism in James Thomson's *The Seasons*," *Huntington Library Quarterly* 72, no. 1 (2009): 1–28.

99. James Thomson, *The Seasons*, ed. James Sambrook (Oxford: Clarendon Press, 1981), Summer, 1442, 1543–1545, 1550–1553. Subsequent references are cited parenthetically within the text.

100. See Karen O'Brien, "'These Nations Newton Made his Own': Poetry, Knowledge, and British Imperial Globalization," in *The Postcolonial Enlightenment: Eighteenth-Century Colonialism and Postcolonial Theory*, ed. Daniel Carey and Lynn Festa (Oxford: Oxford University Press, 2009), 295.

101. Glynis Ridley, "The Seasons and the Politics of Opposition," in *James Thomson: Essays for the Tercentenary*, ed. Richard Terry (Liverpool: Liverpool University Press, 2000), 93.

102. Marie Boas Hall, *Robert Boyle and Seventeenth-Century Chemistry* (Cambridge: Cambridge University Press, 1956), 185. See also the Introduction to this book and Chapter 1.

103. See Henry Power, *Experimental Philosophy in Three Books* (London, 1664), Preface.

104. Isaac Newton, *Opticks; or, a Treatise of the Reflections, Refractions, Inflections and Colours of Light*, 4th ed. (London, 1730), 320.

105. Goodman, *Georgic Modernity*, 59. Joseph Roach anticipates Goodman's reading in "The Artificial Eye: Augustan Theatre and the Empire of the Visible," in *The Performance of Power: Theatrical Discourse and Politics*, ed. Sue-Ellen Case and Janelle Reinelt (Iowa City: University of Iowa Press, 1991), 136–137.

106. Goodman, *Georgic Modernity*, 60–62.

107. Tita Chico, "Putrefaction as Optical Technology," *Configurations: A Journal of Literature, Science, and Technology*, 25, no. 2 (2017): 145–164.

108. Cristobal Silva, *Miraculous Plagues: An Epidemiology of New England Narrative, 1616–1721* (Oxford: Oxford University Press University Press, 2011), 3–10.

109. Vittoria Di Palma, *Wasteland: A History* (New Haven, CT: Yale University Press, 2014), 3–4.

110. Margaret Koehler, *Poetry of Attention in the Eighteenth Century* (New York: Palgrave Macmillan, 2012), 127–28.

111. Ambrose Philips, "A Winter-Piece. An Epistle to the Earl of Dorset," in Joseph Addison, *The Tatler*, ed. Donald F. Bond (Oxford: Clarendon Press, 1987), 1:109 (no. 12; May 7, 1709).

112. Koehler, *Poetry of Attention*, 137.

113. James Thomson, *A Poem Sacred to the Memory of Sir Isaac Newton* (London, 1727), 10.

114. Karen Barad, *Meeting the Universe Halfway: Quantum Physics and the Entanglement of Matter and Meaning* (Durham, NC: Duke University Press, 2007), 71.

115. Letter to Royal Society, February 6, 1672, opening paragraph.

116. Anne Finch, "A Noctural Reverie," in *Miscellany Poems, on Several Occasions. Written by a Lady* (London, 1713), 293.

117. Ibid.

118. Ibid.

119. James Thomson, *The Seasons*, ed. James Sambrook (Oxford: Clarendon Press, 1981), 237.

120. Bruce Robbins, "Comparative Cosmopolitanisms," in *Cosmopolitics: Thinking and Feeling Beyond the Nation*, ed. Pheng Cheah and Bruce Robbins (Minneapolis: University of Minnesota Press, 1998), 252.

BIBLIOGRAPHY

Adams, George. *Essays on the Microscope*. London, 1787.
Addison, Joseph. *The Tatler*. Edited by Donald F. Bond. 3 vols. Oxford: Clarendon Press, 1987.
Addison, Joseph, and Richard Steele. *The Spectator*. Edited by Donald F. Bond. 3 vols. Oxford: Clarendon Press, 1987.
Agorni, Mirella. "Women Manipulating Translation in the Eighteenth Century: The Case of Elizabeth Carter." In *The Knowledges of the Translator: From Literary Interpretation to Machine Classification*, 135–144, edited by Malcolm Coulthard and Patricia Anne Odber de Baubeta. Lewiston: Edwin Mellen Press, 1996.
Aït-Touati, Frédérique. *Fictions of the Cosmos: Science and Literature in the Seventeenth Century*. Translated by Susan Emanuel. Chicago: University of Chicago Press, 2011.
Alberti, Leon Battista. *On the Art of Building in Ten Books*. Translated by Joseph Rykwert, Neil Leach, and Robert Tavernor. Cambridge, MA: MIT Press, 1994.
Algarotti, Francesco. *Il Newtonianism per le dame ovvero Dialoghi sopra la luce e I colori*. Napoli, 1737.
———. *Sir Isaac Newton's Philosophy Explain'd for the Use of the Ladies*. [Translated by Elizabeth Carter]. 2 vols. London, 1737.
Allestree, Richard. *The Ladies Calling*, 4th ed. London, 1676.
Alpers, Svetlana. *The Art of Describing: Dutch Art in the Seventeenth Century*. London: John Murray, 1983.
Anscomb, Lisa. "'As Far as a Woman's Reasoning Can Go': Scientific Dialogue and Sexploitation." *History of European Ideas* 31 (2005): 193–208.
Anstey, Peter. "Literary Responses to Robert Boyle's Natural Philosophy." In *Science, Literature and Rhetoric in Early Modern England*, edited by Juliet Cummins and David Burchell, 145–162. Aldershot, Hampshire: Ashgate, 2007.
Arato, Franco. *Il secolo delle cose. Scienza e storia en Francesco Algarotti*. Genova: Marietti, 1991.
———. "Minerva and Venus: Algarotti's *Newton's Philosophy for the Ladies*." In *Men, Women, and the Birthing of Modern Science*, edited by Judith Zinsser, 111–120. De Kalb: Illinois University Press, 2005.
Aravamudan, Srinivas. *Enlightenment Orientalism: Resisting the Rise of the Novel*. Chicago: University of Chicago Press, 2012.
Armintor, Deborah Needleman. *The Little Everyman: Stature and Masculinity in Eighteenth-Century English Literature*. Seattle: University of Washington Press, 2011.
Astell, Mary. *An Essay in Defence of the Female Sex*. London, 1696.
Bacon, Francis. *The Letters and Life of Francis Bacon*. Edited by James Spedding. 7 vols. London, 1861–1874.
———. *The Works of Francis Bacon*. Edited by James Spedding, Robert Leslie Ellis, and

Douglas Denon Heath. 14 vols. Facsimile edition. Stuttgart-Bad Cannstatt: F. Frommann Verl. G. Holzboog, 1963.
Baker, Henry. *An Attempt towards a Natural History of the Polype: In a Letter to Martin Folkes, Esq; President of the Royal Society*. London, 1743.
———. *Employment for the Microscope*. London, 1753.
———. *The Microscope Made Easy*. London, 1742.
Balderston, Gordon. "Giovanni Battista Guelfi: Five Busts for Queen Caroline's Hermitage in Richmond." *Sculpture Garden* 17, no. 1 (2003): 83–88.
Bannet, Eve Tavor. "Haywood's Spectator and the Female World." In *Fair Philosopher: Eliza Haywood and* the Female Spectator, edited by Lynn Marie Wright and Donald J. Newman, 82–103. Lewisburg, PA: Bucknell University Press, 2006.
Barad, Karen. *Meeting the University Halfway: Quantum Physics and the Entanglement of Matter and Meaning*. Durham, NC: Duke University Press, 2007.
Barrell, John. *English Literature in History, 1730–1780: An Equal, Wide Survey*. New York: St. Martin's Press, 1983.
———. *The Idea of the Landscape and the Sense of Place, 1730–1840: An Approach to the Poetry of John Clare*. Cambridge: Cambridge University Press, 1972.
Barrell, John, and Harriet Guest. "On the Use of Contradiction: Economics and Morality in the Eighteenth-Century Long Poem." In *The New Eighteenth Century: Theory, Politics, English Literature*, edited by Felicity Nussbaum and Laura Brown, 121–143. New York: Routledge, 1987.
Battigelli, Anna. *Margaret Cavendish and the Exiles of the Mind*. Lexington: University Press of Kentucky, 1998.
Baudot, Laura. "An Air of History: Joseph Wright's and Robert Boyle's Air Pump Narratives." *Eighteenth-Century Studies* 46, no. 1 (2012): 1–28.
Bauer, Ralph. *The Cultural Geography of Colonial American Literatures: Empire, Travel, Modernity*. Cambridge: Cambridge University Press, 2003.
Beer, Gillian. *Open Fields: Science in Cultural Encounter*. Oxford: Oxford University Press, 1996.
Behn, Aphra. *The Works of Aphra Behn*. Edited by Janet Todd. 7 vols. London: William Pickering, 1996.
Bender, John. *Ends of Enlightenment*. Stanford, CA: Stanford University Press, 2012.
Benedict, Barbara M. "The Mad Scientist: The Creation of a Literary Stereotype." In *Imagining the Sciences: Expressions of New Knowledge in the "Long" Eighteenth Century*, edited by Robert C. Leitz III and Kevin L. Cope, 59–107. New York: AMS Press, 2004.
———. "Self, Stuff, and Surface: The Rhetoric of Things in Swift's Satire." In *Swift's Travels: Eighteenth-Century British Satire and Its Legacy*, edited by Nicholas Hudson and Aaron Santesso, 93–107. Cambridge: Cambridge University Press, 2008.
Berg, Maxine. *Luxury and Pleasure in Eighteenth-Century Britain*. Oxford: Oxford University Press, 2005.
Bewell, Alan. "A Passion that Transforms: Picturing the Early Natural History Collector." In *Figuring It Out: Science, Gender, and Visual Culture*, edited by Ann B. Shteir and Bernard Lightman, 28–53. Hanover, NH: Dartmouth College Press, 2006.
Bigold, Melanie. "Letters and Learning." In *The History of British Women's Writing*, 1690–

1750, edited by Ros Ballaster, 173–186. Vol. 4 of *The History of British Women's Writing*, edited by Jennie Batchelor and Cora Kaplan. New York: Palgrave Macmillan, 2010.

———. *Women of Letters, Manuscript Circulation, and Print Afterlives in the Eighteenth Century: Elizabeth Rowe, Catharine Cockburn, and Elizabeth Carter*. New York: Palgrave Macmillan, 2013.

Binhammer, Katherine. *The Seduction Narrative in Britain, 1747–1800*. Cambridge: Cambridge University Press, 2009.

Biographia Britannica: Or, the Lives of the Most Eminent Persons Who Have Flourished in Great Britain and Ireland, 2nd ed. 5 vols. London, 1778.

Birch, Thomas. *The History of the Royal Society*. 4 vols. London, 1756.

———. *History of the Works of the Learned*, Art 31 (June 1, 1739).

Birchwood, Matthew. "Vindicating the Prophet: Universal Monarchy and Henry Stubbe's Biography of Mohammed." *Prose Studies* 29, no. 1 (April 2007): 59–72.

Black, Jeremy. *Eighteenth-Century Britain, 1688–1783*, 2nd ed. London: Palgrave, 2008.

Black, Scott. "Quixotic Realism and the Romance of the Novel." *Novel* 42, no. 2 (2009): 239–244.

———. "Romance redivivus." In *The Cambridge History of the English Novel*, edited by Robert L. Caserio and Clement Hawes, 246–261. Cambridge: Cambridge University Press, 2012.

———. "Trading Sex for Secrets in Haywood's *Love in Excess*." *Eighteenth-Century Fiction* 15, no. 2 (January 2003): 207–226.

Bogel, Fredric V. *The Difference Satire Makes: Rhetoric and Reading from Jonson to Byron*. Ithaca, NY: Cornell University Press, 2001.

Bohls, Elizabeth A. "Disinterestedness and the Denial of the Particular: Locke, Adam Smith, and the Subject of Aesthetics." In *Eighteenth-Century Aesthetics and the Reconstruction of Art*, edited by Paul Mattick, Jr., 16–51. Cambridge: Cambridge University Press, 1993.

de Bolla, Peter. *The Education of the Eye: Painting, Landscape, and Architecture in Eighteenth-Century Britain*. Stanford, CA: Stanford University Press, 2003.

Bono, James J. *The Word of God and the Languages of Man: Interpreting Nature in Early Modern Science and Medicine*. Madison: University of Wisconsin Press, 1995.

Bowers, Toni. *Force or Fraud: British Seduction Stories and the Problem of Resistance, 1660–1760*. Oxford: Oxford University Press, 2011.

Boyle, Frank T. *Swift as Nemesis: Modernity and Its Satirist*. Stanford, CA: Stanford University Press, 2000.

Boyle, John, Earl of Orrery. *Remarks on the Life and Writings of Dr. Jonathan Swift*. London, 1752.

Boyle, Robert. *The Correspondence of Robert Boyle*. Edited by Michael Hunter, Antonio Clericuzio and Lawrence Principe. 7 vols. London: Pickering & Chatto, 2001.

———. *The Excellency of Theology Compar'd with Natural Philosophy, (as both are Objects of Men's Study.) Discours'd of In a Letter to a Friend*. London, 1671.

———. *A Proemial Essay*. London, 1661.

———. *Some Considerations Touching the Usefulness of Experimental Natural Philosophy*. 2 parts. London, 1663.

———. *The Works of Robert Boyle*. Edited by Michael Hunter and Edward B. Davis. 14 vols. London: Pickering & Chatto, 1999.

Braunschneider, Theresa. *Our Coquettes: Capacious Desire in the Eighteenth Century.* Charlottesville: University of Virginia Press, 2009.
Brereton, Jane. *Poems on Several Occasions.* London, 1735.
Brewer, David A. *The Afterlife of Character, 1726–1825.* Philadelphia: University of Pennsylvania Press, 2005.
Brown, Laura. *The Ends of Empire: Women and Ideology in Early Eighteenth-Century English Literature.* Ithaca, NY: Cornell University Press, 1993.
Brown, Sarah Annes. "Women Translators." In *The Oxford History of Literary Translation in English:* 1660–1790, edited by Stuart Gillespie and David Hopkins, 111–120. Oxford: Oxford University Press, 2005.
Bury, Emmanuel. *Littérature et politesse: L'invention de l'bonnête home, 1580–1750.* Paris: Presses Universitaires de France, 1996.
Butler, Douglas R. "Plot and Politics in Susanna Centlivre's *A Bold Stroke for a Wife.*" In *Curtain Calls: British and American Women and the Theater, 1660–1820,* edited by Mary Anne Schofield and Cecilia Macheski, 357–370. Athens: Ohio University Press, 1991.
Butler, Samuel. *The Genuine Remains in Verse and Prose of Mr. Samuel Butler.* 2 vols. London, 1749.
Campbell, Mary Baine. *Wonder and Science: Imagining Worlds in Early Modern Europe.* Ithaca, NY: Cornell University Press, 1999.
[Carter, Elizabeth.] *Elizabeth Carter, 1717–1806: An Edition of Some Unpublished Letters.* Edited by Gwen Hampshire. Newark: University of Delaware Press, 2005.
———. *Memoirs of the Life of Mrs. Elizabeth Carter with A New Edition of her Poems.* Edited by Montagu Pennington. London, 1807.
Carter, Elizabeth, and Catherine Talbot. *A Series of Letters between Mrs. Elizabeth Carter and Miss Catherine Talbot, from the year 1741 to 1770.* 4 vols. Facsimile edition. New York: AMS Press, 1975.
Casaubon, Méric. *Treatise Concerning Enthusiasme.* London, 1654.
Casid, Jill H. *Sowing Empire: Landscape and Colonization.* Minneapolis: University of Minnesota Press, 2005.
A Catalogue of Books: The Library of the Late Rev. Dr. Swift. Dublin, 1745.
Cavazza, Marta. *Settecento inquieto. Alle origini dell'Istituto delle Scienze di Bologna.* Bologna: Il Mulino, 1990.
Cavendish, Margaret. *Natures Pictures Drawn by Fancies Pencil to the Life.* London, 1656.
———. *Observations upon Experimental Philosophy.* Ed. Eileen O'Neill. Cambridge: Cambridge University Press, 2001.
———. *Paper Bodies: A Margaret Cavendish Reader.* Edited by Sylvia Bowerbank and Sara Mendelson. Peterborough, ONT: Broadview Press, 2000.
A Censure upon Certaine Passages Contained in the History of the Royal Society, As being Destructive to the Established Religion and Church of England. London, 1670.
Centlivre, Susanna. *The Works of the Celebrated Mrs. Centlivre.* 3 vols. London, 1760–1761.
Chalmers, Alan D. *Jonathan Swift and the Burden of the Future.* Newark: University of Delaware Press, 1995.
Chang, Hasok. "Practicing Eighteenth-Century Science Today." In *Nature Engaged: Science in Practice from Renaissance to the Present,* edited by Mario Biagioli and Jessica Riskin, 41–58. New York: Palgrave Macmillan, 2012.

Chappell, Carolyn Lougee. *Le Paradis des Femmes: Women, Salons, and Social Stratification in Seventeenth-Century France.* Princeton, NJ: Princeton University Press, 1976.

Chico, Tita. *Designing Women: The Dressing Room in Eighteenth-Century English Literature and Culture.* Lewisburg, PA: Bucknell University Press, 2005.

———. "Details and Frankness: Affective Relations in *Sir Charles Grandison*." *Studies in Eighteenth-Century Culture* 38 (2009): 45–68.

———. "Minute Particulars: Microscopy and Eighteenth-Century Narrative." *Mosaic: A Journal for the Interdisciplinary Study of Literature* 39 (2006): 143–161.

———. "'the More I Write, the More I Shall Have to Write': The Many Beginnings of *Tristram Shandy*." In *Narrative Beginnings: Theories and Practices*, edited by Brian Richardson, 83–95. Lincoln: University of Nebraska Press, 2008.

———. "Putrefaction as Optical Technology," *Configurations: A Journal of Literature, Science, and Technology*, 25 (2017): 145–164.

Christie, John R. "Laputa Revisited." In *Nature Transfigured: Science and Literature 1700–1900*, edited by John Christie and Sally Shuttleworth. 45–60. Manchester: Manchester University Press, 1989.

Chudgar, Neil. "Swift's Gentleness." *ELH: English Literary History* 78, no. 1 (2011): 137–161.

Clarke, Alfred. *An Essay towards the character of Her late Majesty Caroline, queen-consort of Great Britain.* London, 1738.

Clery, E. J. *The Feminization Debate in Eighteenth-Century England: Literature, Commerce and Luxury.* London: Palgrave Macmillan, 2004.

Clough, Sharyn. *Beyond Epistemology: A Pragmatist Approach to Feminist Science Studies.* Lanham, MD: Rowman & Littlefield, 2003.

Clucas, Stephen. "Variation, Irregularity and Probabilism: Margaret Cavendish and Natural Philosophy as Rhetoric." In *A Princely Brave Woman: Essays on Margaret Cavendish, Duchess of Newcastle*, edited by Stephen Clucas, 199–209. Aldershot: Ashgate, 2003.

Cohen, Ralph. "David Hume's Experimental Method and the Theory of Taste." *ELH: English Literary History* 25 (1958): 270–289.

———. *The Unfolding of The Seasons.* Baltimore, MD: Johns Hopkins University Press, 1970.

Cole, Lucinda. *Imperfect Creatures: Vermin, Literature, and the Sciences of Life, 1600–1740.* Ann Arbor: University of Michigan Press, 2016.

Colton, Judith. "Kent's Hermitage for Queen Caroline at Richmond." *Architectura* 4, no. 2 (1974): 181–191.

———. "Merlin's Cave and Queen Caroline: Garden Art as Political Propaganda." *Eighteenth-Century Studies* 10, no. 1 (1976): 1–20.

Congreve, William. *The Works of Mr. William Congreve.* 3 vols. 4th ed. London, 1725.

———. *The Works of William Congreve.* Ed. D. F. McKenzie. 3 vols. Oxford: Oxford University Press, 2011.

Connell, Phillip. "Newtonian Physico-Theology and the Varieties of Whiggism in James Thomson's *The Seasons*." *Huntington Library Quarterly* 72, no. 1 (2009): 1–28.

The Contest: Being Poetical Essays on the Queen's Grotto. London, 1734.

Conway, Anne, trans. *The Principles of the Most Ancient and Modern Philosophy.* London, 1692.

Cooper, Anthony Ashley. *Characteristics of Men, Manners, Opinions, Time.* Edited by Philip Ayres. 2 vols. Oxford: Clarendon Press, 1999.

Coppola, Al. *The Theater of Experiment: Staging Natural Philosophy in Eighteenth-Century Britain*. Oxford: Oxford University Press, 2016.
Cosentini, John W. *Fontenelle's Art of Dialogue*. New York: King's Crown Press, 1952.
Cowley, Abraham. "To the Royal Society." In *The History of the Royal Society*. 3rd ed. London, 1722.
———. *Verses, Written Upon Several Occasions*. London, 1663.
Crary, Jonathan. *Techniques of the Observer: On Vision and Modernity in the Nineteenth Century*. Cambridge, MA: MIT Press, 1992.
Craveri, Benedetta. *The Age of Conversation*. Translated by Teresa Waugh. New York: New York Review of Books, 2005.
Cunningham, Andrew. "Getting the Game Right: Some Plain Worlds on the Identity and Invention of Science." *Studies in History and Philosophy of Science* 19, no. 3 (1988): 365–389.
Curll, Edmund. *The Rarities of Richmond: being Exact Descriptions of the Royal Hermitage and Merlin's Cave with his Life and Prophecies. The Second Edition*. London, 1736.
Daston, Lorraine, ed. *Biographies of Scientific Objects*. Chicago: University of Chicago Press, 2000.
———. "Enlightenment Fears, Fears of Enlightenment." In *What's Left of Enlightenment? A Postmodern Question*, edited by Keith Michael Baker and Peter Hanns Reill, 115–128. Stanford, CA: Stanford University Press, 2001.
Daston, Lorraine, and Peter Galison, *Objectivity*. New York: Zone Books, 2007.
Daston, Lorraine, and Elizabeth Lunbeck, ed. *Histories of Scientific Observation*. Chicago: University of Chicago Press, 2011.
Daston, Lorraine, and Katharine Park. *Wonders and the Order of Nature, 1150–1750*. New York: Zone Books, 1998.
Daumas, Maurice. *Scientific Instruments of the Seventeenth and Eighteenth Centuries*. Translated and edited by Mary Holbrook. New York: Praeger, 1972.
Dear, Peter. *Discipline and Experience: The Mathematical Way in the Scientific Revolution*. Chicago: University of Chicago Press, 1995.
———. "From Truth to Disinterestedness in the Seventeenth Century." *Social Studies of Science* 22 (1992): 619–631.
———. "A Philosophical Duchess: Understanding Margaret Cavendish and the Royal Society." In *Science, Literature and Rhetoric in Early Modern England*, edited by Juliet Cummins and David Burchell, 125–144. Aldershot, Hampshire: Ashgate, 2007.
———. "Religion, Science and Natural Philosophy: Thoughts on Cunningham's Thesis." *Studies in History and Philosophy of Science* 32, no. 2 (2001): 377–386.
———. *Revolutionizing the Sciences: European Knowledge and Its Ambitions, 1500–1700*. Princeton, NJ: Princeton University Press, 2001.
De Bononiensi Scientiarum et Artium Instituto atque Academia Commentarii. Bologna: Dalla Volpe, 1731.
Defoe, Daniel. *A tour thro' the whole island of Great Britain*. London, 1724–1727.
DeJean, Joan. *Tender Geographies: Women and the Origins of the Novel in France*. New York: Columbia University Press, 1991.
DeMaria, Robert, Jr. *The Life of Samuel Johnson: A Critical Biography*. Oxford: Blackwell, 1994.

Dennis, Michael Aaron. "Graphic Understanding: Instruments and Interpretation in Robert Hooke's *Micrographia*." *Science in Context* 3 (1989): 309–364.
Derrida, Jacques. *Of Grammatology*. Translated by Gayatri Chakravorty Spivak. Baltimore, MD: Johns Hopkins University Press, 1998.
A Description of the Royal Gardens at Richmond in Surry, the Village, and Places Adjacent. London, n.d. [circa 1736?].
Deutsch, Helen. *Resemblance and Disgrace: Alexander Pope and the Deformation of Culture*. Cambridge, MA: Harvard University Press, 1996.
Dick, Steven J. *Plurality of Worlds: The Origins of the Extraterrestrial Life Debate from Democritus to Kant*. Cambridge: Cambridge University Press, 1982.
Dickie, George. *Art and the Aesthetic: An Institutional Analysis*. Ithaca, NY: Cornell University Press, 1974.
Di Palma, Vittoria. *Wasteland: A History*. New Haven, CT: Yale University Press, 2014.
A Dissertation on Royal Societies. In Three Letters. London, 1750.
Donawerth, Jane. *Conversational Rhetoric: The Rise and Fall of a Woman's Tradition, 1600–1900*. Carbondale: Southern Illinois University Press, 2012.
Douglas, Aileen. "Popular Science and the Representation of Women: Fontenelle and After." *Eighteenth-Century Life* 18 (1994): 1–14.
Downie, J. A. *Jonathan Swift: Political Writer*. London: Routledge & Kegan Paul, 1984.
Drake, Ellen Tan. *Restless Genius: Robert Hooke and His Earthly Thoughts*. New York: Oxford University Press, 1996.
Drennon, Herbert. "Scientific Rationalism and James Thomson's Poetic Art." *Studies in Philology* 31 (1934): 453–471.
Dryden, John. *The Works of John Dryden*. Edited by Edward Niles Hooker, H. T. Swedenberg, and Vinton A. Dearing. 20 vols. Berkeley: University of California Press, 1956–2000.
Duck, Stephen. *Poems on Several Occasions*. London, 1736.
Easlea, Brian. *Science and Sexual Oppression: Patriarchy's Confrontation with Women and Nature*. London: Weidenfeld and Nicolson, 1981.
Edelstein, Dan. *The Enlightenment: A Genealogy*. Chicago: University of Chicago Press, 2010.
Ehrenpreis, Irvin. *Swift: The Man, His Works, and the Age*. 3 vols. London: Methuen, 1983.
Elias, Norbert. *The Civilizing Process: Sociogenetic and Psychogenetic Investigations*. Translated by Edmund Jephcott. Oxford: Blackwell, 2000.
Elsky, Martin. "Bacon's Hieroglyphs and the Separation of Words and Things." *Philological Quarterly* 63 (1984): 449–460.
Evelyn, John. *The Diary of John Evelyn*. Edited by E. S. de Beer. 6 vols. Oxford: Clarendon Press, 1955.
Fabricant, Carole. *Swift's Landscape*. Notre Dame: University of Notre Dame Press, 1995.
Fara, Patricia. *Newton: The Making of Genius*. London: Picador, 2003.
———. *Sympathetic Attractions: Magnetic Practices, Beliefs, and Symbolism in Eighteenth-Century England*. Princeton, NJ: Princeton University Press, 1996.
Fara, Patricia, and David Money. "Isaac Newton and Augustan Anglo-Latin Poetry." *Studies in the History and Philosophy of Science* 35 (2004): 549–571.
Féher, Marta. "The Triumphal March of a Paradigm: A Case Study of the Popularization of Newtonian Science." *Tractrix* 2 (1990): 93–110.

Ferguson, Frances. *Solitude and the Sublime: Romanticism and the Aesthetics of Individuation*. New York: Routledge, 1992.

Fiennes, Celia. *The Illustrated Journeys of Celia Fiennes, 1685–c. 1712*. Edited by Christopher Morris. London: Macdonald & Co., 1982.

Finch, Anne. *Miscellany Poems, on Several Occasions. Written by a Lady*. London, 1713.

Findlen, Paula. "A Forgotten Newtonian: Women and Science in the Italian Provinces." In *The Sciences in Enlightened Europe*, edited by William Clark, Jan Golinski, and Simon Schaffer, 313–349. Chicago: University of Chicago Press, 1999.

———. "Translating the New Science: Women and the Circulation of Knowledge in Enlightenment Italy." *Configurations* 2 (1995): 167–206.

Fissell, Mary, and Roger Cooter. "Exploring Natural Knowledge: Science and the Popular." In *Eighteenth-Century Science*, edited by Roy Porter, 129–158. Cambridge: Cambridge University Press, 2003.

Fitzmaurice, James. "Fancy and the Family: Self-Characterizations of Margaret Cavendish." *Huntington Library Quarterly* 53 (1990): 198–209.

Fontenelle, Bernard le Bovier de. *Conversations on the Plurality of Worlds*. Translated by H. A. Hargreaves. Berkeley: University of California Press, 1990.

———. *Conversations with a Lady, on the Plurality of Worlds. Written in the French by M. Fontenelle*. Translated by John Glanvill. London, 1688.

———. *A Discourse of the Plurality of Worlds*. Translated by Sir W. D. Knight. Dublin, 1687.

Fortescue, James. *Science: An Epistle on Its Decline and Revival*. London, 1750.

Foucault, Michel. *The Foucault Reader*, edited by P. Rabinow. New York: Pantheon Books, 1984.

Fournier, Marian. *The Fabric of Life: Microscopy in the Seventeenth Century*. Baltimore, MD: Johns Hopkins University Press, 1996.

Fowler, Patsy S. "Rejecting the Status Quo: The Attempts of Mary Pix and Susanna Centlivre to Reform Society's Patriarchal Attitudes." *Restoration and 18th-Century Theatre Research* 11, no. 2 (1996): 49–59.

France, Peter. "Moralists and Philosophers." In *The Oxford History of Literary Translation in English: 1660–1790*, edited by Stuart Gillespie and David Hopkins, 361–373. Oxford: Oxford University Press, 2005.

Frank, R. G., Jr. *Harvey and the Oxford Physiologists: A Study of Scientific Ideas*. Berkeley: University of California Press, 1980.

Freeman, Lisa A. *Character's Theater: Genre and Identity on the Eighteenth-Century Stage*. Philadelphia: University of Pennsylvania Press, 2002.

Freud, Sigmund. *Dora: An Analysis of a Case of Hysteria*. Edited by Philip Rieff. New York: Simon & Schuster, 1963.

Frey, Christiane. "The Art of Observing the Small: On the Borders of the Subvisibilia (from Hooke to Brockes)." *Monatshefte* 105, no. 3 (2013): 376–388.

Fulford, Tim. *Landscape, Liberty, and Authority: Poetry, Criticism, and Politics from Thomson to Wordsworth*. Cambridge: Cambridge University Press, 1996.

Galison, Peter. *Image and Logic: A Material Culture of Microphysics*. Chicago: University of Chicago Press, 1997.

Gentleman's Magazine 3 (April 1733).

Gierl, Martin. "Science, Projects, Computers, and the State: Swift's Lagadian and Leibniz's

Prussian Academy." In *The Age of Projects,* edited by Maximillian E. Novak, 297–317. Toronto: University of Toronto Press, 2008.

Gigante, Denise. *Taste: A Literary History.* New Haven, CT: Yale University Press, 2005.

Gikandi, Simon. *Slavery and the Culture of Taste.* Princeton, NJ: Princeton University Press, 2011.

Gillespie, Stuart, and Penelope Wilson. "The Publishing and Readership of Translation." In *The Oxford History of Literary Translation in English: 1660–1790,* edited by Stuart Gillespie and David Hopkins, 38–51. Oxford: Oxford University Press, 2005.

Giovanardi, Claudio. "Note su Algarotti tradotto in Francese." *Nuovi annali della Facoltà di magistero dell'Università di Messina* 1 (1988): 91–125.

Girten, Kristin M. "Mingling with Matter: Tactile Microscopy and the Philosophic Mind in Brobdingnag and Beyond." *The Eighteenth Century: Theory and Interpretation* 54, no. 4 (2013): 497–520.

———. "Unsexed Souls: Natural Philosophy as Transformation in Eliza Haywood's *Female Spectator.*" *Eighteenth-Century Studies* 43, no. 1 (2009): 55–74.

Glanvill, John. *Plus Ultra: or, The Progress and Advancement of Knowledge Since the Days of Aristotle.* London, 1668.

Glide, Joseph M. "Shadwell and the Royal Society: Satire in *The Virtuoso.*" *SEL: Studies in English Literature, 1500–1900* 10, no. 3 (1970): 469–490.

Golinski, Jan V. "Robert Boyle: Scepticism and Authority in Seventeenth-Century Chemical Discourse." In *The Figural and the Literal: Problems of Language in the History of Science and Philosophy, 1630–1800,* edited by Andrew E. Benjamin, G. N. Cantor, and J. R. R. Christie, 58–82. Manchester: Manchester University Press, 1987.

———. *Science as Public Culture: Chemistry and Enlightenment in Britain, 1760–1820.* Cambridge: Cambridge University Press, 1992.

Goodman, Dena. "Enlightenment Salons: The Convergence of Female and Philosophic Ambitions." *Eighteenth-Century Studies* 22 (1988–1989): 329–350.

———. *The Republic of Letters: A Cultural History of the French Enlightenment.* Ithaca, NY: Cornell University Press, 1994.

Goodman, Kevis. *Georgic Modernity and British Romanticism: Poetry and the Mediation of History.* Cambridge: Cambridge University Press, 2004.

Gordon, Scott Paul. "Voyeuristic Dreams: Mr. Spectator and the Power of Spectacle." *The Eighteenth Century: Theory and Interpretation* 36, no. 1 (1995): 3–23.

[Green, Matthew.] *The Grotto, A Poem. Written by Peter Drake, Fisherman of Brentford.* London, 1733.

Griffin, Dustin. *Satire: A Critical Reintroduction.* Lexington: University Press of Kentucky, 1995.

Grundy, Isobel. *Lady Mary Wortley Montagu.* Oxford: Oxford University Press, 1999.

Guerrini, Anita. *Experimenting with Humans and Animals: From Galen to Animal Rights.* Baltimore, MD: Johns Hopkins University Press, 2003.

———. *Obesity and Depression in the Enlightenment: The Life and Times of George Cheyne.* Norman: University of Oklahoma Press, 2000.

Guerlac, Henry, and M. C. Jacob. "Bentley, Newton, and Providence: The Boyle Lectures Once More." *Journal of the History of Ideas* 30, no. 3 (1969): 307–318.

Guillory, John. "Enlightening Mediation." In *This Is Enlightenment*, edited by Clifford Siskin and William Warner, 37–63. Chicago: University of Chicago Press, 2010.

Guyer, Paul. *Values of Beauty: Historical Essays in Aesthetics*. Cambridge: Cambridge University Press, 2005.

Habermas, Jürgen. *Postmetaphysical Thinking: Philosophical Essays*. Translated by William Mark Hohengarten. Cambridge, MA: MIT Press, 1992.

Hacking, Ian. *Representing and Intervening: Introductory Topics in the Philosophy of Natural Science*. Cambridge: Cambridge University Press, 1983.

Hall, A. R., and M. B. Hall. "The Intellectual Origins of the Royal Society: London and Oxford." *Notes and Records of the Royal Society* 23 (1969): 157–168.

Hall, Marie Boas. *Henry Oldenburg: Shaping the Royal Society*. Oxford: Oxford University Press, 2002.

———. *Robert Boyle and Seventeenth-Century Chemistry*. Cambridge: Cambridge University Press, 1956.

Hammond, Brean. "Swift's Reading." In *The Cambridge Companion to Jonathan Swift*, edited by Christopher Fox, 73–86. Cambridge: Cambridge University Press, 2003.

Hanson, Craig Ashley. *The English Virtuoso: Art, Medicine, and Antiquarianism in the Age of Empiricism*. Chicago: University of Chicago Press, 2009.

Haraway, Donna J. *Modest_Witness@Second_Millennium. FemaleMan©Meets_OncoMouse™: Feminism and Technoscience*. New York: Routledge, 1997.

Harding, Sandra. *Sciences from Below: Feminisms, Postcolonialities, and Modernities*. Durham, NC: Duke University Press, 2008.

Harpham, Geoffrey Galt. "So ... What Is Enlightenment? An Inquisition into Modernity." *Critical Inquiry* 20, no. 3 (1994); 524–564.

Harris, Jonathan Gil. *Foreign Bodies and the Body Politic: Discourses of Social Pathology in Early Modern England*. Cambridge: Cambridge University Press, 1998.

Harth, Erica. *Cartesian Women: Versions and Subversions of Rational Discourse in the Old Regime*. Ithaca, NY: Cornell University Press, 1992.

Hawes, Clement. *The British Enlightenment and Global Critique*. New York: Palgrave Macmillan, 2005.

Hawley, Judith. "Elizabeth Carter and Modes of Knowledge." In *Woman to Woman: Female Negotiations during the Long Eighteenth Century*, edited by Carolyn D. Williams, Angela Escott, and Louise Duckling, 157–170. Newark: University of Delaware Press, 2010.

———. gen. ed. *Literature and Science, 1660–1834*, 8 vols. London: Pickering & Chatto, 2003–2004.

Haywood, Eliza. *The Adventures of Eovaai, Princess of Ijaveo: A Pre-Adamitical History*. Edited by Earla Wilputte. Peterborough, ONT: Broadview Press, 1999.

———. *The Female Spectator*. London, 1746.

———. *The History of Miss Betsy Thoughtless*. Edited by Christine Blouch. Peterborough, ONT: Broadview Press, 1998.

———. *Love in Excess*, 2nd ed. Edited by David Oakleaf. Peterborough, ONT: Broadview Press, 2000.

Heffernan, James A. W. *Museum of Words: The Poetics of Ekphrasis from Homer to Ashbery*. Chicago: University of Chicago Press, 1993.

Hellegers, Desiree. *Handmaid to Divinity: Natural Philosophy, Poetry, and Gender in Seventeenth-Century England.* Norman: University of Oklahoma Press, 2000.

Heringman, Noah. "The Commerce of Literature and Natural History." In *Romantic Science: The Literary Forms of Natural History*, edited by Noah Heringman, 1–19. Albany: State University of New York Press, 2003.

———. *Romantic Rocks, Aesthetic Geology.* Ithaca, NY: Cornell University Press, 2004.

Hertz, Neil. "Dora's Secrets, Freud's Techniques." In *Dora's Case: Freud—Hysteria—Feminism*, 2nd ed., edited by Charles Bernheimer and Claire Kahane. New York: Columbia University Press, 1990.

Higgins, Ian. *Swift's Politics: A Study in Disaffection.* Cambridge: Cambridge University Press, 1994.

Hildrop, John. *A Modest Apology for the Ancient and Honourable Family of the Wrongheads.* London, 1744.

Holmes, Richard. *The Age of Wonder: How the Romantic Generation Discovered the Beauty and Terror of Science.* New York: HarperPress, 2008.

Holton, Gerald. *The Scientific Imagination.* Cambridge, MA: Harvard University Press, 1998.

Hooke, Robert. *The Diary of Robert Hooke.* Edited by Henry W. Robinson and Walter Adams. London: Taylor & Francis, 1935.

———. "Discourse concerning Telescopes and Microscopes." In *Philosophical Experiments and Observations.* Edited by W. Derham. Facsimile reprint. London: Cass, 1967. First published 1726.

———. "A General Scheme, or Idea of the Present State of Natural Philosophy, and How its Defects may be Remedied by a Methodological Proceeding in the making Experiments and Collecting Observations." In *The Posthumous Works of Robert Hooke*, edited by Richard Waller, 1–70. London, 1705.

———. *Micrographia: or Some Physiological Descriptions of Minute Bodies.* London, 1665.

Hopkins, David, and Pat Rogers. "The Translator's Trade." In *The Oxford History of Literary Translation in English: 1660–1790*, edited by Stuart Gillespie and David Hopkins, 81–95. Oxford: Oxford University Press, 2005.

Horkheimer, Max. "Reason Against Itself: Some Remarks on Enlightenment." *Theory, Culture & Society* 10 (May 1993): 79–88.

Horkheimer, Max, and Theodor W. Adorno. *Dialectic of Enlightenment.* Translated by John Cumming. New York: Herder and Herder, 1972.

Houghton, Walter E., Jr. "The English Virtuoso in the Seventeenth Century: Part I." *Journal of the History of Ideas* 3, no. 1 (1942): 51–73.

———. "The English Virtuoso in the Seventeenth Century: Part II." *Journal of the History of Ideas* 3, no. 1 (1942): 190–219.

Howell, A. C. "*Res et verba:* Words and Things." *ELH: English Literary History* 13 (1946): 131–141.

Hulme, Peter, and Ludmilla Jordanova, eds. *The Enlightenment and Its Shadows.* London: Routledge, 1990.

Hume, David. *Essays: Moral, Political, and Literary.* Edited by Eugene F. Miller. Indianapolis, IN: Liberty Classics, 1985.

Hunter, J. Paul. "Formalism and History: Binarism and the Anglophone Couplet." *MLQ* 61 (2000): 109–129.

Hunter, Matthew C. *Wicked Intelligence: Visual Art and the Science of Experiment in Restoration London*. Chicago: University of Chicago Press, 2013.
Hunter, Michael. *Establishing the New Science: The Experience of the Early Royal Society*. Woodbridge: Boydell Press, 1989.
———. "Latitudinarianism and the 'Ideology' of the Early Royal Society: Thomas Sprat's *History of the Royal Society* (1667) Reconsidered." In *Philosophy, Science, and Religion in England, 1640–1700*, edited by Richard Kroll, Richard Ashcraft, and Perez Zagorin, 199–229. Cambridge: Cambridge University Press, 1992.
———. "Robert Hooke: The Natural Philosopher." In *London's Leonardo: The Life and Work of Robert Hooke*, edited by Jim Bennett. Oxford: Oxford University Press, 2003.
———. *The Royal Society and Its Fellows, 1660–1700: The Morphology of an Early Scientific Institution*. Chalfont St. Giles: British Society for the History of Science, 1982.
———. *Science and the Shape of Orthodoxy: Studies of Intellectual Change in Late Seventeenth-Century Britain*. Woodbridge: Boydell Press, 1995.
———. *Science and Society in Restoration England*. Cambridge: Cambridge University Press, 1981.
Hutcheson, Francis. *An Inquiry into the Original of Our Ideas of Beauty and Virtue in Two Treatises*. Edited by Wolfgang Leidhold. Indianapolis, IN: Liberty Fund, 2008.
Hutton, Sarah. "Science and Satire: The Lucianic Voice of Margaret Cavendish's *Description of a New World Called the Blazing World*." In *Authorial Conquests: Essays on Genre in the Writings of Margaret Cavendish*, edited by Line Cottegnies and Nancy Weitz, 161–178. Madison, NJ: Fairleigh Dickinson University Press, 2003.
Inwood, Stephen. *The Man Who Knew Too Much: The Strange and Inventive Life of Robert Hooke, 1635–1703*. London: Macmillan, 2002.
Italia, Iona. *The Rise of Literary Journalism in the Eighteenth Century: Anxious Employment*. London: Routledge, 2005.
Jacob, Margaret C. *The Cultural Meaning of the Scientific Revolution*. Philadelphia: Temple University Press, 1988.
———. *The Newtonians and the English Revolution, 1689–1720*. Hassocks, Sussex: Harvester Press, 1976.
Jacob, Margaret C., and Larry Stewart. *Practical Matter: Newton's Science in the Service of Industry and Empire, 1687–1851*. Cambridge, MA: Harvard University Press, 2004.
Jardine, Lisa. *The Curious Life of Robert Hooke: The Man Who Measured London*. New York: Harper Perennial, 2003.
———. *Ingenious Pursuits: Building the Scientific Revolution*. New York: Anchor, 2000.
Jarvis, J. Ereck. "Thomas Sprat's 'Mixt Assembly': Association and Authority in *The History of the Royal Society*." *Restoration: Studies in English Literary Culture, 1660–1700* 37, no. 2 (2013): 55–77.
Jenkinson, Matthew. *Culture and Politics at the Court of Charles II*. Woodbridge: Boydell Press, 2010.
Johns, Adrian. *The Nature of the Book: Print and Knowledge in the Making*. Chicago: University of Chicago Press, 1998.
Johnson, Samuel. *A Dictionary of the English Language*. London, 1755.
———. *The Yale Edition of the Works of Samuel Johnson*, 20 vols. New Haven, CT: Yale University Press, 1956–present.

Johnston, Joseph. "Irish Currency in the Eighteenth Century." *Hermathena* 27, no. 52 (1938): 3–26.
Jones, Matthew L. *The Good Life in the Scientific Revolution: Descartes, Pascal, Leibniz, and the Cultivation of Virtue*. Chicago: University of Chicago Press, 2006.
Jones, Richard Foster. *Ancients and Moderns: A Study of the Rise of the Scientific Movement in Seventeenth-Century England*, 2nd ed. St. Louis, MO: Washington University Press, 1961.
Jones, Robert W. "Eliza Haywood and the Discourse of Taste." In *Authorship, Commerce and the Public: Scenes of Writing, 1750–1850*, edited by E. J. Clery, Caroline Franklin, and Peter Garside, 103–119. New York: Palgrave Macmillan, 2002.
Jones, William Powell. *The Rhetoric of Science: A Study of Scientific Ideas and Imagery in Eighteenth-Century English Poetry*. Berkeley: University of California Press, 1966.
Jordanova, L. J., ed. *Languages of Nature: Critical Essays on Science and Literature*. London: Free Association Books, 1986.
Judson, Margaret. *Crisis of the Constitution: An Essay in Constitutional and Political Thought in England, 1603–1645*. Rutgers, NJ: Rutgers University Press, 1949.
Jung, Sandro. "Print Culture, High-Cultural Consumption, and Thomson's *The Seasons*, 1780–1797." *Eighteenth-Century Studies* 44, no. 4 (2011): 495–514.
———. "Visual Interpretations, Print, and Illustrations of Thomson's *The Seasons*, 1730–1797." *Eighteenth-Century Life* 34, no. 2 (2010): 23–64.
Kareem, Sarah Tindal. *Eighteenth-Century Fiction and the Reinvention of Wonder*. Oxford: Oxford University Press, 2014.
Kaul, Suvir. *Poems of Nation, Anthems of Empire: English Verse in the Long Eighteenth Century*. Charlottesville, VA: University Press of Virginia, 2000.
Keller, Evelyn Fox. "Producing Petty Gods: Margaret Cavendish's Critique of Experimental Science." *ELH: English Literary History* 64 (1997): 447–471.
———. *Reflections on Gender and Science*. New Haven, CT: Yale University Press, 1985.
Kelly, Ann Cline. "Gulliver as Pet and Pet Owner: Conversations with Animals in Book 4." *ELH: English Literary History* 74, no. 2 (2007): 323–349.
Kiernan, Colin. "Swift and Science." *The Historical Journal* 14, no. 4 (1974): 709–722.
King, Shelley, and Yaël Schlick, eds. *Refiguring the Coquette*. Lewisburg, PA: Bucknell University Press, 2008.
Kivy, Peter. *The Seventh Sense: A Study of Francis Hutcheson's Aesthetics and Its Influence in Eighteenth-Century Britain*. New York: Burt Franklin, 1976.
Kneller, Jane. "Disinterestedness." In *Encyclopedia of Aesthetics*, 2:421–426. Gen. ed. Michael Kelly. 6 vols. 2nd ed. Oxford: Oxford University Press, 2014.
Knellwolf, Christa. "Robert Hooke's *Micrographia* and the Aesthetics of Empiricism." *The Seventeenth Century* 16 (2001): 177–200.
Knoespel, Kenneth J. "The Mythological Transformations of Renaissance Science." In *Literature and Science as Modes of Expression*, edited by Frederick Amrine and Stephen J. Weininger, 99–112. Dordrecht: Kluwer, 1989.
———. "The Narrative Matter of Mathematics: John Dee's Preface to the Elements of Euclid of Megara (1570)." *Philological Quarterly* 66, no. 1 (1987): 27–46.
Koehler, Margaret. *Poetry of Attention in the Eighteenth Century*. New York: Palgrave Macmillan, 2012.

Korsmeyer, Carolyn Wilker. "Relativism and Hutcheson's Aesthetic Theory." *Journal of the History of Ideas* 36, no. 2 (1975): 319–330.
Kramnick, Jonathan. *Actions and Objects from Hobbes to Richardson*. Stanford, CA: Stanford University Press, 2010.
Kroll, Richard. "Instituting Empiricism: Hobbes's *Leviathan* and Dryden's *Marriage à la Mode*." In *Cultural Readings of Restoration and Eighteenth-Century English Theater*, edited by J. Douglas Canfield and Deborah C. Payne, 39–66. Athens: University of Georgia Press, 1995.
Lacan, Jacques. *Feminine Sexuality: Jacques Lacan and the Ecole Freudienne*, edited by Juliet Mitchell and Jacqueline Rose. Translated by Jacqueline Rose. New York: Norton and Pantheon 1985.
Lamb, Jonathan. "Locke's Wild Fancies: Empiricism, Personhood, and Fictionality." *The Eighteenth Century: Theory and Interpretation* 48, no. 3 (2007): 187–204.
———. *The Things Things Say*. Princeton, NJ: Princeton University Press, 2011.
Landry, Donna. *Noble Brutes: How Eastern Horses Transformed English Culture*. Baltimore, MD: Johns Hopkins University Press, 2008.
Laslett, Barbara, and Sally Gregory Kohlstedt, Helen Longino, and Evelynn Hammonds, eds. *Gender and Scientific Authority*. Chicago: University of Chicago Press, 1996.
Latour, Bruno. *We Have Never Been Modern*. Translated by Catherine Porter. Cambridge, MA: Harvard University Press, 1993.
Lee, Anthony W. "Who's Mentoring Whom? Mentorship, Alliance, and Rivalry in the Carter-Johnson Relationship." In *Mentoring in Eighteenth-Century British Literature and Culture*, edited by Anthony W. Lee, 191–210. Surrey: Ashgate, 2010.
Levine, Joseph M. *The Battle of the Books: History and Literature in the Augustan Age*. Ithaca, NY: Cornell University Press, 1991.
Lewis, Jayne Elizabeth. *Air's Appearance: Literary Atmosphere in British Fiction, 1660–1794*. Chicago: University of Chicago Press, 2012.
Lloyd, Claude. "Shadwell and the Virtuosi." *PMLA* 44, no. 2 (1929): 472–494.
Loar, Christopher F. *Political Magic: British Fictions of Savagery and Sovereignty, 1650–1750*. New York: Fordham University Press, 2014.
Locke, John. *An Essay Concerning Human Understanding*. Edited by Peter H. Nidditch. Oxford: Oxford University Press, 1975.
London's Glory Represented by Time, Truth and Fame. London, 1660.
López-Vidriero, María Luisa. *The Polished Cornerstone of the Temple: Queenly Libraries of the Enlightenment*. London: British Library, 2005.
Lubey, Kathleen. *Excitable Imaginations: Eroticism and Reading in Britain, 1660–1760*. Lewisburg, PA: Bucknell University Press, 2012.
Lynall, Gregory. *Swift and Science: The Satire, Politics, and Theology of Natural Knowledge, 1690–1730*. Basingstoke, Hampshire: Palgrave Macmillan, 2012.
Lynch, William T. *Solomon's Child: Method in the Early Royal Society of London*. Stanford, CA: Stanford University Press, 2001.
Mackie, Erin. "Gulliver and the Houyhnhnm Good Life," *The Eighteenth Century: Theory and Interpretation* 55, no. 1 (2015): 109–115.
———. *Market à la Mode: Fashion, Commodity, and Gender in* The Tatler *and* The Spectator. Baltimore, MD: Johns Hopkins University Press, 1997.

Malcolmson, Cristina. *Studies of Skin Color in the Early Royal Society: Boyle, Cavendish, Swift.* Farnham, Surrey: Ashgate, 2013.
Mandell, Laura. *Misogynous Economies: The Business of Literature in Eighteenth-Century Britain.* Lexington: University Press of Kentucky, 1999.
Marcialis, Maria Teresa. "Francesco Algarotti's Worldly Newtonianism." *Memorie della Società astronomica italiana* 60, no. 4 (1989): 806–882.
Markley, Robert. "Beyond Consensus: *The Rape of the Lock* and the Fate of Reading Eighteenth-Century Literature." *New Orleans Review* 15 (1998): 68–77.
———. *Fallen Languages: Crises of Representation in Newtonian England, 1660–1740.* Ithaca, NY: Cornell University Press, 1993.
———. "Global Analogies: Cosmology, Geosymmetry, and Skepticism in some Works of Aphra Behn." In *Science, Literature and Rhetoric in Early Modern England*, edited by Juliet Cummins and David Burchell, 189–212. Aldershot, Hampshire: Ashgate, 2007.
———. "Gulliver and the Japanese: The Limits of the Postcolonial Past." *Modern Language Quarterly* 65, no. 3 (2004): 457–479.
Marsak, Leonard M. "Bernard de Fontenelle: The Idea of Science in the French Enlightenment." *Transactions of the American Philosophical Society*, n.s. 49, pt. 7 (1959): 3–64.
Marschner, Joanna. *Queen Caroline: Cultural Politics in the Early Eighteenth-Century Court.* New Haven, CT: Yale University Press, 2014.
Marsden, Jean I. "Ideology, Sex, and Satire: The Case of Thomas Shadwell." In *Cutting Edges: Postmodern Critical Essays on Eighteenth-Century Satire*, edited by James E. Gill, 43–58. Knoxville: University of Tennessee Press, 1995.
Marshall, David. *The Frame of Art: Fictions of Aesthetic Experience.* Baltimore, MD: Johns Hopkins University Press, 2005.
Martin, Benjamin. *Micrographia Nova.* Reading, 1742.
———. *A New and Compendious System of Optics.* London, 1740.
———. *The Young Gentleman and Lady's Philosophy.* 2 vols. London, 1759–1763.
Martin, Julian. *Francis Bacon, the State and the Reform of Natural Philosophy.* Cambridge: Cambridge University Press, 1992.
Mattes, Eleanor. "The 'Female Virtuoso' in Early Eighteenth-Century English Drama." *Women and Literature* 3, no. 2 (1975): 3–9.
Maurer, Shawn Lisa. *Proposing Men: Dialectics of Gender and Class in the Eighteenth-Century Periodical.* Stanford, CA: Stanford University Press, 1998.
McKeon, Michael. *The Origins of the English Novel, 1600–1740.* Baltimore, MD: Johns Hopkins University Press, 1987.
McLeod, Bruce. *The Geography of Empire in English Literature, 1580–1745.* Cambridge: Cambridge University Press, 1999.
McMurran, Mary Helen. *The Spread of Novels: Translation and Prose Fiction in the Eighteenth Century.* Princeton, NJ: Princeton University Press, 2010.
Merchant, Carolyn. *The Death of Nature: Women, Ecology, and the Scientific Revolution.* San Francisco: Harper and Row, 1980.
Merrens, Rebecca. "A Nature of 'Infinite Sense and Reason': Margaret Cavendish's Natural Philosophy and the 'Noise' of a Feminized Nature." *Women's Studies* 25 (1996): 421–438.
Merritt, Juliette. *Beyond Spectacle: Eliza Haywood's Female Spectators.* Toronto: University of Toronto Press, 2004.

———. "Reforming the Coquette: Eliza Haywood's Vision of Female Epistemology." In *Fair Philosopher: Eliza Haywood and the Female Spectator*, edited by Lynn Marie Wright and Donald J. Newman, 176–192. Lewisburg, PA: Bucknell University Press, 2006.

Meyer, Gerald Dennis. *The Scientific Lady in England, 1650–1760: An Account of Her Rise, with Emphasis on the Major Roles of the Telescope and Microscope.* Los Angeles: University of California Press, 1955.

"The Microscope." In *Female Inconstancy Display'd in three Diverting Histories . . . To which is added, Several Diverting Tales and Merry Jokes*, 41–43. London, 1732.

Miguel-Alfonso, Ricardo. "Social Conservatism, Aesthetic Education and the Essay Genre in Eliza Haywood's *Female Spectator*." In *Fair Philosopher: Eliza Haywood and* The Female Spectator, edited by Lynn Marie Wright and Donald J. Newman, 72–81. Lewisburg, PA: Bucknell University Press, 2006.

Miller, James. *The Humours of Oxford.* London, 1730.

Miller, Laura. "Publishers and Gendered Readership in English-Language Editions of *Il Newtonianismo per le Dame*." *Studies in Eighteenth-Century Culture* 42 (2013): 191–214.

Mitchell, Robert. *Experimental Life: Vitalism in Romantic Science and Literature.* Baltimore, MD: Johns Hopkins University Press, 2013.

Mitchell, W. J. T., ed. *Landscape and Power*, 2nd ed. Chicago: University of Chicago Press, 2002.

Montagu, Mary Wortley. *The Complete Letters of Lady Mary Wortley Montagu.* Edited by Robert Halsband. 3 vols. Oxford: Clarendon Press, 1967.

Moore, Sean D. *Swift, the Book, and the Irish Financial Revolution: Satire and Sovereignty in Colonial Ireland.* Baltimore, MD: Johns Hopkins University Press, 2010

More, Henry. *Enthusiasmus Triumphatus; or, A Discourse of the Nature, Causes, Kinds, and Cure of Enthusiasme.* London, 1656.

Morgan, John. "Science, England's 'Interest' and Universal Monarchy: The Making of Thomas Sprat's *History of the Royal Society*." *History of Science* 47 (2009): 27–54.

Mossner, Ernest Campbell. "Hume's 'Of Criticism.'" In *Studies in Criticism and Aesthetics, 1600–1800*, edited by Howard Anderson and John S. Shea, 232–248. Minneapolis: University of Minnesota Press, 1967.

Myers, Natasha. *Rendering Life Molecular: Models, Modelers, and Excitable Matter.* Durham, NC: Duke University Press, 2015.

Myers, Sylvia Harcstark. *The Bluestocking Circle: Women, Friendship, and the Life of the Mind in Eighteenth-Century England.* Oxford: Clarendon Press, 1990.

Neill, Anna. *British Discovery Literature and the Rise of Global Commerce.* Basingstoke, Hampshire: Palgrave, 2002.

Nestor, Deborah J. "Representing Domestic Difficulties: Eliza Haywood and the Critique of Bourgeois Ideology." *Prose Studies* 16, no. 2 (August 1993): 1–26.

Newell, R. W. *Objectivity, Empiricism, and Truth.* London: Routledge, 1986.

Newman, William R. *Promethean Ambitions: Alchemy and the Quest to Perfect Nature.* Chicago: University of Chicago Press, 2004.

Newman, William R., and Lawrence M. Principe. *Alchemy Tried in the Fire: Starkey, Boyle, and the Fate of the Helmontian Chymistry.* Chicago: University of Chicago Press, 2002.

Newton, Isaac. *Opticks; or, a Treatise of the Reflections, Refractions, Inflections and Colours of Light*, 4th ed. London, 1730.

———. *The Principia. Mathematical Principles of Natural Philosophy*. 2 vols. Translated by Bernard Cohen and Anne Whitman. Berkeley: University of California Press, 1999.
Nicolson, Marjorie Hope. *Newton Demands the Muse: Newton's Opticks and the Eighteenth Century Poets*. Princeton, NJ: Princeton University Press, 1966.
———. *Pepys' Diary and the New Science*. Charlottesville: University of Virginia Press, 1965.
———. *Science and Imagination*. Ithaca, NY: Cornell University Press, 1956.
Nicolson, Marjorie Hope, with G. S. Rousseau. *"This Long Disease, My Life": Alexander Pope and the Sciences*. Princeton, NJ: Princeton University Press, 1968.
Niklaus, Robert. "Fontenelle as a Model for the Transmission and Vulgarization of Ideas in the Enlightenment." In *Voltaire and His World: Studies Presented to W. H. Barber*, edited by R. J. Howells, A. Mason, H. T. Mason, and D. Williams, 167–183. Oxford: Voltaire Foundation, 1985.
Noggle, James. *The Temporality of Taste in Eighteenth-Century British Writing*. Oxford: Oxford University Press, 2012.
Norris, Christopher. "Pope among the Formalists: Textual Politics and 'The Rape of the Lock.'" In *Post-Structuralist Readings of English Poetry*, edited by Richard Machin and Christopher Norris, 134–161. Cambridge: Cambridge University Press, 1987.
"Observation in Science and Literature." Special issue of *Monatshefte* 105, no. 3 (2013): 371–488.
O'Brien, John. "Busy Bodies: The Plots of Susanna Centlivre." In *Eighteenth-Century Genre and Culture: Serious Reflections on Occasional Forms: Essays in Honor of J. Paul Hunter*, edited by Dennis Todd and Cynthia Wall, 165–189. Newark: University of Delaware Press, 2001.
O'Brien, Karen. "Imperial Georgic, 1660–1789." In *The Country and the City Revisited: England and the Politics of Culture 1550–1850*, edited by Gerald MacLean, Donna Landry, and Joseph P. Ward, 160–179. Cambridge: Cambridge University Press, 1999.
———. "'These Nations Newton Made his Own': Poetry, Knowledge, and British Imperial Globalization." In *The Postcolonial Enlightenment: Eighteenth-Century Colonialism and Postcolonial Theory*, edited by Daniel Carey and Lynn Festa, 281–304. Oxford: Oxford University Press, 2009.
Ogilvie, Brian W. *The Science of Describing: Natural History in Renaissance Europe*. Chicago: University of Chicago Press, 2006.
Olivier, Marc. "Binding the Book of Nature: Microscopy as Literature." *History of European Ideas* 31 (2005): 173–191.
Orr, Bridget. *Empire on the English Stage, 1660–1714*. Cambridge: Cambridge University Press, 2001.
Packham, Catherine. *Eighteenth-Century Vitalism: Bodies, Culture, Politics*. Basingstoke, Hampshire: Palgrave Macmillan, 2012.
Parageau, Sandrine. "La satire des sciences dans *Observations upon Experimental Philosophy* et *The Blazing World* de Margaret Cavendish." *Études Épistémè* 10 (2006): 75–97.
Paxman, David. "Aesthetics as Epistemology; Or Knowledge Without Certainty." *Eighteenth-Century Studies* 26, no. 2 (1992–1993): 285–306.
Pepys, Samuel. *The Diary of Samuel Pepys*, edited by Robert Latham and William Matthews. 11 vols. London: Bell & Hyman Limited, 1985.

Perry, Ruth. *Novel Relations: The Transformation of Kinship in English Literature and Culture, 1748–1818*. Cambridge: Cambridge University Press, 2004.

Peterfreund, Stuart. *William Blake in a Newtonian World: Essays on Literature as Art and Science*. Norman: University of Oklahoma Press, 1998.

Phillips, Patricia. *The Scientific Lady: A Social History of Woman's Scientific Interests, 1520–1918*. London: Weidenfeld and Nicolson, 1990.

Picciotto, Joanna. *Labors of Innocence in Early Modern England*. Cambridge, MA: Harvard University Press, 2010.

Pincus, Steven C. A. "Republicanism, Absolutism, and Universal Monarchy: English Popular Sentiment during the Third Dutch War," in *Culture and Society in the Stuart Restoration*, edited by Gerald MacLean, 241–266. Cambridge: Cambridge University Press, 1995.

Piper, William Bowman. "Gulliver's Account of Houyhnhnmland as a Philosophical Treatise." In *The Genres of Gulliver's Travels*, edited by Frederik N. Smith, 179–202. Newark: University of Delaware Press, 1990.

Pohl, Nicole. "'Of Mixt Natures': Questions of Genre in Margaret Cavendish's *The Blazing World*." In *A Princely Brave Woman: Essays on Margaret Cavendish, Duchess of Newcastle*, edited by Stephen Clucas, 51–68. Aldershot: Ashgate, 2003.

Pollock, Anthony. *Gender and the Fictions of the Public Sphere, 1690–1755*. New York: Routledge, 2009.

Poovey, Mary. *A History of the Modern Fact: Problems of Knowledge in the Sciences of Wealth and Society*. Chicago: University of Chicago Press, 1998.

Pope, Alexander. *The Correspondence of Alexander Pope*, edited by George Sherburn. 5 vols. Oxford: Clarendon Press, 1956.

———. *A Key to the Lock; Or, a Treatise Proving, Beyond All Contradiction, the Dangerous Tendency of a Late Poem, entitled The Rape of the Lock, to Government and Religion*. London, 1715.

———. *The Twickenham Edition of the Poems of Alexander Pope*. Gen. ed. John Butt. 11 vols. New Haven, CT: Yale University Press, 1961–1969.

Powell, Manushag N. *Performing Authorship in Eighteenth-Century English Periodicals*. Lewisburg, PA: Bucknell University Press, 2012.

Power, Henry. *Experimental Philosophy in Three Books*. London, 1664.

Poynter, F. N. L. "Rysbrack's Bust of Robert Boyle." *Journal of the History of Medicine and Allied Sciences* 24, no. 4 (October 1969): 475–478.

Pratt, Mary Louise. *Imperial Eyes: Travel Writing and Transculturation*. London: Routledge, 1992.

Principe, Lawrence M. "Newly Discovered Boyle Documents." *Notes and Records of the Royal Society of London* 49 (1995): 57.

Pumfrey, Stephen. "Who Did the Work? Experimental Philosophers and Public Demonstrators in Augustan England." *The British Journal for the History of Science* 28, no. 2 (1995): 131–156.

Rancière, Jacques. *The Politics of Aesthetics*. Translated by Gabriel Rockhill. New York: Continuum, 2006.

Ranum, Orest. "The Refuges of Intimacy." In *Passions of the Renaissance*, edited by Roger Chartier, 210–229. Vol. 3 of *A History of Private Life*, edited by Philippe Ariès and Georges Duby. Cambridge, MA: Harvard University Press, 1989.

The Record of the Royal Society of London for the Promotion of Natural Knowledge, 4th ed. London: Morrison & Gibb, 1940.
Rees, Emma L. E. *Margaret Cavendish: Gender, Genre, Exile*. Manchester: Manchester University Press, 2003.
A Reply unto The Letter Written to Henry Stubbe in Defense of the royal Society. Oxford, 1671.
Richardson, Samuel. *Clarissa; or, the History of a Young Lady*. Edited by Angus Ross. New York: Penguin, 1985.
"Richmond Gardens." *The London Magazine: and Monthly Chronologer* 6 (1738): 38–39.
Ridley, Glynis. "*The Seasons* and the Politics of Opposition." In *James Thomson: Essays for the Tercentenary*, edited by Richard Terry, 93–116. Liverpool: Liverpool University Press, 2000.
Rind, Miles. "The Concept of Disinterestedness in Eighteenth-Century British Aesthetics." *Journal of the History of Philosophy* 4, no. 1 (2002): 67–87.
Riskin, Jessica. *Science in the Age of Sensibility: The Sentimental Empiricists of the French Enlightenment*. Chicago: University of Chicago Press, 2002.
Rivett, Sarah. "The Algonquian Word and the Spirit of Divine Truth: John Eliot's Indian Library and the Atlantic Quest for a Universal Language." In *Colonial Mediascapes: Sensory Worlds of the Early Americas*, edited by Matt Cohen and Jeff Glover, 376–408. Lincoln: University of Nebraska Press, 2014.
Roach, Joseph. "The Artificial Eye: Augustan Theatre and the Empire of the Visible." In *The Performance of Power: Theatrical Discourse and Politics*, edited by Sue-Ellen Case and Janelle Reinelt, 131–145. Iowa City: University of Iowa Press, 1991.
———. *It*. Ann Arbor: University of Michigan Press, 2007.
Roberts, Lissa. "An Arcadian Apparatus: Steam Engines and Landscapes in the History of Dutch Culture." *Technology and Culture* 45, no. 2 (2004): 251–276.
Roberts, Marie Mulvey. "Science, Magic and Masonry: Swift's Secret Texts." In *Secret Texts: The Literature of Secret Societies*, edited by Marie Mulvey Roberts and Hugh Ormsby-Lennon, 97–113. New York: AMS Press, 1995.
Robbins, Bruce. "Comparative Cosmopolitanisms." In *Cosmopolitics: Thinking and Feeling Beyond the Nation*, edited by Pheng Cheah and Bruce Robbins, 246–264. Minneapolis: University of Minnesota Press, 1998.
Rogers, John. *The Matter of Revolution: Science, Poetry, and Politics in the Age of Milton*. Ithaca, NY: Cornell University Press, 1996.
Rogers, Katharine M. *Feminism in Eighteenth-Century England*. Urbana: University of Illinois Press, 1982.
Rogers, Moira R. *Newtonianism for the Ladies and Other Uneducated Souls: The Popularization of Science in Leipzig, 1687–1750*. New York: P. Lang, 2003.
Rorty, Richard. "The Continuity between the Enlightenment and 'Postmodernism.'" In *What's Left of Enlightenment? A Postmodern Question*, edited by Keith Michael Baker and Peter Hanns Reill, 19–36. Stanford, CA: Stanford University Press, 2001.
Rosen, David, and Aaron Santesso. "Swiftian Satire and the Afterlife of Allegory." In *Swift's Travels: Eighteenth-Century British Satire and Its Legacy*, edited by Nicholas Hudson and Aaron Santesso, 11–24. Cambridge: Cambridge University Press, 2008.
Rosenthal, Laura J. *Playwrights and Plagiarists in Early Modern England: Gender, Authorship, Literary Property*. Ithaca, NY: Cornell University Press, 1996.

Rousseau, G. S. *Enlightenment Borders: Pre- and Post-Modern Discourses: Medical, Scientific.* Manchester: Manchester University Press, 1991.

Ruestow, Edward G. *The Microscope in the Dutch Republic: The Shaping of Discovery.* Cambridge: Cambridge University Press, 1996.

Sarasohn, Lisa T. *The Natural Philosophy of Margaret Cavendish: Reason and Fancy during the Scientific Revolution.* Baltimore, MD: Johns Hopkins University Press, 2010.

Schaffer, Simon. "The Consuming Flame: Electrical Showmen and Tory Mystics in the World of Goods." In *Consumption and the World of Goods*, edited by John Brewer and Roy Porter, 489–526. London York: Routledge, 1993.

———. "Glass Works: Newton's Prisms and the Uses of Experiment." In *The Uses of Experiment: Studies in Natural Sciences*, edited by David Gooding, Trevor Pinch, and Simon Schaffer, 67–104. Cambridge: Cambridge University Press, 1989.

Schickore, Jutta. *The Microscope and the Eye: A History of Reflection, 1740–1870.* Chicago: University of Chicago Press, 2007.

Schiebinger, Londa. *Has Feminism Changed Science?* Cambridge, MA: Harvard University Press, 1999.

———. *The Mind Has No Sex? Women in the Origins of Modern Science.* Cambridge, MA: Harvard University Press, 1989.

Schierbeek, A. *Measuring the Invisible World: The Life and Works of Antoni van Leeuwenhoek.* London: Abelard-Schuman, 1959.

Schmidgen, Wolfram. *Exquisite Mixture: The Virtues of Impurity in Early Modern England.* Philadelphia: University of Pennsylvania Press, 2013.

Schrödinger, Erwin. *"Nature and the Greeks" and "Science and Humanism."* 1951. Cambridge: Cambridge University Press, 2014.

Secord, James. "Newton in the Nursery: Tom Telescope and the Philosophy of Tops and Balls, 1761–1838." *History of Science* 23 (1985): 127–151.

Shadwell, Thomas. *The Virtuoso.* Edited by Marjorie Hope Nicolson and David Stuart Rodes. Lincoln: University of Nebraska Press, 1966.

Shanahan, John. "'In the Mean Time': Jonathan Swift, Francis Bacon, and Georgic Struggle." In *Swift as Priest and Satirist*, edited by Todd C. Parker, 193–214. Newark: University of Delaware Press, 2009.

———. "Theatrical Space and Scientific Space in Thomas Shadwell's *Virtuoso*." *SEL: Studies in English Literature, 1500–1900* 49, no. 3 (2009): 549–571.

Shank, J. B. "Neither Natural Philosophy, Nor Science, Nor Literature: Gender Writing, and the Pursuit of Nature in Fontenelle's *Entretiens sur la pluralité des mondes habités*." In *Men, Women, and the Birthing of Modern Science*, edited by Judith P. Zinsser, 86–110. DeKalb: Northern Illinois University Press, 2005.

Shapin, Stephen. "The House of Experiment in Seventeenth-Century England." *Isis* 79 (1988): 373–404.

———. "Pump and Circumstance: Boyle's Literary Technology." *Social Studies of Science* 14 (1984): 481–520.

———. *The Social History of Truth: Civility and Science in Seventeenth-Century England.* Chicago: University of Chicago Press, 1994.

Shapin, Steven, and Simon Schaffer. *Leviathan and the Air-Pump: Hobbes, Boyle, and the Experimental Life.* Princeton, NJ: Princeton University Press, 1985.

Shapiro, Barbara. "Natural Philosophy and Political Periodization: Interregnum, Restoration and Revolution." In *A Nation Transformed: England after the Restoration*, edited by Alan Houston and Steve Pincus, 299–328. Cambridge: Cambridge University Press, 2001.

Shoulson, Jeffrey S. "Milton and Enthusiasm: Radical Religion and the Poetics of *Paradise Regained*." *Milton Studies* 47 (2008): 219–257.

Sicca, Cinzia Maria. "Like a Shallow Cave by Nature Made: William Kent's 'Natural' Architecture at Richmond." *Architectura* 16, no. 1 (1986): 68–82.

Silva, Cristobal. *Miraculous Plagues: An Epidemiology of New England Narrative, 1616–1721*. Oxford: Oxford University Press, 2011.

Silvester, Tipping. *Original Poems and Translations*. London, 1733.

Simon, Sherry. *Gender in Translation: Cultural Identity and the Politics of Transmission*. London: Routledge, 1996.

Simpson, A. D. C. "Robert Hooke and Practical Optics: Technical Support at a Scientific Frontier." In *Robert Hooke: New Studies*, edited by Michael Hunter and Simon Schaffer, 33–62. Woodbridge, Suffolk: Boydell Press, 1989.

Siskin, Clifford, and William Warner, ed. *This Is Enlightenment*. Chicago: University of Chicago Press, 2010.

Skouen, Tina. "Science versus Rhetoric? Sprat's *History of the Royal Society* Reconsidered." *Rhetorica: A Journal of the History of Rhetoric* 29, no. 1 (2011): 23–52.

Slagle, Judith B. "'A Great Rabble of People': The Ribbon-Weavers in Thomas Shadwell's *The Virtuoso*." *Notes and Queries* 36 (September 1989): 351–354.

Smith, Courtney Weiss. *Empiricist Devotions: Science, Religion, and Poetry in Early Eighteenth-Century England*. Charlottesville: University of Virginia Press, 2016.

Smith, Frederik N. "Scientific Discourse: *Gulliver's Travels* and the *Philosophical Transactions*." In *The Genres of Gulliver's Travels*, edited by Frederik N. Smith, 139–162. Newark: University of Delaware Press, 1990.

Smith, Hilda L. "Margaret Cavendish and the Microscope as Play." In *Men, Women, and the Birthing of Modern Science*, edited by Judith P. Zinsser, 34–47. DeKalb: Northern Illinois University Press, 2005.

Snow, C. P. *The Two Cultures and the Scientific Revolution*. Cambridge: Cambridge University Press, 1959.

Solomon, Julie Robin. *Objectivity in the Making: Francis Bacon and the Politics of Inquiry*. Baltimore, MD: Johns Hopkins University Press, 1998.

Some Designs of Mr. Inigo Jones and Mr. William Kent. London, 1744.

Spearing, Elizabeth. "Aphra Behn: The Politics of Translation." In *Aphra Behn Studies*, edited by Janet Todd, 154–177. Cambridge: Cambridge University Press, 1996.

Sprat, Danielle. "Gulliver's Economized Body: Colonial Projects and the Lusus Naturae in the Travels." *Studies in Eighteenth-Century Culture* 41 (2012): 137–159.

Sprat, Thomas. *The History of the Royal Society of London, For the Improving of Natural Knowledge*, 3rd ed. London, 1722.

———. *Observations on Monsieur de Sorbière's Voyage into England*. London, 1665.

Stafford, Barbara Maria. *Body Criticism: Imaging the Unseen in Enlightenment Art and Medicine*. Cambridge, MA: MIT Press, 1993.

Steele, Richard. *The Ladies Library*. 3 vols. London, 1714.

Stepan, Nancy Leys. "Race and Gender: The Role of Analogy in Science." *Isis* 77, no. 2 (1986): 261–277.
Stewart, Alan. "The Early Modern Closet Discovered." *Representations* 50 (Spring 1995): 76–100.
Stewart, Larry. "Other Centres of Calculation, or, Where the Royal Society Didn't Count: Commerce, Coffee-Houses and Natural Philosophy in Early Modern London." *The British Journal for the History of Science* 32, no. 2 (1999): 133–153.
———. *The Rise of Public Science: Rhetoric, Technology, and Natural Philosophy in Newtonian Britain, 1660–1750*. Cambridge: Cambridge University Press, 1992.
———. "Seeing Through the Scholium: Religion and Reading Newton in the Eighteenth Century." *History of Science* 34 (1996): 123–165.
Stewart, Susan. *On Longing: Narratives of the Miniature, the Gigantic, the Souvenir, the Collection*. Durham, NC: Duke University Press, 1992.
Stolnitz, Jerome. "On the Origins of 'Aesthetic Disinterest.'" *Journal of Aesthetics and Art Criticism* 20, no. 2 (1961): 131–143.
Stubbe, Henry. *Campanella Revived, Or an Enquiry into the History of the Royal Society*. London, 1670.
———. *The Lord Bacons Relation to the Sweating-Sickness Examined*. London, 1671.
Sudan, Rajani. *The Alchemy of Empire: Abject Materials and the Technologies of Colonialism*. New York: Fordham University Press, 2016.
Sugg, Redding S., Jr. "Hume's Search for the Key with the Leathern Tongs." *Journal of Aesthetics and Art Criticism* 16 (1957): 96–102.
Sutton, Clive. "'Nullius in Verba' and 'Nihil in Verbis': Public Understanding of the Role of Language in Science." *The British Journal for the History of Science* 27, no. 1 (1994): 55–64.
Sutton, Geoffrey. *Science for a Polite Society: Gender, Culture, and the Demonstration of Enlightenment*. Boulder, CO: Westview Press, 1995.
Swift, Jonathan. *The Cambridge Edition of the Works of Jonathan Swift*. Gen. ed. Claude Rawson, Ian Higgins, David Womersley, and Ian Gadd. 17 vols. Cambridge: Cambridge University Press, 2013.
———. *Gulliver's Travels*. Edited by Albert J. Rivero. New York: Norton, 2002.
———. *Gulliver's Travels*. Edited by Claude Rawson. New ed. Oxford: Oxford University Press, 2005.
Terrall, Mary. "Gendered Spaces, Gendered Audiences: Inside and Outside the Paris Academy of Sciences." *Configurations* 3, no. 2 (1995): 207–232.
"The Theory of Musick reduced to Arithmetical and Geometrical Progressions, by the Reverend Mr Tho. Salmon." *Philosophical Transactions*. London, 1705.
Thomas, Claudia. " 'Th'instructive Moral, and Important Thought": Elizabeth Carter Reads Pope, Johnson and Epictetus." *The Age of Johnson* 4 (1991): 137–169.
Thompson, Helen. *Fictional Matter: Empiricism, Corpuscles, and the Novel*. Philadelphia: University of Pennsylvania Press, 2017.
Thomson, James. *A Poem Sacred to the Memory of Sir Isaac Newton*. London, 1727.
———. *The Seasons*. Edited by James Sambrook. Oxford: Clarendon Press, 1981.
Tierney-Hynes, Rebecca. *Novel Minds: Philosophers and Romance Readers, 1680–1740*. Basingstoke, Hampshire: Palgrave Macmillan, 2012.
Tillery, Denise. "Engendering the Language of the New Science: The Subject of John

Wilkins's Language Project." *The Eighteenth Century: Theory and Interpretation* 46, no. 1 (2005): 59–79.

Todd, Dennis. "Laputa, the Whore of Babylon, and the Idols of Science." *Studies in Philology* 75 (1978): 93–120.

Townsend, Dabney. *Hume's Aesthetic Theory: Taste and Sentiment.* London: Routledge, 2001.

Turner, Gerard L'E. "Decorative Tooling on 17th- and 18th-Century Microscopes and Telescopes." In *Essays on the History of the Microscope*, edited by G. L'E. Turner, 70–108. Oxford: Senecio, 1980.

———. "Microscopical Communication." In *Essays on the History of the Microscope*, edited by G. L'E. Turner, 215–232. Oxford: Senecio, 1980.

———. "Micrographia Historica: The Study of the History of the Microscope." In *Essays on the History of the Microscope*, edited by G. L'E. Turner, 1–29. Oxford: Senecio, 1980.

Turner, James Grantham. *Schooling Sex: Libertine Literature and Erotic Education in Italy, France, and England, 1543–1685* Oxford: Oxford University Press, 2003.

Valenza, Robin. *Literature, Language, and the Rise of the Intellectual Disciplines in Britain, 1680–1820.* Cambridge: Cambridge University Press, 2009.

Vickers, Brian. "Swift and the Baconian Idol." In *The World of Jonathan Swift: Essays for the Tercentenary*, edited by Brian Vickers, 87–128. Cambridge, MA: Harvard University Press, 1968.

Vickers, Ilse. *Defoe and the New Sciences.* Cambridge: Cambridge University Press, 1996.

Wall, Cynthia Sundberg. *The Prose of Things: Transformations of Description in the Eighteenth Century.* Chicago: University of Chicago Press, 2006.

Wallace, Beth Kowaleski. "A Modest Defense of Gaming Women." *Studies in Eighteenth-Century Culture* 31 (2002): 21–39.

———. "The Things Things Don't Say: *The Rape of the Lock*, Vitalism, and New Materialism." *The Eighteenth Century: Theory and Interpretation*, forthcoming.

Walton, David. "Copernicus or Cheesecake? Faultlines and Unjust Des(s)erts: Notes towards the Cultural Significance of the Virtuosa." *Cuardernos de Filogia Inglesa* 9, no. 2 (2001): 45–65.

Warton, Joseph. *Essay on the Genius and Writings of Pope.* London, 1756.

Waterhouse, Ellis. *Painting in Britain, 1530–1790*, 4th ed. New Haven, CT: Yale University Press, 1978.

Watt, Ian. *The Rise of the Novel: Studies in Defoe, Richardson, and Fielding.* Berkeley: University of California Press, 1957.

Watts, Ruth. *Women in Science: A Social and Cultural History.* London: Routledge, 2007.

Webster, Charles. *The Great Instauration: Science, Medicine, and Reform, 1626–1660.* London: Duckworth, 1975.

White, Hayden. "Literature and Social Action: Reflections on the Reflection Theory of Literary Art." *New Literary History* 11, no. 2 (1980): 363–380.

Whitney, Charles. *Francis Bacon and Modernity.* New Haven, CT: Yale University Press, 1986.

Wilkins, Emma. "Margaret Cavendish and the Royal Society." *Notes and Records: The Royal Society Journal of the History of Science* 68 (2014): 245–260.

Williams, Raymond. *Keywords: A Vocabulary of Culture and Society.* New York: Oxford University Press, 1976.

Williams, Robert W. "Pope and the 'Microscopic Eye.'" *Sydney Studies in English* 14 (1988–1989): 21–37.
Wilson, Catherine. *The Invisible World: Early Modern Philosophy and the Invention of the Microscope*. Princeton, NJ: Princeton University Press, 1995.
Wood, P. B. "Methodology and Apologetics: Thomas Sprat's 'History of the Royal Society.'" *The British Society for the History of Science* 13, no. 1 (1980): 1–26.
Wordsworth, William. *The Poetical Works of William Wordsworth*. Edited by Edward Dowden. 7 vols. London: George Bell & Sons, 1893.
Wotton, William. *Reflections upon Ancient and Modern Learning*. London, 1697.
Wright, Lynn Marie, and Donald J. Newman, eds. *Fair Philosopher: Eliza Haywood and The Female Spectator*. Lewisburg, PA: Bucknell University Press, 2006.
De Zan, Mauro. "*La messa all'Indice del* Newtonianism per la dame." In *Scienza e letteratura nella cultura italiana del Settecento*, edited by R. Cremante and W. Tega, 133–147. Bologna: Il Mulino, 1984.
Zinshteyn, Mikhail. "The Reality of Coding Classes." *Atlantic*, February 1, 2016.
Zinsser, Judith P. "Emilie du Chatelet: Genius, Gender, and Intellectual Authority." In *Women Writers and the Early Modern British Political Tradition*, 168–190, edited by Hilda L. Smith. Cambridge: Cambridge University Press, 1998.
———, ed. *Men, Women, and the Birthing of Modern Science*. DeKalb: Northern Illinois University Press, 2005.

INDEX

Absolute monarchy, 14, 104; *The Blazing World*, 114–22; divinely appointed, 114–15; French, Dutch, and Ottoman, 120; gender, 115; peaceful, 114–15; science, 118–22; vulnerability, 121

Addison, Joseph and Richard Steele, 13, 49; compared to the *Female Spectator*, 68–69, 186n56; Mr. Spectator, 185–86n51; The *Spectator*, 13, 64–68, 73, 98

Aesthetics, 14, 137–41, 167–68; appeal, 31–32; defined, 137–41; disinterestedness, 136, 137–39, 150; epistemology, 14, 134–37; female body, 148–50; Hogarth's theory, 35; landscape, 151, 155–56, 159–68; mediation, 136–37, 150–51, 154–55; as misleading, 135; pleasure, 138, 150; science, based on, 135–36; science, superior to, 14, 134–68; as scrutiny, 35; sensory perception, 137, 138–41; taste, 72–74. *See also* beauty

Affect: absolute monarchy, 119; epistemology, 79; melancholy (spleen), 144–45; women's minds, 99–101; science, as response to, 154–55

Air pump, 4, 20, 25, 29–31, 39–40; Royal Society showpiece, 38, 157. *See also* scientific instruments

Algarotti, Franceso, 14, 85; biography, 96. *See also* Carter, Elizabeth; *Il Newtonianismo per la dame*; *Sir Isaac Newton's Philosophy Explain'd*

Alpers, Svetlana, 18, 182n120

Astell, Mary, 47

Authority, 2, 6, 12, 34, 46; distributive, 108; hierarchical, 108; science confirms, 111–12, 118–22; scientific spectacle and, 118–22. *See also* immodest witness; modest witness; subjectivity

Bacon, Francis, 21, 26, 77, 101, 156; facts, 32; *Novum Organon*, 21; science and politics, 104–5; Swift's views, 198n65

Baconianism, 17, 34, 169n3

Baker, Henry, 12, 40–42, 48, 55; *An Attempt towards a Natural History of the Polype*, 42; biography, 40; *Employment for the Microscope*, 182n131; *The Microscope Made Easy*, 40–41, 48, 177–78n34; poetry, 134

Barad, Karen, 161, 174n44

Bassi, Laura, 83–84, 96

Beauty, 31–32, 135–56; women's, falseness of, 47; *The Rape of the Lock*, 141–50. *See also* aesthetics

Beau monde: satirized, 54–55, 65–68, 141; reformed, 69–75

Beer, Gillian, 8

Behn, Aphra, 14, 79, 91, 102; authorship, 82; *The Emperor of the Moon*, 28, 44; scientific authority, 81–82; translation theory, 80–82. See also *A Discovery of New Worlds*; *Entretiens sur la pluralité des mondes*; Fontenelle, Bernard de

Birch, Thomas, 82–83, 112, 195n20

The Blazing World (Cavendish), 14, 44, 104–5, 112–22, 157

Bogel, Fredric V., 7, 123

de Bolla, Peter, 35, 140

Bowers, Toni, 187n8, 188nn17–19
Boyle Lectures, 127, 151, 179n61
Boyle, Robert, 3–4, 9–10, 12, 20, 21, 27–31, 32, 34, 37, 102, 156; air pump, 38; *The Christian Virtuoso*, 28–29, 151; civility, 110; *Considerations Touching the Usefulness of Experimental Philosophy*, 35–36; *The Correspondence of Robert Boyle*, 181n110; *The Excellency of Theology*, 9–10, 92; Hobbes, 105; Latour, 105; literariness, 9–10, 18–19, 20, 71, 105; *The Martyrdom of Theodora and Didymus*, 92; metaphors, views on, 28–31; modest witness, 39–40, 110; nature as fable, 9–10; nature as romance, 9–10, 92; *New Experiments Physico-mechanical*, 29–31, 39–40, 46–47; observed particulars, 110; plain style, 27; *A Proemial Essay*, 27–28, 110, 144; Richmond Hermitage, centerpiece of Queen Caroline's, 150–53; romance, 134; scientific author, 20; scientists, good and bad, 35–36; virtuoso, use of, 46–47
Brereton, Jane, 152
British Enlightenment, 2, 5–6; theories of, 171n21. *See also* modernity
Brown, Laura, 146
Burke, Edmund, 140
Butler, Samuel, 28, 44

Camera obscura, 161, 181n109. *See also* scientific instruments
Caroline, Queen, 14, 150. *See also* Richmond Hermitage, Queen Caroline's
Carter, Elizabeth, 14, 82–84, 103; biography, 82–83; Epictetus translation, 83; *An Examination of Mr Pope's Essay on Man*, 82; *Gentleman's Magazine*, 82; mathematics and astronomy, 83; scientific knowledge of, 82–84; *See also* Algarotti, Francesco; *Sir Isaac Newton's Philosophy Explain'd*
Casid, Jill H., 151, 205–206n95
Cavendish, Margaret, 14, 44, 105–6, 112–22, 133; experimental philosophy, 112–13; frontispieces, 197n55; the Newcastle Circle, 196n39; *Observations upon Experimental Philosophy*, 112; rhetorical approach, 196n40; Royal Society, official visit, 112; royalism, 115; status, 115; "A True Relation of My Birth, Breeding, and Life," 197n51. *See also The Blazing World*
Centlivre, Susannah, 13; *The Basset-Table*, 13, 45–46, 58–63
Character, 11; characterization, 13, 45, 49–50, 55, 76, 78–79, 81–82; coquette, 44–46, 63–74; Gimcrack, 44–46, 49–63. *See also* literariness
Charles, II, King, 107, 108–109, 112, 115; return to London, 121
du Châtelet, Émilie, 96, 151
Chico, Tita, 7–8, 146, 170–71n15, 185n35, 185n37, 193n91, 206n107
Civil government, 14, 105–112; commonwealth, 107–8, 110; discourse, 108–9; ideal subjects, 110–12; civil war, 108–9, 117
Clarke, Samuel, 127, 150
Clery, E. J., 189nn35–37, 190n46
Cole, Lucinda, 4
Colonialism, 125–28, 132–33, 158. *See also* imperialism
Combustion, 20, 29, 39–40. *See also* Boyle, Robert
Commonwealth, 107–8, 110, 114, 117; eloquence, 108
Congreve, William, 49; *Incognita*, 92
Consumerism, 23–25, 142, 146, 176n28
The Contest: Being Poetical Essays on the Queen's Grotto, 152–55
Coppola, Al, 4, 183n2
Coquettes, 44–45, 63–74, 76; objects of scrutiny, 65–66; as observers, 67–68, 70–72; recuperation, 68–75; taste, 71–74
Cosmetics, 98, 146. *See also* dressing room; toilet
Cosmology, 13–14; Copernican and Cartesian, 85–86, 98; Newtonian, 98–99
Court culture, 107; *Gulliver's Travels*, Laputa, 125–26; Hanoverian, 126; Henrietta Maria, 115
Cowley, Abraham, 26, 28, 78, 134–36, 140

Daston, Lorraine, 169n3, 169–70n8, 175nn2–3, 175n11, 181n103, 182n135, 184n15, 199n75
Dear, Peter, 169–70n8, 171n20, 175n1, 175n4, 180n73, 181n113, 191–92n63, 197n55

Defoe, Daniel, 30, 142
DeMaria, Robert, Jr., 189n38
Derrida, Jacques, 9
Desaguliers, John Theophilous, 82, 96, 126. *See also* scientific entrepreneurs
Deutsch, Helen, 142
Devis, Arthur, 25–26
Di Palma, Vittoria, 159
Dialogues, scientific, 13, 76, 81, 85, 96, 191nn57–58, 191n62
Difference, 105, 155–68, 174n44; light, 161–62; otherness, 159; satire, 123
Diffraction, 174n44
Disciplinarity, 2–3, 6, 8–10, 173n30; arts and sciences, 136–37; modern university, 8; "two cultures," 8
A Discovery of New Worlds (Behn), 14, 80–82. See also *Entretiens sur la pluralité des mondes*; Fontenelle, Bernard de
Drama, 15, 45, 90
Dressing room, 7–8, 57, 59, 60–61; *The Rape of the Lock*, 145–46. *See also* cosmetics; toilet
Dryden, John, 47, 107, 111, 143
Duck, Stephen, 152, 203n50

Economics, 24; science, 126–27
Ekphrasis, 31, 146
Eloquence, 107–8
Empiricism, 1, 4; Lockean, 27, 139; novels, 4, 170n14–15; realism, 4, 18; as subversive, 175n13
Entretiens sur la pluralité des mondes (Fontenelle), 13, 27–28, 84–95; Algarotti, 97, 98–99; editions, 84–85; frontispieces, 86, 88, 89; translations, 79, 80–82. *See also* Behn, Aphra; *A Discovery of New Worlds*
Epic, 90, 143–44
Epistemology, 14; curiosity, 42; fancy, 113–14; feminism, 174n44, 174–75n48; genre, 114; literariness, 134–37, 155–68; observation, 166–68; politics, 107; sexual desire, 188n16. *See also* knowledge; observed particulars; things
Eroticism, 13–14, 76–78; cosmology, 93–95; microscopy, 47–48, 60–61
Evelyn, John, 20, 198n63
Evidence, 2, 6, 12. *See also* observed particulars; things

Experience, 3, 12, 35–36. *See also* experiment
Experiment, 23; definitions, 3, 17, 21, 169n3, 169n5; discovery, 17, 21; empirical, 26 ; explanation, 17; genre, 12, 15; language, 130; metaphors, 59–60; non literary, 25–26; outlandish, 53, 122–25; practice, 24, 169n1; Royal Society, 49; satire, 122–25; seduction, 77–78, 187–88n11; as wasteful, 122–25. *See also* evidence; experience
Experimental imagination: defined, 1–3. *See also* keywords; imagination; literariness; literature and science studies; science
Experimental philosophy 1, 6. *See also* science

Female Inconstancy Display'd ("The Microscope"), 47–48
The *Female Spectator* (Haywood), 13, 46, 68–75; the *Spectator*, 68–69, 186n56
Feminism, 11–12, 60, 63, 105, 174n44, 174–75n48
Ferguson, Frances, 140
Ferguson, James, 85
Fiennes, Celia, 70
Figurative language, 10, 12, 19, 27–28, 30, 129–31; explanatory role, 27; scientific observation, 37–40, 87–90; wonder, 40–42. *See also* literariness; metaphor
Filmer, Robert, 115
Finch, Anne, 143, 163
Fly's eye, 31–32
Folkes, Martin, 96
Fontenelle, Bernard de, 13, 27–28, 76–77, 79, 84–85, 101–102; Algarotti, 97, 98–99; cosmology, 13, 27, 84–85; *Eloge de Newton*, 85; Haywood's *Love in Excess*, 76–78; *Histoire du renouvellement de l'Académie des Sciences*, 85, 126. *See also Entretiens sur la pluralité des mondes*
Fortescue, James, 24, 199n71
Freeman, Lisa A., 183n1
Freud, Sigmund, 144

Galison, Peter, 8, 169–70n8, 175nn2–3
Gender, 11–12, 18, 25, 46, 67, 135 ; absolute monarchy, 115; defined, 11; Gimcracks, 54; ideology, 12; keyword, 5, 11–12;

melancholy (spleen), 144–45; modesty, 37–38, 181–82n118; politics, 105–6; power, 78–79; scientific subjectivity, 12, 91; seduction, 77–79. *See also* men; patriarchy; women
Genre, 3, 6, 14, 45, 79, 90–91, 105, 133; as epistemology, 113–114. *See also* dialogues, scientific; drama; epic; opera; periodicals; plays; poetry; romance; translations; treatises, scientific
Gentleman's Magazine, 136, 151–55; poetry contest, 152
George, I, King, 128
George Augustus, II, King, 151
Gimcracks, 44–45, 49–63, 77; characterization, 50; examples: Sir Nicholas Gimcrack (*The Virtuoso*), 49–54, 62–63; Lady Science (*The Humours of Oxford*), 54–58, 63; Valeria (*The Basset-Table*), 58–63; gender, 46; literary afterlife, 49; men, 46, 49–50; reformation, 52–53, 57–58; women, 54, 58
Glanvill, John, 80
Globes, 25, 69; politics, 128
Goodman, Kevis, 158, 205–206n95, 206n106
Government: body politic, 123–24; church, 107–8; civil, 106–12; commonwealth, 107–8; factionalism, 106–109, 117, 123–24; monarchical, 107–8, 114–22; science, 104–33; theories of, 104–5. *See also* absolute monarchy; civil war; Interregnum; politics
Greatorex, Ralph, 29
Guidebooks, scientific, 12, 15, 24–25, 83, 85, 178n38; by women, 85
Guillory, John, 201n10
Gulliver's Travels (Swift), 6–7, 14, 105–6, 122–33; Academy of Lagado, 44, 122–23; criticism, 172n25; female body, 123; Gulliver as microscope, 48, 123; literalization, 124–25, 128, 129; things, 129–33

Hacking, Ian, 3, 181n109
Haraway, Donna, 37, 183n2
Harding, Sandra, 105
Haywood, Eliza, 13; *Eovaai*, 11–12; *The History of Miss Betsy Thoughtless*, 63–64; *Love in Excess*, 76–77. *See also* the *Female Spectator*
Hildrop, John, 49
Historicism, 6–7
The History of the Royal Society (Sprat), 14, 26–27, 28, 105–12, 199n71; aesthetics, 134, 140; commissioning, 106; Cowley's prefatory ode, 134–36, 140; economic development, 24; imagination, 41–42; modesty, 41–42; propaganda, 106; purpose, 107; reception, 106–7; science, basis for good poetry, 134; science, modernity of, 23–24; social harmony, 26–27; things, 26–27. *See also Philosophical Transactions*; Royal Society
Hobbes, Thomas, 3–4, 138; Boyle, 105; Margaret Cavendish, 196n39; Latour, 105
Hodgson, James, 126
Hogarth, William, 35
Hooke, Robert, 12, 20, 21, 22–23, 24, 26, 29, 32–35, 37, 167; biography, 22; Cavendish's critique, 112–13; complaints, 24; "Discourse concerning Telescopes and Microscopes," 33–34, 177–78n34; "eroticization of sight," 78; experimenter, 37; "A General Scheme, or Idea of the Present State of Natural Philosophy," 34; literariness, 20, 26; Leeuwenhoek's experiments, 177n33; *Micrographia*, 20, 22–23, 31, 32–35, 66, 78, 135; *Micrographia*, engravings, 34–35; microscope, associated with, 38; microscope, scientist as, 38–39; modest witness, 38–39, 135; rank and status, 37, 49, 115; self-representation, 39; *The Virtuoso*, reaction to, 49; "wonder-monger," 40
Houghton, Walter E., Jr., 183n4, 183n6, 183n8
Hume, David, 72–73
The Humours of Oxford (Miller), 13, 45–46, 62–63
Hunter, J. Paul, 149
Hunter, Michael, 40, 106, 169–70n8, 175n12, 176n28, 183n3, 194n16, 195n21, 196nn31–33
Hutcheson, Francis, 136, 138–41, 150

Huygens, Christiaan, 97, 112, 196n39

Imagination, 2, 4, 10–11, 18–19, 21, 23, 26, 32, 49; allure, 40–42; contemplation, 154–55; control of, 41–42; epistemology, 113–14; materialism, 163–64; observation, 34, 155, 162–68; and reason, 112–14, 131; refusal to use, 129–31; science, as explicator, 113–14; science stimulates, 40–41; scientific education, role in, 86–87, 90, 102–103, 154–55; the *Spectator*, 65; truth, as source, 113–14. *See also* experimental imagination
Immodest witness, 12, 13, 44–75; bad scientists, 44, 47–48; defined, 44–45, 26–49; as female, 38; literary characters, 44–45; modest witness, 46, 90; *See also* modest witness; immodesty; scientist; subjectivity
Immodesty, 45, 46–49, 74–75. *See also* modesty
Imperialism, 14, 61, 105–6, 122–33, 158, 185n41; English, 111; English landscapes, 151, 155–56; English oppression of Ireland, 125–26. *See also* colonialism; government; nationalism; political theory
Interregnum, 107–10, 115; Oxford meetings of natural philosophers, 19–20, 109. *See also* government; politics

Jacob, Margaret C., 24, 169–70n8, 170n13, 177n30, 179n61, 181n113, 190n44, 199–200n81–86, 200nn88–89
The John Bacon Family (Devis), 25–26
Johns, Adrian, 194n5
Johnson, Esther, "Stella," 25
Johnson, Samuel, 3, 47, 82, 100, 106; praise for Elizabeth Carter, 82
Jordanova, L. J., 8, 171n21

Kant, Immanuel, 140, 171n21
Kaul, Suvir, 156, 205–206n95
Kent, William, 150, 203n50
Keywords, 5. *See also* gender; literary knowledge; science; trope
King, William, 44
Knight, W. D., Sir, 80, 188n25

Knowledge: debates about forms of, 5–6; desire for, 79–80. *See also* epistemology
Kramnick, Jonathan, 4, 188n17

Laboratory, 19, 50
Lafayette, Madame de, 90–92
Lamb, Jonathan, 27, 142
Landscape, 151, 155–56, 159–68; difference, 165–68; wasteland, 159–60, 165–68
Latour, Bruno, 105, 132, 180n78
Learned societies: Bologna, 96; dangers of, 117, 124–25; *The Blazing World*, 115–17; *Gulliver's Travels*, 122–25; France and England, 176–77n29
Leeuwenhoek, Antoni van, 24, 48; biography, 177n33
Lewis, Jayne Elizabeth, 4, 29, 202–203n37
Light (Newtonian), 160–61; difference, 161–63
Literariness, 1, 9–10, 12–13, 17–19, 20–21, 25–32, 54, 71; Boyle's "plain style," 27–28; characterization, 44–46; epistemology, 5, 134–37, 155–68; imagination, 26, 135; of the modest witness, 37–42, 105; of the observed particular, 34–35, 105; politics, 107–8; Royal Society's rejection, 25–26; as a scientific tool, 20; technology, 18; visibility, 32. *See also* character; figurative language; genre; imagination; literary knowledge; metaphor; plot; trope
Literary knowledge, 1–3, 5, 10–15, 17–43, 149–50, 155–68; absolute monarchy and, 121–22; as belated, 7, 8, 9; defined, 5; dreams, 65; epistemology, 2–3, 5, 14, 113–14, 134–37, 143, 148; fancy, 113–15, 121–22; keyword, 5; observed particulars as, 90; plots, 62; observation and, 143–50; scientific knowledge, 114; truth, 11. *See also* disciplinarity; genre; imagination; literariness; metaphor; trope
Literature and science studies, 4–5, 6–10, 18
Locke, John, 27, 139, 156; intuitive knowledge, 131; microscopy, critique of, 38–39; Queen Caroline's Richmond Hermitage, celebrated in, 150–51
Lynch, William T., 178–79n45, 179n51, 180n90, 183n3, 194n1, 195n21, 196n34

Martin, Benjamin, 12, 24–25, 126, 141–42, 177n31; *Micrographia Nova*, 177n31, 178n35; *A New and Compendious System of Optics*, 141–42; *The Young Gentleman and Lady's Philosophy*, 25, 85

Mathematics, 6; Elizabeth Carter, 83; politics, 126–28; satire, 115–16, 122, 125; seduction, 95, 97, 99

Mediation, 136–37, 150–51

Memoirs of the Royal Society, 20

Men, 24, 37–38, 46–47, 57, 69, 78, 80, 91, 99, 109–10; obedient, 110–12; seduction, 79, 95; self-absorbed, 125; semen, 48. *See also* gender, patriarchy, women

Metaphor, 1, 10, 11, 12, 13, 14, 18, 20, 28–32, 54, 76; air, 29–31; clarity, 28; globes, 128; modernity, 21–25; mirror, 37–38; observed particulars, 33; referent, 31–32; rejection of, 28; "rhetorical ornaments," 28; science, 18, 28–29, 136–37; wool, 29–31. *See also* figurative language; literariness; literary knowledge; trope

Metonyms, 145

Microscopes, 20, 22, 25; flea, 35; flea glasses, 24; fly's eye, 31–32; Leeuwenhoek's, 177n33; parlour-microscope, 178n40; pleasure, 24; pocket microscopes, 178n40; poems titled, 47–48; price, 24; quality, 177n31; the Royal Society, 38; sales, 24–25; women, 47, 65–68, 178n40. *See also* Baker, Henry; Hooke, Robert; Martin, Benjamin; Power, Henry; microscopy; scientific instruments

Microscopy, 20, 31–32; blindness, 38–39, 157; critiques of, 112–13, 157–58; eroticism, 47–48; fashionable, 24; observed particulars, 32–35, 141–42; satire and, 47–49, 65–68, 116. *See also* Baker, Henry; Hooke, Robert; Martin, Benjamin; Power, Henry; microscopes

Miller, James, 13, 54. *See also The Humours of Oxford*

Mimesis, 37–38; referentiality, 7. *See also* reflection

Miscellenia Curiosa, 20

Mitchell, Robert, 3, 169n6, 172n24

Mock-epic, 141–50

Modernity, 6, 12, 21–25; as the future, 176n24; Latour's theory, 105; modern subjects, 23; as the present, 23–24. *See also* British Enlightenment

Modest witness, 1–2, 3–4, 13, 21, 35–42, 53, 90; aesthetic disinterestedness, 137–41; defined, 37; experimenter, in contrast to, 37; ideal subjects in civil government, 110–12; immodest witness, 46, 90; literariness, 37–42; masculinity, 37; rank and status, 36–37; as a scientific instrument, 38–40; self-erasure, 38, 39–40; threats to, 158–59; training, 37; virtual witnessing, 4, 18–19, 27, 35, 46, 102; *See also* immodest witness; modesty; observation; scientist; subjectivity

Modesty, 37–38, 41–42, 181–82n118. *See also* immodesty

Montagu, Mary Wortley, Lady, 83–84; Francesco Algarotti, 96

Myers, Natasha, 174–75n48

Nationalism, 61–62, 80, 155–57, 166. *See also* government; politics

Natural history, 173n36

Natural philosophy, 1, 6, 21. *See also* science

Nature: agential realism, 174n44; book of, 9; fable, 9–10; as female, 77–78, 102; romance, 9–10, 92; seduction, 77–78, 101–102; study of and civil society, 109

Newton, Isaac, 14, 37, 158; Francesco Algarotti, 96; Hanoverian politics, 127; influence, 126–28; *Opticks*, 158; *Mathematical Principles of Natural Philosophy*, 127; poetry dedicated to, 150–53, 156, 160–61; theory of gravity, 85; popularizations of, 83; the Royal Society, 126, 161; seducer, as a, 101; Swift's hatred of, 126–28; translations, 83–4, 96–102. *See also* Newtonianism; *Il Newtonianismo per la dame*; *Sir Isaac Newton's Philosophy Explain'd*

Newtonianism, 82, 96–103; experiment, 169n5; mathematics, 126–28, 151; optics, 97, 160–61, 165–68, 169n5; philosophical reception, 199–200n81; public demonstrations of, 126–27; *The Seasons*, 156, 158–68. *See also* Newton, Isaac; *Il Newtonianismo per la dame*; *Sir Isaac Newton's Philosophy Explain'd*

Il Newtonianismo per la dame (Algarotti), 14, 85, 96–103; editions, 96; Fontenelle, 97; translations, 79, 80, 82–84, 96. *See also* Carter, Elizabeth; *Sir Isaac Newton's Philosophy Explain'd*

Nicolson, Marjorie Hope, 172n25, 172–73n26, 184n25, 198nn64–65, 203n39, 206n98

Novels, 4; empiricism, 4, 170n14–15; romance, 92

Objectivity, 2, 4, 17–18, 76, 133, 175n2; challenges to, 13, 158–59, 173–74n43; modest witness, 35–42; modesty, imagined as, 37–38; Scholastic tradition, 17; self-interested, 46. *See also* modest witness

Observation, 2; aesthetic theory, 136, 137–41; attentiveness, 35, 144; dangers, 158–59; difficulty, 22; disembodied, 38–40; dream as technology of, 65; embodied, 12, 13, 163–64, 174–75n48; epistemology, 166–68; female, 12; figurative and scientific, 21, 31; flawed, 27–28, 64–65, 159–60, 162–63; German science, 175n11; hybrids, 115–17, 157; imagination, 26, 34, 90, 155, 162–68; literalization, 66, 144–45; literary knowledge and, 143–50, 154–55, 155–68; methodology, 33–34; myopia, 67–68; neutral, 13; pleasure, 42, 69–70, 137–40, 161; poetry, 134; practice, 20–21, 171–72n22; prismatic, 165–68; property owner, of, 155–56; *The Rape of the Lock*, 142–50; "regime of the eye," 35; *The Seasons*, 156–68; the *Spectator*, 64–68. *See also* modest witness; immodest witness; observed particulars; sensory perception

Observed particulars, 1–2, 3–4, 13, 21, 90, 105; defined, 32–35; literary knowledge, 90, 142–43; mediated and textual, 90; metaphors, similar to, 33; microscopy, 32–33, 170–71n15; ontology, 34; as symptoms, 144–45. *See also* things

Oldenburg, Henry, 20, 177n33

Ontology, 130–33, 166–67

Opera, 90

Optics, Newtonian, 97, 160–61, 165–68, 169n5

Ovid, 78, 143

Papal index, 84, 96

Patriarchy, 60, 61–62, 125; political theory, 115; threats to, 67; vulnerability of, 64. *See also* gender; men; women

Pepys, Elizabeth, 22

Pepys, Samuel, 12, 22, 198n63; biography, 22; *Diary*, 21–23

Periodicals, 15, 45

Performance, 51, 53, 59; as a literary device, 45

Philips, Ambrose, 160, 162

Philosophical Transactions, 20, 48; anthologies, 20; Swift's use, 126

Physico-theology, 9, 28, 150

Plays, 15, 45; playhouse culture, 45

Plot, 11, 13, 49, 51, 58, 76; Centlivre's, 61–62; literary knowledge, 62; seduction and, 77, 78–79, 93–95, 96–97, 102–103. *See also* literariness

Poetry, 15; couplets, 149; landscape, 155–68; occasional, 152–55; production of, 155; scientists' view, 134–36

Politics: aesthetics, 140–41; Baconian science, 104–5; the body politic, 123–24; literariness, 107–8; Newtonianism, 126–27; narrative form, 129; science, 104–33; systems, 14; Whiggish, 126–27, 155–56. *See also* absolute monarchy; colonialism; government; imperialism; nationalism

Pope, Alexander, 14, 48; *A Key to the Lock*, 7. *See also The Rape of the Lock*

Power, Henry, 12, 22, 36, 71, 206n103; Margaret Cavendish's critique, 112–13; *Experimental Philosophy in Three Books*, 22, 31–32, 36

La Princesse de Clèves (Layfayette), 90–92

Prism, 160–68, 169n5. *See also* scientific instruments

Putrefaction, 159

Quadrant, 25. *See also* scientific instruments

Querelle des Anciens et des Modernes, 6

Race, 18

Rancière, Jacques, 140–41

The Rape of the Lock (Pope), 14, 66, 136, 141–50, 167–68; dressing room, 145–46

Readership, 80, 91–92, 97–100
Realism, 4; as seeing, 18; limits of, 19. *See also* empiricism; novel
Reason, 113–14, 129, 131–33
Rees, Emma, 115, 197n48
Reeve, Richard, 21–22, 175n15
Reflection, 161, 174n44. *See also* mimesis
Religion, 107, 118, 127
Richmond Hermitage, Queen Caroline's, 14–15, 136, 150; busts within, 204n53; *A Description of the Royal Gardens at Richmond*, 204n60; engravings, 204n61; poems commemorating, 150–55, 167–68; "Richmond Gardens" (*London Magazine*), 204n61. *See also* Boyle, Robert; landscape; Locke, John; Newton, Isaac; physico-theology
Roach, Joseph, 148
Robbins, Bruce, 166
Romance, 14, 15, 90–93; absorptive reading, 92; epistemology, 113–14; as a metaphor for nature, 9–10, 92; the novel, 92; scientific treatises, 113. *See also* literariness; genre; plot; seduction
Rousseau, G. S., 172–73n26, 173n33, 199–200n81, 203n39
Royalism, 109–10, 114–22; confirmed by science, 111–12, 118–22; gender, 115. *See also* absolute monarchy; government; politics
Royal Society, 19–20, 24, 25–27, 37, 47, 96; Baconianism, 21, 34; funding, 19–20; civic institution, 111–12; coffeehouse gatherings, 176–77n29; contributions to, 71; language experiments, 130, 131; Leeuwenhoek's election, 177n33; members, social ranks, 110; methods , 27; Newton's first letter, 161; *Philosophical Transactions*, 20; publishing program, 19–20, 80; satire, 64–65; statues, 25–26; trade, 110–11; weekly meetings, 49; women elected, 196n37. *See also* Boyle, Robert; *The History of the Royal Society*; Hooke, Robert; Power, Henry; Sprat, Thomas
Ruestow, Edward G., 177nn32–33, 184n19

Salon culture, 83, 85

Sarasohn, Lisa T., 116, 196–97n40, 197n47, 197n52
Satire, 6–8, 173n28; experiment, 50; science, 27–28, 44; scientists, 49–58, 76, 115–17, 122–26, 127–28; theory of, 123; women scientists, 54–58
Schaffer, Simon, 169n5, 176n28
Schiebinger, Londa, 112, 169–70n8, 174–75n48, 196n37
Schmidgen, Wolfram, 4, 197n53
Scholasticism, 17, 36, 135
Science, 1–3; advancement of, 51, 166; aesthetics, 134–37, 140–41; art, 47, 134–36; believing, 102–3; blindness, 21, 60; British economy, 24; consumerism, 1, 24–25, 50, 176n28; conversation, as a topic of, 21–23, 68–70; defined, 5–6, 21–23, 171n20; dialogues, 13–14, 76, 85, 96, 191nn57–58, 191n62; dressing rooms, 59, 60–61; education, 13–14, 25, 69–70, 76, 84–103, 154–55, 176n28; enlightenment, 21, 24; epistemology, 5; expense, 50, 52–53; fashionable, 23, 24–25, 41, 54, 59, 65–66, 70–71, 141, 178n40; feminism, 11, 174n44, 174–75n48; gender, 11–12, 18, 84, 91; government, 104–6; history, 8, 17, 21, 169n1, 169–70n8; imagination, 113–14; imperialism, 122–33; keyword, 5–6; limits of, 64–65; literariness, 17–43; literary studies and, 4–5, 6–10, 18, 172–73n26; literature, 134–68; modern, 23–25; nongenerative, 53; politics, 14, 104–33, 156–57; protocols, 18–19, 27; prelapsarian, 9; race, 18; seduction, 76–103; self-interest, 13, 21, 44–45, 51, 53; social benefits, 26–27, 44–45, 106, 108–12, 126–27, 156–57; social dangers, 4, 21, 44–45, 51, 54, 106, 116–17, 124–25; spectacle, 90, 106, 118–22; state power, 104–5; theatricality, 45; trivial, 53, 65–68; trope, 5, 10–11, 14, 15, 136–37; truth, 8; virtual witnessing, 18–19, 27, 35, 46–47, 102; wonder, 40–42, 90, 182n129; available to women, 178n40. *See also* disciplinarity; experimental philosophy; literariness; literary knowledge; natural philosophy; observed particulars; scientists; modest witness

Scientific entrepreneurs, 24–25, 126–27
Scientific instruments, 22, 48, 141–42; bodies as, 66–68; collections, 24–25, 50, 69, 151; conceptual purposes, 38; critiques of, 38–39, 112–13, 157–58; difficulty, 177–78n34; fashionable, 55; implications, 158–59, 161–62, 65–68; light as, 160–61, 163; makers, 22, 24–25, 177n31; metaphors, 28–29, 38–40, 54, 90; ownership of, 50, 176n28; reliability, 28, 177n31; sales, 24–25; satires, 47–48, 51, 116; scientists imagined as, 38–40; scotoscope, 22; sensory perception, 38, 112–13. *See also* air pump; camera obscura; microscope; prism
Scientists, 12–13; absent-minded, 48, 52, 125; attentive, 36, 144; *The Blazing World*, 115–22, 157; Boyle's definition, 36; coquettes, 44–45, 63–74; failed, 13, 35, 44, 49–58; fake, 51, 55–56; fashionable and urbane, 23, 24; gender, 46, 91; gentlemen, 37–38, 47, 110–12; Gimcracks, 44–45, 49–63; *Gulliver's Travels*, 122–26; hybrids, 115–17, 157; immodesty, 45, 46–49; mad, 184n15; masculine, 37; as microscopes, 38, 157–59, 167; modern and enlightened, 24; modest witnesses, 35–42; obedient, 111–12; poet, as model for, 135–36; privilege, 37; professionals, 37; rank and status, 36–37, 46–47; reformation, 52–53; satires, 49–58, 122–26, 127–28; seducers, 77–78, 187–88n11; self-interested, 48, 76; virtuoso, 46–47; women, 58–63, 68–72, 178n40. *See also* immodest witness; science; modest witness
Scripture, book of, 9
The Seasons (Thomson), 15, 136, 155–68
Secord, James, 176n28
Seduction: affective and intellectual, 77, 99–101; defined, 14, 78–79; narrative, 11–12, 14, 93–95, 102–103; romance, 90–94; science, 11–12, 14; scientific education, 76–103, 187–88n11
Self-interest, 13, 44–45
Sensory perception, 38–39; aesthetics, 136, 137–41; affect, 100–101; flaws, 66–68, 112–13, 160, 162–63; influx of, 158; taste, 72–74

Sexual desire, 13, 14, 50–51, 52, 76–77, 78; as educational model, 14, 84–103; epistemology, 188n16; microscopy, 47–48
Shadwell, Thomas, 13, 45. *See also The Virtuoso*
Shaftesbury, third earl of (Anthony Ashley Cooper), 136, 137–38, 150
Shank, J. B., 190–91n54, 191n56, 192n70
Shapin, Steven, 181n115, 195n29, 204–205n73
Shapin, Steven and Simon Schaffer, 3–4, 18–19, 37, 105, 169n3, 170n9–12, 175n3, 179n53, 180n90, 181n107, 181n113
Shapiro, Barbara, 196n32, 196n35
Silvester, Tipping (author of "The Microscope"), 47–48
Sir Isaac Newton's Philosophy Explain'd (Carter), 14. *See also* Algarotti, Francesco; Carter, Elizabeth; *Il Newtonianism per le dame*
Smith, Courtney Weiss, 4
Snow, C. P., 8, 173n30
Some Designs of Mr. Inigo Jones and Mr. William Kent, 204n61
Spleen (condition), 144–45
Sprat, Thomas, 12, 14, 23–24, 26–27, 28, 41–42, 133; aesthetics, 134, 140; *Observations on Monsieur de Sorbière's Voyage into England*, 195n25; politics and science, 105–12, 133; rhetoric, 195n25. *See also The History of the Royal Society*
Stepan, Nancy Leys, 18
Steele, Richard, 69, 181–82n118
STEM (science, technology, engineering, and math), 8, 173n32
Stewart, Larry, 24, 169–70n8, 176–77nn28–30, 178n39, 181n112, 190n44, 200nn82–85, 200nn88–89
Stubbe, Henry, 105, 194n14
Subjectivity, 64, 74. *See also* immodest witness; modest witness; scientists
Subvisibilia, 20, 33–35
Sudan, Rajani, 4
Swift, Jonathan, 25, 44, 105–6, 122–33; Bacon, 198n65; *Bickerstaff Papers*, 127–28; Margaret Cavendish, 124; *Journal to Stella*, 178n43; "The Lady's Dressing Room," 47; *A Modest Proposal*, 127; Newton, hatred of, 126–28; Wood's

copper coinage, 127–28. *See also Gulliver's Travels*

Taste, 68, 71–74, 158
Telescopes, 11, 25, 90; image, 27–28; satire, 116. *See also* scientific instruments
Things, 2, 13, 26–27, 34; Bacon's definition, 178–79n45; epistemology, 149–50; literary knowledge, 142–43; Pope's, 141–50; Swift's, 129–33, 142; temporal change, 143; as trophies, 150. *See also* observed particulars
Thompson, Helen, 4, 172n24
Thomson, James, 15; *A Poem Scared to the Memory of Sir Isaac Newton*, 160–61. *See also The Seasons*
Todd, Dennis, 198n65
Toilet, 47, 55, 98, 142, 145–46. *See also* cosmetics; dressing room
Translations, 13–15; pay for, 80, 83; politics of, 84; theory, 80–84; translator's authority, 84. *See also* genre
Travel narratives, 87
Treatises, scientific, 12, 15. *See also* genre
Trope, 3, 10–11, 14, 15, 31; defined, 10; ekphrasis, 31, 146; keyword, 5, 10; science, 21. *See also* literariness; metaphor

Virtuoso, defined, 46–47
The Virtuoso (Shadwell), 13, 45, 49–54, 62–63; Gimcrack's characterization, 50; literary afterlife, 49

Vitalism, 3, 112, 169n6, 172n24, 202–203n37
Voltaire, 96, 151

Ward, Ned, 44
Warton, Joseph, 156
Watt, Ian, 4, 170n14
Wealth, 13
Whigs, 128, 155–57
Whiston, William, 126
White, Hayden, 7, 173n27
The Whores Rhetorick, 78
Wilkins, John, 130
Williams, Raymond, 5, 171n19
Wollaston, William, 151
Women, 11–12; adornment, 145–48; agency, 60, 63; bodies, 149–50; consumerism, 146; learning, 84–103; marriage market, 63–64; microscope, under the, 47, 65–68; minds, 99–101; modesty, 38, 181–82n118; objectification, 150; rank, 85, 115, 191–92n63; readers, 80, 97–100; science available to, 178n40; science education, 76–78, 80–81, 83–84, 84–103; scientific translators, 80–84; scientists, 25, 54–58, 68–72; seduction, 78–79; sexuality, 50–51, 144, 148; sisters, 85; spinsters, 186n55; unmarried, 12, 25, 58; widows, 55. *See also* gender; men; patriarchy
Wonder, 40–42, 182n129
Wotton, William, 49
Wren, Christopher, 34–35

The authorized representative in the EU for product safety and compliance is:
Mare Nostrum Group
B.V Doelen 72
4831 GR Breda
The Netherlands

www.ingramcontent.com/pod-product-compliance
Lightning Source LLC
Chambersburg PA
CBHW030235240426
43663CB00037B/966